RIVAL AMBASSADORS

AT THE COURT OF QUEEN MARY

Antoine de Noailles

Rival Ambassadors at the Court of Queen Mary

By E. HARRIS HARBISON

PRINCETON UNIVERSITY PRESS · PRINCETON

LONDON: HUMPHREY MILFORD, OXFORD UNIVERSITY PRESS

1940

SET UP AND PRINTED BY PRINCETON UNIVERSITY PRESS
AT PRINCETON, NEW JERSEY, U.S.A.

TO

H. H. H.

PREFACE

*I*T sometimes happens that one historian unwittingly writes another's preface. Over two generations ago a distinguished French student of Tudor history wrote two sentences which may well serve as introduction to the present work: "In our opinion the capital mistake made by most English historians of Mary Tudor is that they have never been able to envisage their nation from any other point of view than that of its activity, and consequently that they have not been able to write the history of a reign which, like that of Mary Tudor, presents only the spectacle of anarchy and violence at home and of cowardice and weakness in the face of the foreigner. They have not known how to explain to themselves and to their readers that while the rôle of passivity may not be glorious for a nation, it may well be very important; that in default of being one of the gamblers, a nation may be the stake of a struggle between other nations; and that in the time of Mary Tudor, England had come to occupy such a position."[1]

Since these words were written, many other nations have learned what it is to occupy the position of Marian England. It is not the business of the historian to draw parallels, and few have been drawn in succeeding pages; but the reader may sense the fact that the problems of past ages are not altogether remote from our own. To see contemporary war and diplomacy in perspective—a perspective which reaches far beyond the past few generations—is something more than an intellectual challenge today; it is a psychological necessity.

The reign of Mary has been called a "barren interlude" in Tudor history, and so it undoubtedly was. But the student of Tudor absolutism, of the growth of English national sentiment, or of the progress of Protestantism in England cannot afford to neglect a period in which these developments were checked for a time

[1] Paul Friedmann, *Les dépêches de Giovanni Michiel* (Venice, 1869), pp. xviii-xix.

by forces which have come to be known as "medieval." It is illuminating to study Tudor absolutism in reverse as well as in obverse, in the reigns of Mary and her brother as well as in the reigns of her grandfather, her father, and her sister. In tracing the growth of English national consciousness, it is important to devote attention to the one ruler in Tudor history who deliberately outraged—and thereby fostered—the patriotism of her subjects. And in any attempt to account for that alliance of Protestantism and nationalism which has marked English history since the reign of Elizabeth, the reign of Mary the Catholic must ever be of crucial significance.

In the years when Mary wore the crown all of these developments were profoundly influenced by England's relations with her more powerful neighbors, France and Spain; yet in spite of this fact, no thorough study has been made of the diplomacy and intrigue which dominated the "barren interlude" (see Note on the Sources). The present work is an attempt to fill this hiatus. In form it is a duobiography of Simon Renard and Antoine de Noailles, the Spanish-Imperial and French ambassadors who fought out one of the century's most dramatic diplomatic duels at Mary's court. In substance it is a study of the diplomatic technique utilized by Habsburg and Valois to attain the hegemony of Europe by winning the mastery of England. In extent it reaches from the accession of Mary in 1553 to the outbreak of war between France and England in 1557.

The research in European archives upon which the following pages are based was made possible through the generosity of Harvard University and the donor of the Bayard Cutting Travelling Fellowship (1935-1936). I am grateful to the officials of the Public Record Office and the British Museum in London, the Archives du Ministère des Affaires Etrangères and the Bibliothèque Nationale in Paris, and the Bibliothèque Publique of Besançon for permission to consult books and manuscripts. The History Alumni Committee of Princeton University provided a term's leave-of-absence from teaching duties in which to accomplish the later stages of writing; and the Princeton University Research Committee has contributed generously to the cost of publication.

Of the many individuals who have contributed advice and suggestions, I am particularly indebted to Professor Roger B. Merriman of Harvard University who first suggested to me the need for further scholarly work in the reign of Mary and who has given freely of his time and knowledge, particularly during the early stages of the manuscript's preparation. To Professor J. E. Neale of University College, London; to Professors Raymond J. Sontag, Joseph R. Strayer, Ira O. Wade, and R. S. Willis, Jr., of Princeton University; and to Mr. Joseph A. Brandt, Director of the Princeton University Press, I am indebted for valuable suggestions and sympathetic interest. To Mr. and Mrs. Royall Tyler of Budapest, who graciously allowed me to make use of their transcripts of Spanish and Imperial material for the years 1555-1558, I owe sincerest thanks for their unfailing kindness during my stay abroad. For the long hours which my wife has spent with the manuscript full expression of gratitude would be impossible; apart from constant assistance in matters of detail, she has contributed much of whatever accuracy and grace there may be in the translations from the French. I regret that for reasons of cost it has been impossible to give the French or Spanish texts of all passages quoted from unprinted documents; but the translations have been made as literal as is consistent with intelligible English.

E. H. H.

Princeton, N.J.
September 1940.

CONTENTS

CONTENTS

ILLUSTRATIONS

RIVAL AMBASSADORS

AT THE COURT OF QUEEN MARY

ABBREVIATIONS

For full titles of works briefly cited in the text and not noticed here see the Bibliography. For description of manuscripts cited see the Note on the Sources.

Aff. Etr.: Archives du ministère des affaires étrangères, Paris, France. Unless otherwise noted, references are to Correspondance politique, Angleterre.

Antigny, Tyler: Royall Tyler's transcripts for 1555-1558 at Antigny-le-Château, par Arnay-le-Duc, Côte d'Or, France.

A.P.C.: Acts of the Privy Council of England, new series, J. R. Dasent, ed., 32 vols., London, 1890-1907.

Bib. Nat.: Bibliothèque Nationale, Paris, France.

——, f.f.: fonds français.

——, nouv. acq.: nouvelles acquisitions.

B.M.: British Museum, London, England.

D.N.B.: Dictionary of National Biography, 63 vols., London, 1885-1900.

Docs. inéds.: Colección de documentos inéditos para la historia de España, 112 vols., Madrid, 1842-1895.

Dom. Cal.: Calendar of State Papers, Domestic, 1547-1590, 2 vols., London, 1856.

For. Cal.: Calendar of State Papers, Foreign, Edward VI, and Mary, 2 vols., London, 1861.

Gachard and Piot: *Collection des voyages des souverains des Pays-Bas,* L. P. Gachard and Charles Piot, eds., 4 vols., Brussels, 1874-1882.

P.R.O.: Public Record Office, London, England.

——, S.P.: State Papers.

——, Tyler: Royall Tyler's transcripts for 1554.

Span. Cal.: Calendar of State Papers, Spanish, 11 vols., London, 1862—.

Tytler: P. F. Tytler, *England under the reigns of Edward VI and Mary,* 2 vols., London, 1839.

Ven. Cal.: Calendar of State Papers, Venetian, 9 vols., London, 1864-1898.

Vertot: René Aubert de Vertot, *Ambassades de Messieurs de Noailles en Angleterre,* 5 vols., Leyden, 1763.

Weiss: *Papiers d'état du cardinal de Granvelle,* Charles Weiss, ed., 9 vols., Paris, 1841-1852.

Wiesener: Louis Wiesener, *La jeunesse d'Elisabeth d'Angleterre,* Paris, 1878.

CHAPTER I

THE DIPLOMACY OF DYNASTS

ON July 6, 1553, the only legitimate son of Henry VIII, a precocious but pitiful figure of a boy-king, breathed his last at Greenwich. For the first time in English history the legal successor to the throne was a woman. She was Mary the Catholic, daughter of Henry VIII and Catherine of Aragon. Plain, honest, outspoken, and pious, she was the most admirable and the least attractive of the Tudors. If she made good her claim to the crown, she would marry, of course. The "regimen of women" was as unfamiliar to Englishmen as it was monstrous to John Knox; and the idea that a woman might rule alone, unaided by a husband and without prospect of bearing an heir to her throne, was unthinkable—until a Virgin Queen had successfully ruled England for many years. Half-English and half-Spanish as she was, it was natural that Mary had once been affianced to her first-cousin on her mother's side, the Emperor Charles V. But after Henry VIII divorced his Spanish Queen, a second marital alliance between England and Spain soon lost its attractions. Now that her father and half-brother were dead, however, there was every reason to believe that Mary would look to Spain or the Empire for a bridegroom. During the spring and summer of 1553, therefore, the monarchs and diplomats of almost all Europe suddenly became interested in the dramatic events which were unfolding in London. Most interested of all were the heads of the two most powerful dynasties on the Continent, Charles V, Emperor of Germany and King of Spain, and Henry II, King of France.

*   *   *

The dominating political fact of the first half of the sixteenth century was the struggle for European hegemony between the rival dynasties of Habsburg and Valois. As we look back upon it today, there was hardly a diplomatic episode, no matter how insignificant or remote, which was not in some way related to this rivalry. A vacancy in the Polish throne, a religious revolution in a petty German state, a trade concession at the Sublime Porte, a papal election, a rebellion in Ireland, a discovery of gold in the New World, or a shipwreck on the coasts of the Old, any one of these events might tip the balance in favor of the Emperor or the Most Christian King and set the diplomatic couriers scurrying over the face of Europe. To the leading dynasties and ruling classes of the time, the stakes seemed high; to us of a later generation they seem incredibly paltry. Ministers wrote endless dispatches, ambassadors blundered through endless audiences, and generals directed endless indecisive campaigns to determine who should rule in Navarre or Milan, what should be the political fate of Burgundy or the Nether-lands, what religion should prevail in Germany and what petty dynasty in a dozen petty Italian states. But underneath all the insignificant episodes, written between the lines of every verbose dispatch, was one vital issue: who was to be the acknowledged arbiter of Europe's destinies, the Emperor or his Valois rival? If the issue had ever been clearly decided (which it was not), the stream of Europe's history would have cut channels quite different from its course as we know it today.

The monarchs who directed, the ministers who planned, and the envoys who executed the foreign policies of sixteenth-century governments were motivated by most of the same forces which dictate the actions of statesmen today. But they did not think as we do. Their conscious motives were the product of a climate of opinion which can be sensed only by an effort of the historical imagination. It is difficult for the modern historian to divest him-self of the prejudice that nationalism and economic imperialism have always been the bases of diplomacy, as they are today. It is the fashion of an age in which the mass and the machine are king to scorn the political and biographical approaches to history and to see a social and economic explanation for the actions of in-dividuals and governments everywhere and at all times. Historical science has gained immeasurably by this recent emphasis, but it has lost something as well: the touch and feel of remote ages. History must inevitably be "contemporary thought about the past"; but contemporary thought about the past is most truly history when it projects itself in imagination from the thought-forms of its own age into those of the past. The embryonic sense of nationality and the expanding commercial capitalism which mark the Age of the Reformation were not the only motive forces of its diplomacy. Important they undoubtedly were, and earlier historians too often neglected them. But to sixteenth-century statesmen themselves, the motive forces of the age were dynastic prestige and religion—and the modern socio-economic historian neglects them at his peril.

Nowhere does this become more evident than in attempting to define the general factors which underlay the foreign policy of any particular state in the sixteenth century. Diplomacy was the personal prerogative of the monarch, and to describe the character of the monarch is often to describe the character of his country's foreign relations. The marriage or conversion of a king—one is almost tempted to say his dietary habits and his glandular structure—affected the relations of nations as intimately as geographical and economic factors. Geography, commerce, and public sentiment formed a frame-work within which any sovereign was compelled to plan his diplomacy, but within this frame-work he was remarkably free.

*　　*　　*

France in 1553 was the largest national monarchy in Europe. Writers on the origins of national sentiment delight to argue about whether the monarchy created the French nation or whether the French people created the national monarchy. Whatever the truth may be, the victory of national over dynastic interests was not complete until the French Revolution; sixteenth-century monarchs were often nationalists by accident but always dynasts by design. It was Henry II who first extended the frontiers of France almost to the Rhine by seizing the bishoprics of Metz, Toul, and Verdun in 1552, and it was the fashion of older text-books to say that he was therefore the first French monarch who had a clear

conception of the "natural boundaries" of France. But the tendency
of modern scholarship is to see chance rather than deliberate purpose in Henry's "watering his horses in the Rhine." Whatever its
ex post facto significance to patriotic poets like Ronsard, the attack
on Lorraine was a mere incident in a foreign policy which was
motivated not by national sentiment but by dynastic and personal
considerations.[1]

Everything we know of Henry II's character and up-bringing
confirms this judgment.[2] His most prominent traits—love of
tournaments and the chase, a lively sense of personal honor, and a
stubborn loyalty to servants who had remained faithful to him—
belonged rather to the Age of Chivalry than to modern times. He
sent his armies against the Spaniards in Italy largely because
appeals made by the Italian exiles who crowded his court touched
his romantic sense of chivalry; and his hatred for Charles V was
rooted in bitter memories of the four years he had spent in Madrid
as the Emperor's prisoner (1526-1530) and in the uneasy suspicion
that his cold, calculating rival was no gentleman.

His life as Dauphin had been curiously similar to Mary's life as
Princess. Both had incurred their father's disfavor, both had spent
long years in exile from court, and both had been denied that
intimate contact with political affairs which is usually the pre-
requisite of successful statesmanship. In Mary's case, the result
was a fanatical longing to erase the stain of her father's heresy;
in Henry's, a more mundane desire to reverse his father's policies,
ruin his father's ministers, and enjoy the worldly pleasures which
had so long been denied him. In both there was a certain lack
of political objectivity, a stubborn devotion to friends who had
remained faithful in adversity, a tendency to be swayed by a few
trusted intimates. But there the parallel ends. Whereas Mary set
her course and followed it with all the stubbornness characteristic

---

[1] See Gaston Zeller, *La réunion de Metz à la France* (Strasbourg, 1926); and Lucien
Romier, *Origines politiques des guerres de religion*, 2 vols. (Paris, 1913-1914). There is
a brief summary of the problem in Henri Sée and Armand Rebillon, *Le seizième siècle*
(Paris, 1934), 187.

[2] On the subject of this and the following paragraphs, see Romier, *Origines politiques*,
Vol. I, Chaps. I and II, and pp. 174-7; François Decrue, *Anne de Montmorency*, Vol. II,
passim; and Ernest Charrière, ed., *Négociations de la France dans le Levant*, Vol. II
(editor's comments, *passim*).

of her family, Henry never really had a policy. As one writer has remarked, he was "an ordinary man" called by the accident of birth to govern a kingdom.[3] Intelligent but indolent, lacking in political experience and somewhat diffident about his own opinions, he left it to those whom he trusted as individuals to steer the ship of state whither they would. The only care he took was to see that *all* those who had remained faithful to him as Dauphin were on the quarter-deck with him, and the result was that the ship tacked violently from side to side.

French foreign policy under Henry II, in other words, was the product of court intrigue. By 1550 there were two organized factions among his advisers. Each cordially hated the other and each had about an equal share of the King's favor. If Anne de Montmorency, Constable and Peer of France, was Henry's "prime minister," the Guises were his personal favorites. The former was the balance-wheel of French diplomacy, the latter were its driving-force.

Montmorency controlled the diplomatic machinery of the government. Ambassadors and secretaries of state were generally his creatures. Foreign ambassadors turned to him for statements of the royal policy before they approached the King; individuals and factions which had an interest in foreign affairs were compelled (as Henry's Queen, Catherine de' Medici, once remarked), "to go through the Constable's door"; and the *conseil des affaires* (a committee of the King's Council which determined all important questions of policy) was dependent upon him for carrying out its decisions.[4]

The most important fact about Montmorency in 1553 was that he was old. The advancing years had brought wealth, power, and a large family, and the Constable was content. His genius lay in diplomacy and administration, not in war and court intrigue. He knew that any disturbance in the *status quo* in foreign or domestic affairs would profit his brilliant young rivals, the Guises, and shake the security of his position. It was characteristic of him that

[3] Romier, *Origines politiques*, I, 24.
[4] On Montmorency's position see in particular Decrue, *Montmorency*, II, 38-41; and Romier, *Origines politiques*, I, 34-42.

he had profound respect for Charles V's wisdom and experience and that his respect was returned. It was also characteristic that he excelled in the patient preparation of military campaigns and failed miserably in their execution. In spite of an ambition typical of an aristocratic age to advance his family's fortunes, he had many of the elements of true statesmanship—a profound patriotism, a concern for the interests of the nation as a whole, and an honest desire to keep France at peace. "I desire peace," he once told a papal nuncio, "because I am a Christian, because I am an old man, and because I find myself in a good situation."[5] There was no war in Henry II's reign which the Constable did not try to prevent, no peace offer to which he turned a deaf ear, no peace conference which he did not either initiate or support.

It was otherwise with the Guises. Charles de Guise, Cardinal of Lorraine, was the brains of the family. Tactful and soft-spoken where Montmorency was candid and haughty, he had a charm of manner and a subtlety of approach which gave his family the advantage whenever it was a question of back-stairs intrigue, of winning the favor of the King's elderly mistress, or of negotiating a secret treaty with the Pope. He was the typical Renaissance prelate: cultured, urbane, and ambitious to the core. If he was the statesman of the family, his elder brother François, Duke of Guise, was its popular hero. Young as he was, the Duke was already the ablest general in France, the acknowledged leader of the younger, war-loving nobility, and the idol of the Catholic populace. While the Cardinal bid the cards, the Duke played them—and he seldom fell short of the contract if the problem were one of sheer military ability.

All over Europe the House of Lorraine had interests and ambitions which would profit by the right kind of upset in the *status quo*. Mary, sister of Charles and François, was Queen Regent of Scotland. Her daughter, Mary Stuart, was betrothed to the Dauphin—one of the many reasons which the Guises had to claim special favor with the King. The family's claims extended not only to Scotland and Lorraine but also to Italy, and it was François's

[5] Romier, *Origines politiques*, I, 38.

cherished ambition to obtain the crown of Naples, and his brother's, to obtain the papal tiara. Athwart each of these ambitions lay the power of Spain—in Italy, on the Rhine, perhaps even in Scotland's neighbor England, now that a Queen who was half-Spanish claimed the throne. It went without saying that the Cardinal and the Duke were always the leaders of the war-party in the *conseil des affaires,* the inveterate foes of Montmorency's policy of caution and compromise.[6]

Henry II was never so uneasy as when either faction showed signs of getting the upper hand at his council-table through the absence of a leader on the opposing side. Neither his trust in Montmorency's judgment nor his personal attachment to the Guises ever wavered. The result was that although the Constable never really had a party of his own (except for a handful of civil servants and relatives such as Secretary L'Aubespine and his famous nephew, Gaspard de Coligny), and although he usually found himself in a minority of one in Council, his jealous young rivals were never able to break his grip on the machinery of state, in spite of their popularity among the French aristocracy, their control of the Church, and their powerful foreign connections, particularly with the Curia. Sometimes Henry's foreign policy was the Constable's, sometimes it was the Cardinal of Lorraine's, but more often it was both—a dual diplomacy, inherently contradictory, pursued at one and the same time by different agents in different parts of Europe. The French ambassadors in London during Mary's reign, appointees of the Constable but also personal friends of the Guises, were to suffer from this dualism on more than one occasion.

There was, however, one fairly consistent tendency in French foreign policy after the death of Francis I: a shift in interest from south to north, from Italy to the northeastern frontier and the British Isles. Once at the beginning of his reign and once toward the end Henry became involved in Italian adventures, but so far as the Guises and the Italian *fuorusciti* permitted him, he showed "a spontaneous tendency to direct his military activity toward the

6 Romier, *op. cit.,* I, 45-57; Decrue, *Montmorency,* II, 12-14.

North and in particular against the English."[7] To extend the boundaries of France on the northeast, and in particular to dislodge the English from their footholds on the Continent, was his deepest ambition. The recovery of Boulogne from England in 1550 was the first step; seizure of the Lorraine bishoprics, the second; an attack on Calais would be the third.

Here Montmorency and the Guises differed only on methods, not on the objective. The Constable preferred to gain the desired ends by diplomacy, by playing England off against the Empire, by cooperating with any English government which was not actively hostile until the time was ripe for a diplomatic or military *coup*. The Cardinal and the Duke, on the other hand, generally advocated the threat or use of military force, for reasons already suggested. However, there was a compromise policy on which both Montmorency and his rivals could usually agree: underhanded intrigue with one or another of the religio-political factions which fought for control of the English government after the death of Henry VIII. The Constable insisted only that so long as France was involved in war with the Emperor on other fronts, such intrigue should be curbed whenever it ran the risk of provoking a breach in diplomatic relations with England. The Guises did not care.

Other more impersonal forces—religious, social, and economic—had an important, but not a determining influence on French diplomacy. Henry II, Montmorency, and the Guises were all Catholics, but the secular tone of the age is nowhere more evident than in the willingness of all of them to make alliances with the infidel and the heretic in order to embarrass the Emperor. Catholic piety in French governing circles required merely that, for the sake of public opinion, a decorous cloak of secrecy be cast over negotiations with the Turk and with the Protestants in Germany and England. Ancient popular enmities were hardly more determining. French national sentiment had been forged on the anvil of war with England, but the French and English governments had got on with each other unusually well during the first

[7] Romier, *op. cit.*, I, 29. cf. Decrue, *op. cit.*, II, 39-41.

half of the sixteenth century and the economic interests of the rising middle classes generally favored peace. The nobility was the one class which profited from war in an age when lucrative military offices were still the preserve of the aristocracy and plunder generally found its way into the pockets of generals and captains. The nobles' revenues were fixed, and prices were rising; any foreign adventure, therefore, was apt to arouse their enthusiasm. But this enthusiasm did not necessarily determine the particular objectives of military ventures.

* * *

If French foreign policy was predominantly dynastic and personal in its motivation, Habsburg diplomacy was almost exclusively so. The vast conglomeration of kingdoms, principalities, and colonies in the Old World and the New that was Charles V's Empire has long been the prototype of dynastic pretensions, and its ruler, the personification of dynastic statecraft.[8] While others had conquered (in the words of the famous proverb), the House of Austria had married; and Charles of Burgundy at sixteen was heir to three of the proudest ruling families in Europe, those of Austria, Burgundy, and Spain. Now at fifty-three he was Emperor of Germany, King of Spain, Lord of the Netherlands, and ruler of half Italy. A generation of experience in ruling his scattered dominions had taught him much—the force of the rising sentiment of nationality, the stubbornness of the new heresy, the importance of the expanding middle class—but his ideals were still what they had always been, supra-national, Catholic, and dynastic.

In 1553 Charles was old, crippled by gout, and weary of life. He had reached the apogee of his prestige in Europe six years before in the year following his victory over the rebellious German princes at Mühlberg, but since then he had left the initiative to his enemies—to the Turks, the Lutherans, and the French. He had spent his life in the dogged pursuit of one aim, to preserve the vast inheritance which had fallen to him and to pass it on unim-

---

[8] On this and what follows, see Edward Armstrong, *The Emperor Charles V*, 2 vols. (London, 1902); Karl Brandi, *The Emperor Charles V* (New York, 1939); and in particular, R. B. Merriman, *Rise of the Spanish Empire*, III, 398-413.

paired to his son, Philip of Spain. The spirit which guided his every thought and action (in the felicitous phrase of a recent historian) was that of "sturdy defensiveness."[9] No proposal to the German Diet, no instructions to his representatives in Spain or Italy, no dispatch to his ambassadors abroad seems ever to have been motivated by anything but the desire to preserve what God in His infinite wisdom had given him. *Austriae est imperare orbi universo* was the proud motto of his family, the dream of many of his ministers, and the nightmare of his enemies. But scholars are still in doubt about how deeply the prudent and rather unimaginative Christian gentleman who fell heir to such heavy responsibilities was moved by the vision of world-empire. Certainly in the twilight of his life Charles was tired, tired as was Spain herself, tired as even all of Europe was after more than a generation of religious and dynastic strife.

Perhaps it was Charles's temperamental inability to seize the initiative except when some crisis stirred his sense of duty and roused him from his natural lethargy which saved Europe from being dominated by one man in the early sixteenth century. The Spanish army was the best of its age; the fortune in gold and silver which poured in from Spain's trans-Atlantic colonies was the envy of other monarchs; and the Netherlands were the money-market and commercial hub of Europe. But in spite of the potential resources of his dominions, Charles had his back to the wall in the 1550's.

France was consistently successful in the war which broke out in 1551. The Emperor's long struggle with the Lutherans in Germany was resulting in stalemate. His persistent attempts to persuade the Electors to recognize his son Philip as his successor in the Holy Roman Empire had met with obstinate refusal, and there was constant friction over this and other issues with his brother Ferdinand, King of the Romans and ruler of Austria, to whom much of the Imperial authority in Germany was already committed in practice. Charles's government in the Netherlands was woefully short of funds and Spain was as reluctant as ever to consider his wider dynastic interests as her own. Like Elizabeth

[9] Merriman, *op. cit.*, III, 408-9.

of England after him, he always put his deepest trust in the healing power of time, in the subconscious conviction that most political difficulties can be solved only by a sort of "resolute irresolution."[10] In 1553 he was waiting patiently for some change in the European kaleidoscope which would enable him to establish Philip's authority in his dominions and allow him to lay down the responsibilities which he had borne so long.

With the accession of his cousin to the throne of England the opportunity for which he was waiting seemed to have arrived. The crisis in London was of far more direct interest to him than to Henry II, Montmorency, and the Guises. England lay athwart the life-line of the Habsburg Empire, the sea-route from Spain to the Netherlands. Cut off from the money-markets in Flanders, Spanish gold was sterile; and Spanish man-power was essential to the defense of the Low Countries against French attack. To bring England into the Habsburg orbit would solve the problem of imperial defense and forge the last link in the iron chain which already came close to encircling France.

In the conduct of foreign affairs, Charles was his own prime minister. Any hesitations and contradictions in Habsburg diplomacy were primarily the result of the Emperor's character and the conflicting interests of his many dominions, not of court intrigue. To be sure there were factions in Brussels as there were in Paris. Among Charles's ministers there were Spaniards, Flemings, and Burgundians, and each group was jealous of the others. If Montmorency had a counterpart in the Imperial administration it was Antoine Perrenot de Granvelle, Bishop of Arras and later (1561) Cardinal Granvelle. As a native of the Franche-Comté he was disliked by Flemish nobles and Spanish grandees alike, but there was no rivalry at Brussels comparable to that of Montmorency and the Guises until Philip took over the reins and began to displace his father's servants with Spaniards. Although Granvelle controlled the diplomatic machinery of the Emperor's court, he never had the personal ascendancy over his master which the Constable had over Henry II. He was comparatively

---

[10] The phrase is used of Elizabeth in J. R. Seeley, *The Growth of British Policy* (one-vol. ed., Cambridge, 1922), 180.

young, a cleric of rather humble birth; and his sovereign was
older, wiser, and (even in ill-health) considerably more interested
in affairs of state than the King of France. Both decision and inde-
cision in Habsburg diplomacy were the Emperor's.

*   *   *

It is difficult for a later generation to remember that Henry
VIII's England was at best a second-rate power, with only about a
fifth the population of France and a mere fraction of the colonial
resources possessed by Spain and Portugal. In 1553 the kingdom's
prestige on the Continent was something even less than second-
rate, and this fact, too often forgotten by insular historians of the
nineteenth century, is fundamental to any understanding of
Mary's reign.[11]

The first two Tudors had managed to make their small island
kingdom a factor to be reckoned with in European diplomacy.
Henry VII had restored its foreign prestige after the War of the
Roses, and Henry VIII, Wolsey, and Thomas Cromwell were
often able to command a high price for English aid to one or
another of the continental powers. A strategic geographical position, a sizable navy which could usually command the Channel
in a crisis, an amateur army of rather doubtful efficiency but
sturdy personnel, and a flourishing commerce were England's
assets in the diplomatic game. A political system too closely dependent upon the character and survival of the monarch was her
chief liability—a fact which became only too evident to foreign
powers after the death of Henry VIII.

The decline, as Pollard has shown, began even before 1547.[12]
The King left Protector Somerset a staggering legacy of debt,
domestic discontent, and foreign danger. However much Somerset did to preserve order at home and prestige abroad during his
two years of power (1547-1549), there can be no disputing the
disastrous effects of the Duke of Northumberland's rule (1549-

---

[11] Continental historians have naturally been struck more often by this fact than their
English brethren. See e.g. the works of Constant and A. O. Meyer cited in the Bibliography; and in particular, Friedmann, *Les dépêches de Giovanni Michiel*, pp. xviii-xix.

[12] A. F. Pollard, *England under Protector Somerset* (London, 1900), Chap. II.

1553). In four short years, thanks to the ambition of a rapacious and unscrupulous adventurer, England became the laughing-stock of Europe, an object of contempt to intriguing foreign diplomats. The shifts and makeshifts which English statesmen used to keep their nation free of foreign control were almost pathetic: hollow promises, still hollower threats, and offers of mediation which no one took seriously. English agents abroad quickly lost their influence and most of them were acutely conscious of the fact. Foreign ambassadors in London, if they were intelligent and alert, quickly acquired an influence far beyond what they had been able to exert when Henry VIII was on the throne. Most foreign statesmen and some Englishmen assumed that England was destined to gravitate sooner or later within the orbit of either the Habsburg or the Valois monarchy. None could foresee that an English Queen would one day hold the balance between the two great dynasties on the Continent. Like a restless invalid tossing from side to side on a bed of pain, England turned from France to Spain and back again; and like false friends, France and Spain sat by the bedside offering the advice of Job's comforters and scheming within themselves how to seize upon the inheritance of the deceased.

A few incidents of Edward VI's reign are particularly eloquent of the contempt which both French and Spanish monarchs had acquired for England's weakness, especially after Somerset's fall in November 1549.[13]

The Protector had followed the normal and traditional orientation of English policy, an Anglo-Imperial alliance against France, with considerable vigor and success. For centuries the wool-trade had bound England and the Netherlands in the closest of economic ties; the English middle classes, if they thought about it at all, were pro-Imperial and anti-French;[14] and Somerset's chief sup-

---

13 On English foreign relations between 1547 and 1553, see A. O. Meyer, *Die Englische Diplomatie in Deutschland;* Decrue, *Montmorency;* Pollard, *op. cit.;* Constant, "Le mariage de Marie Tudor et de Philippe II"; Charles Sturge, *Northumberland* (Univ. of London, thesis); Gachard and Piot, *Voyages,* Preface, Vol. IV; *Ven. Cal.,* Preface, Vol. V; *For. Cal., Ed. VI;* and particularly, *Span. Cal.,* Vols. IX to XI. (Full titles in Bibliography.)
14 On this both French and Imperial ambassadors were fairly well agreed in 1553. *Span. Cal.,* XI, 19; Vertot, II, 43.

port was drawn from the mercantile community. Naturally his enemies at home inclined toward a French alliance, if only from spite. There is evidence, for instance, that Admiral Seymour's plot against his brother, the Protector, in January 1549, gained the support of the French ambassador, Odet de Selve;[15] and still better evidence that when Somerset was railroaded to his death by Northumberland at the close of the year 1551, another French ambassador played a disreputable part in hastening the execution.[16]

There is some disagreement among scholars about the underlying motives of Northumberland's foreign policy, but none about its results. The Duke's only biographer maintains that he was fundamentally no more pro-French than Somerset, that his ideal was to avoid entangling alliances of any sort, and that he was finally driven into a French alliance by the necessities of his domestic policy. The Duke's cynical support of the radical wing of the Protestant party and his persecution of Mary, the hope of the Catholics, alienated the Emperor and made it necessary to seek support in France, since "few if any believed that, without foreign assistance, England was strong enough to resist either France or the Empire."[17] Another writer implies, on the other hand, that Northumberland turned the realm into "little more than a French province" from personal preference.[18] Whatever the motives—the Duke is one of the most inscrutable characters in English history—the results were disastrous. Within a few years there seemed to be nothing to prevent Henry II's actually making a French province out of England if he had the will. When an adventurer named Thomas Stukeley told Northumberland in September 1552 that the King of France meant to attack Calais and seize Falmouth, Dartmouth and Plymouth, the Duke was easily persuaded that the report was false and proceeded to make what profit he could out of the incident by informing Henry himself of the informer's story.[19] In fact, England might well have been swallowed up by her ancient enemy during Northumberland's

[15] *Span. Cal.*, IX, pp. xxxiii *ff*.   [16] *ibid.*, X, pp. xli *ff*.
[17] Sturge, *Northumberland*, 95, 125-7, 165.
[18] Royall Tyler, in *Span. Cal.*, IX, p. lxi; X, p. xxxi.
[19] *Span. Cal.*, X, p. lv, and p. 564, note.

rule had it not been for two factors: the war which broke out between Henry II and Charles V in 1551 and the dualism in French policy which has already been mentioned. The war on the Continent absorbed all of Henry's energy and resources, and Montmorency persuaded him that it was the better part of valor to preserve England's friendly neutrality rather than to take advantage of her weakness by an act of unprovoked aggression.

The paramount threat to English independence between 1549 and 1553, then, came from France, the ally of the tyrant Northumberland whom the vast majority of Englishmen hated. Within a few short months the threat was to come from Spain, ally of the Queen who was hailed by her people as their savior from Northumberland's tyrannies. When it came, this second threat was more dangerous than the first. The domination of England was of more positive interest to Charles V than to Henry II; Mary, unlike Northumberland, was personally and unalterably prejudiced in favor of the continental power which was beginning to cast its shadow over the realm; and the majority of English statesmen and merchants had been brought up to fear the Empire less than France. Furthermore, there were some in the Emperor's service who were already as contemptuous of England's ability to resist foreign domination as were Henry II's advisers.

The story of the Imperial ambassador's plot to spirit the Princess Mary out of England in the summer of 1550 is a fair illustration of the low opinion which Charles's servants had of the English government's strength and watchfulness. The game was dangerous and fortunately Mary's household servants persuaded her not to take part in it, but the fact that Charles approved the venture, prudent as he was, proves how ready he was to gamble for high stakes where England was concerned.[20] A year later his sister Mary, Queen Dowager of Hungary and Regent of the Netherlands, suggested that in order to protect the trade-route between Spain and the Netherlands and to anticipate the French, it would be wise to seize a port on the southern coast of England. "Many people are of the opinion," she wrote, "that the kingdom of England would not be impossible to conquer, and especially now that it is a prey

[20] ibid., X, pp. xii-xx, and 124-35.

to discord and poverty." The way might be prepared by some "intelligent ambassador . . . such as Renard"; then someone attached to the Habsburgs might try his hand at conquering the nation and marry the Princess Mary to establish his power.[21] The Emperor's war with France combined with his lack of money made any trial of the scheme impossible for the time being, but the incident shows clearly enough what was in his mind and the mind of his advisers after 1551. Given the funds, the opportunity, and the right man as ambassador, England might be added to the Habsburg estates. The funds were never forthcoming, but on July 6, 1553, both the opportunity and the man appeared when Edward VI died at Greenwich and Simon Renard arrived in London.

* * *

When the crisis came in England, both Henry II and Charles V had exceptionally able representatives on the spot. Greater French ambassadors than Antoine de Noailles and greater Imperial or Spanish ambassadors than Simon Renard appeared at the courts of Tudor rulers, but never before or after did two diplomats of such marked and equally matched ability appear at the same time and with so much at stake. The result was perhaps the most dramatic and significant diplomatic duel of the century.

The personality of an ambassador was never so important a factor in the relations between governments as it was during the dawn of modern diplomacy; and apart from the significance of their characters for an understanding of what follows, Noailles and Renard are of considerable interest as examples of the amateurs who were Europe's earliest resident ambassadors. A French scholar once remarked that there were three stages in the evolution of the sixteenth-century diplomat: first the soldier, second the lawyer or ecclesiastic, and finally the expert and cultivated statesman.[22] There were no sharp dividing lines, but Antoine de Noailles belonged primarily to the first class; Renard and Mary's Chancellor, Stephen

---

[21] *Span. Cal.*, X, 378-9, and note.
[22] M. D. Nisard, quoted by Tamizey de Larroque in his *Lettres inédites de François de Noailles,* 13-14, note.

Gardiner, to the second; the Cardinal of Lorraine and Antoine de Noailles's brother François, to the third.

*   *   *

The life of Antoine, Seigneur de Noailles, might be written as a commentary on the ancient motto, *noblesse oblige*.[23] A sense of the position to which he was born and its responsibilities, an innate and inarticulate loyalty to King and country, an honest and undogmatic devotion to the religion of his forefathers, these were the guiding stars of his life. Experience, responsibility, and honor came to him early, not because he was precocious or more than moderately ambitious, but because he was the eldest son of an ancient and illustrious family, a family whose lineal descendants today can trace their ancestry back to the eleventh century. Friendships, recognition, and high office—everything, in fact, but material reward—came to him without striving and without price. He was human enough to appreciate the world's acclaim and to complain rather bitterly in later life about the royal ingratitude for his "pains and trouble," but even in moments of disappointment and discouragement his strong sense of duty and his temperamental optimism saved him from the resentment born of thwarted ambition. When the world was against him, when the Queen of England was impugning his integrity or when factious Bordeaux magistrates were blackening his character, he remembered that he was the scion of an ancient and honorable house, the intimate of the great men of his day, the friend of his King; and the thought preserved his self-confidence and self-respect. In a word, the fact that he was Seigneur de Noailles explains much in his character and career.

[23] The most important source for the life of Antoine de Noailles is "Divers mémoires pris sur les originaux pour la vie d'Antoine de Noailles," Bib. Nat., f.f., No. 6948. For later accounts see "Relation des ambassades des Seigneurs de Noailles . . . ," Bib. Nat., f.f., nouv. acq., No. 9520 (the manuscript from which the first volume of Vertot's *Ambassades* was printed with many omissions); a brief biography (which touches on many details not included in the above finished draft, and which is written in the same hand) in Bib. Nat., f.f., nouv. acq., No. 328, fols. 48-60; and Tamizey de Larroque's article, "Antoine de Noailles à Bordeaux," which is based upon Bib. Nat., f.f., No. 6948. See Note on the Sources and Bibliography.

The present village of Noailles in the Department of Corrèze was once a Roman villa called Nobiliacum, and it was near there in the old province of Limousin that Antoine de Noailles was born on September 4, 1504, the eldest of nineteen children. All three of his brothers who survived infancy—Hugues (b. 1511), François (b. 1519), and Gilles (b. 1524)—entered upon ecclesiastical careers and were eventually drawn into diplomacy, a fact which induced one enthusiastic eighteenth-century historian to remark that France in the sixteenth century "had need of hardly more than one family to fill all its embassies."[24] Antoine's education was the personal concern of his father, Louis de Noailles, who must have taught him the patriotism and the sense of duty which were so much a part of his character, along with the Latin, the Italian, and the Spanish of which he acquired so good a command. Like most of his fellow-countrymen who became diplomats, he knew no English and never bothered to learn more than a few phrases of it. His practical and rather unimaginative mind, so unlike the inquiring and reflective mentality of his more famous brother François, was probably the result of his training. War, diplomacy, and administration, rather than literature and the arts, were the natural vocations of an eldest son; and Antoine was both soldier and diplomat before he was thirty. His military career began at the age of sixteen in Italy and he never lost his taste for the thrill of war. In his time diplomacy was an adjunct of war in a more intimate sense than it is today, and after he had proved his military ability by organizing the defense of Provence against a Spanish attack in 1536, minor diplomatic missions followed thick and fast. In the course of his service, both Montmorency and the Dauphin (the future Henry II) came to know and respect his talents.

In his early thirties he fell in love, and it was characteristic of him that not even a crusty prospective father-in-law who had other ideas about marrying his daughter could discourage him. The battle raged for four years, and it finally required no less than twelve *lettres de cachet* from Francis I to bring the doughty parent to terms. On May 31, 1540, the marriage contract was

---

[24] One of Vertot's collaborators, in Bib. Nat., f.f., No. 6948, fol. 246.

signed. It proved to be a happy match, blessed with eight children. Jeanne de Gontaut was a devoted wife and mother, but she took little part in her husband's career except to share in his triumphs and disappointments. In England she occasionally visited the Queen and sometimes sent the Chancellor a gift of preserves when he was ill, but her letters (charmingly misspelled) were concerned mostly with domestic details and maternal cares. After her husband's death she became one of Catherine de' Medici's ladies-in-waiting.[25]

After Henry II came to the throne Antoine de Noailles's commissions became steadily more important. In 1547 he was created a Councillor and *maître d'hôtel ordinaire*. The next summer, when the Admiral, D'Annebaut, fell into disgrace, Noailles was commissioned, along with his cousin Boisdauphin, to fit out two fleets at Brest and Havre which were to transport French troops to Scotland and to bring the child Queen, Mary Stuart, back to France. The commission was temporary and Noailles did not captain the ships which he equipped and victualled. But the technical knowledge which he gained of naval problems in general was of considerable value to him later in the innumerable maritime disputes which he was called upon to handle as ambassador. As reward for his services, he was made Governor of the Château du Ha in Bordeaux (1549), the King's Lieutenant General in Guienne (November 1551), and finally, Governor of Bordeaux (January 1552). In the fall of 1552 he was one of those who threw themselves into Metz with the Duke of Guise to defend the city against the Emperor's attack. Before the siege was raised on January 3, 1553, he had been designated to succeed Boisdauphin as ambassador to England.

Noailles was neither better nor worse equipped for the London post than his predecessor. He had fought the English at Boulogne and had sent off a fleet to Scotland, but he had never been in England.[26] There is reason to suspect, however, that the Constable

[25] Tamizey de Larroque, "Antoine de Noailles à Bordeaux," 452-5; Bib. Nat., f.f., No. 6948, fols. 16-24, 281-3. Jeanne's letters to François de Noailles from London are in Aff. Etr., IX, fols. 396, 423, 524, 542, 567; and Vertot, V, 194-5.

[26] In 1549 Van der Delft, the Imperial ambassador in London, wrote that "a gentleman of the chamber of the most Christian King . . . called Monsieur de Noailles" had

picked the best man he knew for a difficult and possibly dangerous position; and the fact that Noailles was left in London for three years seems to indicate that Montmorency was sure he had found the right man.

In a sense, he had. Antoine de Noailles had a good many of the qualities which made for successful diplomatic careers in his time. His character was a curious compound of contradictory traits: subtlety and naïveté, strong hatreds and warm affections, deep conscientiousness tempered by occasional *insouciance,* and a formal and forbidding dignity in public which belied a dry wit in private. To the average English councillor who had to deal with him, his most prominent trait must have been a blunt and caustic tactlessness, overlaid (except in moments of temper) with a veneer of polished urbanity. He could be bitingly ironic, coldly cordial, or even friendly in a distant sort of way; but he could never be charming, as his younger brother François was. He was what would be called today a man's man. He seems never to have taken the trouble to understand or cultivate the women whom he met in England. His information from ladies of the court came invariably through intermediaries, and his contempt for Mary as a stateswoman made it impossible for him to feel any pity for her as a woman until she became a forlorn and tragic figure, ignored by her husband and cheated of her hope of becoming a mother. He characteristically blamed her for being too womanly in yielding to her husband's every dictate and too unwomanly in her treatment of rebels and heretics. He was no more successful in understanding either the Chancellor, who was a lawyer and an ecclesiastic, or Cardinal Pole, who was something approaching a saint. In a word, he was a soldier and a patriot, and he had difficulty understanding those who appeared to be neither.

Fundamentally he was a man of action, not a man of thought. Reflection was always painful to him and he was never happy when the situation called for patience rather than activity. He

gone to court that day with Odet de Selve, the French ambassador (*Span. Cal.,* IX, 341). Delft must have received the news by word of mouth and misunderstood the name because Selve's companion was actually Louis II de Salazar, Seigneur d'Asnois (G. Lefèvre-Pontalis, ed., *Correspondance politique d'Odet de Selve,* 481-4).

dictated the great majority of his dispatches to secretaries and seldom took up his own time or that of his sovereign by philosophizing or by expounding what he thought the fundamental principles of French policy should be. Sanguine by temperament, practical and unspeculative by mental habit, he tended to confine himself to the problem of the moment; and even when he was most discouraged, he could always find comfort in even the most trivial bit of activity which might help remedy the situation.

Perhaps it was because he lacked considered opinions, because both his religion and his patriotism were matters of instinct rather than of reflection, that he got on well with both factions at the French court, with his military and diplomatic colleagues, and with the staff of his embassy in London. Montmorency once remarked that the ambassador was "of his own bringing up" and that he had always found him "honest and gentle."[27] The Duke of Guise and the Cardinal of Lorraine seem to have had hardly less respect for him than the Constable himself, and D'Oysel, ambassador to Scotland and creature of the Guises, was his firm friend. But it is significant that Noailles was most attracted to a man who belonged to neither faction at court, the Cardinal of Tournon.[28] If his brother François had "a kind of intellectual kinship" with Montaigne, Antoine had much the same kinship with the less literary moderates and trimmers of his time and could inspire the confidence and liking of extremists on both sides of the religious and political fence.[29] With the exception of one courier whom he suspected (probably falsely) of being a traitor,[30] his soldiers, his secretaries, and his spies served him with unwavering loyalty. His capacity for inspiring personal devotion was most

[27] Tytler, II, 356.

[28] He considered Tournon "la plus nette et solide cervelle d'homme d'estat que je cognoisse à nuit en la chrestienté." Tamizey de Larroque, "Antoine de Noailles à Bordeaux," 478-9.

[29] See Tamizey de Larroque, "Antoine de Noailles à Bordeaux," 479-80; *idem, Lettres inédites de François de Noailles,* 14; Vertot, I, 20; Bib. Nat., f.f., No. 6948, fol. 257.

[30] The man's name was Hogius. "Je n'ay peu prévoir en vous," he wrote Noailles in May 1554, "aulcung signe de bien veillance envers moy, ains au contraire ung perpétual mécontentement, une secrete déffiance et soubçon. . . . Du cas dont me tenez pour suspect j'en suis net comme l'enfant. . . ." Aff. Etr., IX, fols. 176-7. cf. *Span. Cal.,* XI, 75, 426; Vertot, II, 281, 299, 301; III, 211-12; and Aff. Etr., IX, fols. 61, 182.

apparent in his own family. François and Gilles looked up to him as both father and brother. The eldest brother always had the advancement and success of the younger two at heart, and he always looked forward with particular pleasure to François's visits. When there seemed to be a possibility in January 1556 that all three brothers might be in London at the same time, he counted eagery upon enjoying "a boon which can not often come to us."[31]

Antoine de Noailles was withal a more human figure than the portraits of him which have come down to us would suggest.[32] The lustreless and inscrutable eyes, the sallow cheeks and handsome beard, the heavy dignity of his countenance as sketched by contemporaries belied the rather naïve amateur in diplomacy and intrigue who stuck to his task only from a dogged sense of duty. He had a taste for good wine, a liking for card games, a knowledge of horseflesh, a zest for the chase, and a boyish interest in the pageantry of court life in a foreign country.[33] But he was never happy in London. The climate agreed with him no better than it did with most Frenchmen and he was particularly subject to "fluxions des yeux." While his body was in England, his heart was in France, either with the King's "gallant and puissant army" or in his native Limousin, "waging war on the hare and the partridge."[34] Once when diplomacy palled too much, he wrote Henry II that he needed a change of air because of a cold, left his most trusted servant La Marque in charge of the embassy, and travelled to a fair some hundred miles from London to buy some horses. It rained all the way and his party had to ride through mud up to their horses' bellies, but what chagrined him most was to see "700 or 800 of the best horses in England" pass by on their way to other purchasers. (Someone had misinformed him on the date, and the fair was over ere he arrived.) The student who appreciates humor, conscious and unconscious, will find much to enjoy

[31] Antoine to François de Noailles, 14 Jan. 1556, Aff. Etr., IX, fol. 582.

[32] There is an engraving of Antoine de Noailles (see frontispiece) in Bib. Nat., Collection Clairambault, No. 1139, Vol. 39: No. 1651, fol. 46v. See René Fage, Les Noailles peints par Oudry (Brive, 1922).

[33] See e.g. Vertot, II, 104; III, 313-14; V, 195; and D'Oysel to Noailles, 11 Oct. 1553, Aff. Etr., IX, fol. 82.

[34] Vertot, III, 257-8; Antoine to François de Noailles, 1 Sept. 1555, Aff. Etr., IX, fol. 517.

in Noailles's correspondence: Henry II sympathized with his "cold," and the ambassador answered solemnly that he would take better care of himself.[35]

It is tempting to say that Noailles resembled the traditional English squire in his personal tastes, his mental habits, and his dislike of living in a foreign country.

* * *

Simon Renard was a complete contrast to his rival in almost every way. Both were fundamentally French in language, thought, and culture. Both had seen military service and both were diplomats by necessity rather than by choice. But the differences were far more striking than the similarities.

Renard was an *homme nouveau,* his career, a sixteenth-century "success story." Brilliant and ambitious to the core, he climbed to fame through his own talents and the favor of a friend, only to sink to a pitiable end through his own faults of character and the bitter enmity of this same friend—Cardinal Granvelle.[36]

He was Noailles's junior by nine years, being born at Vesoul in the Franche-Comté about 1513.[37] We know nothing of his ancestry and parentage. At the University of Louvain, where he became *docteur ès droits,* he established a close friendship with the later Cardinal Granvelle. Granvelle's father, Imperial Chancellor from 1530 to his death in 1550, came to know and respect the ability of his son's friend, and in 1540, after Renard had been practising law for several years in his native city of Vesoul, the Chancellor had him appointed *Lieutenant du baillage d'Amont,*

---

[35] Antoine to François de Noailles, 6 Oct. 1555, Aff. Etr., IX, fol. 540. For the sequel, see *ibid.,* IX, fols. 545, 549, 554.

[36] Renard's life has been studied in some detail by three writers: "Vunière" (pseudonym for Neuvier), Mathieu Tridon, and Lucien Febvre. There is a brief account in Weiss (I, pp. xxxi-xxxiii). See Note on the Sources, pp. 354-5.

[37] Tyler (in *Span. Cal.,* X, p. x, note) argues that Renard was born in 1523 on the ground that the well known portrait of him attributed to Antonio Moro and now at Besançon (see p. 32) is inscribed "1553 AETATIS SUE 3°." I am convinced that Tyler is wrong. The "3°" was apparently once a "39." Renard, married to a wife of eighteen at that time, may have ordered the painter to soften the lines of age and alter the inscription. And his appointment in 1540 as Lieutenant d'Amont (no sinecure) becomes unintelligible if he was only seventeen. See "Vunière," *Etude historique,* 3; Tridon, "Renard," 116, 188-9, and notes; Febvre, *Philippe II,* 141, and notes.

a district of the Franche-Comté. In 1547 he was made *maître des requêtes ordinaires de l'hôtel* for Burgundy; the next year he was put in provisional charge of the government of the Duchy of Milan, created a Councillor of State, and sent to the Diet of Augsburg; and in January 1549, he was raised to the peerage with the rank of *chevalier* and the title of Seigneur de Barmont. At the end of the same month he was appointed ambassador to France.

Years later Renard wrote of this appointment (affecting the third person singular in referring to himself):

> When it became apparent that His Majesty was pleased by his services, a commission as ambassador to France was foisted upon him. . . . He was removed from court and sent to France against his will . . . , without instructions, and at a time when the temper of the French was inclining toward restlessness and war.[38]

There was no word of truth in the whole statement, unless it was in the last phrase. Strained relations between France and the Empire made war practically inevitable, and Renard's appointment offered little opportunity for real diplomatic achievement. But there is no evidence that he was anything but pleased by the honor at the time, and his full and careful instructions showed how concerned the Emperor was to postpone the eventual breach in Franco-Imperial relations as long as possible.

Renard fulfilled his first major diplomatic appointment quietly and without *éclat,* but capably enough to be considered the premier diplomat in the Imperial service when war finally broke out in 1551, two years and eight months later.[39] Soon after he arrived in Paris he found out that peace was at the mercy of an upset in the delicate balance between Montmorency and the Guises. He knew that Henry II's romantic whims were no less dangerous to the peace of Europe than his own master's stubborn sense of honor. The result was that he became convinced that war was inevitable and that there was little he could do as ambassador to stay its outbreak. His "gloomy advices" in 1550 and 1551 were

---

[38] Weiss, V, 18.

[39] Tridon, "Renard," 165. On Renard's first mission to France, see Tridon, *op. cit.,* Part I, Chap. I; and Decrue, *Montmorency,* II, 98-100. His correspondence from Paris is published in Weiss, Vol. III, and *Span. Cal.,* Vols. IX and X.

no more than objective statements of the truth as matters turned out, but Granvelle thought that by irritating the Emperor they were hastening the breach which they were meant to prevent.[40]

It was in Paris that he acquired his first interest in England, together with a lively sense of the danger to Habsburg interests of an Anglo-French alliance. He was actually better informed about the real state of affairs in London than Scheyfve, the Imperial ambassador on the spot.[41] It is not surprising, therefore, that three weeks after war broke out between France and the Empire Mary of Hungary suggested to Granvelle that Renard was the man for the London post.

For the moment, however, the Bishop of Arras had other plans for his friend. After Renard had rejoined the Emperor's court at Innsbruck in the fall of 1551 he was sent to the Council of Trent, then to his native Franche-Comté to convoke the Estates and raise money for the war. The following year he was with Charles at the siege of Metz while his future rival, Antoine de Noailles, was within the city walls. There he fell ill, probably with the gout which troubled him most of his life, and remained in retirement until June 1553, when he was drafted for service as one of three extraordinary Imperial ambassadors to England.

It appears that the Emperor had to promise him "exemplary reward" in order to persuade him to forget his bad health and cross the Channel.[42] Why this was necessary might be a mystery if we did not know something of his real ambitions from his later career. In his "autobiography," written in the form of a letter to Philip in 1562, he constantly reiterated the conviction that all his major diplomatic appointments, as well as his numerous minor missions in Germany and Italy, were deliberately contrived by Granvelle because Granvelle was jealous of his influence at court. There is no question that the Bishop of Arras was a jealous minister, but there is equally little question that Renard had what would be called today a persecution complex. He undoubtedly antedated Granvelle's enmity in writing a decade after the events. Their cor-

[40] Weiss, V, 18. The evidence in this case rests upon Renard's statement of some years later, but there seems to be no good reason to doubt it.

[41] *Span. Cal.,* X, p. x.   [42] *Span. Cal.,* XI, 250; Weiss, V, 21.

respondence suggests that the estrangement did not actually begin until after 1553 and that it was not complete until at least three years later.[43] But there was this much truth in Renard's later account: his deepest ambition was always to be "at the center of great affairs," to rise to a position of trust in the Emperor's Council at Brussels.[44] It was already obvious in 1553 that diplomacy was his *forte,* but he did not consider it his profession any more than did Noailles or any other sixteenth-century diplomat. If an embassy abroad bade fair to bring him fame and favor with the Emperor or his son, he would throw his whole heart into it, no matter how great the difficulties and dangers. But all too often diplomacy seemed to be a devious road to his end.

Renard was in every way a remarkable person. In the words of his first biographer, Abbé Boisot, "He was a very clever man, adroit, vehement, fine-spoken, but fond of mockery and turbulent"[45]—a judgment which has been echoed with curious unanimity by later writers.

His mind was brilliant and supple. Unlike Noailles he had the ability to look far ahead, to grasp the significant element in a mass of detail. In all of the French ambassador's dispatches there was nothing to compare with the penetrating analysis of the state of Europe and of the Habsburg cause which Renard drafted for Philip early in 1555. The original, written in the ambassador's own rapid and illegible hand with numerous erasures and changes, is an eloquent example of its author's habits of work and thought.[46] Since he was an acute and sensitive observer, with an infinite capacity for hard, painstaking work, his perspective was never distorted by neglect of detail. The great majority of his dispatches he drafted in his own hand, unwilling apparently to trust even the humdrum business of news-reporting to a secretary. This inexhaustible nervous energy seems to have been characteristic in

---

[43] Febvre, *Philippe II,* 144 *ff.* cf. Renard's "autobiography," Weiss, V, 12-26.

[44] "Vunière," *Etude historique,* 39.

[45] Quoted by Weiss (I, p. xxxii) and many others. Boisot was the first scholar to examine Renard's papers. See Note on the Sources.

[46] Weiss, IV, 359-67. Original in Besançon, Bibliothèque publique, Fonds Granvelle, Vol. 73.

Simon Renard, by Antonio Moro(?)

general of those industrious Comtois from the valleys of the Jura who served Charles V so well in administration and diplomacy: his fellow-countryman Granvelle sometimes drew up forty or fifty letters a day and was reputed to be able to dictate dispatches to five secretaries in five different languages at the same time.

In a day when diplomacy was a far more personal affair than today, Renard's greatest asset was his power of expression. His legal training helped him to veil a subtle purpose beneath a frank and persuasive eloquence. Marshalling arguments, anticipating objections, turning the flank of an opponent's case, these were his most congenial mental occupations. His forensic strokes were those of a professional while Noailles's seemed those of an amateur by comparison. His resourcefulness in argument was of little use to him so long as he was dealing with a practiced diplomat like Montmorency, but it was to prove a startlingly effective weapon in dealing with a woman who knew little of the wiles either of lawyers or of ambassadors. Sir Philip Hoby, who had met Renard abroad, foresaw the danger. "If England should be ruled by such a councillor, woe, woe to England," he wrote, in anticipation of Mary's coming to the throne.[47]

There was another reason why Renard was peculiarly fitted to fill the post of ambassador to a woman ruler. Like Mary, he had known persecution, or thought he had; and he was endowed with an extraordinary and almost feminine sensibility which gave him an instinctive understanding of the Queen's mental and emotional processes. From the moment of their first meeting there was a certain *rapport* between the two. If Noailles, like Gladstone, too often considered Mary as a public institution, Renard, like Disraeli, knew how to please and flatter the woman in the Queen.

The other side of the picture is not so pleasing. Like many high-strung and sensitive persons, Renard could not avoid the feeling that most of those he had to deal with were his intellectual inferiors. Even abroad he had to be "at the center of great affairs" and he could not work in harness with others. Two of his secre-

---

[47] Quoted by Froude, *History of England*, V, 488.

taries proved traitors and he had quarrels, more or less serious, with his predecessor in London, with his various temporary colleagues in the post, with the Emperor's Spanish secretary, and finally with Granvelle himself. He harbored the conviction that a man of his worth provoked envy and he was abnormally sensitive to personal slights and injuries. Success, therefore, had the effect of both intoxicating and embittering him, while failure induced him to blame others rather than himself.[48] Since his task in England could never have been accomplished by a committee, his inability to delegate work to others was at first an advantage rather than a hindrance to the cause he served. But it eventually spelled serious difficulties for Habsburg diplomacy and disaster for Renard himself.

Another of his traits which was to stand out in bold relief while he was ambassador in London was a tendency to resort to abject pessimism whenever he thought that the course of events offered little chance for the satisfaction of his own insatiable ambition. Like most realists, he had a natural habit of looking on the dark side of things. But he seems to have reasoned half-consciously to himself that if the future bore out his melancholy predictions, he would acquire the reputation of being a prophet; if it did not, he could take credit for the change and point to the insuperable difficulties overcome.[49] When the times called for an awareness of every possible future hazard, as they did during his early months in England, Renard (unlike Noailles) was at his best. When the need was for faith and optimism, as it was in France during his first embassy and in England later on, he was generally at his worst.

The character of Antoine de Noailles is revealed as clearly in his amusements as in his habits of work, but it is hard to avoid the conclusion that Renard's life was all work and no play—or rather that he found a bitter kind of amusement in his work, which absorbed him completely. He soon found that Englishmen were "no sharper than other folk,"[50] and he seems to have taken a grim sort of pleasure in dealing with members of a people which every

---

[48] Febvre, *Philippe II*, 144.   [49] cf. Tyler's judgment in *Span. Cal.*, XI, p. xxviii.
[50] *Span. Cal.*, XI, 298.

foreign diplomat of the time considered unreliable, barbarous, and venal. It is dangerous to generalize, however, in view of the fact that nothing but his official correspondence has survived. The sombre, handsome, and composed lines of his face as painted by a Flemish artist in 1553 suggest intelligence and energy in repose, but they give no hint of humor or *Gemütlichkeit*. A Spaniard who stayed at the London embassy in the spring of 1554 left a picture of his host's social graces which spoke volumes: "The ambassador has entertained me well, and he understands the art; but although he did not say so openly, I saw he was hoping for some readier recognition of his services."[51]

We know little of his relatives except that he had a sister and two brothers, one of whom he employed to help decipher dispatches in England. He was married a few years before he went to London, and if a portrait by a master of the art can reveal personality, one can be pardoned for believing that his wife, Jeanne Lullier, was endowed with all the serenity, modesty, and charm which her husband lacked. She was with Renard in London for a year (October 1553 to October 1554), bore him six children in all, and survived him by some years.[52] Their three sons left no posterity and in 1618 a son-in-law was allowed to assume the ambassador's arms: the famous name which Simon Renard struggled so hard to win died with his sons.[53]

* * *

These, then, were the personalities and forces which were to shape the course of events in England after the death of Henry VIII's son. Perhaps the most striking feature of the drama which was enacted in London from 1553 to 1557 was that the two leading characters were miscast. While the rival ambassadors' rôles did not

[51] Juan Hurtado de Mendoza to Granvelle, 19 Mar. 1554, P.R.O., Tyler, p. 251.

[52] Jeanne Lullier's portrait (by Antonio Moro), like Renard's, is at Besançon. Thanks to Noailles's deliberate delay in procuring a safe-conduct for her trip to England, the ship in which she crossed the Channel was threatened and almost captured by some French warships (Noailles to Cardinal of Lorraine, 24 Oct. 1553, and Cardinal of Lorraine to Duke of Guise, 9 Nov. 1553, Aff. Etr., IX, fols. 85, 95; Vertot, II, 222, 231; *Span. Cal.*, XI, 324). On her departure from England, see Vertot, III, 341, and Aff. Etr., IX, fol. 284.

[53] "Vunière," *Etude historique*, 3-4.

prove to be so uncongenial as one might have expected, it is one of the many ironies of history that the Seigneur de Noailles, honorable descendant of an ancient and honorable family, was called to fill the part of conspirator and intriguer; while to the *parvenu* Seigneur de Barmont fell the rôle of confidant and "spiritual confessor" of royalty.

CHAPTER II

NORTHUMBERLAND'S CONSPIRACY

APRIL TO JUNE 1553

IT was the Duke of Northumberland's famous conspiracy to exclude Mary Tudor from the throne which brought Noailles and Renard to England.

Almost two years before Edward VI died there were rumors in England that Northumberland meant to tamper with the succession, and when the boy-king fell ill in February 1553, the rumors increased. The Duke knew that his power, if not his very life, depended upon the survival of the sickly youth over whom he exercised such a strange fascination. Almost all the nobility were his enemies; the merchants distrusted him; the commoners hated him as the personification of the inclosure movement; the Catholics considered him the Anti-Christ; and even the Protestant minority whom he had favored were beginning to despise him. If his control over the crown should suddenly be destroyed, if the Princess whom he had consistently maltreated should come to the throne, he knew that there was hardly anyone in all England who would show him mercy.

When the idea occurred to him of settling the crown on a puppet ruler no one knows, but it was the logical outcome of his four turbulent years of power. The candidate was fixed upon by a process of elimination. Elizabeth, next in line to the throne after Mary by hereditary right and Henry VIII's Will, could not be trusted to bend to his dictates as Edward had. Mary Stuart, granddaughter of Henry VIII's elder sister Margaret, had the best title after Elizabeth, but she was half-French and betrothed to the Dauphin. However, Henry's younger sister, the first Mary Tudor, had had a daughter, Frances, who was the wife of one of Northumberland's few supporters, Henry Grey, Duke of Suffolk. Obviously it would be tempting fate for Northumberland to put on the throne the wife of a friend who was just as un-principled as he was himself, but the lady had a daughter who would serve his purpose. The girl (known to history as the Lady Jane Grey) might be married to Guildford Dudley, Northumberland's only unmarried son, and used as the instrument of her father-in-law's tyranny.[1]

Even a reckless gambler like Northumberland knew that there were almost insuperable difficulties in the way of any such desperate scheme. The vast majority of the people looked to Mary as the legitimate successor; Charles V would certainly resist any attack on her rights with every means at his disposal; and even the King of France, who could of course be counted upon to favor any attempt to exclude the Emperor's cousin, might very well make capital out of the inevitable chaos by placing Mary Stuart on the throne. Until he was sure that Edward was dying and that he had nothing to hope for from Mary or Elizabeth, the Duke held his hand. But in April the King began to spit blood, and about the 26th announcement was made of the betrothal of Guildford Dudley and the Lady Jane.

Even yet Northumberland was probably not irrevocably committed to desperate measures. He sent reassuring messages to Mary and circulated rumors that the ancient friendship between England and the Empire might be cemented sometime in the future by a marriage between the Princess and Philip, Prince of Spain.[2] In order to win the good will of both Charles V and Henry II and to obviate foreign intervention, he had offered his services as honest broker to both sides in settling their dispute on the Continent. Until May, "he had an anchor thrown out in all quarters from which a wind might blow."[3]

While the Duke was wavering, the French and Imperial ambassadors in London were guessing. Boisdauphin, Henry II's

[1] All that is known of Northumberland's conspiracy has been carefully sifted by previous scholars. See J. G. Nichols, *Literary Remains of King Edward VI* (London, Roxburghe Club, 1857), II, 561-71; the same author's edition of *The Chronicle of Queen Jane* (London, Camden Society, 1850), 85-102; Pollard, *Pol. Hist.*, 80-93; and Froude, *History of England*, V, 478-515.

[2] *Span. Cal.*, XI, 35-6.

[3] Froude, V, 481.

representative, had far more influence at court than his rival Scheyfve, and it is natural to suppose that more accurate information about Northumberland's aims reached Paris than Brussels.[4] But since Boisdauphin's papers are lost, there is no evidence to prove that Henry II had definite word of the conspiracy before Charles V. Northumberland was a master of dissimulation; he knew the French of old, and it is unlikely that he took the French ambassador into his confidence until he felt that he had to. Neither Boisdauphin nor Scheyfve was a man of outstanding ability, and in the spring of 1553 both were anxious to get home. But even before the betrothal of Guildford and Jane was announced, it was not difficult for any foreign ambassador to put two and two together from the rumors which filled London. Both Henry II and Charles V were certainly aware by the beginning of May, if not before, that a major crisis was approaching in England.[5]

The news from across the Channel stirred far less interest in Brussels than in Paris. Charles V was suffering from a particularly severe case of gout and could hardly attend to even the most trivial matters. His affairs in Germany and Italy were in chaos, his resources were exhausted by his recent unsuccessful siege of Metz, he had no army or navy ready for service, and he knew that when summer came all his troops would be needed to defend the Netherlands against the French. Unless France intervened actively in England, the Emperor would apparently have to trust the English people themselves to defend his cousin's rights, and Scheyfve's reports of Northumberland's unpopularity led him to

---

[4] cf. Nichols, *Literary Remains*, p. cxcii, note (a); *Span. Cal.*, XI, 5, 11; Sturge, *Northumberland*, 224, note. Sir Philip Hoby's dread of Renard's coming to England (above, p. 29) may have been inspired by his observation of the sinister influence acquired at court by Boisdauphin: the worst term of opprobrium he could think of three years later for an ambassador was "a worse than Beau Daulphin" (*Facsimiles of National Manuscripts*, III, No. xl).

[5] Scheyfve's suspicions mounted fairly steadily after February (*Span. Cal.*, XI, 8-9, 12, 16-17, 35). On his diplomatic ability, see *Span. Cal.*, X, p. ix, and XI, p. viii. Boisdauphin was rewarded for his services in England by being made a Gentleman of the Chamber on his return, but he was modest about his achievements and confessed to Noailles that he had been taken in by an Italian informer during the spring. (Noailles to Boisdauphin, 30 June 1553, Aff. Etr., IX, fol. 37.)

believe that he might do so with some confidence, for the time being at least.[6]

The French court, on the other hand, immediately showed its interest in what was happening in London. On April 6 Antoine de Noailles, who had been appointed to replace Boisdauphin three months before, left St. Germain-en-Laye to take up his post. The documents contain no hint as to whether his departure was connected with the approaching crisis, but it seems likely that it was, in view of the fact that Edward's illness was already common knowledge. The new ambassador arrived in London on April 30, exhausted by a tertian ague and the rigors of his three weeks' journey.[7]

Noailles's instructions have not survived, but he seems to have been directed to let Northumberland understand that Henry II was vitally interested in the problem of the succession. On May 4 Boisdauphin and Noailles sent a message to the Duke in which they hinted delicately that they knew something of his problem. Rumors about Edward's condition were exciting Mary's friends, they pointed out; if the King was too ill to receive the new ambassador from France, a pretended interview should be arranged in order to frighten "those who hoped to inherit the crown." The implication was that if Northumberland meant to exclude Mary, Henry II was ready and willing to be associated with the scheme. The Duke saw the logic of the suggestion and on May 7 the audience which was not an audience was staged at Greenwich. After the ambassadors had dined with the Council the Lord Chamberlain announced that Edward was waiting to receive them, the whole company retired to another room, and there the councillors thanked the envoys for their assurance of Henry II's good will. It was perfectly obvious from the speakers' faces that the King was very ill. In private conversation, the Duke went so far as to ask the ambassadors what they would do if they were in his shoes, and they made all the suggestions which they considered to be "of favor and advantage" to Henry II's interests.

[6] See e.g. *Span. Cal.*, XI, 19.

[7] Vertot, II, 1, 28-9; Henry II to Boisdauphin, 6 Apr. 1553, Bib. Nat., Collection Dupuy, No. 844, fol. 71.

Ten days later they were finally admitted to the dying King's bedside in order that Noailles might present his credentials and Boisdauphin take his leave.[8]

Significantly enough, the first clear invitation to an Anglo-French understanding thus came apparently not from Northumberland but from the French. Montmorency gathered from the ambassadors' account of their interview with the Duke at Greenwich that he was about to cross his Rubicon and that he would soon be asking definitely for French support. To take advantage of the diplomatic opportunity, the Constable immediately dispatched Claude de L'Aubespine, First Secretary of the French Council, to England.[9] Armed only with verbal instructions, L'Aubespine reached London about May 21, the day Jane Grey was married to Guildford Dudley. He had an interview with the full Council on the 28th, left the city with Boisdauphin on June 6, and was back at Ecouen by the 15th.[10]

While he was in England L'Aubespine reached some sort of understanding with Northumberland. In an attempt to determine the nature of this understanding, the few surviving scraps of direct evidence may be interpreted to mean everything or nothing. The Secretary's trip, Noailles wrote Henry II, "has been no less necessary for the present than presumably it will be useful and profitable to you in the future." A little later the ambassador referred to the "honest and fine offers" which Henry had made to the Duke, and the King wrote that he was happy "that the union there is such as you write me." Scheyfve heard that L'Aubespine had made "offers of service, going as far as to say in so many words that the Duke's cause should also be the King's." But there is no hint about how much Northumberland told the Secretary

---

[8] Vertot, II, 3-7, 27; *Span. Cal.*, XI, 40, 44.

[9] On May 16. The English ambassadors at Poissy, who were not in Northumberland's confidence, were told that the purpose of L'Aubespine's mission was merely to present Henry II's sympathy to Edward VI in his illness (*For. Cal., Ed. VI*, 280, 289; Tytler, II, 178-82; *Calendar of Salisbury Manuscripts*, I, 121).

[10] *Span. Cal.*, XI, 46; *For. Cal., Ed. VI*, 286; Vertot, II, 35; Noailles and Boisdauphin to Montmorency, 27 May 1553, and Noailles to Montmorency, 4 June 1553, Aff. Etr., IX, fols. 26, 27.

of his "cause," what "offers" were made, or how close was the "union" of interests which resulted.[11]

Certainly the understanding was not so close as it appeared to those on the outside. The interests of Northumberland and the King of France were like parallel lines which run in the same direction but never meet. Both were vitally interested in excluding Mary Tudor from the throne, but the substitution of Lady Jane Grey was at best but a *pis aller* for each of them. Northumberland knew well enough that Henry II would take advantage of any confusion to press the claims of Mary Stuart. He was further aware that the introduction of any great number of French troops into England, even with the purest intentions in the world, would so infuriate the people that his own head would be in as much danger as if he allowed Mary to succeed peacefully to the crown that was rightfully hers. In a sense, his choice of the Lady Jane was determined by the necessity in which he found himself of preventing *both* the French and the Spanish from interfering with his ambition. The French, furthermore, were almost as suspicious of Northumberland as he was of them. While he was passing through Boulogne on his way to England, Noailles heard some news that made him believe the Duke was not to be trusted, and two months later he was still somewhat afraid that the naval and military preparations in England might possibly be aimed at France. He found Northumberland "close-lipped and reserved in everything," and for almost two months after his arrival he matched the Duke's taciturnity with a cautious reserve of his own.[12]

What Northumberland really needed was a clear promise of help from France in case the Emperor should intervene in Mary's behalf. He had not yet formally approached the King or his fellow-councillors on the subject of altering the succession, and he knew that such a promise might help quiet the fears of the waverers and perhaps frighten Mary's friends at home and abroad into inactivity. L'Aubespine was eager to offer this much assur-

[11] Noailles to Henry II, 6 and 30 June 1553, Aff. Etr., IX, fols. 28, 35; Henry II to Noailles, 2 July 1553, *ibid.*, IX, fol. 39; *Span. Cal.*, XI, 51.
[12] Vertot, II, 33-4, 48.

ance,[13] especially since it would probably cost nothing. He and
Noailles made much of Charles V's sinister intentions for propaganda purposes, but they must have suspected that the real danger
to Northumberland's pretensions came not from a crippled Emperor with an exhausted treasury in Brussels, but from the English
people themselves. L'Aubespine, in fact, was willing to promise
more than the Duke was willing to ask for explicitly. The French
hoped that Northumberland might possibly be trapped into a
declaration of war against the Emperor. They knew, furthermore,
that they stood to profit not only by his success but also by the
chaos which would attend his failure. The Secretary, therefore
(to judge by later events), seems to have suggested to Northumberland that French troops would be forthcoming in case he
found himself in a desperate situation, even though Charles V
had not intervened. Since many members of the Council were
anti-French, however, L'Aubespine probably gave them to understand (on May 28) that Henry II's offer of assistance was
strictly conditioned upon Imperial interference.[14]

Obviously a great many complicated factors were involved in
L'Aubespine's discussions: the French desire to encourage Northumberland, the Duke's need for a counterweight against Spain,
the lingering French suspicions of his sincerity, and the English
Council's fear of foreign intervention in any form. Henry II had
given an unscrupulous adventurer a blank check, hoping that
either his success or his failure would bring an opportunity to
reduce England to French control.[15]

The news of the French Secretary's mission finally roused
Charles V from his apathy. His gout had intensified his normal
tendency to postpone decisions and his long experience had given
him a livelier sense than Henry II had of the danger of stirring
national sentiment by foreign intervention, particularly in England. But now the danger to his cousin was all too clear, and the
vision of what her accession to the throne might mean to Habsburg interests was suddenly dazzling. If he could not send troops,

---

[13] See *Span. Cal.,* XI, 51, 71.
[14] On the Council's attitude, see Lodge, *Illustrations of British History,* I, 226-7; and
cf. note 31 below.
[15] See *Span. Cal.,* XI, 77, 79.

he could at least send diplomats, proverbially the most effective warriors the Habsburgs possessed. On June 23 three extraordinary ambassadors left Brussels, to arrive in London only a few hours before Edward VI died. Of the three, Jacques de Marnix de Sainte-Aldegonde, Sieur de Thoulouse, was a mere figurehead; Jean de Montmorency, Sieur de Courrières (a distant cousin of the Constable's), scarcely less so; Simon Renard, the real leader.[16]

Every line of their lengthy instructions testified to the Emperor's prudence, far-sightedness, and ripe political wisdom. The ambassadors' two main objectives were, of course, to get Mary on the throne and to thwart Henry II's attempt to turn England into a French province. A third—to subject England to Habsburg influence by a suitable marriage for Mary if she became Queen—was kept in the background. The envoys were made to understand before they left Brussels that because of the war with France it was impossible for Charles to send a "strong expedition" to England, even if Mary were in the direst straits. Their only weapons, therefore, were to be tact, persuasion, and propaganda. They were to assure the English Council of the Emperor's good will, to remind them that "the French are England's ancient enemies," and to remove all fears from their minds of Imperial intervention. If they were stopped before reaching London, they were to spread the report that Charles favored an English candidate for Mary's hand; if not, they were to repeat the assurance in London and to persuade Mary to make any promise necessary to ensure her accession, even to the point of guaranteeing the religious and political *status quo*. There was no hint or suggestion that the ambassadors were to use threats: hollow warnings that the Emperor might use force, it was assumed, would only drive Northumberland to extremes, alienate the people, and give the French the opportunity they were waiting for. Flemish troops could not put Mary on the throne, but the English people could;

---

[16] On the motives which induced Charles to send the three ambassadors, see *Span. Cal.*, XI, 101, 126-7; Tridon, "Renard," 169 *ff.*; Vertot, II, 45. An English adventurer named William Pelham apparently gave the Emperor's sister, Mary of Hungary, full details about Northumberland's plot some time in May. (*Span. Cal.*, XI, 354.) On Pelham see "French Intrigue at the Court of Queen Mary," *Amer. Hist. Rev.*, Vol. XLV (April 1940), 548.

and the mere presence of three distinguished Imperial ambassadors in London would be hint enough of their sovereign's concern for her best interests. The envoys would naturally have to be "guided by circumstances which may change rapidly." Once Mary was on the throne, they might play the various English candidates for her hand off against each other and arrive at "a better solution."[17]

Events had moved rapidly in London before the Imperial ambassadors arrived. The story of how Northumberland won over the King, the privy councillors, and the lawyers is too well known to need repetition in detail. Early in June Edward was induced by an appeal to his Protestant piety to draw up a "devise" settling the succession by will on the heirs male of the Suffolk line, on the implied theory that no woman had a right to rule in England. But there were no heirs male in the family, the Duke's time was getting short, and in the last analysis, he wanted a woman ruler whom he could control through her husband. A scheme which was already hopelessly illegal and desperately unpopular was made utterly illogical by forgery. By alterations and insertions in the original "devise," the crown was left by Edward "to the Lady Frances's heirs males *if she have any before my death*: to the Lady Jane's *and her* heirs males."[18] In spite of determined opposition from at least five loyal supporters of Mary—the Marquis of Winchester, Lords Arundel, Bedford, Shrewsbury, and Sir Thomas Cheyne—the leading councillors were bullied into giving their consent by threats, by bribery, or by timely marital alliances, such as the betrothal of Lord Pembroke's son to Lady Catharine Grey, Jane's younger sister. On June 12 Edward himself ordered the assembled law-officers of the Crown to draw up letters patent along the lines of the "devise," and on the 21st a hundred peers, ministers, judges, ecclesiastics, and leading citizens were forced to put their signatures to the King's Will.

Meanwhile Noailles was no better informed about what was taking place at court than Scheyfve. Until the leading ministers

---

[17] *Span. Cal.*, XI, 60-5, 81.

[18] Alterations noted in italics. See Nichols, *Literary Remains*, 571-2; Pollard, *Pol. Hist.*, 83-6; and Froude, *History of England*, V, 499 ff.

were won over and the Will signed, Northumberland could not risk taking into his confidence an ambassador who represented the claims of Mary Stuart. Furthermore Noailles was new to his position, reserved by temperament, and suspicious of the Duke's sincerity, though not of his ability. It was easy for both French and Imperial ambassadors to guess the significance of the long, secret meetings at court during the first three weeks of June, but when Noailles finally obtained audience with the Council on the 18th he was left to gather how far advanced the plot was by inference. He noted the "trumpets and other music" at dinner and guessed that the general gaiety was the result of the ministers' final submission to Northumberland's will. He was not told so, any more than Scheyfve would have been. But he learned somehow of the Will's signature within twenty-four hours, while his rival heard of it definitely only two weeks later.[19]

After the leading men of the country had become technical accomplices in the conspiracy, both Northumberland and Noailles began to sound each other out. Letters of June 15 reached the ambassador from Henry II and Montmorency saying that they were pleased by L'Aubespine's report of what he had accomplished in England and that Noailles was to use all his dexterity in preserving the advantages gained. A personal letter from the King to Northumberland was enclosed.[20] Noailles immediately tried to get into touch with the Duke, but the latter was afraid to let the ambassador come out to Greenwich for fear that Mary's friends in the Council would become suspicious. The news that Henry II's troops had suffered a serious reverse at Thérouanne[21] on June 20 probably disturbed him, however, and on the evening of the 26th he made a special trip to London to visit Noailles at the latter's house.

[19] Vertot, II, 40-1, 49; *Span. Cal.,* XI, 69. Noailles appears to have written Henry II the news that the Will was signed in a last-minute postscript to his dispatch of June 22 which was not recorded in the minute. On June 30 he wrote the King that Edward had made his Will nine days before, "as I wrote you" (Aff. Etr., IX, fol. 35). This passage is wrongly included as part of his dispatch of June 26 by Vertot (II, 48-9).

[20] Vertot, II, 35-8.

[21] Noailles wrote Montmorency on the 26th that the Imperialists had been spreading the news in London (Aff. Etr., IX, fol. 33).

Noailles presented Henry's letter, which urged the Duke to come out openly against the Emperor by declaring war. Northumberland replied that he could not do this without the Council's consent but he would allow Noailles to present Henry's arguments in public sometime later at Greenwich. Noailles was confident that the Council would eventually come around.[22] By expressing his suspicion of recent naval and military preparations in the city (which Northumberland denied), he then managed to draw from the Duke the first frank confession of his purposes.

I sounded him out so far on the illness and exhaustion of [the King] and also on the proposal which your Majesty had M. de L'Aubespine make to him that he finally disclosed much to me. He told me that they had provided so well against the Lady Mary's ever attaining the succession, and that all the lords of the Council are so well united, that there is no need for you, Sire, to enter into any doubt on this score. Upon which I did not forget to tell him (in order to sound him out still further) how pleased your Majesty would be if the crown [tel chapeau] should fall to him himself, adding that the people of the country felt the same way. He thanked your Majesty for this very humbly, but said that he thought himself too unworthy of such an estate and that he would consider himself unfortunate to think of it. I believe, Sire, that [the succession] will pass at first through a regent until the people have been pacified—they would not be easy to tame in their first fury.[23]

At no time was it more evident than during this two-hour interview that the French were more eager to help Northumberland than he was to accept their assistance. It was characteristic of Noailles that he was beginning to be carried away by the excitement of the crisis. He was still aware, to be sure, of the weaknesses in the Duke's position. He was worried by the news Northumberland passed on to him that an Imperial delegation was on its way to London, and a few days later when he was refused a second interview, he assumed that the Duke was still afraid of the Imperialist party in the Council, who were "numerous enough." But in spite of all misgivings, Noailles was becom-

---

[22] Vertot, II, 44, 47. This, it seems to me, is the only possible solution of a difficult problem. If Henry's "requeste" (Vertot, II, 47) had been for territorial compensation, Northumberland would never have promised to let Noailles present it to the Council. Perhaps L'Aubespine had already hinted at an English declaration of war as a *quid pro quo*.

[23] Noailles to Henry II, 28 June 1553, Aff. Etr., IX, fol. 34.

ing convinced that Northumberland would win and that it was well to get on the right side of England's future ruler by any means whatever, even by the most dangerous flattery. His instructions could easily be interpreted as *carte blanche* to go as far as he wished in this.

> Since the departure of MM. de Boisdauphin and de L'Aubespine [he reported on June 30], I have not failed to entertain him [Northumberland] in similar terms and on the same subject which they spoke about to him. And at the first audience which is granted me, I shall do so again in still broader terms.[24]

Six days after these words were written, on Thursday, July 6, at about nine in the evening, Edward VI expired. The Council did its best to keep the news from spreading, but it reached the ears of the Imperial ambassadors the following morning and by evening it was all over London.[25] Noailles had been waiting a week for an interview which Northumberland had promised him, but on Friday the Duke sent twice to tell him it would have to be postponed. Affairs at court, he said, were "so important" that he could not leave Greenwich for several days, but if the ambassador had anything urgent on his mind, he could come to court on Saturday or Sunday.[26]

Noailles was worried. Henry II had written him on June 23 that, according to first-hand news from Brussels, Charles V's purpose in sending Renard and his two colleagues to England was to pursue "the intrigue already begun with the Lady Mary to provide that the succession there may not slip out of his hands."[27] Noailles himself was afraid that the Emperor, to save his cousin from death or imprisonment, intended to hand her over to Northumberland to be married off as he pleased, perhaps to the Duke's eldest son, whose marriage to Somerset's daughter could be dissolved—"a thing which is more to be feared than a thousand others which might happen in this affair." Northumberland might jump at such an offer, Noailles thought, because he knew the Duke of Suffolk hated him bitterly for passing over his

[24] ". . . J'en feray encores de plus grandes." Noailles to Henry II, 30 June 1553, Aff. Etr., IX, fol. 35.

[25] *Span. Cal.,* XI, 72, 75; Vertot, II, 52.   [26] Vertot, II, 50-52.
[27] Vertot, II, 45.

wife, the Lady Frances, and giving the crown to his daughter, Jane; even Suffolk himself might sell out to the Emperor and support the scheme in order to revenge himself upon Northumberland.[28] When these fantastic fears were increased on Friday evening by rumors that the King was dead, Noailles hesitated no longer. Armed with an extract from Henry's letter, he presented himself immediately before the Council at Greenwich in order to get ahead of the Imperial ambassadors and to repeat to Northumberland "all the honest and fine offers which Your Majesty has been pleased to order me to make him" (as he reported to his King). He began by discussing the Emperor's designs and then had the extract read:

After it was read [he reported] I could easily see in their faces the great satisfaction and joy each of them experienced in hearing such offers presented on behalf of such a great prince as you, Sire. They remained silent, both because of the reports I gave them about the Emperor's plots and because of the pleasure they had received; and the Duke, who was the first to speak, told me that they would retire and consult together in order to give me the reply which a matter of such great favor to them deserved. As he passed by me he pressed my hand and gave me to understand the great pleasure which my recital had given him, then suddenly he turned back to me and asked me to give them [a copy of] what I had had read. But I knew, Sire, how important such documents are and what glosses might be made on them by several of this company whom I know to be too devoted to the service of the Emperor, so I prayed him to withdraw his request, saying that these offers and many larger ones were addressed expressly to him and that I would discharge myself of them whenever it should please him. He was content with this, left me without carrying the conversation further, and turned to the other lords. After a while when they had reached their decision, the Duke, speaking for all of them, thanked your Majesty very humbly for all the honest, great, and generous offers which you are pleased to make them, and feeling his position strong, he urged you to consent to share with them in the vicissitudes of their fortunes.[29] They asked me, Sire, as your minister, to keep you in this good

[28] Noailles to Henry II, 7 July 1553, Aff. Etr., XV, fol. 44 (original). This dispatch (actually written over three days, July 6-8) was recklessly altered and cut in the published version (Vertot, II, 50-3) in order to cover up Noailles's eagerness to offer Northumberland French assistance. There are important lacunae at p. 51, line 8, and at p. 52, line 3 from bottom in Vertot's version; and the whole last half of the document is suppressed. See Note on the Sources.

[29] ". . . et se sentant fort [?] vous a tenu de voulloir assister avecques eulz aus occurences de leurs fortunes. . . ." The reading, fort, is doubtful.

will and said that in accordance with this great friendship and favor which
you have been pleased to bestow upon them, they desire to ask your aid
and to employ your forces when the occasion presents itself. Upon which
you may be sure, Sire, that I did not fail to assure them that they never
had an alliance with a prince who kept his word more scrupulously and
literally and who would go further beyond its fulfillment if need be than
your Majesty. In short, Sire, I left them in such a frame of mind that I
could discover nothing in them opposed to the weal, prosperity, and advancement of your affairs; nor were they disposed, in my opinion, to welcome
the proposals which the [Imperial] deputies will make to them. . . .

Since I believe that the end of this affair must come now or within
a few days, and since I think that the King, your good son, is dead and
that the lords wish to cover up the fact and keep it secret, it seems to me
very necessary that your Majesty write a letter to all the said lords in general
on the subject of the extract which you sent, in order to encourage them,
and that you write them either what I have already given them to understand on your behalf or any other such expressions which it seems your
Majesty should write them.[30]

Noailles was greatly pleased with the results of the interview.
He was confident that the Council felt better now that they were
assured of assistance from France. He went on to say that his
promises would probably help reconcile Northumberland and Suffolk, and that Mary, who was rumored to have fled to Flanders,
would never willingly put herself into Northumberland's hands.
Uninvited, he had offered material support from his sovereign and
the Council had risen to the bait, probably under pressure from
the worried Northumberland. Little did he suspect that the next
time he saw the Duke it would be on the scaffold.

Actually the French ambassador had overestimated his triumph
over the councillors and misinterpreted the looks of pleasure on
their faces. Shortly after the interview letters were drafted in
Council to the English ambassadors in France which showed the
real feelings of most of the ministers:

You shall declare that his Majesty's Ambassador [Noailles] has here
showed unto us that which he had in charge from his Majesty [Henry II]
by his letters, touching the detection of certain practices of the Emperor
intended with the Lady Mary to the danger of this realm, for the avoiding
whereof his Majesty, like a Prince of great honor, offers *such help as he*

[30] Noailles to Henry II, 7 July 1553, Aff. Etr., XV, fols. 44-5.

may conveniently; where surely his Majesty shows himself so worthy of praise and thanks, of us and all this realm, as we shall never forget this his great friendship in so difficult times, although we doubt not but that the estate and power of this realm shall, by God's goodness, prevail against all manner of practices or attempts, *either by the Emperor or any other,* either foreign or outward enemies whatsoever the same be.[31]

In times of revolution men tend to overvalue the possession of the physical instruments of force. Because Northumberland was master of the armed forces of the realm (a few companies of militia, a score of ships, and what munitions there were in the Tower), both Noailles and the newly-arrived Imperial ambassadors were convinced for a week after Edward's death that he would win out. After Jane was proclaimed Queen on July 10, Noailles wrote optimistically about "the new King," Guildford Dudley, and persuaded himself that Mary (who had been warned in time and had fled to Norfolk) was doomed. As late as July 13 he was still hopeful about inducing Northumberland to declare war on the Emperor. His Imperial rivals were so frightened that they kept to Scheyfve's house for five days, then went out for a brief walk with a few Spanish merchants, "to help themselves to show a little spirit," as Noailles maliciously reported. They decided that Mary had no hope of gaining support "because of religion" and because of Northumberland's strength, so they wrote her that her brave intention of declaring herself Queen was dangerous. They realized that the dispatch of Flemish troops would only aggravate the situation, but they suggested a naval demonstration. Pessimism and perplexity were written between the lines of every one of their dispatches for almost two weeks, as well as misjudgment of Mary's position more fundamental even than Noailles's. "The actual possession of power," they decided, "was a matter of great importance, especially among barbarians like the English"; in any contest between "right" and "arms," victory would rest with the latter, in England at least. Had Mary heeded

[31] Lodge, *Illustrations of British History,* I, 226-7. Italics inserted. The first phrase actually reads "his Majesty's Ambassadors have here showed"—an obvious slip in view of what follows. The Council was referring to Noailles's interview of July 7, not to that of L'Aubespine, Boisdauphin, and Noailles on May 28.

their pusillanimous advice (which fortunately she did not) her
cause would have been lost.[32]

One suspects that Renard, who immediately assumed the leadership of his colleagues, was responsible for most of this pessimism.
Certainly Scheyfve, mediocre as his talents may have been, knew
the situation better. Before Renard arrived he had written that
"three quarters of the nation" favored Mary, that at least five influential councillors were on her side, and that "a little favor"
from the Emperor would "avert many disasters."[33] But his more
brilliant colleague knew the uses of adversity, as we have seen,
especially when adversity could be artfully exaggerated. Furthermore, he had learned the lesson of obeying instructions literally
when he was in France, and his present instructions left little
doubt about the need for extreme caution.

Perhaps, as an American writer seems to suggest, Noailles and
Renard were right in believing that "the actual possession of
power" would be decisive, and wrong only in their estimate of
the power Northumberland actually possessed. In 1552, because
of his reckless finance, Northumberland had had to disband the
mercenary army which he was quietly gathering. "Against money
and metal, the weight of guns and mercenaries, Mary and her
followers could not have raised their heads. But without money,
and hence without mercenary soldiers, Northumberland had no
chance against the divinity that doth hedge a king, and the magic
of the Tudor name."[34] Perhaps on the other hand, as an English
writer implies, even a mercenary army could not have saved the
Duke in the end from the fury of the people. It was "not a profound diagnosis," he points out, to assume (as foreign observers
did) that the power of the Tudor monarchy rested upon the subservience of a people which had risen against half its kings since
the Norman conquest.[35] Whether it was the Duke's lack of funds

[32] Vertot, II, 57-61; Noailles to Vendôme, 13 July 1553, Aff. Etr., IX, fol. 45; Span.
Cal., XI, 72-80.

[33] Span. Cal., XI, 50, 52, 57, 66, 70-1.

[34] F. C. Dietz, "Finances of Edward VI and Mary," Smith College Studies in History,
III (1917-1918), 97.

[35] Pollard, Pol. Hist., 88.

or the English people's love of liberty which was ultimately decisive, the tide began to turn between July 12 and 14.

At the height of the crisis Renard did something to retrieve his mistakes in judgment by helping to initiate a revolution in the Council which was to prove the determining event in Northumberland's downfall. On July 12 Lord Cobham and Sir John Mason visited the Imperial ambassadors on behalf of the Duke. They explained Edward's Will, told the envoys that their credentials were no longer valid since Edward was dead, and threatened them with England's "barbarous laws" should they attempt to communicate with Mary. Renard's reply showed something of the coolness and daring which were characteristic of him at his best. He outlined his instructions with skillful emphasis upon the Emperor's good will toward the English nation as a whole, as well as toward Mary, and tactfully implied that the Council had been misled by the French, not by one of their own number, into a misinterpretation of Charles's intentions. He urged them "rather to welcome the advances of their old friends than to seek new alliances," and added that his master was informed by "news from France" that the purpose of Henry II's advances toward England was to stir up trouble and to place Mary Stuart on the throne. This last was a telling blow to two councillors who secretly favored Mary Tudor. They sat confused and staring at each other for a moment, then protested they had made a mistake in saying that the envoys must consider their mission terminated and begged them not to leave London until they (Cobham and Mason) had reported Renard's "profitable and praiseworthy" words to the Council.[36]

After the interview the two ministers went immediately not to Northumberland but to five other friends of Mary in the Council: Bedford, Arundel, Shrewsbury, Pembroke, and Secretary Petre. The next day these seven, unknown to the Duke, summoned the Imperial ambassadors. Northumberland was still in London, but the councillors said he had left the city with the Duke of Suffolk to oppose Mary, who was gathering a considerable number of supporters at Framlingham in Suffolk. Renard spoke again on

[36] *Span. Cal.*, XI, 83-6.

behalf of his colleagues and rehearsed the main points he had made the day before. He dressed up the story of Henry II's sinister intentions by saying that the Emperor had intercepted some letters from Northumberland to France which gave away the whole intrigue of placing the young Queen of Scotland on the throne. This "happy invention"[37] made a considerable impression. Again the councillors urged the ambassadors not to depart and promised to report the results of the interview "to the other lords of the Council." There is no evidence that they did so, however. When Northumberland left London the next morning after a vain attempt to persuade the Duke of Suffolk to lead the army against Mary, he knew nothing of his colleagues' conversations with the Emperor's envoys. The revolution behind his back had already begun, and only Suffolk's threats and the fear of Northumberland's wrath if he returned in triumph kept the Imperialist party in the Council from proclaiming Mary immediately. Renard wrote later that "no harm was done by the point touching the Queen of Scotland's claim," and for once in his life he was guilty of an understatement. His lie had hit upon the truth, Mary's friends in high places had been frightened by the prospect of French intervention into taking independent action, and when the time came to throw off the mask, they could do so in the assurance that Charles V's motives were at least somewhat more disinterested than Henry II's.[38]

While the Imperial ambassadors were talking to the seven councillors, Northumberland was unwittingly furnishing proof that Renard's accusations and warnings were not far from the truth. On July 13, unknown to his opponents in the Council, he dispatched a personal representative to France to ask Henry II for the troops which Noailles had led him to believe would be forthcoming in case of need. The agent chosen for the purpose was his distant cousin, Sir Henry Dudley, an adventurer with considerable naval and military experience who was to become famous

---

[37] The phrase is Tyler's (*Span. Cal.,* XI, p. xvii, note).

[38] *Span. Cal.,* XI, 88, 94, 115. Nine years later Renard boasted that he had thwarted Northumberland, saved Mary, checked the French intrigues, and restored England to union, concord, and devotion to the Emperor (Weiss, V, 21).

as the leader of one of the most serious conspiracies of Mary's reign.[39]

Dudley reached the French court at Compiègne about the 18th and was admitted to see the King. A few days later he visited the Constable, who was with the army at Amiens, then went on to Calais, where he was arrested about the 26th by the Governor, Lord William Howard. In the middle of August he was examined by Mary's Council in London and offered a "circumstantial and likely tale" of his mission, which was later confirmed by Wotton, the English ambassador in France.[40] At first he maintained that when he left London Northumberland "did not think he would be in need of prompt assistance from the French, as he took no account of the Queen [Mary] or of the forces she might be able to call together to support her." Later he confessed that he was sent to remind Henry II of "a promise he had given the Duke to succor him with money and men if it were necessary and he became hard pressed to establish the said Jane," and that "the Duke had promised to hand over to the French Calais, Guines, and Hammes, the English possessions on the mainland, and Ireland."[41]

Whether Northumberland was actually so desperate as to offer such a bribe to the King of France, no one will ever be sure. As early as the end of May there were rumors that he was ready to hold out Ireland as a bait to the French, and after Dudley's arrest, the report that Calais had been offered to Henry was spread by Mary's Council, along with a story that Boisdauphin had poisoned Edward VI.[42] The government had obvious motives for spreading such tales after the Duke's downfall, and they rest entirely upon Imperial sources. But there was unquestionably some truth in them.

[39] On Dudley, see *D.N.B.* and C. H. Garrett, *Marian Exiles,* 147-9. On his mission to France, see *Span. Cal.,* XI, 87, 94-5, 113, 116, 123-4, 135, 172-3, 208-9; *Machyn Diary,* 39.

[40] *Span. Cal.,* XI, 173. Wotton's dispatch has been lost, and there is no record of Dudley's deposition apart from the Imperial ambassadors' letters.

[41] *ibid.,* XI, 173, 208. Renard does not state definitely that Dudley himself made this latter confession, but this seems to be the implication.

[42] *ibid.,* XI, 46; Antonio de Guaras, *Accession of Queen Mary* (R. Garnett, ed.), 86; Noailles to Montmorency, 3 Aug. 1553, Aff. Etr., IX, fol. 53.

When Dudley presented his plea to Henry II, the King promised with suspicious alacrity to send troops to Queen Jane's aid even if he had to forsake his campaign against the Emperor and lead the relief forces in person. This, in spite of the fact that while he was speaking news came of a second French defeat at the hands of the Imperial forces at Hesdin (on July 17).[43] His apparent eagerness is easily explained if Dudley suggested to him that Calais would be the ideal base for any French operations in support of Northumberland. From there Henry's forces could block any move of the Emperor's, stop Mary if she tried to flee to Flanders, and stand ready to cross the Channel at twenty-four hours' notice. This assumption seems to be proved by the fact that when Dudley went to Calais on his return trip, he carried a letter from Montmorency to Lord Howard offering to introduce a friendly force of French soldiers into Calais in order to prevent "any but Englishmen" from setting foot in England and establishing a "foreign king" there in the existing confusion. Howard, "true loyal gentleman" that he was, immediately arrested the bearer of the letter and wrote the Constable in the picturesque language which was all his own that if the French tried to seize Calais by any such subterfuge, he would with God's grace make them repent it.[44] Granted the weakened state of the Pale's defenses[45] and Henry's known ambition to drive the English off the Continent, it seems likely that Northumberland, already as black a character as any in English history, must bear the added reproach of this final treason.

The tide had begun to turn in London before Dudley reached the French court. Shortly after Northumberland left the city at the head of his meagre forces, news reached the Council that the fleet stationed off the east coast had deserted to Mary. "Eche man then began to pluck in his hornes," as a contemporary chronicler noted.[46] On the 16th Cobham and Mason again visited the

---

[43] *Span. Cal.*, XI, 173.

[44] Vertot, II, 85-8; *Span. Cal.*, XI, 208. Noailles wrote Henry II on July 18 suggesting that Howard might be "persuadé à vostre intention" (Vertot, II, 74-5). Perhaps the letter reached Montmorency before he wrote Howard on the 24th.

[45] *Span. Cal.*, XI, 124; *A.P.C.*, IV, pp. xvii, 260, 303-4.

[46] *Chronicle of Queen Jane*, 9.

Imperial ambassadors to apologize for their earlier conduct and to promise the envoys personal protection if they departed for Flanders. Renard decided that he, Courrières, and Thoulouse would not leave for several days and would travel slowly on the way to see what the Duke's fate was to be. Meanwhile he refused to communicate with Mary when a messenger came to ask what assistance the Emperor was prepared to give her. Although he knew that Charles was still determined not to risk rousing the people by dispatching troops from the Netherlands, Renard thought Mary's case was so desperate on the 19th that he drafted part of a dispatch asking for help. The appeal did not have to be sent, however. That afternoon Shrewsbury and Mason came to tell the envoys that the Council had decided to proclaim Mary. The Emperor's representatives were sure it was a "miracle," "a work of the Divine Will," and could hardly believe they were not dreaming.[47] Two hours later the official announcement was made at Cheapside and even Protestant London rejoiced. The bells were rung, the organs played, and the people dined and danced in the streets while bonfires blazed. When the news reached Northumberland next day at Cambridge he threw up his cap for the new Queen, and that evening Arundel arrived to arrest him in her name.[48]

One of the first to "pluck in his hornes" after Mary's proclamation was the French ambassador. He had sensed that all was not well with Northumberland several days before his Imperial rivals, and when Mary was proclaimed, he wrote that it was the outcome "always to be feared from the reign of this Queen Jane."[49] The revolution, he decided, was attributable to divine intervention and to the English character:

> The atmosphere of this country and the nature of its people are so changeable that I am compelled to make my dispatches correspondingly wavering and contradictory. . . . I have witnessed the most sudden change believable in men, and I believe that God alone has worked it.[50]

[47] *Span. Cal.*, XI, 79-81, 83, 92-3, 95-6, 105.

[48] *Chronicle of Queen Jane*, 9-12; *Machyn Diary*, 37; *Wriothesley's Chronicle*, II, 88-9; Vertot, II, 79-80.

[49] Vertot, II, 79. cf. Noailles to Bishop of Orléans, 13 July 1553, Aff. Etr., IX, fol. 47.

[50] Noailles to Montmorency, 3 Aug. 1553, Aff. Etr., IX, fol. 53; and Noailles to Orléans, 29 July 1553, Vertot, II, 93.

Noailles had, in fact, been placed in a position from which the only retreat in ordinary diplomatic practice was resignation. In the eyes of Mary, of her supporters in the Council, and of the people at large he was an accomplice to Northumberland's treason. It was popularly believed that at the height of the crisis Henry II had several thousand troops ready for a descent on England, and it was little wonder that the London populace turned with fury upon Frenchmen of all stations resident in the city. "You could not believe the foul and filthy words which this nation cries out every day against our own," Noailles wrote his master.[51] No wonder, too, that Noailles began to fear that England, far from entering the war on the French side, might soon join the Emperor. The sharp irony of many of his later dispatches appeared for the first time when he remarked that Mary would probably let herself be ruled by Charles V,

unwilling as she is to recall that in all her own miseries, troubles, and afflictions as well as in those of the Queen, her mother, the Emperor never came to their assistance, nor has he helped her now in her great need with a single man, ship, or penny.[52]

Noailles's was a fundamentally sanguine nature, however. He decided that Mary would have enough to do during the fall in establishing her power, filling her treasury, and restoring the old religion to offer much opposition to French interests on the Continent. Certainly she was not strong enough to break with France immediately, and if she married an Englishman, she might never be forced to do so.[53] Since he was practically cut off from communication with France for several weeks and since his sovereign's few brief letters from camp gave him no guidance, Noailles chose his own course.[54] As between Montmorency's policy of cooperation with any government which seemed likely to preserve England's neutrality and the Guises' policy of hostility to Habsburg satellites wherever they might be in Europe, he resolved to follow the former and to brazen it out with Mary's Council. On July 23 he sent off his most trusted courier, La

---

[51] Noailles to Montmorency, 23 July and 3 Aug. 1553, Aff. Etr., IX, fols. 50, 53.
[52] Noailles to Montmorency, 3 Aug. 1553, Aff. Etr., IX, fol. 53.
[53] Vertot, II, 80-1, 90-2; *Span. Cal.*, XI, 116.
[54] See Vertot, II, 69, 75-6, 82-3, 95-6, 97-8.

Marque, with a letter which was obviously designed to fall into the government's hands. In it he pointed out that Mary had received the crown by the law of nature, and said that he knew Henry II would be even more delighted by her accession than he had been by Jane's.[55] On July 29 he and D'Oysel, the French ambassador to Scotland (who was on his way from Edinburgh to Paris), travelled a day's journey outside the city to kiss the new Queen's hand at New Hall. Neither Mary nor her councillors showed a trace of their real feelings, and Noailles reported that he had received a "good welcome."[56]

The Imperial ambassadors had arrived at New Hall the evening before. Mary had just learned of Montmorency's attempt to introduce French troops into Calais and asked that her cousin guarantee English possession of "the key to France." Next day Renard and his colleagues were formally received along with the French ambassadors, and Renard had a private conversation with the Queen.[57] It was a significant augury of the future: a short three weeks ago it had been Noailles who had the ear of England's ruler. The diplomatic rivalry between the ambassadors of France and Spain had begun in earnest.

The circumstances in which the rivalry began had much to do with determining its later course. For one thing, the miraculous revolution in Mary's fortunes left an indelible impression on both Noailles and Renard. Both were struck by the part which "the people" had played in the crisis. Trained as they were (like most continental diplomats) to think primarily in terms of despotic government and armed force, they were nevertheless impressed by the fact that in England the Third Estate seemed to have a mind of its own. To Renard this was to be a lesson of caution, to Noailles, a spur to adventure. If the English were as fickle and as unruly as they appeared to be, if God were in the habit of working His miraculous will more often in England than

---

[55] Vertot, II, 83-4, 88-9. One of his dispatches (that of July 18-19) had already been intercepted at Rye and turned over to Renard, who was unable to find any clue to the French cipher (Vertot, II, 73-5, 88, 95, 97, 107; *Span. Cal.*, XI, 133, 160).

[56] Noailles to Montmorency, 29 July 1553, Aff. Etr., IX, fol. 52; Vertot, II, 99.

[57] *Span. Cal.*, XI, 121, 123-4, 127-8.

in other countries, then anything might happen in this barbarous nation ruled by a woman.

For a moment, albeit a short one, it seemed as if the island kingdom were about to recover its lost prestige and independence. The legitimate heir had come to the throne, and not a foreign soldier had landed to help or hinder her. Although she was half-Spanish and a Catholic, she was hailed with joy by patriots and Protestants alike, largely because everyone knew something of how close Northumberland had come to selling his country to the French. If she remembered her people's hatred of foreign influence, dramatized at the moment she came to the throne by the Londoners' attacks on Frenchmen, she might take her place beside her father as one of England's great rulers; if she did not, she might suffer Northumberland's fate. *Vox populi vox dei,* proclaimed the placards as she made her triumphal entry into London on August 3. Few anticipated that within a month a preacher would be crying, *Vox populi vox diaboli.*[58]

[58] *Span. Cal.,* XI, 134, 217.

CHAPTER III

THE QUEEN AND HER MARRIAGE

AUGUST TO OCTOBER 1553

The first of the two great kings now reigning in France and Spain who gains England to his side will not only trim his fellow's locks but shear him to the skin.[1]

SO wrote Antoine de Noailles's brother almost two decades after Mary's accession when the Kings of France and Spain were wondering whom Queen Elizabeth would marry. The words may serve, however, as a perfect expression of the thoughts which passed through the minds of both Renard and Noailles as they kissed the hand of Elizabeth's sister at New Hall. Upon her choice of a husband seemed to depend the fate not only of England but of all Europe as well.

There was no dearth of candidates for her hand. During the fall of 1553 no less than seven were prominently mentioned, three of them Englishmen and four foreigners. But only two were of any real importance, and there was but one vital issue in the Queen's choice: was her husband to be a fellow-countryman or a foreigner?

Most of Mary's advisers and the vast majority of her people would, of course, favor an Englishman, but it was hard to find the right candidate. Cardinal Reginald Pole, who was later to become Mary's closest adviser in spiritual affairs and the instrument of England's reconciliation with the Church of Rome, was talked of as a possibility in some Catholic circles. Lord Arundel's son was mentioned. But the hopes of Catholics and patriots alike soon focused upon Edward Courtenay, shortly to become Earl

[1] Memoir by François de Noailles, 16 Aug. 1571, in Charrière, *Négociations de la France dans le Levant,* III, 170, note.

of Devon, handsome son of the Marquis of Exeter, who had suffered execution in 1539. His qualifications were that he was a
Catholic, that royal blood ran in his veins, and that he had suffered persecution under Mary's father. Half his twenty-seven years
of life had been spent behind prison bars, however, and it was not
surprising that not long after Mary released him from the Tower
he aroused her contempt by his dissolute amusements, his childish
petulance, and his foolish ambition. There is not the slightest
evidence that the Queen ever gave a serious thought to marrying
him, but the foreign diplomats and the people were awakened to
this fact only slowly. Courtenay, in fact, was beaten before he
entered the race, but he was nevertheless the candidate of an important faction in the Council, of a large majority of the knights
and burgesses who were members of Parliament, and of the middle
classes who shaped public opinion in Tudor England.

The four foreign candidates were all Habsburg adherents:
Don Luis of Portugal; Emmanuel Philibert of Savoy; the Archduke Ferdinand, second son of the Emperor's brother, the King
of the Romans; and Philip, Prince of Spain. If the Queen should
decide to look abroad for a husband, the first three were far more
suitable from the English point of view than the last. None of the
three embodied the threat to English national independence which
Philip represented as heir to the Spanish dominions in the Old
World and the New. Don Luis as yet had no estates of his own,
Emmanuel Philibert was an exile from his, and if Ferdinand
acquired an inheritance, it seemed likely that it would be in Burgundy and the Netherlands, England's ancient allies, where he
was far more popular personally than Philip. But not one of them
had any real chance of pressing his suit to a successful conclusion
if only because the Emperor controlled all the diplomatic channels
between England and the Habsburg dominions. Don Luis and
the Archduke did make overtures to the English government and
Paget was interested for a while in the Duke of Savoy, but all
three were late in the field and not one found support with either
the English, the Imperial, or the French government.[2] It soon

[2] On Don Luis, see the article of E. Pacheco y de Leyva cited in the Bibliography,
and *Span. Cal.*, XI, p. xxxiv, and index; on Emmanuel Philibert, *ibid.*, XI, 202, 219,

became clear that if Mary should prefer a foreigner, Charles V would name the successful candidate—and Charles's choice was his son, Philip.

The Emperor's choice was determined by considerations which have already been suggested. In Charles's mind, Philip's suit for Mary's hand was essentially a stroke of "sturdy defensiveness," a measure of defense against French aggression and against divisive forces within the Habsburg dominions. French conquests in Lorraine, the Anglo-French alliance under Edward VI, the betrothal of Mary Stuart and the Dauphin, Henry II's support of Northumberland's conspiracy—all these were threats to the Emperor's interests which could not be ignored.[3] But the enemies within his own gates were almost as dangerous as those without. His Spanish son was no more popular in Germany than he was in the Netherlands. The Electors had already made it clear that they would not accept Philip as Holy Roman Emperor, and now it seemed possible that the Low Countries might prefer a son of the Emperor's brother Ferdinand to Philip as their ruler. The threat from Paris and the threat from Vienna were closely related in that it was Henry II's natural interest to favor the Austrian Habsburgs over the Spanish in the family quarrel over who was to succeed to the Emperor's power outside Spain.[4] A marriage between Philip and Mary would meet both threats. It would checkmate Henry II's ambitions in the British Isles; it would "pair off" England and the Netherlands for mutual protection against their enemies, as Charles himself expressed it; and it would compensate Philip for his loss of the Imperial crown.[5] Incidentally it would help to raise the prestige of the Spanish Habsburgs above the

and Arture Segre and Pietro Egidi, *Emanuele Filiberto,* 2 vols. (Turin, 1928); on the Archduke Ferdinand, Tridon, "Renard," 177-9. The King of Denmark was another candidate, of no importance.

[3] See Renard's memoir to Philip of eighteen months later in Weiss, IV, 393-4; and cf. Antoine Varillas, *Histoire de Henri II* (Amsterdam, 1693), I, 342: "Cette fausse démarche [Henry's support of Northumberland] fut la première et la principale cause de l'Alliance entre l'Espagne et l'Angleterre"—an interesting observation in an otherwise worthless book.

[4] Charles V's gravest fear was that the Archduke Ferdinand might possibly become ruler of both England and the Netherlands (*Span. Cal.,* XI, pp. xx, 223-4, 227-8; Tridon, "Renard," 178; Charrière, *Négociations de la France dans le Levant,* II, 284-5).

[5] *Span. Cal.,* XI, 226-7, 389.

Austrian and thus perhaps strengthen Philip's candidacy for the Imperial dignity later on. The Spanish marriage negotiations were first and foremost an answer to a crucial problem of Imperial defense.

Naturally the French did not see the matter in this light. To Henry II and his ministers Philip's suit could have but one meaning: encirclement. Clearly, both Montmorency and the Guises would resort to any and every means to block a marriage of such threatening implications, but their choice of methods was strictly limited. A preventive war was out of the question. It would only drive the English into the Emperor's arms unless it resulted in a decisive French victory, and there was little hope of that. Friendly representations to Mary from French diplomats would hardly be enough to turn her from marriage with her cousin, in view of her family background and the circumstances of her accession. There was only one hope: the English people. They had risen once to put her on the throne; they might rise again to overthrow her if she determined to marry a foreigner.

As aiders and abettors of England's most unpopular ruler in generations, the French could apparently expect little support from the ministers who knew, and the common people who suspected something of Henry II's designs in England while Northumberland was ruler of the land. But the prospect was not so hopeless as it seemed. Vain as it was for the French to attempt to influence Mary herself, the Queen was not the government, and the government was not the people. England, as Renard and Noailles soon learned, was in some mysterious sense "populaire." There was a Council, a Parliament, and something the resident ambassadors found to be a third entity, "le peuple."[6] Venetian and Spanish envoys might differ about how much actual power was possessed by Council and Parliament,[7] but to the diplomats the

[6] See e.g. Span. Cal., XI, 339, 344; and Vertot, II, 238.

[7] Michiele considered English sovereigns "absolute lords" whose councillors had no more independent power than Turkish Bashaws; but Soranzo reported that Mary deferred "in everything" to her Council. (Ven. Cal., V, 559; VI, Part II, 1052.) Renard often complained about Mary's subservience to her Council, and a Spanish observer wrote in August 1554, "the King and Queen have no more authority in this realm than if they were vassals, for the councillors govern and are lords of the kingdom, and even of the King and Queen." (Muñoz, Viaje de Felipe II en Inglaterra, p. 111.) Soranzo

plain fact was that England's government was not absolute, either
in theory or in practice. The game of diplomacy and intrigue at
Mary's court was always profoundly conditioned by this fact.

After the death of Henry VIII, government by the Crown-in-
Council had degenerated into government by conciliar faction
and compromise. A system of administration so closely dependent
upon the intelligence and will of the monarch as Tudor government was, had little chance of working effectively when the ruler
was a boy or a woman. The Privy Council which evolved under
Henry VIII was designed to act as "the ears, the person, and the
voice itself of the King,"[8] not even remotely as a modern policy-
making cabinet. When, in the absence of a strong monarch, the
councillors attempted to act as a governing body (as they did
during Edward's reign), the result was inevitable: faction and
confusion. Mary's natural generosity and the insecurity of her
position combined to make matters worse. She could not refuse
official reward to servants and friends who had been faithful to her
in adversity; and many members of Northumberland's Council
were either too influential in the counties or too valuable for their
administrative experience to be dismissed. The result was that she
raised the normal membership of the Privy Council to almost
fifty. In such an unwieldy body, the real work naturally had to
be done by a small group of six or eight of the abler and more
active members. But this group had at first no official standing,
and the average attendance at most of the Council's meetings was
remarkably large. This meant that the informal cabal which was
attempting to manage affairs of state was hampered in any attempt
to arrive at clear-cut decisions and to keep these decisions a secret.

Both the cabal and the Privy Council as a whole were split into
two fairly well defined factions. One, led (with one interruption)
till his death in 1555 by the Chancellor, Stephen Gardiner, was
made up in large part of Mary's household servants, most of them
devoted Catholics and few of them possessed of any political experience. Gardiner's zealous interest in restoring the old religion,

and Michiele were fairly well agreed that Parliament had little independent influence.
(*Ven. Cal.*, V, 553-4; VI, Part II, 1053.)

   [8] The phrase is Michiele's (*Ven. Cal.*, VI, Part II, 1052).

his narrow legalism, and his honest patriotism were characteristic of the group, as also his lack of finesse and flexibility in political matters. The other faction, led by William, Lord Paget, a shrewd and supple *homme nouveau* who managed to get on well with four successive sovereigns, consisted of the nobles and civil servants who felt that they had a natural or acquired right to govern the country. In Pollard's comparison, they were like the French *politiques* of a later day who preferred political sanity to spiritual salvation.[9]

The foreign connections of the two factions were significant for the diplomatic rivalry which was beginning in London. Gardiner's party looked to Rome, Paget's to Brussels. The Catholic patriots believed that a reconverted and regenerated England could and should stand upon her own feet. They feared and hated the political—though not the religious—influence of the foreigner, whether it came from Paris, Brussels, or Madrid, and looked to a religious restoration as the solution of all the country's ills. Paget, on the other hand, was honestly convinced that England was too weak to stand by herself and that since the nation must choose between France and Spain, it was less dangerous to choose Spain, whose ruler was England's traditional friend. As officeholders, his associates were jealous of Mary's former household servants; as landlords, they feared the restoration to the Church of their abbey lands; and as statesmen, they dreaded the national and personal insecurity which might be the result of Gardiner's intemperate religious zeal.

Charles V's interests naturally lay with Paget's party, just as Henry II's lay with Gardiner's. But the community of interest was tenuous in both cases, particularly the latter. Paget (like most of his followers) was an Imperialist partly because he was a patriot and a man of ambition; if the Emperor's designs should threaten

[9] Pollard, *Pol. Hist.*, 113-15; *Span. Cal.*, XI, pp. xxv-xxvi; *A.P.C.*, IV, pp. xxxi-xxxv. Gardiner's party included Waldegrave, Rochester, Englefield, Southwell, Bourne, Gage, Jerningham, Winchester, Baker, Cheyne, and Peckham. Paget's included Arundel, Bedford, Pembroke, Sussex, Howard, Shrewsbury, Derby, Huntingdon, Hastings, Cornwallis, and Petre. This list is drawn from widely scattered sources and does not pretend to do more than indicate the normal affiliations of the members mentioned. After Gardiner deserted Courtenay's cause in November 1553, Waldegrave assumed the leadership of the Catholic patriots for a time (*Span. Cal.*, XI, 431, 443-5).

English independence and his own advancement, he would desert the Spanish cause. Gardiner, on the other hand, hated the French as much as he hated the Spanish. In supporting Courtenay, his friend and fellow-prisoner, as the most suitable candidate for the Queen's hand, his object was to exclude the influence of both Valois and Habsburg. In searching for spies and agents in England, Noailles found friends both among the Chancellor's Catholic followers and among the Protestant gentry who were as jealous of peers with Imperial pensions as they were of bishops with fat revenues; but he ran the risk of losing them the moment they suspected that there was any real danger of foreign intervention from Paris.[10]

Noailles and Renard soon learned that Parliament was a factor of considerable, even if secondary, importance in English government. Although dominated by the Privy Council and incapable of taking the initiative, the two Houses could on occasion play a significant obstructive rôle, especially when the Council itself was divided. The sessions were short but fairly frequent, and the members showed a spirit of independence which increased steadily throughout the reign. Mary was afraid of her Parliaments as neither her father nor her sister was, and justifiably so. For a month or so each year the members aired her policies and her Council's quarrels in public, and in view of the unpopularity of her aims, it was no wonder that she dreaded the effect such debate might have upon the people. Neither Lords nor Commons could permanently block a proposal upon which Queen and Council were agreed, but in a rough way they could both reflect and lead public opinion. To foreign ambassadors, therefore, Mary's first four Parliaments had a political importance out of all proportion to their constitutional significance.

No careful study has yet been made of popular opinion in Tudor England—how it was formed, how it was manipulated by royal propaganda, and how it influenced the actions of Tudor statesmen. Merely to state the problem is to indicate its complexity and perhaps the impossibility of its solution. But there can be no question

---

[10] On Noailles's spies and agents, see the present writer's "French Intrigue at the Court of Queen Mary," *Amer. Hist. Rev.*, Vol. XLV (April 1940), 533-51.

that during the middle years of the century when government and people were at odds, foreign observers were right in assuming that "the people" constituted an independent element in English politics, distinct from Crown, Council, and Parliament.

Neither Renard nor Noailles had any very clear conception of what constituted the English *demos,* but both were agreed upon the monster's characteristics. The English, Renard wrote, were "faithless and lawless folk, uncertain in religion, shifty and inconstant, of a jealous nature, haters of strangers, and of old detesters of all authority, even that of English princes."[11] A score of passages could be cited from the dispatches of Spanish, French, and Venetian ambassadors as commentaries on Renard's text. John Bull would be horrified, in fact, by the descriptions written by continental diplomats of his sixteenth-century ancestors. They were barbarous, treacherous, volatile, gullible, venal, and altogether unreliable. Perhaps the only traits a middle-class Englishman of the nineteenth century would have recognized in Mary's contemporaries were a love for the underdog, a hatred of tyranny, and a profound contempt for foreigners.[12]

The mental picture of the English people which Renard and Noailles shared in common had considerable effect upon their conduct as diplomats. If Renard hoped, with many misgivings, that Englishmen were gullible and venal enough to accept a Spanish King, his rival was overly confident that they were too provincial and unruly to do so without a fight. The Imperial ambassador was by far the more acute observer of the two. He noticed the fact that public opinion was to all intents and purposes that of the middle classes in the south and east, and he sensed the sharpened class consciousness in both nobility and commons which was one aftermath of the inclosure controversy of the preceding reign. But he could do little to win over the Protestant

---

[11] Renard and Egmont to Charles V, 8 Mar. 1554, P.R.O., Tyler, p. 206.

[12] "Tous ceux qui ont escrit l'humeur des peuples insulaires les ont généralement blasmez de légerité et inconstance, mais pardessus tous autres ceux qui habitent cette isle ont esté griefvement reprins de mensonge et de toute diversité" (François de Noailles to Montmorency, 21 July 1555, Aff. Etr., IX, fol. 494). See also p. 229 below. Egmont and Ruy Gómez were agreed upon English venality (*Docs. inéds.,* III, 449-50, 529). See Wiesener, 167-8, note, for further references.

middle classes, and he sedulously avoided fostering the class interest even of Imperialist nobles like Paget in order to gain his ends.[13] Noailles, on the other hand, was less penetrating in his observations, but more successful in his manipulation of public opinion. He acquired some understanding of the patriotism and economic interest of the middle classes, and his Catholicism did not stand in the way of his consorting with English heretics. But like Renard he never tried to make use of the prevailing economic discontent and class feeling. To anyone else it might have been a temptation to save England from Charles V's clutches by fostering social revolution, but not to Noailles. Once when a lazy Scottish courier aroused his ire, he betrayed his aristocratic prejudices unmistakably: "I was so annoyed with him that I would gladly have given him four lashes—and he would have deserved it—if we had been in a land of liberty."[14] Few Englishmen then or now would have relished his definition of a "land of liberty."

England was indeed a fertile field for foreign intrigue in the summer of 1553 with its unmarried Queen, its factious and unwieldy body of ministers, its dependent but obstructive representative assembly, and its unruly populace.

*   *   *

On Thursday, August 3, the Queen, dressed in violet velvet and accompanied by a brilliant procession, made her formal entry into London. Renard and his three colleagues took part in the ceremony while Noailles, who had no course but to stay away, watched the procession from his window in the Charterhouse. The Queen's grace and modesty seemed "more divine than human" to the Imperial ambassadors, and the people's joy was "hardly credible."[15] Three weeks later the Duke of Northumber-

---

13 On April 22, 1554, shortly after Wyatt's rebellion, Renard wrote Charles V that "the whole danger was in London and its surroundings" (P.R.O., Tyler, p. 362). On his sense of the hatred between classes, see Renard to Charles V, 28 June and 18 Sept. 1554, P.R.O., Tyler, pp. 484 and 152 (second half); and Weiss, IV, 278, 294-5. cf. An Account of the Negotiations at Brussels of Lord Paget, 14 Nov. 1554, P.R.O., Tyler, pp. 243 ff. (second half).

14 Noailles to D'Oysel, 21 Dec. 1554, Aff. Etr., IX, fol. 329.

15 *Span. Cal.*, XI, 150-2.

land went unwept to the scaffold. The diplomatic initiative had passed with a vengeance from the French ambassador to his Imperial rivals.

Renard's immediate task was threefold: to see that Mary was "definitely and firmly seated on the throne"; "to put her into a marrying humor"; and to make sure that, once she was in such a humor, she chose the right person.[16] As time went on, a fourth objective of a more personal nature forced itself upon him: to get rid of his three colleagues in the Imperial embassy.

The Queen was as popular as any English sovereign who had ever ascended the throne before her. She had told Renard at New Hall that "after God she desired to obey none but" her cousin, the Emperor, "whom she regarded as a father."[17] And it is easy to see in retrospect that her choice of Philip of Spain as the husband who would satisfy all her deepest longings was inevitable, granted her religious ideals and her ancestry. But Renard's task was by no means so easy as it appeared. The Protestant minority had tasted power in the previous reign; to establish a ruler on the throne who was both a woman and a Catholic would require considerable tact and political sagacity; and Mary was honest (as she always was) in protesting on several occasions that she had no personal desire to marry.[18] True, she saw that marriage was her religious and patriotic duty. The cause closest to her heart, the restoration of the old religion in England, would require the advice and help of a husband, and both the salvation and public peace of the country seemed to depend upon her bearing a child since her sister Elizabeth was known to have heretical leanings and her cousin Mary Stuart was betrothed to the Dauphin of France. But the Emperor's aims were not hers, and if it should ever dawn upon her how profoundly secular and political they really were, she might turn upon the one she regarded as her father.

Renard could not give his whole attention to the marriage question until he was sure that the Queen was firmly established on her throne. Undue severity toward Northumberland's unwill-

---

[16] The phrases quoted are from *Span. Cal.*, XI, 194, 154.
[17] *Span. Cal.*, XI, 132. [18] See *Span. Cal.*, XI, 132, 213, 289.

ing accomplices or undue haste in overturning the Protestantism established by law during the previous reign would jeopardize Mary's position and cheat the Emperor out of the fruits he expected to gather from her accession to the throne.

Charles V was unduly worried that his cousin would indulge in mass executions of Northumberland's followers. At the end of July he wrote his ambassadors, "For God's sake let her moderate the lust of vengeance which probably burns in her followers." Renard knew the Queen's "great goodness and natural clemency," however, and proceeded to turn his master's warning into a counsel of severity. Quoting the example of Theodosius, he reminded her that "power and tyranny had sometimes more force, especially in affairs of state, than right or justice." He warned her that to spare the Lady Jane (as she intended) would be to risk "scandal and danger," and advised that Northampton and Pembroke be brought to justice along with the Duke himself. His advice was not followed, and in the course of time both he and the Emperor came around to each other's point of view. Renard had to confess that Mary had gained popularity by sparing Northampton and Northumberland's sons; and Charles wrote, "In the name of God, let her not deceive herself with the delusion of clemency."[19] By sparing all but two of the Duke's followers, the Queen certainly gained rather than lost. Her clemency proved the delusion Charles feared it would be only after she had openly flaunted the national sentiment of her people.

It was more difficult to curb the Queen's religious zeal. If the Emperor and Renard had a theory of government for England it was that of Elizabeth, the Queen whom they feared and persecuted as Princess: to deal strictly with the traitor and to spare the heretic. Mary's natural inclinations ran exactly counter to her sister's in this respect. In dealing with rebels and traitors who threatened her government, her throne, and her very life itself, she was in very truth "the most merciful of the Tudors." But in the case of wayward souls of humble estate and political insignificance who had strayed from the path of salvation (and

[19] *Span. Cal.*, XI, 122, 159, 167-9, 179, 215-16.

who might lead others astray), she was as conscientiously severe
as any high-minded inquisitor of the Middle Ages.

One reason she never fully realized the great gulf fixed between her own aims and those of her cousin was the diabolical
skill with which Renard presented the Emperor's advice in
matters religious. It is hardly too much to say that Charles's
objects were exclusively dynastic and secular, but his ambassador
knew how to dress up each suggestion in terms of religious
benefit. The Emperor's real aim, she was told, was her own: to
see England peacefully restored to the Roman communion. To
accomplish this, she must move slowly, temporize with the
heretics, let Parliament set the pace. How little Charles really
cared about Parliament became evident when he hinted that
she might consider Northumberland's expedient of calling an
assembly of "special deputies," to be chosen mostly from the
Catholic North and West. But during the crisis of Northumberland's conspiracy his ambassadors had assured the Council that he
favored leaving all important questions to Parliament; and his
own experience in Germany had taught him the necessity of
obtaining some form of public assent to any "innovations."[20]

The religious question, Renard pointed out to the Queen,
might be divided into three heads: *"Ad cultum verae religionis*
[i.e. restoration of the mass and of Catholic doctrine and practice
in general], the authority of the Pope, and the restitution of the
ecclesiastical property."[21] Since the majority of the people disliked
the ritualistic experiments of the preceding reign, the mass might
be restored without fear, provided it were done under show of
parliamentary initiative. The ambassador persuaded her, therefore, not to solemnize her brother's funeral under the old rites,
as she had intended, and his counsels of prudence probably had
something to do with the moderation of her proclamation on

[20] *Span. Cal.*, XI, 109-11, 119, 123, 171. Renard simply passed on the Emperor's
suggestion about an assembly of notables for what it was worth, and fortunately nothing
came of it.

[21] This analysis was actually made two months later, but it summed up Renard's
approach to the question from the beginning. *Span. Cal.*, XI, 279.

religion of the middle of August.[22] As for the other two objects, Renard suggested that they would require "time, moderation, and perhaps the display of authority" for their accomplishment. He explained that the Emperor's unwillingness to allow the Papal Legate, Cardinal Pole, to cross immediately to England was motivated solely by a desire to avoid any incident which might arouse an anti-papal furore in England and endanger the eventual reconciliation; and his arguments did much to allay the Queen's bitter disappointment that Pole was not allowed to fulfil his mission for over a year.[23]

By September Renard was satisfied that the first part of his program—to see that Mary became Queen in fact as well as in name—was accomplished.[24] He had already made some progress toward attaining his second aim—to put her into a marrying mood.

From the very beginning the only real choice in Mary's own mind was not between Courtenay and Philip, but between marrying her cousin and ending her days in chastity. It is not clear just how early Renard grasped this fact, but his conduct throughout could not have been better adapted to the situation as it was. Granvelle had almost certainly discussed the possibility of a match between Philip and Mary with him before he left Brussels, and at his first private interview with the Queen at New Hall he approached the subject of her marriage delicately and with caution. The Emperor, he said, was mindful of the fact that "great part of the labor of government could with difficulty be undertaken by a woman," and therefore he urged her to "entertain the idea of marriage." Her reply led Renard to believe that she was too "great-hearted, proud, and magnanimous" to marry one of her own subjects.[25]

[22] *Span. Cal.*, XI, 116-19, 156, 157-9, 194. On the date of the proclamation, see *ibid.*, XI, 187, note; and *Chronicle of Queen Jane*, 24, note.

[23] The Emperor's delay of Pole at Dillingen is thoroughly discussed in the prefaces to *Span. Cal.*, Vol. XI, and *Ven. Cal.*, Vol. V.

[24] See the Imperial ambassadors' optimistic report of September 9 in *Span. Cal.*, XI, 214-19.

[25] *Span. Cal.*, XI, pp. xxiii, 131, 153-4.

At his second private audience with her on August 13 he reopened the subject, not by a casual reference to Courtenay as he had intended, but by mention of her duty to the nation and a broad hint that a foreigner would best help her fulfil her obligation. At the mention of marriage Mary laughed, "not once but several times." But she was evidently as embarrassed as she was pleased, and the ambassador, with unerring feeling for her mood of the moment, pressed his advantage no further than to promise that when the time was ripe his master would suggest a Catholic, not too young, whom she would have an opportunity of meeting before making up her mind.[26]

Charles thought Renard was going too fast. He was afraid that word of the ambassador's conversations with Mary might leak out and rouse the people before the Queen's authority was firmly established. He feared that Renard might disparage Courtenay in Mary's presence and thus arouse her undying resentment in case the young Englishman eventually captured her affections. All talk of marriage should be dropped, he wrote, until the subject was proposed to the Queen by Council or Parliament, and Renard must not promise that Philip or any other foreign candidate would come to London (and risk the possibility of a refusal) before the marriage treaty was signed. Granvelle tempered his master's rebuke by assuring Renard that he had done "very well so far."[27]

The real difficulty was that no one in Brussels or London yet knew whether Philip would be available as a candidate for Mary's hand. His recent negotiations for the hand of Doña Maria, the Portuguese Infanta, were common knowledge in England, and although he had already decided to break them off because of difficulties over the dowry, Renard was unable to deny the rumor that he was betrothed until Charles V had received letters from Spain. The letters were slow in coming. On July 30, the day after definite news of Mary's triumph reached Brussels, Charles wrote his son suggesting the advantages of a marriage with the Queen of

[26] *Span. Cal.,* XI, 154, 165-6, 171. At almost the same moment Noailles was writing Montmorency that the Queen had "hardly listened" to the Imperial envoys' proposals and that she would probably marry Courtenay (Vertot, II, 111).

[27] *Span. Cal.,* XI, 180-1, 183.

England; on August 22 Philip replied, "I am so obedient a son that I have no will other than yours"; and on September 11 his reply reached Brussels.[28] Not until September 20 did Charles send Renard the necessary instructions and letters for an official presentation of Philip's name to the Queen. For two months, therefore (July 20 to September 20), Renard was in the position of a card-player who fears that the ace of trumps which is up his sleeve may have disappeared when the moment comes to play it. He was faced with the delicate task of stimulating the Queen's interest in Philip, blocking all other rivals for her hand, and at the same time resisting any attempt of Queen and Council to draw him out on the subject of Philip's intentions.

In the game of diplomatic hide-and-seek which ensued Renard was at his best, but it is small wonder that he became discouraged and irritable. Time was of the essence of his problem since the topic of the Queen's marriage was on everyone's lips, Council and people alike favored an English candidate, and Courtenay's popularity was not yet tarnished by public knowledge of his faults. An ambassador from the King of the Romans had arrived in London with the known intention of presenting the Archduke Ferdinand as a candidate. Gardiner's party in the Council was daily becoming more suspicious of the Imperial ambassadors. On the last day of August the Chancellor told the Queen that in view of her age she must not delay her marriage and hinted broadly to her that Courtenay was the only suitable candidate. Mary was so embarrassed by his importunity that she appealed to Charles for a letter proposing in general terms that she marry, which might "divert" Courtenay's friends in the Council.[29]

Worst of all, perhaps, there were suspicious signs of a rapprochement between the Council and Henry II's representatives. On August 15 M. de Gyé and Jean de Morvillier, Bishop of Orléans, arrived in London, ostensibly to congratulate Mary upon her accession. Their mission proved an unexpected social success. They congratulated Mary upon her determination to restore the

---

[28] *Span. Cal.,* XI, 126-7, 177-8, 230.

[29] *ibid.,* 190, 192, 201-7. Renard blocked the efforts of Ferdinand's ambassador by the simple expedient of always being present when the envoy saw the Queen.

òld religion and promised that in this holy task she would find in the King of France "all the comfort and aid which she could expect and desire from a Christian prince." There was something in Renard's suspicion that their words were not entirely inspired by "Christian zeal," but Mary received them graciously and assured them that "war was not becoming to a woman." Courtenay and several members of the Council were wined and dined at Noailles's house, and the Imperial ambassadors complained that their rivals were "more courted and visited" than they. When the two special envoys departed two weeks later, Noailles's determination to win over the new government by tact and judiciously veiled threats seemed to be bearing fruit and, on the surface at least, Anglo-French relations were never more cordial.[30]

The French mission would hardly have troubled the Imperial ambassadors had it not been for the rising tide of sentiment in favor of Courtenay in the Council. On the day of the Queen's entry into London, Paget remarked to Renard that a marriage with Philip would be "the finest match in the world" and the words misled the ambassador into thinking that the Council could easily be persuaded to approve a foreign marriage. Granvelle immediately warned him to be more reserved in talking to so shrewd a person as Paget, and it was not long before Renard was disillusioned about the sentiments of the Councillors as a whole.[31] Wisely he decided to ignore their opposition and to concentrate upon winning the Queen herself. He and his colleagues pled with her not to pay so much heed to her ministers, and she promised to keep them more "at a distance" provided the ambassadors would promise not to raise the question of her marriage at a public audience. She was afraid, she explained, that her countenance might betray her emotions.[32]

---

[30] Vertot, II, 119-23; *Span. Cal.,* XI, 189-9, 193, 202-3, 209, 228. Early in August Noailles intended to tell the Queen that "[Dieu] sçaura tres bien luy envoyer quelques troubles en ses entreprinses s'il veoyt qu'elle en vueille abuser" (Noailles to Montmorency, 3 Aug. 1553, Aff. Etr., IX, fol. 53); but when faced with her, he put his thoughts into more diplomatic language and came away convinced of the sincerity of her desire to preserve the peace with France (*Span. Cal.,* XI, 152; Vertot, II, 103).

[31] *Span. Cal.,* XI, 154, 165-6.   [32] *Span. Cal.,* XI, 201, 202, 205.

The strain of keeping the Queen interested in Philip without being able to mention his name began to tell upon Renard early in September. During a private audience at Richmond he finally had recourse to his original plan of mentioning Courtenay in order to gain some inkling of her real inclinations. Mary made it abundantly clear that she thought little of the young Englishman and the conversation turned naturally to the foreign candidates. Renard ran over the list, deliberately omitting Philip's name, and Mary immediately remarked that she was sorry His Highness was already married to the Portuguese Infanta. The ambassador protested that to the best of his knowledge this was not so, but the Queen went on to marshal other objections such as the Prince's youth, his nationality, and his many political responsibilities. Her obvious interest in the subject, her frequent interruptions, and the *non sequiturs* in her thought tested the defenseless diplomat's mental agility to the limit, but he kept his head sufficiently to remark that Philip was "an old married man with a son . . . six or seven years of age."[33]

By the middle of September Renard might well have prided himself upon the progress he had made towards attaining his three original objectives. The Queen was established, ready to marry, and deeply interested in Philip. But already the success of the marriage negotiations was seriously jeopardized by a quarrel between Renard and Scheyfve which had been ripening slowly for two months.

Before the Imperial ambassadors left Brussels in June, Granvelle had probably given them to understand that Renard was to be their leader. In any case, it was Renard who drafted the dispatches signed by all four, dominated all collective decisions on policy, and was chosen to represent his colleagues when the Queen asked that "one or two" of them be sent to talk with her in private at New Hall.[34] After Mary's entry into London Renard began to write personal letters to Granvelle on the subject of the marriage and Granvelle replied in kind. Whether this private correspondence was part of the Emperor's original plan or whether it was the result of Renard's ambition to monopolize the marriage

---

[33] *Span. Cal.*, XI, 212-13.   [34] See *Span. Cal.*, XI, pp. xxiii-xxiv, and 130.

negotiations, it became evident by the end of August that diplomacy of such delicacy could never be conducted by a committee.

Scheyfve, of course, was still the resident ambassador, and the Council persisted in looking upon the commission of Courrières, Thoulouse, and Renard as temporary and limited. Now that a negotiation was on foot which would make any diplomat's reputation, Scheyfve had begun to regret his repeated requests for recall of the past spring. He had a pardonable suspicion that Renard was trying to elbow him out of his position and his jealousy took the form of a constant insistence upon the disadvantages and dangers of the match with Philip. This had the effect of making Renard unusually sanguine in his formal letters to Charles and to Philip himself, while in his personal notes to Granvelle he was as gloomy as Scheyfve himself. The Queen, he wrote, was a "novice all round" and would be "thrown off her throne one fine morning" unless God preserved her; if Philip was as unpopular and King Ferdinand's sons as popular in the Netherlands as everyone said, something should be done, he intimated, to reconcile the two branches of the Habsburg family.[35]

Courrières and Thoulouse seem to have taken Renard's side in the quarrel, but the real trouble came from Scheyfve's inquisitive and impertinent secretary, Jehan Duboys. Duboys had passed on to his master a ridiculous piece of gossip to the effect that Renard had obtained a pardon for Northumberland's accomplice, the Marquis of Northampton, and had received a gift of plate as a token of Northampton's gratitude—a story which added fuel to the flames of Scheyfve's jealousy. Early in September the secretary added a paragraph at Scheyfve's command to a dispatch which Renard had drafted. It was only a third-hand story about Courtenay having remarked that the Imperial ambassadors "were here to treat of the marriage of the Queen with the Prince of Spain, but that no such marriage would take place,"[36] but Renard lost his temper with Duboys for tampering with the minute. A

[35] Span. Cal., XI, 207-11, 214, 227-9.

[36] ibid., 205. The remark was made to Lord Dacre (see papers relating to Duboys, note 37).

little later the Queen mentioned Renard's remark that Philip "had a son and was old enough" to Duboys, who frequently went to the palace on routine affairs. When Duboys reported the remark to the other ambassadors, Renard again flew into a rage, accused the secretary of lying, and said that "he had never spoken to the Queen about the match or mentioned the Prince's son." "Not a word about any proposal of marriage," he warned his colleagues more than once, "ought to be spoken to the Queen or any of her ministers, for such was his Majesty's pleasure." Duboys maintained that Mary had asked him on several occasions whether Renard had any instructions "to make a proposal of marriage on behalf of the Prince or another"; when the secretary replied that he did not know, she remarked upon how strange it seemed that Renard, "alone and as it appeared without instructions, should be conducting so weighty a negotiation." "She wished," Duboys reported, that "the other ambassadors might be present, or at any rate Scheyfve, as he was resident ambassador."[37]

In order to bring matters to a head, Renard seems to have persuaded his colleagues to write the Emperor on September 4 suggesting that all of them but Scheyfve be recalled. A few days later he repeated his request for recall in a private note to Granvelle, protesting that Scheyfve's suspicions of his ambition were unfounded.[38] As one writer suggests, Renard's expressed desire to leave the negotiations in Scheyfve's hands had every appearance of being a "calculated caprice," designed to rid himself of his colleagues and to permit his reaping the glory of the Spanish match alone.[39] But he was unquestionably disheartened by the difficulties in his way in London, and possibly his ambition was gravitating back to Brussels. He had come to England expecting to stay only a month or so. His wife and children were still in Flanders and his affairs there were not settled. Part of his salary as Imperial Councillor and as ambassador to France was still unpaid, and he was deep in debt. Granvelle later maintained that

[37] This was the gist of what Duboys told Granvelle six months later during an informal investigation of Renard's activities. Two Papers of March [?] 1554, P.R.O., Tyler, pp. 282-6; Renard to Charles V, 8 Mar. 1554, *ibid.*, p. 217. cf. *Span. Cal.*, XI, 205-6, 214, 227-9.

[38] *Span. Cal.*, XI, 202-3, 214, 229.   [39] Tridon, "Renard," 179.

it was he who had stiffened Renard's flagging courage when the ambassador wanted to "drop the whole matter."[40] The reader may judge for himself how much of private ambition or of public policy there was in his conduct. The only fact of importance to Charles and Granvelle in the middle of September was that the friction between Scheyfve and Renard had become an insuperable obstacle to the successful prosecution of the marriage negotiations.

*   *   *

Meanwhile Noailles was working as hard as Scheyfve (but naturally with less success) to discover what was happening behind the scenes at court. Because of their fear of war with France, the Council treated him with studied cordiality, and the ambassador was soon lulled into the belief that his sins of the past three months were forgotten, if not forgiven. Henry II and Montmorency were absorbed in their campaign against the Imperial forces on the Flemish border and the conviction grew in the minds of King, Constable, and ambassador alike that there was little to fear from England for the time being.[41]

A cloud crossed Noailles's horizon on August 9 when he heard a rumor that the Imperial ambassadors had proposed Philip's name to the Queen and that Mary had been unfavorably impressed by her first meeting with Courtenay. But within a few days Courtenay's name was on the lips of everyone with whom the ambassador associated and his fears were dissipated.[42] The reception accorded M. de Gyé and the Bishop of Orléans strengthened his belief that French diplomacy, backed by English popular opinion, had more than an even chance of placing an Englishman on the throne by Mary's side.

Suddenly his confidence was shattered. In the middle of the night of September 6-7 a gentleman of the court named Sir John

[40] *Span. Cal.,* XI, 249; Weiss, IV, 299.

[41] Vertot, II, 105-6, 114, 139. On August 3 Noailles wrote Montmorency (Aff. Etr., IX, fol. 53): "Ceste nation se propose et délibère de nous faire la guerre, tant ilz en ont d'envye (comme grandz et petitz déclairent)"; but he added that the Council, led by Paget and Arundel, would oppose war, and his optimism grew steadily as time passed.

[42] Vertot, II, 109, 111-12.

Leigh came to his house to tell him that Charles V's ambassadors had formally proposed Philip as a suitor for the Queen's hand, promising that the Prince would give up his other titles, reside in England, and hand over the Netherlands to Mary as a dowry. The news was, of course, inaccurate in every detail, but it gave Noailles a truer picture of the Emperor's real intentions than the truth itself could have done. Somehow rumors of Mary's conversation with Renard of a few days before had reached Leigh's ears, probably through one of his friends among the Queen's ladies-in-waiting. Although not a member of the Council himself, Leigh was a close friend of several of Gardiner's followers who had served in Mary's household before she became Queen, such as Rochester, Englefield, and Waldegrave. Like them he was both a Catholic and a patriot, and he shared their fear that the Queen's marriage with Philip would subject England to the dynastic and secular aims of Habsburg diplomacy and thus wreck the religious restoration. Unlike his friends in more responsible positions, however, he felt free to confide in Noailles and to promise the ambassador that he would do everything he could to prevent the marriage. He begged that his name be kept a close secret because of his position at court.[43]

The morning after Leigh's visit Noailles embarked upon a strenuous course of activity. Characteristically, he did not wait to work out a far-sighted plan based upon rational analysis of English political forces and personalities. There were apparently two avenues of opposition to a Habsburg match which were open to him: the way of diplomacy and the way of intrigue. Inconsistent as the one was with the other in theory, Noailles acted for the next two and a half years upon the well-grounded assumption that there was no essential contradiction in diplomatic practice between persuasion and force—between assuring Mary that the King of France was the best friend she had in the world and fostering sedition against her government.

In his "long and angry" dispatches of the next few days he suggested various diplomatic expedients. Someone, preferably his

---

[43] Vertot, II, 143-4. On Sir John Leigh, see "French Intrigue at the Court of Queen Mary," *Amer. Hist. Rev.*, Vol. XLV (April 1940), 542-5.

brother François, should be sent over immediately to help him persuade the Queen not to let herself fall into Charles V's trap. Henry should provide him with letters of credence addressed to ten councillors (whom he named) as well as to Pembroke and Clinton, who were still out of favor. It would be "à propoz" for Catherine de' Medici to send Mary her picture, together with "a few presents of crêpes, collars, cuffs, and like trinkets" to flatter the Queen's known taste for personal finery.[44] Rumors circulated by the Imperial ambassadors in London that a peace settlement was imminent on the Continent should be scotched; peace—or even rumors of peace—would help the Emperor to persuade the English Council that he was not trying to drag England into a war with France by proposing a marriage between Mary and his son.[45] Ships should be fitted out in Brittany and Normandy to intercept Philip in case Mary should decide suddenly in his favor and the Prince should sail unexpectedly for England under color of visiting the Netherlands. (The state of Noailles's mind was revealed by his fear that Philip and Mary "se trouvassent ung soir couchez ensemble" before anyone in France knew that the Prince had left Spain.) Finally, he asked whether he might give the English government formal warning that Henry would never permit Philip to set foot in England.[46]

There was much that Noailles could do on the spot before replies to his various proposals came from France. After writing Leigh's information to Henry II he invited an associate of Courtenay's whom he had won over to visit him that night by a secluded garden gate at the back of his house. He asked the man to tell Courtenay the news and to urge him to have his friends begin building up a party of supporters in the Parliament which was

[44] Noailles to Montmorency, 7 Sept. 1553, Aff. Etr., IX, fol. 69; Noailles to L'Aubespine, 8 Sept. 1553, *ibid.*, IX, fols. 70-1; Vertot, II, 145-6. None of these suggestions except the last found favor at the French court (Montmorency to Noailles, 17 Sept. 1553, Aff. Etr., IX, fol. 73), for reasons discussed below. The Councillors whom Noailles mentioned were Norfolk, Gardiner, Winchester, Cheyne, Arundel, Shrewsbury, Derby, Sussex, Paget, Rochester, and "Wantour" [?] (Lord William Howard?), (Noailles to L'Aubespine, above).

[45] Vertot, II, 162, 165-6, 168, 181, 195; *Span. Cal.*, XI, 278, 281, 303-4; *For. Cal., Mary*, 13. Henry II had no intention of making peace and so was more than ready to second this suggestion.

[46] Vertot, II, 159, 182, 204-5. The King vetoed this last suggestion unreservedly.

to meet within a month.[47] Next day, the 8th, he called upon Soranzo, the Venetian ambassador, argued that a marriage between Philip and Mary would so distract French attention that Italy would be left to Charles V's mercy, and persuaded the envoy that it was his interest to help thwart the match.[48] The following day he called upon Gardiner, passed on the rumors he had heard, and painted a prophetic picture of the woes which a Spanish marriage would bring to the Queen, to the nation, and to the Chancellor himself. Gardiner cautiously admitted that he agreed with everything Noailles said, but his reserve misled the ambassador into believing that he had deserted Courtenay's cause for Philip's. A second interview two weeks later did nothing to remove Noailles's misunderstanding of Gardiner's patriotism. When the Chancellor talked "with great emotion" of Mary's desire to effect a peace settlement between France and Spain, Noailles interpreted his words as an attempt to pave the way for the success of Philip's suit. Henry II wrote that there was no danger in working with Englishmen like Gardiner who were "attached to the welfare of their country," but Noailles was discovering (as he had discovered in the case of Northumberland) that cooperation was difficult with English ministers whose interests were parallel to, but not identical with his own.[49]

Thanks partly to Noailles's efforts, London was filled with rumors that the Emperor's ambassadors had proposed Philip's name to the Queen several weeks before any such proposal had actually been made. Pamphlets warning Englishmen of the Emperor's perfidiousness and the horrors of Habsburg rule in other parts of Europe began to appear in the streets; Courtenay's supporters in and out of the Council girded themselves for a fight in Parliament to compel Mary to marry an Englishman; and Renard's task was made doubly difficult before it had really begun by the surreptitious propaganda campaign which began to bear fruit in popular restlessness by the end of September.

We should like to know just how much Noailles had to do with directing or inspiring this campaign, but any answer to the

---

[47] Vertot, II, 174-5.   [48] ibid., 175-8.
[49] ibid., 157, 164-6, 169-70, 178-81.

question must be based upon inference and conjecture. There
was a remarkable similarity between the ambassador's arguments
to Gardiner anent the Spanish match and those of a "Discourse
of an English Gentleman" which appeared after the opening of
Parliament. The trouble-makers of all sorts who visited his house
through its garden gate included at least one who was both
pamphleteer and member-elect of Parliament, and it is not impossible that Sir Peter Carew, Sir Edward Rogers, and Sir Edward
Warner—all members of Parliament and all later involved in
treason—were among his callers. Noailles himself certainly did
not write broadsides; and the organization of Courtenay's
party in Parliament was the work of Gardiner, Englefield, Waldegrave, and Pembroke, none of whom would have been inclined
to ask the French ambassador for support. But Noailles appears
to have maintained a rudimentary publicity bureau which supplied the pamphleteers with arguments; and as he and his secretary went about "from one house to another of the councillors
and leading men of the country" harping upon the dangers of the
Spanish match, he was certainly in close touch with the leaders
of a group of heretics, patriots, and disappointed office-seekers
who eventually turned from parliamentary opposition to rebellion.[50]

There was one fatal flaw, of course, in all of Noailles's plans
for cheating the Emperor of his prey: their success depended
ultimately upon a handsome, vain, and dissolute youth of
twenty-seven. If Noailles had been able to read Mary's emotions
as shrewdly as Renard, he might have touched the most sensitive
spot in her conscience by impressing upon her that it was her
religious and patriotic duty not to marry at all. But it was univer-
sally assumed that she would marry, and the French ambassador
naturally felt himself compelled to support the only candidate
apart from Philip who seemed to have a chance. Furthermore,
from the French point of view, Courtenay's weakness of character was a positive advantage, just as the weakness of Jane's claim
to the crown had been. The new "King Edward" might bring

[50] On the subject of this paragraph, see *Amer. Hist. Rev.*, Vol. XLV (April 1940),
547-9.

England to as pitiful a state as the old and Henry II might yet realize his dream of subjecting the island to French influence. Noailles was perfectly aware of the danger of publicly committing his master to Courtenay's support, but there was a streak of naïveté in his nature which led him to overestimate Courtenay's chances of success and (as time went on) to trust the young suitor with too many confidences.[51]

When Henry II and Montmorency received Noailles's momentous news, they were with the army. The enemy was in retreat and good news was pouring in from Corsica, Italy, and Germany. Whether because Henry was blinded by his victories or because Montmorency was inclined to make allowances for his friend's impulsive nature, both refused to believe the truth of the ambassador's report. The King decided that the rumor which reached Leigh's ears had probably been started by the Imperial ambassadors themselves "to advance their cause, which is scarcely going well in any quarter." However, he ordered Noailles to investigate carefully and, if the story proved to be true, to do everything possible "under cover" to break up the negotiations.[52] He did not bother to write again until almost two weeks later and was still unconvinced even then. He approved the ambassador's efforts to impress the dangers of the Spanish match on responsible persons like the Chancellor, but he forbade the use of threats in any form and lectured Noailles severely upon the perils of allowing unknown informers to troop in and out of his house.[53]

Although Montmorency fell ill late in September, the instructions sent to London continued to bear the marks of his prudence so long as he remained at court. The Guises (to judge by later events) undoubtedly urged a more active policy when Henry finally became persuaded at the end of September that Mary was not so indifferently disposed to a marriage with Philip as he had hoped. But the King was visiting his stricken minister four times

---

[51] Courtenay soon began to betray Noailles's intrigues to Mary (*Span. Cal.*, XI, 292, 313).

[52] Vertot, II, 148-55; Montmorency to Noailles, 17 Sept. 1553, Aff. Etr., IX, fol. 73. The French campaign in the north was actually making little if any progress, but the Constable was remarkably optimistic about it (Decrue, *Montmorency*, II, 146-50).

[53] Vertot, II, 191-6.

a day and his letters of October 2 were still dominated by Montmorency's habitual fear of provoking a war with England. Noailles was warned that he had gone quite far enough with Gardiner. Hereafter he was to conduct his conversations "tactfully . . . adroitly . . . modestly"; understatement would be more efficacious than overstatement with English ministers, hints more provocative to their imagination than threats "since this nation is so wild"; the whole matter depended on the will of a woman, and women (according to the husband of Catherine de' Medici) "always desire and do what you wish to prevent them from doing and to make them think wrong." But Henry approved Noailles's efforts to get up an opposition in Parliament and agreed that the best way to stop Philip was to support Courtenay. L'Aubespine summed up his master's advice in a sentence: "He wants you to proceed with a little more restraint in the present affair, with which I agree, no less, however, than you yourself, who will know well how to act with the necessary prudence and skill."[54]

No sooner had Noailles convinced his sovereign that Mary was likely to marry Philip than he began, ironically enough, to doubt his own conviction. The pageantry, gaiety, and holiday spirit of the ceremonies attending the Queen's coronation on October 1 were too much for him. Quick to resent personal injuries, Noailles was peculiarly sensitive to the friendliness of others, and as he basked in the warmth of Mary's smile, the councillors' cordiality, and Renard's studied affability, he regained much of his normal optimism. The Queen, he was proud to report, showed more favor to him than to the Imperial ambassadors themselves, and after dining with Paget and several others of the lords, he came away convinced that the Council would never give its consent to a foreign marriage. The Queen, to be sure, was personally inclined to Philip, as were Rochester, Arundel, Norfolk, and their wives, "who would be more to be feared

[54] Vertot, II, 204-7; L'Aubespine to Noailles, 2 Oct. 1553, Aff. Etr., IX, fol. 76. On Montmorency's illness and the temporary ascendancy of the Guises at court, see Romier, *Origines politiques,* I, 39. The King's instructions were not at all "a mere blind, intended to be shown to the Queen," as Miss Stone suggests in her *History of Mary I* (pp. 261-2). Henry's remarks about the contrariness of womankind were not calculated to soothe Henry VIII's daughter.

than their husbands under these circumstances." But Parliament would never approve a foreign match, he was told by some friends of Courtenay, and Mary would not dare to flout its opposition. A member of the Council told Soranzo that the marriage "had gone up in smoke"; and Noailles believed that it was for Courtenay's sake that the Queen had cancelled a tournament which was to have been part of the festivities—"knowing him to be as maladroit as can be believed, a young lord who has never mounted a big horse." All the news he heard seemed to agree that Renard had overshot the mark and that Courtenay was rapidly growing in favor. He had no suspicion that, far from being outwitted, his rival almost had victory within his grasp.[55]

* * *

Forty-eight hours after Philip's reply reached Brussels on September 11 the Emperor decided to recall Scheyfve, Courrières, and Thoulouse, to leave Renard in London as resident ambassador, and to open formal negotiations with the Queen on the subject of her marriage. Until then the steps taken by Renard in the matter had remained a remarkably close secret between Mary, Charles, and Granvelle. Renard's colleagues knew little more about Granvelle's instructions to him than Noailles himself, and even Charles's sister, his trusted Regent of the Netherlands, had not been informed. Granvelle now warned the ambassador that what had passed between them thus far "had better be kept a secret eternally for many reasons."[56]

After writing to recall the three envoys, Charles spent a week preparing a remarkable set of instructions to Renard. In effect, he approved and enlarged upon the plan of concentrating on the Queen and temporarily ignoring the Council which the ambassador was already following. With the cautious foresight for which he was noted, he suggested and answered a dozen imaginary arguments against the match with Philip and sketched

[55] Noailles to Henry II, 7 Oct. 1553, Aff. Etr., IX, fols. 80-1. cf. Vertot, II, 213-16, 217-18.

[56] *Span. Cal.*, XI, 230-3, 355. Tyler (*ibid.*, 355, note) substitutes Bave for Viglius as one of the "four" in Charles's confidence, but cf. Weiss, IV, 299.

a glowing picture of its future benefits to both England and Spain as forensic ammunition for his representative. Above all, Renard was to convince the Queen that her cousin's only object was her own good. If she felt that a Spanish match was politically impossible, the ambassador was to ask her to suggest another; otherwise he was to trust her advice on ways and means of winning the consent of Council, Parliament, and people. A "plain answer" from Mary was Renard's objective after September 20.[57]

It was impossible for him to carry out Charles's instructions until his three colleagues were on their way to Brussels, but any hopes he had in this respect were rudely shattered by an amusing farce which took place in the Queen's audience chamber on September 21. When the three asked Mary's leave to depart, she replied that she still had need of their counsel and begged them to remain for her coronation. Blissfully unaware of the Emperor's real intentions, they answered that they would "not merely stay for the coronation, but longer."[58] They were as good as their word. Courrières and Thoulouse did not leave London until October 23, Scheyfve not until the 27th.[59]

Meanwhile Renard did what he could to prepare for the final assault. Since he could not confer with Mary in private without arousing his colleagues' suspicion, he went to Paget directly after the coronation and said that the Emperor had ordered him to consult some member of the Council, preferably Paget himself, upon the subject of the Queen's marriage. The lie served its purpose of loosening the minister's tongue. Paget proceeded to rehearse the arguments against a Spanish match which Noailles had suggested to him at dinner the day before, particularly the fact that it would inevitably embroil England with France. He went on to suggest some fears of his own about the rift between the Spanish and Austrian branches of the Habsburg family and about Philip's qualifications, ending by praising Don Luis of Portugal as the ideal candidate. Renard assumed rightly that his objections were meant to be constructive rather than destructive,

[57] *Span. Cal.,* XI, 243-8. cf. Tridon, "Renard," 180.
[58] *Span. Cal.,* XI, 232, 250-1; Vertot, II, 171.
[59] *Span. Cal.,* XI, 315, 319; Vertot, II, 224.

answered them briefly, and returned next day by the councillor's back door for further conversation. This time Paget made the fruitful suggestion that Charles should open matters by writing personal letters to the Queen and to seven councillors whom he named.[60]

Thanks to his own initiative, Renard had acquired an exceptionally shrewd campaign manager. During the next four months Paget was his closest adviser and collaborator, reporting on the state of official and popular opinion and directing the Imperial propaganda campaign. Renard made full use of his new adviser's cautious pessimism to impress the difficulty of his task upon Charles and Philip,[61] and one result was that Paget's objections, partly inspired by Noailles, became the real germs of the marriage treaty.

Renard was genuinely humbled by Paget's picture of the diplomatic and domestic pitfalls which beset his path. Opposition to a foreign marriage had been steadily crystallizing in the Council during September. As rumors of Philip's candidacy began to circulate among the people, Gardiner's party became more sure of itself and open quarrels broke out at the Council table. The Chancellor had wanted Parliament summoned before the coronation, and it was only with the greatest difficulty that Renard had persuaded the Queen that Gardiner's real purpose was to subject her to Parliament's will.[62] The ambassador could do nothing as yet to cope directly with the conciliar opposition, but he repeated his plea to Mary that she ignore the captious criticism of the "patriots" and make the crucial decision herself. "The matter is a weighty one," he wrote to Charles, "and other brains than mine were needed to direct it."[63]

On October 10 Renard managed to see the Queen in private and gave her the gist of his master's instructions. It was his first frank proposal to her of Philip's suit. This time her objections

[60] *Span. Cal.*, XI, 265-72. The councillors Paget suggested were Arundel, Shrewsbury, Gardiner, Rochester, Tunstall, Petre, and himself. Charles disapproved of Renard's lack of candor with Paget for fear it might destroy the latter's confidence (*ibid.*, XI, 283).
[61] See *Span. Cal.*, XI, 261-4. [62] *ibid.*, 201, 205 ff., 238 ff., 252, 254-5.
[63] *ibid.*, 271.

were Paget's, rehearsed to her a day or so before, and because they
were perfectly familiar to him, Renard gave free rein to his
eloquence in rebuttal. He answered the political objections soberly
and saved his real efforts for a glowing description of Philip
as a paragon of all the virtues, "middle-aged, being twenty-six,"
and "too wonderful to be human." He protested that although
this might sound like the language of a subject or servant, he
was in reality "minimizing" the Prince's graces. Next day, at her
own request, he sent her a written summary of his arguments.
Its theme was that an alliance with one of her own subjects would
be a "mere marriage" and no defense against her "four certain
and open enemies"—the heretics, Northumberland's followers,
Henry II, and Elizabeth—or against her own people, "folk of
changeable and contradictory temper, seekers after innovation
and vindictive."[64]

The Queen had at last come to the point of making the fateful
decision which would determine the future course of her reign.
On the 13th Paget argued the advantages of the Spanish match
to her at length. An eminent scholar suggests that it was Paget,
"an older and suppler diplomat," who hit upon the phrase which
Mary's troubled mind was seeking when he urged her "not to
look at it merely as a marriage, but as a solemn alliance which
might be made to be of the greatest advantage to her kingdom
and subjects" as a counterweight to the Franco-Scottish alliance.
But Renard had already presented the diplomatic argument with
considerable skill, and in the moment of decision it was Mary's
religious ideals and womanly affections which turned the scale.[65]
That evening she summoned Renard to come to her in secret. The
conversation turned upon the terms of the future marriage treaty,
but the subject closest to the Queen's heart was obviously Philip
himself. She took Renard by the hand and adjured him to tell
her whether all he had said about the Prince was true. He pledged
his word that it was, whereupon she pressed his hand and said,
"That is well." In the silence which followed Renard sensed that

64 *Span. Cal.,* XI, 288-93, 300-2.
65 Tyler, in *Span. Cal.,* XI, p. xxxv. cf. *ibid.,* XI, 293, 294-7.

she was deeply moved. A month later she confessed to him that he "had made her fall in love with His Highness."[66]

Renard's three colleagues finally took leave of the Queen at a banquet on October 17. Up to the very end Scheyfve and Courrières had been trying to discover through Duboys what was passing between Renard and Mary, and on one occasion Renard had had to put the secretary off by remarking that "marriages were made in Paradise."[67] On Friday the 27th, immediately after Scheyfve had set out for Brussels, Renard went to the Queen and officially presented the Emperor's proposal. She cut short the speech he had prepared, saying that "she had wept over two hours that very day, praying God to inspire her in her decision"; "she believed she would agree to the proposal," and added that she would hold Renard, "her second father confessor," hostage for Philip's virtues. Renard was caught off his guard when the Queen left him to face six members of the Council after their talk was finished. But he kept his presence of mind, flattered Gardiner and Rochester by privately presenting them with the letters which Charles had written at Paget's suggestion, and disarmed the whole group by saying that he had not yet spoken to the Queen and that the Emperor meant to leave the whole matter of her marriage in their hands. He foresaw that many of them would soon scramble to get on the bandwagon, but he was struck by a second wave of humility as he contemplated the staggering difficulty of his next task—to win the English governing classes to the marriage. "This problem is so difficult as to pass my capacity," he wrote Charles; "I once more implore your Majesty to forgive my shortcomings."[68]

The following Sunday evening, the 29th, Mary gave Renard her "plain answer." Historians and biographers have done the scene full justice, but their attention has been focused upon the Queen, not upon the excited but suave ambassador kneeling by her side before the Holy Sacrament, repeating the words of the *Veni Creator* with her and Mistress Clarence, and rising to receive her solemn promise to marry Philip and "love him perfectly." One

<hr>

[66] *Span. Cal.*, XI, 296-8, 357.   [67] *ibid.*, 297, 310-11.
[68] *ibid.*, 319-22.

inevitably wonders what was in Renard's mind as Mary told him with burning sincerity that she believed all he had told her of Philip, that she trusted the Emperor would be "a good father to her," and that "she felt herself inspired by God" in her decision. It was certainly neither humility nor conscientious misgivings. "The joy this declaration gave me," he wrote, "was such as your Majesty may imagine." Perhaps Charles was indeed able to imagine the nature of his ambassador's joy in the light of his closing words:

Sire, *for my reward* for these good news I will only ask your Majesty favorably to accept my services and excuse my shortcomings.[69]

Next day Renard sat beside Noailles at the Lord Mayor's banquet and entertained his rival with "an infinity of remarks about the necessity for peace." It was just over seven weeks since the French ambassador had made the remarkable prediction that Mary would make up her mind within six weeks or two months, but he had no suspicion yet of how good a prophet he had been.[70]

[69] *Span. Cal.,* XI, 328-9. Italics inserted.   [70] Vertot, II, 145, 233.

CHAPTER IV

PRELUDE TO REBELLION

NOVEMBER 1553 TO JANUARY 1554

"ON the beginning of Novembre was the furst notyce emong the people towching the maryage of the quene to the king of Spayne."[1] Thus a contemporary chronicler laconically recorded an event which marked a turning-point in the rivalry between Renard and Noailles.

Rumors of the negotiations had, of course, been rife in London for over a month, but no "notyce" that the Queen had made up her mind reached the people until a week or ten days after the scene before the Sacrament on October 29. Until news of her decision to marry a foreigner had penetrated to the houses of London burghers and country squires there was no common ground upon which the rival ambassadors could meet. For three months Renard had been engaged behind closed doors in "cabinet diplomacy" while his opponent looked on suspiciously from the outside. After the Queen's choice of a husband became known to everyone in the realm the two ambassadors found themselves engaged in a more equal combat to sway English public opinion.

Renard had won the Queen, and his triumph was a *chef-d'œuvre* of diplomacy. His second task—to win the consent of the Council —proved to be easier than he anticipated. But his third—to win "the assent of the people"—turned out to be beyond his capacity. Early in November he recognized, rather tardily, that this last was "the great difficulty," but Charles had fortunately defined the problem rather narrowly: "If, with her people's approval, or, in the event that the Queen decided upon it, *without bringing a commotion about,* it [the match] could be arranged, we judge it

[1] *Chronicle of Queen Jane,* 32.

to be the plan most suitable to the present condition of her affairs."[2] Both Renard and his master knew that they could never gain the support of a majority of the people, or even perhaps of the Council, but they hoped that enough of the leading councillors and noblemen could be persuaded, bribed, or frightened into the Imperial camp to leave the middle classes leaderless and impotent. The danger was that if the people's patriotism were really stirred, a resolute handful of the gentry might be able to stir up the dreaded "commotion."

The task of gaining the Council's approval reduced itself in practice to that of winning the Chancellor. Gardiner was not only Courtenay's strongest supporter; he was the most powerful figure in the government. His followers probably never constituted more than a minority of the Privy Council as a whole, but in the early months of the reign he dominated the informal cabal which was managing affairs of state, and as the Queen's mouthpiece in Parliament (which had convened on October 5), he wielded an influence which was all the more dangerous because a large majority of the members had already shown themselves opposed to a foreign marriage. He was not invulnerable, however. The position of his supporters in the Council—and to a certain extent his own—depended primarily upon the Queen's favor, not upon their political ability or hereditary influence. Unlike Paget's party, therefore, they were particularly vulnerable on any issue in which they differed from their mistress. Renard knew that Gardiner's desertion would probably spell the defeat of the Catholic patriots' opposition in Council and Parliament.

Mary left the strategy of attacking the opposition in the Council to Renard and Paget. As the first step in the campaign, it was decided to subject Gardiner to the ambassador's eloquence. On Sunday, November 5, the two spoke frankly to each other for the first time; and for the first time Renard met his match in argument. Gardiner went straight to the weakest spot in his opponent's armor—the Emperor's hypocrisy about his real motives in suggesting the marriage. "The marriage," he said, "would not suffice to provide a remedy for both your Majesty's [the Emperor's] af-

[2] *Span. Cal.*, XI, 244-5, 344. Italics inserted.

fairs and religion"—and it was "much more important to remedy religious affairs than to arrange a foreign match." In marrying Philip, the Queen would involve England in everlasting strife with France and invite French intrigue with English heretics. Englishmen were traditionally Imperialist in their leanings, and the Emperor would do better to be satisfied with their good will "without seeking any closer alliance." Gardiner hinted broadly enough that in seeking this "closer alliance" Charles V was following his own selfish interests, all his promises and altruistic professions to the contrary notwithstanding. Renard argued in vain that all the Chancellor's objections applied equally well to an English candidate, that what England needed above all was "security" against French aggression, and that "for reasons [Gardiner] might understand unaided, it was more likely that the alliance would further religious affairs than injure them." Gardiner admitted that "much might be said on both sides," but said he must stick by his convictions as an Englishman and a Catholic. "Nevertheless, if he saw that the Queen wished to marry a foreigner he would not demur."[3]

Gardiner was too much the typical Englishman to be swayed by rational argument, but he knew the meaning of loyalty to his sovereign and it was Mary who finally brought him around. After his own failure Renard wisely kept in the background, planning every step in private with Mary and Paget, but allowing the Queen to do the talking. When the Chancellor came to her, she told him frankly that she would never marry an Englishman and took him to task for preferring the people's will to her own. Renard talked to him two days later and got the impression that he had "half changed his mind."[4]

Gardiner's conversion could not be completed, however, so long as the threat of a parliamentary attack hung over the Queen. At the end of October Courtenay's friends in the House of Commons had drawn up a petition to the Queen that she marry an Englishman, but Mary had managed thus far to put them off on the plea

[3] *Span. Cal.*, XI, 337-42. cf. J. A. Muller, *Stephen Gardiner and the Tudor Reaction*, 238-40.
[4] *Span. Cal.*, XI, 342-3, 347-8.

of illness.[5] In an attempt to cut the ground from beneath the Commons' feet, it was arranged (probably at Paget's suggestion) that Renard should formally present the Emperor's proposal to the Queen in the presence of six members of the Council, whereupon she was to make it plain that she meant to accept Philip. The plan was carried out on November 8, but it was robbed of much of its effectiveness by the fact that none of Courtenay's supporters but Gardiner himself was among those present.[6] Renard was convinced, however, that the inner Council had been won over and that nothing remained but the drafting and signature of the treaty. Confident of success, he thought it safe to allow Cardinal Pole to come as far as Brussels on his way to England.[7]

Mary could not put off her faithful Commons forever, and after word of her interview with Renard had been allowed to leak out, it was thought safe to receive the petitioners. On November 16 the delegation of twenty members was allowed to come to the palace and the Speaker, Sir John Pollard, spoke his piece. The scene and all its picturesque details are familiar to readers of the classic accounts. The Speaker was candid and long-winded; his arguments against a foreign match, Renard noted, were learned in Gardiner's school. When he suggested "that it would be better for her Majesty to marry a subject of hers," the Queen could stand it no longer. Rising in her place, she remarked drily that "Parliament was not accustomed to use such language to the kings of England"; she knew her duty to the kingdom, but "to force her to take a husband who would not be to her liking would be to cause her death, for if she were married against her will she would not live three months, and would have no children." Gardiner's discomfiture was complete. Lord Arundel, Paget's closest associate, told him acidly that "he had lost his post of Chancellor that day, for the Queen had

---

[5] Vertot, II, 233-4, 237-8, 241, 256; *Span. Cal.,* XI, 333, 343.

[6] The five present were Gardiner, Paget, Arundel, Petre, and Thirlby. Rochester was to have been included, but he and the other leading members of Gardiner's faction were probably engaged at the time in the passage of the act on religion in Parliament.

[7] *Span. Cal.,* XI, 342-4, 347-9, 356-7. cf. Vertot, II, 236, 260. Rochester was probably won over by this time, as both Noailles and Renard thought, but Renard was over-sanguine in thinking that Englefield and Waldegrave were also ready to desert Courtenay.

usurped it"; and a few days later tears came to his eyes when the Queen taxed him with having inspired the Speaker.[8]

The spectacular failure of Parliament's petition was the decisive event in the Spanish marriage negotiations. Never before had a Tudor ruler flaunted popular opinion as expressed in Parliament so openly and at the same time so inexpertly. When Mary, during the course of her reply to the Speaker, "called the members of the nobility to witness whether they had ever seen such doings," she was allying herself with the representatives of feudalism against the nationalistic middle classes in a way which would have shocked her father and grandfather.[9] Every avenue of constitutional opposition to her will was blocked when Gardiner was bullied into submission and Sir John Pollard sent back empty-handed to the House of Commons, but the cost was considerable. National opposition to the Spanish match was not scotched, but driven underground and intensified.

*　　*　　*

About the time when Renard felt sure that he had won over the leading councillors (November 8), Noailles became convinced that his rival had won the Queen. The information which finally resolved his doubts was hardly more than circumstantial evidence of the vaguest sort—a rumor that Courtenay's mother had fallen out of favor, a report that Mary had remarked to someone at court that she would never marry Courtenay or any other Englishman, a story that Pole had been delayed at Dillingen because the Queen feared he might oppose her marriage with Philip—but the information came, it appears, from Sir John Leigh, and Noailles considered Leigh's reports "more trustworthy than any other's because of his entrée and familiarity with the Queen."[10] But the ambassador had taken his master's warnings to heart, and the conviction

---

[8] *Span. Cal.*, XI, 363-4, 372; Vertot, II, 269-70. cf. Froude, VI, 123-5. Probably Gardiner had loyally accepted his defeat immediately after learning Mary's determination to marry Philip, as he protested to her on November 19; but he undoubtedly hoped that the petition might turn the scales at the last moment. cf. Muller, *Gardiner*, 241.

[9] The nobles present, Renard reported, "said she was right." *Span. Cal.*, XI, 364.

[10] Vertot, II, 239-48.

that Mary had decided to marry Philip made no immediate difference in his conduct. He hoped rather wistfully to discover some other way than violence to make the Queen see reason, "because there is so little trustworthiness in the people of this nation."[11]

Early in November Henry II was still of the opinion that, so long as there was no definite proof of Mary's intention to marry Philip, it was better to persuade and flatter than to threaten and intrigue. He was pleased by Parliament's reversal of Henry VIII's divorce because he saw that it brought Mary Stuart one step nearer the English throne, but he hoped that the Queen would not go through with her rumored intention of having Elizabeth declared a bastard by parliamentary statute. "The danger in this," he wrote, "is that, in wishing to push the matter further, [Mary] may benefit her sister's condition and make it something else than it remains by this first judgment."[12] His whole concern was to avoid the possibility of any unfortunate "incident" which might drive Mary into the arms of his enemy, hence he showered the English ambassador in France with professions of his good will, vigorously denied some rumored French intrigues in Ireland, and warned Noailles once more to turn a deaf ear to all "impassioned people."[13]

It was becoming more and more difficult, however, for Noailles to ignore the growing desperation of Courtenay's supporters. Step by step he was being drawn into their confidence. In the first week of November they were talking boldly about the inevitability of a popular rising; but since a rebellion was notoriously difficult to stage in winter, they still hoped that Parliament might accomplish their ends more peaceably.[14] Some of the bolder spirits were plotting to murder Paget, and a plan was taking shape to have Courtenay marry Elizabeth, carry her off to Devonshire, gather about him all the discontented elements, and resist Philip's landing by force. Pembroke and Clinton were said to be ready to join the plot, as well as "nearly all the valiant soldiers of the realm"; and preparations had been made to give the Spaniards a rousing welcome at Plymouth should they land there. The conspirators

[11] Vertot, II, 242.   [12] Henry II to Noailles, 14 Nov. 1553, Aff. Etr., IX, fol. 96.
[13] ibid.; Vertot, II, 248-53.   [14] Vertot, II, 238.

were already inquiring whether Henry II would support them with French warships.[15] Noailles had good reason to fear that Courtenay's "youth and inexperience" would be the ruin of the plot. Less than a week later the young Earl decided to flee to France, leaving the execution of the scheme to others. He was dissuaded at the last minute by Noailles's vigorous protest that he would lose all by flight, just as Mary would have done had she fled abroad after the death of Edward VI.[16] Obviously, the untoward "incident" which Henry II wished to avoid might occur at almost any moment.

Three days after the Commons' petition had been presented, Noailles appeared at court to repeat his sovereign's professions of good will to the Queen. His choice of both time and occasion was unfortunate. It was Sunday, the court was crowded, and Gardiner and some of his colleagues were still smarting from their recent humiliation. Noailles had unfortunately given the impression that he had something of importance to tell the Queen, and she had "prepared and dressed herself with greater care than pleased her." He must have sensed how anticlimactic his speech (which avoided all mention of the marriage) seemed to his audience, because he became confused, stumbled for words, and aroused the company's laughter. The Council later told the Queen that "his negotiation had been unfortunate and irrelevant," and Gardiner added that he "had not spoken a word of truth." In writing Henry II Noailles suppressed the more embarrassing details of his experience, mentioned the lines of anxiety in Mary's face, and remarked that he would be very much surprised if she went through with the marriage in the face of the storm of opposition which was gathering around her head.[17] But he was obviously discouraged. Montmorency's policy of watchful waiting had finally proved its fruitlessness. Neither the Queen nor her ministers were persuaded of the sincerity of Henry's professions, and the malcontents were rapidly getting out of hand. The beginning of December was to witness a significant *volte-face* in French policy.

---

[15] *ibid.*, II, 245-6. Although Noailles does not say so definitely, this information seems to have come from Leigh.

[16] Vertot, II, 253-4, 255-6, 259.   [17] *Span. Cal.*, XI, 370-2; Vertot, II, 267-71.

During the last week of November, while Renard was waiting
for the draft marriage treaty to be sent from Brussels and Noailles
was awaiting further instructions from his King, Paget seized the
initiative. The events of the early part of the month had naturally
upset the balance of factions in the Council. Mary was compelled
to turn from her former household servants to the Imperialist
nobles for support, and Paget stepped nimbly into Gardiner's
shoes as her closest adviser.[18] Convinced of the advantages of the
Spanish marriage, Paget was nevertheless determined to safeguard
English national interests. He set to work now in the conviction
that a treaty could be drawn which would bulwark England
against French aggression without arousing French resentment,
and satisfy Charles V without provoking the English people to
rebellion. For a while he got the better of both Renard and Noailles
and it seemed as if his efforts would be successful.

The idea occurred to him that the best way to safeguard English
national integrity and allay the popular discontent was to confirm
Elizabeth's right to the crown (in case Mary died without children
by Philip) and to marry the Princess to Courtenay. If this scheme
were incorporated into the Anglo-Spanish engagements, he
thought, Courtenay's supporters would be disarmed, Elizabeth's
numerous friends in Parliament would be pleased, and French
intrigues would be blocked by the exclusion of Mary Stuart from
any immediate claim to the crown.

He had suggested the advantages of a marriage between Elizabeth and Courtenay to Renard as early as the end of October.
Probably it was about this time that Sir Philip Hoby and Sir Richard Morison broached the idea at his instigation to Courtenay
himself, as the latter confessed seven months later.[19] Finally the
councillor persuaded Mary, in spite of her ineradicable distrust of
Elizabeth, to discuss the scheme with Renard on November 25.
Renard shrewdly suspected that Paget (who was present at the
interview) was thinking a good deal about his own future in case
Elizabeth should some day come to the throne. He therefore re-

[18] Vertot, II, 240-1, 355.

[19] Courtenay added that, had it not been for Hoby and Morison, he would never
have been guilty of the ingratitude which caused him to be imprisoned. Renard to
Charles V, 20 June 1554, P.R.O., Tyler, p. 466.

plied warily. It was a "weighty matter," he said, and needed reflection; it would accomplish all the good results Paget said it would *if* Elizabeth and Courtenay remained loyal to the Queen. Naturally the idea of uniting in marriage the two persons in England who were the most likely focal points for a popular rebellion did not captivate either Mary or Renard, and after the Emperor definitely vetoed the scheme a month later, Paget was one of the first to say that he thought little of it himself. But the fact that he was able to persuade Mary to give it consideration and that Renard felt it unwise to veto the plan immediately on his own responsibility indicates the astonishing ascendancy which Paget had gained over both of them.[20]

The day after Mary discussed the scheme with Renard, Noailles asked Paget to dinner. Paget refused to come alone, but accepted when the ambassador invited several other guests. Almost all of them belonged to the Imperialist wing of the Council, and Noailles sat between Paget and Arundel, his leading English opponents. The conversation was inconsequential, but some inquisitive remarks of the ambassador gave Paget the idea that something might be accomplished by further talk.[21] On December 1, he visited Noailles and entertained him with "fine speeches" for an hour and a half. He sounded the ambassador out on the French government's attitude toward the Spanish match and waxed eloquent about Mary's determination to keep the peace with France, marriage or no marriage. He and the Council, he said, knew nothing as yet of the Queen's decision, but they were of one mind with her in their desire to keep out of the quarrel on the Continent and, if possible, to arrange a settlement between the warring parties. With disarming frankness he spoke of the rumors of French intrigues in England, adding that he was sure Noailles was "prudent and discreet enough" not to forget that "the duty of a good ambassador was to promote peace and friendly feeling." Noailles was not fooled by Paget's implication that Mary had made no decision, but he was completely taken in by the councillor's studied astonishment upon learning that Henry II felt some resentment about the

20 *Span. Cal.*, XI, pp. xlii-xliv, 292, 323, 328, 334-5, 393-5, 453, 454, 472.
21 Vertot, II, 275, 291, 292; *Span. Cal.*, XI, 400.

marriage. He thought that Paget already regretted his part in the proceedings and that he and his followers might yet be induced, even at this late date, to sabotage the negotiations in return for "a round sum of money."[22]

Thus far Paget had been remarkably successful in preparing the way for the particular kind of "solemn alliance" between Tudor and Habsburg which he desired. He had won the Queen's confidence, he had kept Renard alive to the interests of England (and of himself), and he had helped to initiate informal conversations on peace between Wotton and Henry II at Fontainebleau by temporarily diverting Noailles's attention from the marriage to the benefits of a European settlement.[23] But it was useless to insure the kingdom against Charles V's ambition and to allay Henry II's resentment unless English patriotism were pacified at the same time. Since the hopes of the patriots were still centered in Courtenay, Paget's whole strategy depended upon winning the young Earl's loyalty. The two had a long conversation during the last week of November, and Paget believed he had "converted" the young man whose friends had so recently been plotting to murder him. He was mistaken, of course. Paget was a match for hardened diplomats like Renard and Noailles in the game of gentlemanly prevarication, but he was completely hoodwinked, it appears, by a volatile and impressionable youth of 27 who was always ready to agree with anything his last visitor told him.[24] How much more successful he was with Elizabeth, we do not know. A few days before the Princess left London on December 6 he and Arundel called upon her, and it is not at all unlikely that some hint about the advantages of her marrying Courtenay was dropped in the course of the conversation.[25]

---

[22] Vertot, II, 275-80, 291-8, 300-1; *Span. Cal.*, XI, 410-11. Henry II wisely vetoed Noailles's suggestion of bribery as too dangerous (Vertot, II, 315-16).

[23] Vertot, II, 296, 324-31; Tytler, II, 261-73; *Span. Cal.*, XI, 466-9.

[24] *Span. Cal.*, XI, 399-400.

[25] *ibid.*, XI, pp. xliv, 418; Vertot, II, 309-10. Perhaps Paget also suggested a marriage with Emmanuel Philibert, Duke of Savoy, as an alternative to one with Courtenay. Sir James Croft later told Noailles "que la praticque du mariaige de Madame Elizabet avecques le prince de Piedmont a esté mise en avant par les Impériaulx . . . qu'on en avoit parlé à ladite dame avecques beaucoup de belles promesses de la part de l'Em-

Renard soon realized that he could not trust a class-conscious *arriviste* like Paget to solve his third major problem—that of winning the people. He was pardonably chary about trusting himself entirely to an adviser in whom native ability, experience, and self-interest were so inextricably combined. A marriage between Courtenay and Elizabeth was actually part of the malcontents' plans for stirring up trouble, and the idea of using such a match as insurance against popular revolt was undoubtedly brilliant, but certainly dangerous. Renard preferred the safer course of drafting, and then of publicizing a treaty which would surprise the people by its generosity and its concern for English feelings. He had something of the faith of a twentieth century dictator in the power of propaganda. "When the people," he told Gardiner, "were thoroughly informed of all the benefits that would be conferred by an alliance with his Highness . . . they would be glad and prefer it to one within the kingdom, recognizing it to be such as the times required."[26] He spent the month of December seeing to it that the marriage articles were "such as the times required."

The draft treaty reached Renard on December 1. Although its text came from Brussels, its substance had been worked out weeks before in London. Mary, Gardiner, and even Noailles himself might have claimed the authorship of one or another of the articles, but Paget's hand was evident in all of them and Renard's was the unifying intelligence which drew together the separate suggestions into an intelligible whole. Early in November Renard had sketched the essentials of a marriage contract to Gardiner, and by the time the Emperor's draft reached London its terms were no surprise to anyone in the English government.[27]

pereur." Noailles to Montmorency, 12 Jan. 1554, Aff. Etr., IX, fol. 117. Renard could never have made such a suggestion when he saw Elizabeth himself on December 6, but Paget might have done so in order to have a second string to his bow.

[26] *Span. Cal.*, XI, 339-40.

[27] *Span. Cal.*, XI, 347, 365, 381, 387-92. The treaty is published in Rymer's *Foedera*, XV, 377 *ff*. Tyler has translated the Latin version (P.R.O., Tyler, pp. 3-6). The English version signed by twenty-three members of the Council in P.R.O., S.P.Dom. 11, Vol. I, No. 20, is undoubtedly the draft approved by the Council on December 7. Its provision that the marriage be contracted "by wordes of the presente tence" was later modified at the Council's own demand. cf. *Span. Cal.*, XI, p. xlvi; and see below.

There was little difficulty in getting the articles approved by the full Council on December 7. Renard had presented them to the "inner council" four days before, and Paget and Gardiner took it upon themselves to answer all objections in the larger meeting. Three minor amendments were accepted by the ambassador on his own responsibility, and a week later the revised articles were approved by the Emperor's Council in Brussels.[28] On December 21 the Emperor's commissioners—Egmont, Lalaing, Courrières, and Nigri—left Brussels, and on the second day of the new year they arrived in London. Within a week they had agreed to several more minor changes and had reached a final agreement with Gardiner and the English commissioners. On January 12 the treaty was signed, and on the 15th it was publicly proclaimed.[29]

The significance of the marriage treaty for the future lay in its spirit rather than in its letter. After the articles had been sent off to Renard, Charles V, looking forward to his own early retirement to Spain, was reported to have remarked, "England is also on the way to Spain."[30] To gain the supreme end expressed by his remark, the Emperor was willing to make almost any concession the English demanded. But there was a point beyond which it was dangerous for him to go: he could not afford to win English public opinion at the cost of alienating his own subjects in the Low Countries and in Spain—a consideration which his Franc-Comtois ambassador in London was slow to grasp. The marriage was unpopular in the Netherlands, especially among the bourgeois who disliked the Spaniards; but its commercial advantages were obvious and Charles took care to explain its benefits to the Flemish nobles.[31] In Spain and among the Spaniards in Brussels the opposition was more serious. The Spanish grandees' pride was hurt by the concessions to English national sentiment which the Emperor considered necessary; and Eraso, Charles's Spanish secretary, resented the fact that of the four special commissioners sent to sign

[28] Span. Cal., XI, 412, 414-16, 432-3, 435-6.

[29] ibid., XI, 428-31, 446-8; Gachard and Piot, IV, 286-90, 293, 299; Renard to Charles V, 9 Jan. 1554, and Francisco de Aresti to Molina, 29 Jan. 1554, P.R.O., Tyler, pp. 30, 80; Vertot, III, 22. The English commissioners were Gardiner, Arundel, Paget, Rochester, and Petre (For. Cal., Mary, 45).

[30] Span. Cal., XI, 414.   [31] Span. Cal., XI, 386-7, 398

the treaty in London, not one was a Spaniard. The Emperor was acutely aware of the danger of "wounding national susceptibilities," both in England and Spain, but the problem was almost impossible of solution.[32]

Two significant attempts which he made to spare Spanish feelings illustrated clearly the dilemma in which he found himself.

The first was an attempt to divide the marriage articles into two separate and distinct agreements. The first agreement, the formal treaty itself, provided that during Mary's lifetime Philip should "haue and enioye ioyntely together with the said moost noble Quene his wief the stile, honor, and kingly name of the Realme" of England and should "ayde" his wife in the administration, "saving nevertheles the rightes, lawes, privileages, and customes" of the realm. The disposition of "all the benefices and offices, landes, revenues, and fruicts" of the land were to remain in Mary's hands, to be granted only to native-born Englishmen. The eldest son born of the marriage was to inherit England, Burgundy, and the Netherlands; and if Don Carlos (Philip's son by his first wife) should die childless, this same eldest son was to become ruler also of Spain and its dependencies. The second agreement, a supplementary set of articles to be sworn to by the Prince before his marriage, included the more specific and humiliating demands of the English. This "other contracte," as it was called, stipulated that Philip should "receyve and admitt into the seruice of his householde and courte gentlemen and yeomen of the said Realme of Englande in a convenyent number, and them as his propre subiectes shal esteme, enterteyne, and nourishe, and shall bring none in his retynue nor haue none with him that will do any displeasure or wronge to the subiectes of the said Realme, and if they do he shall take order to correct them with condigne punishment and see them expelled his corte." Furthermore, he was not to take Mary out of the realm without her consent, nor to "beare or carrye over out of thaforesaid realme the jewelles and preciouse thinges of grete estimacion," nor to remove "any shippes or gonnes." In case Mary died childless, "the said Lorde Prynce shal not chalenge unto him any right at all in the said kingdome." From the diplomatic

---

[32] Span. Cal., XI, pp. xlvi, 384, 391.

point of view, however, the most important article was that which read as follows:

Item, that the Realme of Englande, by occacion of this matrimonie, shall not dyrectlie or indirectlie be entangled with the warre that now is betwixt the moost victorious Lord the Emperour, the said Lorde Princes father, and Henry the Frenche King, but he, the said Lorde Philipp, asmuche as shall lye in hym on the behalf of the said Realme of Englande, shall see the peace betwene the said Realmes of Fraunce and England obserued, and shall give no cause of any breache. . . .[33]

This last clause constituted a kind of supplement to one of the articles in the formal treaty which provided that, between the dominions of the two contracting parties,

there shalbe from hencefourth an entier and syncere fraternitie, vnitie, and moost streight confederacie forever (god willing) hapelie to endure, So as they shall mutually one of them aide another thoroughe and in all thinges which to themselfes and thier honour, and to the confermacion and encrease of thier astates, realmes, famulies, countries, and dominions, and of thier heires and successours, shalbe moost agreable, [according to the Anglo-Flemish treaties of 1542 and 1546].[34]

At the last minute Gardiner objected that this article in the formal treaty might be interpreted so as to drag England into war with France, and asked that the "other contracte" be incorporated into the treaty itself. The Imperial commissioners refused and the English gave in. The difference was not serious because the Council was primarily interested in the substance rather than the form of the agreement. The "other contracte" was sworn to by Philip five months later at Santiago, and the English always considered it an integral part of the treaty in fact.[35]

The second attempt Charles made to spare Spanish feelings was to insist that the marriage by proxy be performed *per verba de praesenti*, not (as the English demanded) *per verba de futuro*. The apparently trivial question of whether the present or the future tense should be used in the ceremony was of considerable symbolic importance. Philip, backed by his father, was unwilling to trust himself to the mercies of the English until the ceremony

[33] Marriage treaty, P.R.O., S.P.Dom. 11, Vol. I, No. 20.   [34] *ibid*.
[35] Gachard and Piot, IV, 288; Philip's Ratification, 25 June 1554, P.R.O., Tyler, pp. 477-8.

by proxy had been performed in its most binding form, while the English wanted the real contract to be concluded only after the Prince's arrival in England. Renard, eager to accede to any demand which would pacify English opinion, exceeded his instructions and agreed to the Council's demand, but the Emperor refused to support him. An *impasse* was avoided when Mary promised Renard privately that she would have a secret ceremony performed *per verba de praesenti,* and two months later the marriage by proxy was actually celebrated in this form.[36]

*   *   *

As the old year gave place to the new, the question which haunted the minds of almost everyone in England except the Queen herself was whether the marriage treaty represented anything more than a scrap of paper. Sometime before Mary angrily dissolved Parliament on December 6, one of the members rose and asked this "smart question" (as reported by Sir Thomas Smith): "In case, said he, the bonds should be broken between the husband and wife, each of them being Princes in their own country, who shall sue the bonds? Who shall take the forfeit? Who shall be their judges? And what shall be the advantage?"[37] The question was echoed shortly after the dissolution when Gardiner revealed the terms of the formal marriage treaty to a gathering of some of the leading nobles and argued vigorously in support of the match. In the stony silence which greeted his remarks, Lord Windsor (who had the reputation of being something of a blockhead) blurted out the thought which was in everyone's mind: "You tell us many fine words on the part of the Queen and many large promises on the part of the Emperor and his son; but if it happens that they choose not to carry out what they promise, what pledges and assurances will you have of them to compel them to hold by their agreements?" The company broke into laughter, not in derision, but in amused surprise at the aptness of the remark.[38]

[36] *Span. Cal.,* XI, 424, 436; Philip to Charles V, 6 Jan. 1554, P.R.O., Tyler, p. 10; Egmont and Renard to Charles V, 8 Mar. 1554, *ibid.,* p. 213; Gachard and Piot, IV, 312; Weiss, IV, 201.

[37] Strype, *Memorials* (ed. 1816), IV, 87-8.   [38] Vertot, II, 317-18, 319-20.

During the Christmas holidays the French were particularly persistent in asking the same question. Henry II was already strongly tempted (as we shall see) to cast in his lot with those in England who were contemplating violent resistance to Mary's will, but the fear of provoking a war which both English and French wished to avoid still acted as a restraining influence at Fontainebleau. On December 17 Henry and Montmorency summoned Wotton, the English ambassador, and sounded him out on the question whether England would keep the peace with France after Mary was married to the son of France's archenemy. "What provision," the Constable asked, "can be made for such a matter but a few lines written, which Spaniards use to keep as long as they make for their purpose?" Wotton was very meagrely informed about the progress of the marriage negotiations, and his interrogators took full advantage of his embarrassment. The King's countenance was "very sad," and Montmorency took the pose of being sorry for England, now about to pass under the Habsburg yoke like Sicily, Naples, and Lombardy. He was sorry, too, for Wotton who (being a bachelor) could not be expected to understand how easy it was for a husband to get around his wife. The ambassador came away with the impression he was expected to gain, that the King of France misliked the marriage "marvelously" and expected it to lead to war.[39]

Noailles had already been instructed to ask Mary the same question and to let her understand, "tacitly and cleverly," that Henry was a friend to be valued and a foe to be feared. He carried out his commission at Richmond on December 22. The Queen protested that far from wishing to break with France, her most cherished dream was to see peace established on the continent through English mediation. Paget and Gardiner eagerly supported her offer of mediation and Noailles was persuaded that the English would not pick a quarrel until the following summer at least.[40]

Henry II was not satisfied, however. After his talk with Wotton he ordered Noailles to be more specific in his questions. Would

[39] Vertot, II, 324-9; Tytler, II, 261-76.
[40] Vertot, II, 312-15, 334-41; Noailles to Mary of Lorraine, 24 Dec. 1553, Aff. Etr., IX, fol. 106; Span. Cal., XI, 451-2,

Philip be permitted to make use of the English navy? Would commerce be interrupted? Would Frenchmen in England be molested? And (most important of all) would Mary consent to have Philip sign a solemn treaty with the King of France promising never to break the peace between the two countries? Noailles put the questions to the Queen shortly after Christmas, as if on his own initiative, and Mary answered all of them in the negative. Her refusal to sign a fresh treaty with France was supported by the Council, but Noailles refused to take no for an answer. His persistence provoked Paget to ask drily whether he expected Philip to give the French hostages for his good behavior, and his temper was ruffled further when Paget remarked that the marriage would reconcile France and Spain just as the betrothal of Mary Stuart to the Dauphin had reconciled England and Scotland. Paget stopped the argument in the end by revealing (apparently on his own responsibility) that the marriage treaty included a clause which expressly satisfied the French demands. It would be shown to Noailles in due season, he said.[41]

Paget's revelation accomplished something, if not all of its purpose: Henry II was satisfied that there was no immediate danger of England's being drawn into war. Noailles had already forwarded a copy of the formal treaty to Fontainebleau, but the article in the "other contracte" guaranteeing peace with France was news to the French court. Henry told Wotton he was surprised at Mary's refusal to sign a fresh treaty with France: "for the common sayeinge is, a good creditour feareth not to entre ynto an obligation, for he entendeth to paye well, but an ylle creditour is loth to be bounden, that entendeth not to paye." But he instructed Noailles to accept the article as sufficient guarantee, provided a clause be added including Scotland as France's ally, and provided an attested copy of the amended article be given to the ambassador.[42] Since the treaty was already signed and ratified by the Emperor before he

[41] Vertot, II, 329-30, 349-56; *Span. Cal.*, XI, 474-5; *For. Cal., Mary*, 35-6. Noailles's dispatch in Vertot, II, 349, is wrongly dated December 26. It was probably written on the 29th.

[42] Wotton to Mary, 26 Jan. 1554, P.R.O., S.P. 69, Vol. III, No. 138 (the summary of this dispatch in *For. Cal., Mary*, 51-2, omits all details of the interview described); Vertot, III, 35-6; Gachard and Piot, IV, 334.

wrote, his demand was never considered. Six months later, when the King had finally seen the article, he wrote Noailles, "It is neither so explicit nor so significant [*bruslent*] that a conscience much less easy than theirs [Philip's and Mary's] may not pardon itself easily enough for breaking it [the article] when they wish."[43]

Philip's reaction to the marriage treaty was very much what the French feared it would be. There had been no time to consult him upon the terms of the agreement. He undoubtedly suspected the fact that his father and Renard were deliberately suppressing or minimizing the dark side of the news from England. His pride could not but be hurt by Charles's warning that he must bring only "honest servants" with him to England and by the humiliating clauses in the treaty on the same subject. Finally, he probably shared the general feeling in Spain that the treaty practically disinherited his son, Don Carlos.[44] On January 4 at Valladolid he had his secretary draw up a secret protest *ad cautelam* against the agreement in the presence of Ruy Gómez and the Duke of Alva.

... Until the articles had been drawn up and granted by his Majesty, he [Philip] had not known of them, and he intended to grant the said power [to conclude the treaty] and swear to observe the articles in order that his marriage with the said Queen of England might take place, but by no means in order to bind himself or his heirs to observe the articles, especially any that might burden his conscience ... desiring that it should forever be recorded, as a plain, clear, and certain fact to stand as long as the world should last, that his Highness had given the above-mentioned oath in order, as he had said, that his marriage with the Queen might take place, and not of his own free will. ....[45]

Protests of this sort against oaths sworn under duress had a history dating back to the time of the Crusades, and they were a perfectly familiar and accepted part of diplomatic practice in the sixteenth century. Henry VII, in fact, had had an exactly similar document drawn up when his younger son contracted to marry Mary's ill-fated mother, Catherine of Aragon. But Philip's protest was probably more sincere than most, and he soon made clear to his father

---

[43] Henry II to Noailles, 10 June 1554, Aff. Etr., IX, fol. 204.

[44] See *Span. Cal.*, XI, 391, 403-7, 409, 432, editor's comment.

[45] A writing *ad cautelam*, 4 Jan. 1554, signed by Secretary Molina and enclosed with a copy of the marriage contract in the Archives at Simancas. P.R.O., Tyler, pp. 7-8.

which particular article of the treaty was the greatest burden upon his conscience:

We are raising no objections over here; but if it chanced to be possible to omit the last article concerning the observation of peace with the King of France, it would appear to me that the article is not suitable, as it is so greatly in favor of the King of France.[46]

*   *   *

At the turn of the year there were indeed many elements in the situation which were "greatly in favor of the King of France." The threat of foreign war and domestic rebellion hung heavy over the English government while Mary was celebrating Christmas at Richmond and her ministers were talking peace with the foreign diplomats.

The Queen's refusal to consider a bilateral agreement with France was probably a mistake, from the point of view of English national interest. There was much to be said for Noailles's implication later on that an Anglo-French treaty would have benefitted Mary more than Henry II in that it would have "bridled" her subjects and warded off the danger of a revolt backed by France.[47] But Habsburg interest required that no bar be placed in the way of England's coming to the aid of the Netherlands in case of invasion by France (as stipulated in the treaties of 1542 and 1546), and neither Paget nor Mary dared do anything which might arouse Charles's resentment.

The practical failure of the Imperial propaganda campaign in England was pregnant with still more serious consequences. Gardiner's address to the nobility (which we have noted) and a moving speech by Mary to the Council on December 17 made a noticeable impression on the upper classes. Many of the lords were impressed by how favorable the marriage articles were to England; the Council replied to the Queen "with one voice that they would do their duty and die at her feet to serve her"; and Renard noticed that both lords and ministers were hastening to show their approval of the marriage—"some out of fear, others out of hope,

[46] Philip to Charles V, 6 Jan. 1554, P.R.O., Tyler, p. 10.
[47] Vertot, III, 184-5. Noailles's arguments here were obviously not altogether sincere.

others won over by reason, others out of hypocrisy, and others out of desire to please."[48] Apparently the Emperor's objective had been attained: the match had been arranged, the governing classes had been won over, and no "commotion" had been brought about. But Renard knew that the people were still unreconciled and that the opposition had merely been driven underground.

There were, in fact, two fatal flaws in his campaign to win the people. In the first place, he was never able to find an answer to the "smart question" asked by a member of the Commons and repeated by Lord Windsor. Odet de Selve, ambassador to England under Edward VI and a shrewd observer of the English scene, was surprised that Queen and Council had paid so much attention to terms and so little attention to sanctions in negotiating the marriage treaty; the English, he hinted, should have demanded Gravelines, Dunkirk, Bruges, or some other Flemish city as a pledge of the Emperor's sincerity.[49] His sentiments were undoubtedly echoed by everyone who pondered the "smart question." In the second place, in spite of Renard's efforts to hasten the drafting and publication of the treaty, its public proclamation came too late. On January 14 Gardiner read the articles to an assembly of lords, and on the following day he repeated his words to the Mayor and aldermen of London. Within a week hundreds of letters were dispatched to "sundry persons of credit to be by them published in sundry parts" of the realm, but before the week was up, the letters had begun to speak of a "traiterous conspiracy," fostered by "certain lewd and ill-disposed persons."[50]

[48] Span. Cal., XI, 439-40, 443-4.
[49] Charrière, Négociations de la France dans le Levant, II, 304-5.
[50] Francisco de Aresti to Molina, 29 Jan. 1554, P.R.O., Tyler, pp. 80-1; Gachard and Piot, IV, 299; Vertot, III, 22; Chronicle of Queen Jane, pp. 34-5; P.R.O., S.P.Dom. 11, Vol. II, Nos. 5-8.

CHAPTER V

WYATT'S REVOLT

*C*HE King of France," wrote Renard early in December 1553, "is fitting out his best ships; so that before Easter arrives there shall be such a tumult in England as never was seen."[1] For once the Imperial ambassador's pessimism was not exaggerated. Just two months before Easter the specter which haunted him—a popular rebellion aided and abetted by France—became a reality.

Since the death of Henry VIII, popular respect for royal and conciliar authority had waned appreciably in England. Northumberland had taught the average Englishman to associate high political office with economic greed, religious radicalism, and subservience to the foreigner. Treason to an anointed monarch was still as abhorrent to the majority of the people as ever, but the motives which might drive a minority to rebellion—class consciousness, religious zeal, and national sentiment—were more powerful and more widespread than they had been for a decade.

The forces which opposed the Queen's marriage with a foreigner in the fall of 1553 were divided into three groups: Gardiner's faction in the Council, supported by courtiers like Sir John Leigh and by leaders of the parliamentary majority like Sir John Pollard; a party of discontented nobles including Suffolk, Northampton, Pembroke, Clinton, and other former adherents of Northumberland; and a handful of restless and adventurous knights and gentlemen who had known each other during the previous reign, some of them friends or retainers of the nobles mentioned. So long as there was hope of influencing the Queen through Parliament the three groups worked together rather

---

[1] *Span. Cal.,* XI, 426.

closely, but after the failure of the Commons' petition it became evident that the Queen's enemies had come to a parting of the ways and that neither the Catholic patriots nor the disappointed nobles were the stuff of which rebellions are made.

The opposition of Gardiner's faction was stubborn because it was deeply rooted in principle, but the Catholics were aware that any rising against the influence of the Spaniard would almost surely turn into an attack upon the influence of the priest. Loyalty to their mistress and devotion to the old religion combined to strengthen their distaste for violence. Court intrigue, backstairs opposition, lively criticism in Council and Parliament of every Imperial proposal, and the circulation of anti-Spanish propaganda were the limits of their activity. Typical of their methods was Sir John Leigh's "intrigue" (as Renard called it) to have Cardinal Pole brought over immediately to England in December, in order to strengthen the Catholic opposition to the Spanish match at court.[2] Typical also was a rumor, circulated probably by some of Gardiner's supporters, that Charles V had demanded forty or fifty young English gentlemen including Courtenay as hostages for Philip's safety in England. When one of Noailles's informers reported the story, it had acquired circumstantial and homely details:

> Several gentlemen of this country are going to Spain, some as ambassadors, some as hostages, [to remain] until the King of Spain is established and obeyed here; since they do not expect to come back till then, they will speak good Spanish when they return. The fathers of those who are going as hostages are doing what they can to break this article, which it is difficult [for the government] to defend.[3]

All in all, the waverings of Gardiner's party represented the waverings of most of the Catholics in the land, torn between dislike of their Queen's marital inclinations and devotion to her person and her religion.

[2] *Span. Cal.*, XI, 471. cf. Vertot, II, 271.

[3] "Quy n'est sans inconvénient de débat." Berteville to Montmorency, 12 Jan. 1554, Aff. Etr., IX, fol. 116. See also Vertot, II, 322; Noailles to Mary of Lorraine, 18 Dec. 1553, Aff. Etr., IX, fol. 104; Noailles to Henry II, 12 Jan. 1554, *ibid.*, fol. 114ᵛ; *For. Cal., Mary*, 53; Gachard and Piot, IV, 307. There was no mention whatever of hostages on the part of Charles during the negotiation of the marriage treaty, but see below, p. 141.

The nobles who had supported Northumberland were hardly more inclined to violence than the Catholics. The Duke of Suffolk and his brothers were desperate and foolhardy enough to risk their lives in a rebellion, but the others knew that a popular rising might easily turn into an attack on property and privilege. Pembroke and Clinton, for instance, had too large a stake in the existing social order and too much lingering hope of preferment to desert the Queen in her hour of danger, and it was comparatively easy for Renard and Mary to bribe several of the others back to loyalty by hints of reward.[4]

It was the third group which actually planned and organized the rebellion which broke out prematurely in January. Most of them had held some sort of office during the previous reign and most of them inclined to the new religion; but very few had lost estates or property when Mary came to the throne, and patriotism rather than Protestantism was the true religion of the majority. With few exceptions, they were not desperate men by nature, as the records of many of them in the next reign were to prove, but they had less to lose than men like Leigh and Pembroke. It was the coincidence of patriotic, religious, and personal motives for objecting to the Spanish marriage which drove them to treason.[5]

Some of Courtenay's friends had already been toying with ideas of violence before the Commons' petition was presented and their schemes had reached Noailles's ears through Sir John Leigh, as we have seen. But it was the failure of the petition which drove them to formulate specific plans for a rebellion toward the end of November. About two weeks after Sir John Pollard came back empty-handed from the palace nine men met in London to concert plans for a rising.[6]

[4] *Span. Cal.*, XI, 412, 431, 441.

[5] On the family connections between several of the conspirators, see Pollard, *Pol. Hist.*, 108. On the association in official business during Edward VI's reign of several who were later involved in Wyatt's and Dudley's conspiracies, see e.g. *For. Cal., Ed. VI*, 123. Biographical details which follow are drawn from *D.N.B., A.P.C., Cal. of the Patent Rolls, For. Cal., Dom. Cal.*, and *Span. Cal.*

[6] According to the later indictments, Carew, Arnold, Croft, Pickering, Winter, Rogers, and Thomas conspired with Wyatt and Harper on November 26 to levy war on the Queen (*Cal. of the Patent Rolls, Philip and Mary*, II, 47, 124-5, 177, 201-2, 293). An

The reputed "principal organizer" of the conspiracy was William Thomas, a "hot and fiery" Welshman who had once been connected with Pembroke's household, had served as Clerk of the Privy Council during Edward's reign, and had acted for a while as the young King's "political instructor." An ultra-Protestant and an enthusiastic patriot, he appears to have been much influenced by Machiavelli's political thought, perhaps also by Christopher Goodman's ideas on tyrannicide. If it is true (as it appears to be) that he suggested to some of his fellow-conspirators in December that the assassination of the Queen would be the simplest way of attaining their objectives, it is not hard to believe that he was the moving spirit among the plotters.[7] To judge simply by the French ambassador's reports, however, Sir James Croft, Lord Deputy of Ireland from 1551 to 1552 and later Queen Elizabeth's Comptroller, was the real manager of the conspiracy.[8]

The conspirators' strength lay in their connections—with Privy Councillors and members of Parliament, with Elizabeth and Courtenay, with the country gentry of the western and south-eastern counties, and with the French. Sir Peter Carew and Sir Edward Rogers, for instance, were both members of Parliament in the fall of 1553; like Croft, both seem to have been personally acquainted with Elizabeth, or at least with members of her household; and both had considerable influence in their native Devon. Carew had distinguished himself by his outspoken opposition to the Spanish match in the House of Commons and the assumption is that he was in close touch with Gardiner's faction in the Council and possibly with Noailles as well.[9] Sir Thomas Wyatt, who

indictment normally cannot be trusted as evidence of the facts, but there is reason to believe that the charges in this case were based upon depositions of the conspirators which were either suppressed or destroyed by Gardiner in order to shield Courtenay. Soranzo implied that it was the petition's failure which drove the conspirators to treason (*Ven. Cal.*, V, 560).

[7] *A.P.C.*, IV, p. xxviii; *D.N.B.*; E. R. Adair, in *Tudor Studies*, 147-52, and *passim*; Garrett, *Marian Exiles*, 163. Adair concludes that Thomas "may have been guilty" of the charge of attempted assassination but that "the Crown certainly failed to prove it." Garrett assumes that he was guilty. Noailles, who got wind of a plot to murder Paget, heard nothing of the scheme of assassinating the Queen; but this does not necessarily prove that such a scheme was never contemplated.

[8] Wyatt seems to have hinted that Croft was the real ringleader (Tytler, II, 313-14).

[9] See above, p. 80.

stoutly protested later that he was only the "4th or 5th man" in the plot and that it was Rogers who asked him to join at Courtenay's request,[10] was popular in his native Kent and related to the most influential families in the county. Several of his associates were related to Mary's ambassadors in Paris and Brussels, and his friend Sir William Pickering, had served as English ambassador in France during Northumberland's last two years of power. Sir Nicholas Throckmorton, a fellow-diplomat, was a frequent and welcome visitor at Hatfield before Elizabeth, whom he was later to serve with such distinction, had become Queen. Sir Nicholas Arnold was Sheriff of Gloucestershire, Sir William Winter, Vice-Admiral of the fleet, and Sir Edward Warner had been Lieutenant of the Tower at the end of Edward's reign.

The earliest plans of the conspirators as they were revealed to Noailles focused upon a rising in Devonshire. It was in the West, still smarting (it was supposed) from the brutal suppression of the rebellion of 1549, that Philip would probably land, and it was in the West that Carew, Rogers, and Courtenay himself had relatives, friends, and estates. Perhaps it was only when Protestant Kent began to appear a more fertile field for rebellion than the Catholic West that Wyatt was taken into the plot. At any rate, it was agreed by Christmas that the leaders were to put themselves at the head of simultaneous popular risings in their home counties—Carew in Devon, Croft on the Welsh Border, the Duke of Suffolk in the Midlands, and Wyatt in Kent—and that they were then to converge upon London. Palm Sunday, March 18, was set as the date for the revolt.

There was undoubtedly more agreement about means than about ends. The avowed aim was to depose Mary and to put Courtenay and Elizabeth on the throne, but the leaders knew that Courtenay was as untrustworthy as he was popular and that Elizabeth would probably be too cautious to commit herself to them. Suffolk might press the claims of his daughter, Lady Jane, and the French might support Mary Stuart in the crisis. Most of the conspirators seem to have acted on the assumption, however,

---

[10] cf. Proctor's History of Wyatt's Rebellion in *An English Garner*, VIII, 46; *Cobbett's State Trials*, I, 862-3; and *Chronicle of Queen Jane*, 69.

that once Mary was overthrown Elizabeth would cast in her lot with them, marry Courtenay, and thus bulwark England forever against the influence of the foreigner.

The conspirators did not immediately ask for French assistance. Their blow was timed to coincide with the return of warm weather and the expected arrival of Philip himself, and so there was no pressing need for an understanding with the French government. They were all agreed upon the danger of allowing French troops to set foot in England. Carew, who was probably more Francophile than the rest,[11] advised asking for French "armour, ammunitions, and money." Throckmorton, however, was skeptical about Henry II's ability to furnish such assistance in view of the drain of war upon his resources and warned Carew "to beware that he brought any Frenchmen into the realm forcibly, inasmuch as he could as evil abide the Frenchmen after that sort as the Spaniards." Carew hastily assured him that "as touching the bringing in of Frenchmen, he meant it not, for he loved neither party, but to serve his own country and to help his country from bondage."[12] Since their success depended upon an appeal to English patriotism, the conspirators were even more wary than Northumberland had been about asking for military support from France. If they were in any doubt about the sentiments of the people, an incident which took place during January on the Kentish coast would have enlightened them. When a French frigate, hotly pursued by a Flemish warship, brought in a Flemish prize to Margate for sale, the bailiff and the local inhabitants helped the Flemings to tear the frigate to pieces and to put the French captain and his men to flight.[13] Even after rebellion had raised its head several members of the Council were confident that the rebels would resist the landing of French soldiers.[14]

[11] Although he had fought the French, he had travelled widely in France and spoke the language fluently. See Hooker's Life of Carew in *Calendar of the Carew Manuscripts*, I, pp. lxvii ff.

[12] Trial of Throckmorton, in *Cobbett's State Trials*, I, 883.

[13] Noailles to Montmorency, 21 Jan. 1554, Aff. Etr., IX, fol. 120. For further references to the incident, see *ibid.*, IX, fols. 12ᵛ, 127, 132; Vertot, III, 61, 83-5; Gachard and Piot, IV, 300; *For. Cal., Mary*, 61; Tytler, II, 353. The French captain was Villegaignon.

[14] Imperial ambassadors to Charles V, 29 Jan. 1554, P.R.O., Tyler, p. 77 (Gachard and Piot, IV, 321).

A request for French money, munitions, and warships was a different question, however. As early as the beginning of November some friends of Courtenay had asked Noailles whether the French fleet would help to prevent Philip from setting foot in England and Noailles had passed the question on to his government.[15] The truth was that in spite of the ambassador's studied attitude of reserve in November, the plotters had every reason to believe that the King of France would support them to the limit of his ability when the time came, and therefore they made no further approach to Noailles until Christmas.

Meanwhile a significant change had taken place in the attitude of the French government. Montmorency's illness had had little immediate effect upon Henry II's foreign policy, as we have seen. But when the Constable, discredited by the results of the summer's military campaign and discouraged by the indolence of his associates at court, retired to his château at Chantilly in October in order to regain his health, the Guises quickly seized their opportunity to dominate the King. And when his strength returned, it was to Paris that the Constable went in November, not to Fontainebleau, where Henry had gone for the winter in company with the Cardinal of Lorraine and the Duke of Guise.[16] The shift in the balance of parties at court was soon reflected in a more aggressive attitude toward England. When La Marque arrived at Fontainebleau with the news that Mary was determined to marry Philip and that Courtenay's friends were plotting to resist the Prince's landing by force,[17] it was the Guises who guided Henry's hand in penning his instructions to Noailles of November 23.

If you see [Henry wrote] that the Queen is resolved to marry the Prince of Spain and also that there is a likelihood that Courtenay has the will and means to upset the apple-cart [*brouiller les cartes*], you may say still more confidently that you are sure that for such a great benefit to the realm [of England] I would not deny my favor either to him or to the other gentlemen who know the evil which the marriage could bring to the realm and would

[15] Vertot, II, 246.
[16] Decrue, *Montmorency*, II, 146-50; Romier, *Origines politiques*, I, 39; Vertot, II, 240, 263.
[17] Vertot, II, 239-48.

like to oppose it. However, since things are as they are, you must act prudently and with great caution, and must not reveal what my intentions are in this respect unless you see that there is a real chance of stopping the Queen's marriage. . . . As to the offers which several people have made to you there, show yourself as cool in their reception as possible until you see when the plans are likely to come to a head and what chance of success they have. For you can well believe that I would not like to let slip any good opportunity to stop something so pernicious and destructive to my interests as this marriage. But all this cannot be done at once; time will teach us the best course. Our chief aim must be to see that Courtenay and those who have the power, if they see things going badly, take example from the recent tragedies over there and not let themselves be anticipated and arrested. They have to do only with a woman who is badly provided with good counsel and men of ability, so it should be easy for them to guard against discovery if they are prudent enough and have enough blood in their nails.[18]

Strictly interpreted, these instructions gave Noailles hardly more freedom of action than he was already exercising; broadly interpreted, however, they left the direction of French policy in his hands. If the conspirators were able to persuade him that their plans were reasonably sure of success—and during Northumberland's conspiracy Noailles had proved that the wish was too often father to his thought—he could be assured that he had *carte blanche* to promise any assistance they asked for.

The King's letter made little immediate impression upon him, however, when it reached London on November 30. The conspirators had not yet confided their full plans to him and he was gloomy about the prospects of a rising. He was so afraid Courtenay might give away the scheme for a revolt in Devon that he thought it might be well for the young Earl to do the very thing he had opposed his doing a few weeks before—flee to a safe retreat abroad. Two weeks later the prospect brightened somewhat when informers reported that all Courtenay had to do was to marry Elizabeth, take her with him to Devon, and the crown would be theirs; but Courtenay, already watched by government spies, refused to seize his opportunity and his cowardice was Noailles's despair.[19]

[18] Henry II to Noailles, 23 Nov. 1553, Aff. Etr., IX, fol. 99.
[19] Vertot, II, 289-90, 310.

The mystery which surrounds Noailles's relations with the conspirators during December is well-nigh impossible to penetrate, but one fact emerges clearly from the evidence: during the Christmas holidays, while the Imperial commissioners were on their way from Brussels to London to sign the marriage treaty, the plot passed from the stage of thought to that of action and the plotters confided the gist of their plans to the French ambassador. Arnold testified later that it was on December 22 that Thomas suggested the assassination of the Queen, and about the same time Carew left London for Devon, to be followed a few days afterward by Thomas himself.[20] On the 23rd a naturalized Frenchman called upon Noailles to tell him that the mayor and aldermen of Plymouth were so determined to resist Philip's landing in their port that they wanted Henry II to send them a French garrison for their protection.[21] The same day Noailles was informed that Sir James Croft had plans for stirring up "infinite troubles" in England and Ireland and wished to enter the French King's service.[22] About the same time an Englishman appeared at Fontainebleau, told Montmorency he represented "8 or 10 English gentlemen," and offered to bring over to the French service "8 or 9 good warships" which he and his associates hoped to have on the sea before the end of January.[23]

[20] *Tudor Studies,* 148.

[21] Vertot, II, 342. It is almost certain that Noailles's informer was Jean de Fontenay, Sieur de Berteville, a French intriguer who had obtained naturalization in 1549. In his dispatch of December 23 Noailles enclosed a letter (now lost) from Berteville to Montmorency in which Berteville asked to be pardoned for past misdeeds and taken back into the French service. In his reply Montmorency remembered that "the person" who had written the letter had given him information "while he was in France" (Montmorency to Noailles, 30 Dec. 1553, Aff. Etr., IX, fol. 112). Early in January Noailles conferred with Berteville at Montmorency's orders, and Berteville gave him a second letter describing the conspirators' activities for transmission to the Constable (Berteville to Montmorency, 12 Jan. 1554, *ibid.,* IX, fol. 116). On Berteville's career, see *Amer. Hist. Rev.,* XLV (April 1940), 540-2.

[22] Henry II to Noailles, 30 Dec. 1553, Aff. Etr., IX, fol. 111. It is not clear whether it was Croft or someone else (possibly Berteville) who gave Noailles this information. The ambassador's record of Croft's proposals was probably added to his dispatch of December 23 (Vertot, II, 334 *ff.*) in the form of a postscript which somehow did not get copied into the original minute.

[23] Montmorency to Noailles, 30 Dec. 1553, Aff. Etr., IX, fol. 112. The Englishman mentioned was perhaps one of the piratical Killigrew brothers, who were in France a month later (Renard to Charles V, 1 Mar. 1554, P.R.O. Tyler, p. 194).

Noailles's experience as Admiral pro-tem of the French navy had taught him the importance of sea-power during any crisis in Anglo-French relations, and he was quick to grasp the significance of the conspirators' plans. He knew there was strong anti-Spanish feeling among English sailors and he had already advised Henry II that a show of French strength in the Channel would encourage the malcontents in England.[24] Reports soon began to reach London that the Norman ports were humming with activity.[25] Devon was still the center of the conspirators' hopes and control of the channel an integral part of their strategy. If their few vessels could find shelter in French ports and support from French warships, Imperialist nobles who embarked in the West for Spain could be spirited off to Brest (as Noailles suggested),[26] Spanish commerce could be preyed upon, the rebels could be supplied with munitions from across the Channel, and some sort of resistance could be offered to Philip's fleet when it arrived. Once the rebels' ships had taken up positions along the west coast, it would be safe for Courtenay to join Carew and for the malcontents to take up arms.[27]

Meanwhile, thanks to the Constable's return to court early in December, French policy had veered once more in the direction of caution. Montmorency was able to persuade Henry not to commit himself to the conspirators until the resources of diplomacy were exhausted. The invitation to Mary to sign a fresh Anglo-French treaty was undoubtedly made at the Constable's suggestion, and until word reached Fontainebleau that the Queen had refused the proposal, Henry was content to hold his hand. His dispatch of December 30 (the last written instructions to reach Noailles before the rebellion broke out) was more cautious than that of November 23. Noailles was ordered to investigate Croft's plans more closely,

[24] Vertot, II, 289, 312.
[25] *Span. Cal.*, XI, 470; Renard to Charles V, 9 Jan. 1554, P.R.O., Tyler, p. 29; Gachard and Piot, IV, 294.
[26] Vertot, II, 322.
[27] On January 12, 1554, Berteville wrote Montmorency:
   "Celuy de quy je vous écryvy dernièrement qui a esté prisonnyer si longuement [Courtenay] a été prest etre envoyé en otage en Espaigne, mais cela est rompu. Il n'est en trop grande faveur de quelques grans, mais du commun, assez. J'espoire qu'il aura congié aler en son pays [Devon] *premyer que ces marans viennent,* où il séjournera tant qu'il plaira à Dieu." Aff. Etr., IX, fol. 116. (Italics inserted.)

to hint that the King of France was liberal in rewards to those who did him service, but not to make "any other and more specific promise." Montmorency congratulated the ambassador upon his noncommittal reply to the Mayor and aldermen of Plymouth and warned him, "It is very necessary to act with great reserve in reply to such overtures until one sees more foundation in them, as I advised you in my preceding letters." If the conspirators approached Noailles on the subject of finding shelter for their ships in French ports, he was "always to encourage them in this plan without opening himself too much" to them.[28]

By the time these instructions reached London a week later, the English government had got wind of the plot, the conspirators were on the point of asking for immediate French support, and Noailles was ready to take the bit in his teeth.

Carew's departure for Devon had aroused the government's suspicions and information soon reached the court that he was involved in a plot of some heretics "to induce Courtenay or the Lady Elizabeth to act as their leader."[29] On January 2 he was ordered to appear before the Council for questioning. Noailles soon foresaw the results which this action would have upon the conspirators:

The Queen and the lords of her Council [he wrote on January 12] are working to break up the plot of those who are conspiring against the marriage . . . , and thus those who are in the plot will have to take up arms sooner than they think.[30]

The time for action had come, two months earlier than expected, and Noailles had recaptured his mood of September. Everything he heard convinced him that the conspirators would have the support of the people.[31] And on January 7 at the crucial moment

[28] Henry II and Montmorency to Noailles, 30 Dec. 1553, Aff. Etr., IX, fols. 111, 112. During the third week of January an Englishman came to Fontainebleau with a letter from Pickering, reported that three or four of the rebels' ships were at sea, and asked shelter for them in French ports. Noailles was immediately ordered to promise such shelter (Henry II and Montmorency to Noailles, 22 Jan. 1554, Aff. Etr., IX, fols. 123, 125).

[29] Renard to Granvelle, 7 Jan. 1554, P.R.O., Tyler, p. 24; *A.P.C.*, IV, 382, 385.

[30] Noailles to Montmorency, 12 Jan. 1554, Aff. Etr., IX, fol. 118.

[31] On December 24 Noailles wrote Mary of Lorraine, "Je la [Mary] pense plus Espaignolle que Anglaise, et qu'elle porte une hayne conceue de loing temps à sa propre

D'Oysel, the French ambassador to Scotland, arrived from France
to give him verbal instructions and moral support.

D'Oysel undoubtedly gave Noailles a picture of Henry II's intentions which differed (in emphasis at least) from Montmorency's
dispatches. When the fateful instructions of November 23 were
sent off from Fontainebleau, the Cardinal of Lorraine and the
Duke of Guise intended to send D'Oysel back immediately to their
sister Mary, the Queen Dowager of Scotland, via London. He was
to be "further instructed on the King's intention in everything"
and was to confer with Noailles on his way.[32] For some reason he
was detained at court for three weeks and the presence of enemy
ships in the Channel delayed him two weeks more on the French
coast,[33] but once he reached London the French embassy became
a veritable beehive of activity. There is reason to believe that he
rather than Noailles took the lead in dealing with the plotters
during his week's sojourn in the city. He had come direct from
Fontainebleau; he was merely passing through and could thus
act with more freedom than the resident ambassador; his later letters prove that, like his friends the Guises, he was convinced that
only a bold and aggressive policy could meet the Habsburg threat
to French interests in Scotland; and the later accusations of the
English government were aimed even more at him than at
Noailles.[34]

Before D'Oysel set out for Edinburgh on January 14 Noailles
had him "hear, see, and touch with eye and finger . . . all the
plots and machinations" which were on foot, introducing him

nation. De quoy elle n'est en rien déceue, car ses subgetz ne luy portent pas meilleure
volunté." Aff. Etr., IX, fol. 106.

[32] Vertot, II, 263.

[33] For details of D'Oysel's journey, see D'Oysel to Noailles, 29 Dec. 1553, Aff. Etr.,
IX, fol. 110; Noailles to Henry II, 12 Jan. 1554, ibid., fol. 114; Noailles to D'Oysel, 22
Jan. 1554, ibid., fol. 121; Vertot, III, 17; Renard to Granvelle, 7 Jan. 1554, P.R.O.,
Tyler, p. 25.

[34] For his opinions, see e.g. D'Oysel to Noailles, 28 Feb., 2 Mar., 5 Mar., 21 Mar.,
and 20 May 1554, Aff. Etr., IX, fols. 142, 143, 148, 21 (copy misdated 21 Mar. 1553),
185. For the government's charges against him, see François [actually Antoine] de
Noailles to Montmorency, 16 Mar. 1554, ibid., IX, fol. 13ᵛ; Vertot, III, 139; and
D'Oysel to Noailles, 20 May 1554 (above). In his letter of 12 Jan. 1554 to Henry II
(Aff. Etr., IX, fol. 114), Noailles referred the King to a letter which D'Oysel was
writing on the same day. Unfortunately this important report has been lost (cf. Vertot,
III, 14, 17, 21).

personally to all their "principal authors and leaders."[35] Minor
figures in the plot—Englishmen, Frenchmen, and Scots—kept the
French diplomats in touch with the ringleaders, and Croft, Rogers,
and Pickering each visited the embassy in person.[36] A long conversation with Croft was the climax of the week's activities.

It is easier to determine what the conspirators asked for than
what Noailles and D'Oysel promised them. Frightened by the
order for Carew's appearance before the Council, Croft asked for
an immediate assurance of French support—in ships, munitions,
and money.

> The principal authors and leaders of the plot [Noailles reported] are
> afraid of having a great lack of arms, artillery, munitions, and money, and
> they beg the King most humbly to furnish them with these commodities
> in view of his interest in the matter and his friendly concern for the com-
> mon weal and repose of this realm.[37]

Apparently Noailles and D'Oysel were more than ready to
promise the assistance requested on their own initiative, but remembering the main point of their instructions they questioned
Croft closely to determine what chances the plot had of success.
Croft replied by discussing his accomplices' plans at length—"the
ends of their intention and how they hoped to handle their enterprise and the means they had of carrying it out." The plan was, he
said, that "each of them was to retire to the place where he knew
he had support and that the Lady Elizabeth and the Earl of Devonshire were to flee [from court] at the first opportunity."[38] Probably
Croft sensed the necessity of convincing the ambassadors that the
plot had what Montmorency called "foundation." At any rate he
said his associates had hopes of winning over some of the Council
and hinted broadly that not only Courtenay but even Elizabeth
herself were in his friends' confidence. He seems to have told

[35] Vertot, III, 17.   [36] *Amer. Hist. Rev.*, XLV (April 1940), 548-9.
[37] Noailles's Instructions to La Marque, 15 Jan. 1554, Aff. Etr., XV, fol. 267. This
passage is omitted from Vertot's published version of the dispatch (Vertot, III, 23), as
also from his manuscript copy (Aff. Etr., XII, fol. 150). Wiesener, who overlooked the
originals upon which Vertot's work was based, cites Lingard's faulty version of the
passage (Wiesener, 175, note 1). Three other passages in the same dispatch are either
omitted or falsified by Vertot.
[38] ". . . délibèrent se retirer chacun à l'endroit où il a intelligence et se sauver du
premier jour Madame Elizabet et le conte Dompcher. . . ." Noailles to Henry II, 12
Jan. 1554, Aff. Etr., IX, fols. 114-15.

Noailles that he was "very familiar" with Elizabeth and her servants, and that he intended to stop by Ashridge on his way to Wales in order to warn her to withdraw further into the country as soon as the rising began—an intention which he actually carried out later.[39] When Noailles asked him what he knew about the possibility of Elizabeth's marrying the Duke of Savoy, he replied that the Imperialists had actually made such a proposal to her, but that

no matter what sign she shows of listening to it, she is determined not to accept anyone suggested to her from this quarter . . . because she knows full well that it would be her ruin and that all the Emperor intends to gain from the proposal is to abuse and deceive her while his son, the Prince of Spain, assures and establishes his position here; furthermore she sees the fine claim she has to the crown and the expectation she has of gaining it, especially if the matters undertaken for her come to a successful end.[40]

Obviously Croft knew a good deal about Elizabeth's intentions, but the historian inevitably wonders whether his information came from the Princess herself or from her friends. However, whether he really knew whereof he spoke or whether he was indulging in wishful thinking calculated to impress the French envoys, he managed to persuade them that the conspiracy had "foundation" enough to be deserving of support.

Noailles and D'Oysel could not give the conspirators any formal and official promise of assistance, but in diplomacy there are infinite gradations between a promise and a hint. Noailles had already been empowered to suggest to them, as on his own responsibility, that since Henry II's interests were what they were, any determined rebellion against Mary would find support from France; and this is clearly what he did.

I shall continue to encourage Croft and his companions in this good intention [he wrote on January 12] without discovering or opening myself further than your Majesty has been pleased to command me, until the time

[39] On January 22 Noailles wrote D'Oysel, "Encores craintz je beaucoup que le personnaige [Elizabeth] que celluy à qui je vous fiz parler [Croft] doibt veoir au partir d'icy ne soit empesché" (Aff. Etr., IX, fol. 121). The identifications noted would seem to be established by the fact of Croft's visit to Ashridge (J. A. Muller, *Gardiner,* 248 and notes). On Croft's hopes about the malcontents in the Council, see Vertot, III, 15.

[40] Noailles to Montmorency, 12 Jan. 1554, Aff. Etr., IX, fol. 117.

and occasion arrives when one can be really assured about the foundation of their designs. However, Sire, if you think that I am too reserved and that my being a little more frank in an underhand way might further and encourage their schemes, please advise me how I should act. . . . It seems to M. d'Oysel and myself, Sire, that it would be most *à propos* if you would have ready at Brest, St. Malo, or Morlais persons of quality to whom those in the plot might send news of the disposition of their affairs (this would be easy in view of the small expanse of water between them), so that [the conspirators] might be encouraged with your favor and help; in addition, those whom you commission will be able to discover the right moment for your interests [to intervene], a moment which may be such that you, Sire, will be very glad not to lose it.[41]

Three days later the faithful and indefatigable La Marque was dispatched to Fontainebleau for instructions, and Noailles made it still more clear what he hoped the answer would be.

La Marque will say further that it seems to the Seigneurs de Noailles and d'Oysel that his Majesty should encourage, covertly and underhandedly, the authors and leaders of this enterprise, since they are not persons of mean quality; and that (if it pleases his Majesty) he should come to an understanding about the best means of favoring them as soon as possible with arms and other things which his Majesty finds most available in his provinces of Normandy and Brittany.[42]

There is good reason to believe that Noailles and D'Oysel actually offered more than the conspirators asked for. Croft and his friends did not want the cooperation of French troops and there is no evidence in Noailles's dispatches that they asked for anything more than money and supplies; but it seems clear that the French ambassadors offered to create diversions on the Scottish border and the Calais Pale as soon as the conspirators should resort to arms.[43] Both Croft and Wyatt were later reported to have confessed that D'Oysel had promised them *men* as well as money and arms,[44] and

[41] Noailles to Henry II, 12 Jan. 1554, Aff. Etr., IX, fols. 114-15. Slightly differing versions of this same suggestion are to be found in Noailles to Montmorency, 12 Jan. 1554, *ibid.*, IX, fol. 118, and in Vertot, III, 23-4.

[42] Instructions to La Marque, 15 Jan. 1554, Aff. Etr., XV, fols. 267ᵛ-8. This passage is omitted by Vertot (III, 23). In the sentence immediately following, Vertot writes "et pour descouvrir ce qu'on doit attendre de ceste entreprinse . . . ," while the original minute reads "et pour dextrement exécuter telle entreprinse . . ." (cf. Noailles's letter of January 12 to Henry II quoted immediately above).

[43] Renard to Charles V, 24 Feb. 1554, P.R.O., Tyler, p. 184 (Tytler, II, 307).

[44] Noailles heard that Croft had confessed after his arrest "qu'en parlant à M. Doysel et à moi nous luy avions présenté pour ses esmotions gens, armes, et faveur" (Noailles

Renard heard that Henry II had told the plotters he had twenty-four ships and eight companies of infantry "ready to land in England and to go to their assistance."[45] Most of the reports of French military and naval preparations which Renard's spies and English friends brought in to him in January and February—rumors of two hundred ships being fitted out, strong detachments being sent to Scotland, and thousands of crowns being distributed among the malcontents[46]—were either false or greatly exaggerated. Henry II's indolence, Montmorency's moderating influence, and the exhaustion of French resources in the war with Charles V certainly precluded the possibility that French troops in any great number were ready to strike at England by the end of January. But D'Oysel and the Guises were undoubtedly watching for an opportunity to fish in troubled waters—to strengthen the French position in Scotland and to strike at Calais should the rebels succeed in crippling Mary's government. During February and March reports poured into England of French preparations to attack Calais[47] and of Scottish preparations to break the peace in the North; and the fact that D'Oysel tried to suborn several important English officials in the northern counties while on his way to Edinburgh[48] suggests that these preparations were part of a plan previously agreed upon, either in Fontainebleau or at the French embassy in London. In

to Montmorency, 4 Oct. 1554, Aff. Etr., IX, fols. 273ᵛ-4). Renard heard that Wyatt confessed that D'Oysel had promised "money, assistance, and men" (Tytler, II, 306). The surviving confessions of Croft and Wyatt make no mention of these facts, but we have reason to believe that some of the rebels' depositions were destroyed or suppressed by Gardiner and his friends in the Council to shield Courtenay.

[45] Imperial ambassadors to Charles V, 29 Jan. 1554, P.R.O., Tyler, p. 77 (cf. Gachard and Piot, IV, 320).

[46] P.R.O., Tyler, as follows: Egmont to Philip, 7 Jan. 1554 (*Docs. inéds.*, III, 449); Renard to Charles V, 9 Jan. 1554 (p. 29); same to same, 18 Jan. 1554 (Gachard and Piot, IV, 299, 301); Renard to Philip, 23 Jan. 1554 (p. 62); Imperial ambassadors to Charles V, 27 Jan. 1554 (*Docs. inéds.*, III, 456); Renard to Charles V, 8 Feb. 1554 (a second letter of this date, P.R.O., Tyler, pp. 131-2); Renard to Philip, 19 Feb. 1554 (*Docs. inéds.*, III, 499).

[47] See e.g. *For. Cal., Mary*, 58, 64-6, 77; Vandeville to Mary of Hungary, 16 Feb. 1554, P.R.O., Tyler, p. 154; Renard to Charles V, 15 Mar. 1554, *ibid.*, p. 239; Granvelle to Mary of Hungary, 22 Mar. 1554, *ibid.*, p. 270; Vertot, III, 96, 100-1; Senarpont to Noailles, 6 Mar. 1554, Aff. Etr., IX, fol. 149; Charrière, *Négociations . . . dans le Levant*, II, 308-9.

[48] Noailles to D'Oysel, 22 Jan. 1554, Aff. Etr., IX, fol. 121; D'Oysel to Noailles, 28 Feb. and 5 Mar. 1554, *ibid.*, IX, fols. 142, 148; Vertot, III, 161; Renard to Philip, 23 Jan. 1554, P.R.O., Tyler, p. 62.

January 1554, as in July 1553, the French were more eager to offer military "assistance" than English traitors were to ask for it.

When La Marque reached Paris on January 22 with Noailles's report on his conversations with the conspirators, news had already reached the French court that Mary was unwilling to sign a new treaty with France. Convinced that war with England was inevitable Montmorency hesitated no longer. He had received a letter from Pickering (presumably outlining the plot) and he knew that some of the rebels' ships were already at sea.[49] French naval officers were immediately summoned, ships of sixty tons and over were forbidden to leave port without permission, royal officials were sent to the Norman coast as Noailles had suggested, and the government began to look for ready money. On January 26 La Marque left Paris with five thousand gold crowns for the conspirators and a dispatch ordering Noailles to throw himself unreservedly into the plot.[50] The courier could not know, as he sped toward London, that England was already in the throes of rebellion. The French King's decision had come too late.

*   *   *

Rebellion was in the air even before La Marque had left London (on January 15). Gardiner's announcement of the terms of the marriage treaty to the Mayor and aldermen of the city only added more fuel to the fire it was meant to quench. By the middle of January it was finally clear to the public that there was no turning back for the Queen. Italian and English merchants complained openly that the Spanish alliance would be their ruin; heretics bewailed the coming enslavement of England to a Spanish Catholic; and news arrived from the West that Carew had openly defied the Council's order to appear before them and had turned traitor. Renard was thoroughly convinced that a widespread rebellion was imminent, organized by a shadowy band of resolute leaders, fos-

---

[49] "J'ay parlé au gentilhomme anglois qui m'a apporté la lettre du sieur de Piderin et luy fais dépescher la lettre dont il m'a escript, et d'autre part luy ay donné les moyens qu'il aura à tenir au lieu où il va pour l'exécution de ce qu'il vous a promis." Montmorency to Noailles, 22 Jan. 1554, Aff. Etr., IX, fol. 125.

[50] For. Cal., Mary, 52; Vertot, III, 34-7. La Marque did not reach London until after Wyatt had surrendered.

tered by the French and Venetian ambassadors, and backed by all the military and naval might of France. Afraid that Mary might be terrified by the reports which had reached him, he confided his fears for the time being only to Paget, giving him the names of "all those who have an understanding with the King of France." But when he learned that Carew had composed a letter warning the Queen that he and his friends would never allow the Spaniards to set foot on English soil and "deflower their daughters," the ambassador told Mary everything he knew.[51]

The conspirators who were still in London knew now that they must act at once or not at all. The middle classes in the city seemed ripe for revolt, French support was assured, and the English government was apparently preparing to strike. On the 19th Wyatt and Pickering left London for Kent while Croft remained to watch developments.[52] The wheels of rebellion were already beginning to move when Gardiner finally took action. Worried by Carew's treason, Renard's report to the Queen, and the restlessness in London, and anxious to regain the place in Mary's favor which Paget had usurped, Gardiner summoned Courtenay on the 21st and managed to worm out of him the fact that he had been approached by some unnamed individuals on "several things touching religion and the marriage." There was probably more to the confession than Gardiner revealed, but this was all he told Renard two days later, fearful perhaps that a knowledge of Courtenay's full guilt might give Paget and Renard a powerful weapon to use against him and against the other councillors who had supported the young Earl's candidacy during the fall.[53] The conspirators learned of Courtenay's betrayal almost immediately, and through them the report reached Noailles (twenty-four hours before Gardiner spoke to Renard) that "this young fool of a Lord Courtenay"

[51] Renard to Charles V, 18 Jan. 1554, P.R.O., Tyler, pp. 45 ff. (Gachard and Piot, IV, 298-303). Renard was severely rebuked by the Emperor for his attempt to spare Mary's feelings by withholding unpleasant information from her (Gachard and Piot, IV, 315). The French agents whose names he gave Paget seem to have been merely minor figures like Bernardo, Bonvisi, and Spinola. With the exception of Carew, he did not know who the ringleaders were until after the rebellion broke out.

[52] Noailles to Montmorency, 21 Jan. 1554, Aff. Etr., IX, fol. 120.

[53] Renard to Charles V, 23 Jan. 1554, P.R.O., Tyler, p. 59 (Gachard and Piot, IV, 308); Wiesener, 177-8.

had revealed "the enterprise of Peter Carew and his companions."
On the 22nd Wyatt held a meeting of his followers on the Medway, and that night Croft left London to warn Elizabeth that the rising was about to break out.[54] Proclamations calling upon all true Englishmen to rise against the Spaniard were scattered throughout Kent and on the 25th Wyatt raised his standard at Rochester.

Renard was the only man in all England whom Mary could trust in the crisis. Gardiner had lost her confidence by his support of Courtenay and many of his friends in the Council were in sympathy with the rebels, if not in actual communication with them. Paget had never shared her views on religion and was notoriously apt to go over to the winning side in any political upheaval. The council was paralyzed by jealousy and suspicion. Most of the members were afraid of the use Mary might make of a levy of troops, and the result was that virtually nothing had been done to protect the Queen against the storm threatening her throne and her life itself. On January 24 Noailles wrote gleefully of the confusion at Westminster:

> The Earl of Arundel is still feigning illness and Paget has absented himself [from court] for four or five days. They are greatly concerned, as is also their mistress, to sense and discover what is being prepared and plotted. The Queen, the Emperor's ambassador, and the [Imperial] deputies, together with all the Flemings who are in this country, are taking pains to reconcile themselves the best they can with the malcontents, but I hope they will prove to have taken thought too late.[55]

Gardiner's friends openly accused Paget's party of having sown the seeds of rebellion by their support of the Spanish marriage, and the Imperialist nobles countered by attributing the trouble to Gardiner's religious fanaticism. Suspicion of each other's motives made both Gardiner and Paget unwilling to confide in either Renard or the Queen. The Chancellor waited two days before telling Renard about his talk with Courtenay, and Paget did not inform

---

[54] Noailles to D'Oysel, 22 Jan. 1554, Aff. Etr., IX, fol. 121; Froude, VI, 149. On January 24 Noailles wrote Montmorency, "Sans la faute de cueur de ce jeune homme de Courtenay, toutes choses estoient conduittes à souhait" (Aff. Etr., IX, fol. 127). But as I have tried to indicate, the rising was precipitated by other factors: Carew's flight, the government's activities, and the conspirators' assurance of French help.

[55] Noailles to Montmorency, 24 Jan. 1554, Aff. Etr., IX, fol. 127. See Froude, VI, 154, for a vivid account of the government's unpreparedness.

the ambassador about the rising in Kent until two days after the event. When the Queen reproached him for his negligence, he fell on his knees, said that he had been doing his best to raise troops but that he had only one voice in the Council and could not do everything by himself; he would not divulge the reason why the Council had not communicated with the Imperial ambassadors, he said, "though his life depended on it." Obviously Courtenay's supporters had managed to veto any immediate announcement of the news from Kent to Renard for fear that the Emperor might send troops to England.[56]

Faced with a rebellion which threatened to destroy every vestige of Imperial influence in England and humbled by his responsibility, Renard showed himself at his best. He was sure that he and he alone could save the Queen, and his industry, his vigilance, and his courage were unflagging. To the waverers in the Council he was a prophet of doom, to the Queen, a pillar of strength. With so much at stake he was able temporarily to conquer his temperamental pessimism, but it was a hard task. Every remedy which he had suggested had been blocked by circumstances beyond his control. He had tried in vain to hasten Philip's arrival in England in the hope (shared by Paget's party) that the danger of insurrection would vanish if the Prince were established in England before the advent of warm weather. His earlier trust in the efficacy of government propaganda was rudely shattered when the success of the rebels' whispering campaign became evident, particularly in London and the East. Like Noailles and like most statesmen of the time, Renard and his master were both firm believers in the theory that rebellions are the work of individual agitators rather than of underlying social and political forces. If only Elizabeth were imprisoned; if only Courtenay were sent abroad on a diplomatic mission; if only the Emperor would take into his service some of the turbulent Englishmen who were potential leaders of rebellion, the trouble would be averted. But the government had no evidence against Elizabeth, arrangements to send Courtenay

---

[56] Imperial ambassadors to Charles V, 27, 29, and 31 Jan. 1554, and Renard to Charles V, 5 Feb. 1554, P.R.O., Tyler (cf. *Docs. inéds.*, III, 456; Gachard and Piot, IV, pp. 319 ff. and 330 ff.).

abroad were made too late, and Charles V did not warm to his ambassador's suggestion that he hire English trouble-makers.[57]

Military preparedness would, of course, have been the most effective remedy and Renard had kept urging it unceasingly during January, but here he was fighting against insuperable odds as we have seen. To still the bedlam which reigned unchecked at the council table Renard thought of bribery. But the money he had asked for early in January did not arrive until too late; the one hundred ducats a day and "10,000 for gaming" which his four colleagues were said to have been given was probably already exhausted in entertainment; and it is doubtful whether the use of bribes would have been effective in any case at the height of the crisis.[58] If all else failed he could, of course, call upon the Emperor for help, but both he and Charles knew that to send German mercenaries to England was to play straight into Henry II's hands. Renard's one real hope lay in using his boundless influence over the Queen to help her save herself, and this he did with consummate finesse.

By the end of January the situation was serious indeed. Carew had thrown up the game and fled to France, it was true; and Suffolk's rising in the Midlands was soon to be snuffed out. But the news from Kent was more and more disturbing. On the 27th a force of Londoners was sent down under the Duke of Norfolk to face Wyatt, but their captains had already been suborned by Noailles's agents[59] and on the 29th they deserted to the rebels with the cry, "We are all Englishmen." Next day Wyatt and his followers, some two or three thousand strong, began their march on London with no one to say them nay.

Frightening evidence had already reached Renard that the French had a definite understanding with the traitors and that Gardiner's faction in the Council was deliberately sabotaging every effort to put down the rebellion and to search out the ringleaders.

[57] *Span. Cal.,* XI, 473; Renard to Charles V, 23 Jan. 1554, Charles V to Imp. ambs., 31 Jan. 1554, and same to Renard, 18 Feb. 1554, P.R.O., Tyler (Gachard and Piot, IV, 306 ff.; Weiss, IV, 195 ff., 215). For examples of anti-Spanish propaganda, see Renard to Granvelle, 7 Jan. 1554, P.R.O., Tyler, p. 24; and Tytler, II, 277-8.

[58] Vargas to Philip, 19 Jan. 1554, P.R.O., Tyler, p. 52; Gachard and Piot, IV, 290, 306-7, 313; *Docs. inéds.,* III, 449-50; Weiss, IV, 182-3.

[59] *Amer. Hist. Rev.,* XLV (April 1940), p. 548.

On January 26 one of Noailles's couriers was arrested by government troops near Rochester, stripped of his dispatches, and thrown into jail at Gravesend.[60] The next evening his packet was delivered to Gardiner. Noailles's letter was not the most incriminating which he had written during the past month, but it was easy for the Chancellor to read between the lines as he went feverishly about the business of decipherment. The conspirators had been forced to take up arms, Noailles had written, because of Courtenay's betrayal; Elizabeth had withdrawn further from London and friends were flocking to her; everything was going well, thanks to God.[61] What excited Gardiner and Mary most of all was an enclosure— a letter from Elizabeth to the Queen, translated into French. How had Noailles come by it? Did he have spies in the Council itself, or was there some secret channel of communication between the Princess and the French embassy? Gardiner was particularly disturbed by the mention of Courtenay. In sending Renard a copy of his decipherment he left the name of his young friend blank, but the ruse failed to deceive Renard. Having got hold of the original dispatch shortly afterward through the Queen, he found no difficulty in deciphering the name, and when he asked Gardiner for an explanation, the Chancellor changed color with embarrassment. Renard's suspicions that the Catholic patriots were trying to shield Courtenay, if not the rest of the conspirators as well, seemed to him to be confirmed.[62]

As Wyatt's rabble moved slowly up the southern bank of the Thames from Rochester, three groups within the circle of the

[60] Noailles to Senarpont, 30 Jan. 1554, Aff. Etr., IX, fol. 131; Vertot, III, 49, 60; For. Cal., Mary, 60; P.R.O., S.P.Dom. 11, Vol. II, No. 22.

[61] Vertot, III, 43-6. Elizabeth had not yet moved, but the Council knew that she intended to do so and Noailles's words seemed to connect her plans with the rebels' (Muller, Gardiner, 247). Three French packets in all were intercepted during the crisis: one containing Noailles's letter to Henry II of January 26 and a "dummy dispatch" to be shown to inquisitive officials (a vain precaution, as it turned out) (Aff. Etr., XV, fol. 283); another containing letters from Noailles of January 28 and 30; and finally a letter (probably another "dummy dispatch") from Henry to Noailles of January 26 (For. Cal., Mary, 55).

[62] This intercepted dispatch had an interesting history. See in general Renard's (or his colleagues') dispatches to Charles V of 29 Jan., 31 Jan., 5 Feb., 22 Mar., 7 Apr., and 1 May 1554, P.R.O., Tyler (some passages printed in Gachard and Piot, IV, 323, 331-2, 335, and in Tytler, II, 383 ff.). See also Vertot, III, 134; and The Letters of Stephen Gardiner, J. A. Muller, ed., 459-60. The question how Elizabeth's letter fell into Noailles's hands and who translated it is discussed in Appendix I.

Queen's advisers struggled to gain control of the government's policy. Renard, spurred on by his four Imperial colleagues and stirred by a personal appeal from Mary herself, tried to persuade the Council to accept military assistance from Charles V. Gardiner's party, none of them military leaders and all of them fearful of Imperial intervention, urged a policy of temporizing with the rebels. Paget's friends—Pembroke and Clinton in particular—confident of their military prowess and contemptuous of Wyatt's strength, opposed either the introduction of Imperial troops or a compromise with the rebels.

On the 29th Renard wrote his master a cautious plea for help, in view of the fact that war between France and England seemed inevitable.[63] Next day at dinner with the Council he asked whether Charles or Philip could do anything to help the Queen—since the rebels were obviously "encouraged, counselled, and supported by others besides those under present suspicion." Gardiner coldly rejected his proposal, pointedly omitting any reference to the Emperor and making it clear that although an Imperial fleet equal to the French might render the Queen real service, German troops "would not be acceptable."[64] The Chancellor had already advised Mary to flee to Windsor and his friends were suggesting refuges even more remote, such as Calais. On the 31st his party in the Council drew up an offer of compromise to Wyatt. The rebels were to be told that the Queen would be glad to appoint a committee to discuss the question of her marriage with them and that if any valid objections were offered she would "not refuse to gyve eare" to them. It was explained to Renard that this proposal was merely to gain time and to discredit Wyatt before the bar of public opinion should he refuse to accept it. The Council already had sent out proclamations contending that the rebellion was an heretical and subversive movement, unconnected with any legitimate patriotic grievance.[65] The rejection of such a peace offer by the rebels would prove the government's case. Renard fell in with the proposal and

---

[63] Imp. ambs. to Charles V, 29 Jan. 1554, P.R.O., Tyler, p. 79 (Gachard and Piot, IV, 323). In spite of his earlier misgivings, Charles V immediately offered Mary German mercenaries when the news of Wyatt's rising reached Brussels on February 1 (Weiss, IV, 197-8, 203, 204).

[64] Imp. ambs. to Charles V, 31 Jan. 1554, P.R.O., Tyler, pp. 89-90.

[65] Gachard and Piot, IV, 321.

persuaded Mary to approve it, although she took care to assure
him (and the Emperor) that her determination to marry Philip
was unshaken. To prove that nothing had been added to the document by Gardiner or herself, she showed a translation of it to the
ambassador before it was sent to Wyatt.[66] One inevitably wonders
whether some of the Catholic patriots did not hope that Wyatt
would accept the offer and thus reunite public opinion against the
Spanish marriage. "We have a suspicion," Renard wrote just before the proposal was broached to him, "that the rebels are being
favored by the leading men here so as to put through the marriage
with Courtenay."[67]

Before Wyatt's reply reached the court, the four Imperial commissioners had fled before the approaching storm. Their orders
were to stay until the marriage had been concluded by proxy; but
Philip's powers had not yet arrived, the people were irritated by
their presence in London, and their lives were obviously in danger
should Wyatt capture the city. On the night of the 31st they embarked hastily on some small Flemish vessels in the Thames and
early the next morning they dropped down to sea. "We must bow
to the will of God," Egmont wrote Philip, "I am the most unhappy
man in the world." Two days later they reached Flushing, all of
them miserably seasick.[68]

A few hours after their ships slipped down the river Mary made
her famous appeal to the people of London at the Guildhall.
Renard had already "exhorted her to show her fortitude" when
she seemed ready to give way to despair,[69] but it was the arrival of
an arrogant and uncompromising reply from Wyatt to her proposal of the day before which induced her to appeal to her subjects
in person. She read the traitor's reply in full—the rebels demanded
the Queen herself as a hostage, together with a return to the religion of her brother's reign—and spoke movingly of the reasons
which had led her, against her natural inclinations, to contemplate
marriage. Her courage, her passion, and her sincerity made a deep

[66] Renard to Charles V, 5 Feb. 1554, P.R.O., Tyler, pp. 111 ff. (Gachard and Piot,
IV, 330-2); Mary to Hastings and Cornwallis, n.d., P.R.O., S.P.Dom. 11, Vol. II, No. 9.
[67] Imp. ambs. to Charles V, 31 Jan. 1554, P.R.O., Tyler, p. 90.
[68] Nigri to Granvelle, 27 Jan. 1554; Imp. ambs. to Charles V, 31 Jan. and 3 Feb. 1554;
Egmont to Philip, 1 Feb. 1554, P.R.O., Tyler. cf. Vertot, III, 44, 51, 53.
[69] Imp. ambs. to Charles V, 31 Jan. 1554, P.R.O., Tyler, p. 91.

impression—and yet she was not entirely honest. She told Renard both before and after her address that nothing could shake her determination to marry Philip, but she did not tell him—nor did anyone else—that she had promised her people to follow their will as expressed in Parliament.

> On the word of a Queen I promise you [she said] that if it shall not probably appear to all the nobility and commons in the high court of parliament that this marriage shall be for the high benefit and commodity of the whole realm, then I will abstain from marriage while I live.[70]

Renard was too conscientious a diplomat not to have reported this disturbing passage to his master if Mary or Gardiner had told him the truth, but the official version given him was somewhat different. The Queen promised, he wrote, that "if people had not *understood* the causes and occasions [of her marriage], she would *repeat* them to a Parliament."[71]

The effect of her appeal was felt at once. The Catholics, the propertied classes, and even the patriots in the city began to lose what sympathy they had for the rebels. Five hundred peasants were said to have deserted Wyatt on the night of the Queen's speech and when the rebels arrived in Southwark two days later they found the bridge closed against them. They had missed the tide "which, taken at the flood, leads on to fortune."

One chance remained, however. If Wyatt could cross the river swiftly and unexpectedly, the Londoners might yet open their gates to him. On February 6 he stole up the Thames to Kingston, crossed the stream in the dead of night, and started back toward the city from the west. When the news reached court in the small hours of the morning, the frightened Council, led by Gardiner, went to the Queen and begged her to escape from Westminster by boat. "She, without losing her presence of mind for a moment," Renard remarked complacently, "sent for me." "Unless she wanted to lose

---

[70] Foxe, *Acts and Monuments* (ed. 1838), VI, 414-15. Foxe's account is confirmed in general by Noailles (Vertot, III, 50, 56, 62, 66), by Machyn (*Diary,* 53), and by Pole's informers (*Ven. Cal.,* V, 460). See also *Eng. Hist. Rev.,* Vol. XXXVIII (1923), 255. Proctor makes no mention of such a promise (*An English Garner,* VIII, 77), but the evidence is almost incontrovertible that it was made, much as Foxe reports it.

[71] Gachard and Piot, IV, 332. (Italics inserted.) Charles V believed, or pretended to believe, that Mary had *intended* to make the promise reported by Foxe, but was dissuaded (*Ven. Cal.,* V, 462).

her kingdom," he advised her, she must not take refuge in flight
"while any force or expedient remained to be tried." Gardiner
and others of the Council were "greatly perturbed" when she told
them the ambassador's opinion, but her trust in the Catholic patriots was exhausted. In her moment of peril she turned to her men-
at-arms, to Pembroke and Clinton, in command of her troops.
When they implored her to trust herself to them and not to flee,
she summoned up her courage, forgot her mistrust of Paget's
secular-minded friends, and announced her decision to remain.[72]
Twelve hours later Wyatt was a prisoner, his followers dispersed
or captured, his cause apparently shattered forever.

It was one of the true ironies of her tragic career that Mary was
saved in her time of direst need by two former adherents of her
bitterest enemy, Northumberland, and by a foreign ambassador
who cared little for her own deepest interests. The rebels' lack of
arms and experienced leadership, Gardiner's tactical proposal of
pardon, and the Queen's own courage played decisive parts in her
victory, but in the last analysis it was Renard, the only person she
could trust, who was responsible for the outcome if any individual
was responsible. "His presence and counsel have been a great
support to me in my latest calamity," she wrote Charles. And yet
how little she realized the deep gulf fixed between her inmost
longings and the aims of her "spiritual confessor." On the evening
of the final battle he suggested to her "that it would be better for
the present to say nothing about the marriage," but she replied
that she "would not consent to dissemble, but meant to work,
with God's help, to bring about its consummation." Perhaps she
already repented her enforced "dissembling" during the crisis,
just as she had bitterly repented her submission to her father's will
many years before. "There never was a more steadfast lady than
the Queen," Renard wrote.[73]

[72] Renard to Charles V, 8 Feb. 1554, P.R.O., Tyler, pp. 127-9 (fragments in Weiss,
IV, 209-11; and Docs. inéds., III, 481-6).

[73] Mary to Charles V, 11 Feb. 1554, P.R.O., Tyler, p. 137; Renard to Charles V, 8
Feb. 1554 (two letters of the same date), ibid., pp. 127-30, 131-2. For the tributes of the
Council, Charles V, Philip, and Eraso to Renard's work, see Weiss, IV, 212, 214; Philip
to Renard, 12 May 1554, P.R.O., Tyler, p. 404; and "Francisco de Madrid to Philippo del
Prado" (Eraso to Philip), 17 Feb. 1554, ibid., p. 159.

In the history of popular risings in Tudor times, Wyatt's Rebellion was in a sense unique. Neither before nor after was the Tudor monarchy ever so clearly aligned against the national sentiment of the middle classes. Whenever the people took up arms against their ruler on other occasions, the latter could generally pose with some show of justice as the defender of the national interest against interests which were either less than national or more than national, either provincial or universal. But Mary could not plead mere patriotism in her defense, and would have scorned to do so. The government's insistence that the revolt was instigated by religious and social radicals backed by the might of France was an admission of the weakness at home and humiliation abroad to which the Spanish marriage negotiations had brought the realm. Apparently the English sense of nationality was now no more than a flame to be fanned or extinguished at will by foreign powers and their diplomatic representatives to suit the dictates of dynastic power politics.

The surprising thing is how small was the effect of the rebellion —its near-success and its failure—upon the course of Habsburg and Valois diplomacy in England, how little it taught the chief actors in the drama. Englishmen and foreigners alike drew the lessons each of them wished to draw. To Mary and Gardiner the rising proved the need of more religious severity. To Renard and Paget it proved the need for stricter treatment of political offenders. To Noailles it proved the need of more aggressive intervention on the part of France in English affairs. Mary blinded herself so far as she could to the political roots of the trouble, Renard still hoped that official repression would effectively stifle the popular demand for a native King, and Noailles forgot that English patriotism might prove to be a double-edged weapon in French hands. Within a very short space of time Mary would be flying once more in the face of middle class opinion, Renard would be scheming further how to fasten the Habsburg yoke on an unwilling people, and Noailles would be intriguing again with irresponsible leaders of the national opposition.

In the meanwhile, however, Wyatt's defeat, like Northumberland's six months earlier, had an important though transitory effect upon the relative positions of the rival ambassadors. For the moment Renard, thanks to his conduct in the crisis and to his hold over the Queen, was well-nigh dictator of English policy. His rival, personally discredited, socially ostracized, and politically defeated, looked forward resignedly to dismissal by the English government or recall by his own.

To Renard the events of February 7 were "an evident miracle";[74] to his impenitent rival they illustrated the more unsearchable side of God's ways to man:

> . . . If it had pleased you [he wrote Henry II] to lend an ear to many of the Queen's enemies a long while ago, I am certain that she would not have a single warship in her power today, nor would so many valiant and important persons be in her prisons and on the scaffolds, but rather free to take from her the same crown which recently they won her. I say so, Sire, because I am a better witness of it all than any other. . . . Perhaps [God] is permitting her marriage to this Prince in order to punish them both together through some occasion which He has wished to conceal from men, to let them know how much more sure are the instruments of His vengeance than those forged by their inventions and practices.[75]

[74] *Docs. inéds.,* III, 483.
[75] Noailles to Henry II, 9 Mar. 1554, Aff. Etr., IX, fol. 154. See also Noailles to D'Oysel, 5 Apr. 1554, *ibid.,* IX, fol. 409.

CHAPTER VI

AFTERMATH OF REBELLION

FEBRUARY TO APRIL 1554

IT has been remarked that the bitterest human passions and hatreds often follow, rather than accompany, the violent upheavals of history. An historian of recent diplomatic history writes that so far as the German people were concerned, "hostilities with France began only after the armed conflict ended" in 1918.[1] It would be equally true to say that the hostilities, domestic and international, of which Wyatt's rebellion was a manifestation, really began only after Wyatt had laid down his arms on February 7, 1554.

The rebellion was the turning point of Mary's reign in both domestic and foreign affairs. The fact that a few thousand ill-equipped rebels could come within an ace of depriving the Queen of her crown was dramatic illustration of how dependent the Tudors were upon popular support. The revelation embittered Mary and stripped her for the time being of the illusion that her people would eventually appreciate her motives in choosing Philip for her husband. She tried desperately to believe the official explanation of the insurrection—that it was directed against the Catholic religion, not against the Spanish match—but whether it was heresy or anti-Spanish sentiment which had to be extirpated before Philip could land in England, the arguments in favor of the use of force were now unanswerable. The "most merciful of the Tudors" at heart was soon to become the "Bloody Mary" of popular history. After her death the common people remembered that it was mainly the rank and file who suffered after Wyatt's failure, and again after the revival of the heresy statutes a year later. Treason was never condoned by the people in Tudor times, but the

[1] R. J. Sontag, *European Diplomatic History* (New York, 1933), 212.

hundred odd rebels who were hung for their treasonable patriotism
in the spring of 1554 were easily confused in the popular mind with
the two hundred martyrs who were burned for their religion in
succeeding years. Those who exhorted Latimer to courage at the
stake and thrilled to his dying words perhaps remembered Wyatt's
execution and the many who had pressed to dip their handker-
chiefs in his blood.[2] Henry VIII's breach with Rome had laid the
foundation for that confusion of Protestantism and nationalism
which was such a prominent characteristic of Elizabeth's reign,
but the process of confusion was greatly accelerated during the
months following Wyatt's rebellion while the clergy were talking
about reviving the statutes against heresy and the executioners
were exhibiting their ghastly work at the gates of London. In the
minds of many of Mary's subjects, Spain and Catholicism would
soon be fused into a single symbol of frightfulness.

Renard and Noailles played modest parts in this development,
but it was by their failures rather than by their successes. If Renard
could have had his way, the ringleaders of the conspiracy would
have been executed and possibly the rank and file might have been
spared, Gardiner's religious zeal would have been curbed at the
very beginning, and Mary would have been provided with a standing army for future emergencies. He could not get his way, and
the later plots and popular tumults of Mary's reign were the
measure of his failure. If Noailles had been successful in his effort
to overthrow Mary and put Elizabeth and Courtenay on the throne
with French support and under French domination, Englishmen
might have forgotten their new-found hatred of Spain for yet another generation. The waverings of French policy in the spring of
1554 help to account for the fact that during most of the reign
English patriots were able to look to France as a friend without
fearing her as a menace to their liberties.

[2] François de Noailles reported on April 12, 1554, that the spectacle at Wyatt's execution was "tres desplaisant à presque tous ceulx qui luy ont assisté, ce qui fut assez
tesmoigné par le grand nombre des personnes qui vindrent secretement tremper leurs
mouchoirs en son sang, comme jurans et promettans en icelluy la vengeance de la mort
de ce vaillant et hardy Capitaine, qui n'avoit faict aucun doubte de s'exposer à tout
péril pour la conservation de la liberté publique." Aff. Etr., IX, fol. 161. On the total
number of Wyatt's followers who were executed, cf. Renard's estimate of 100-200 and
François de Noailles's of 400 (Docs. inéds., III, 502; Tytler, II, 309; Vertot, III, 124).

If Philip had landed in England during the month following Wyatt's defeat, he would have found a devoted but disillusioned bride, a crestfallen Imperial ambassador, a Council torn by faction and haunted by the fear of war, and a people cowed but dangerously restive after the recent insurrection. When he did arrive the following July, the situation had so improved that there was surprisingly little in the attitude of Queen, Council, and people to worry him, no serious disorders, no real threats to his safety, and no open insults to his own person. The passage of time was primarily responsible for the improvement, but Renard must be given a great deal of the credit.

The nervous strain which he had undergone during the rebellion left Renard discouraged, diffident, and cynical. Neither he nor Noailles could immediately grasp the extent and significance of the Queen's victory. It was true, he wrote, that the west and north had remained loyal; the inhabitants of Plymouth had promised to give Philip an honorable reception, and even the Londoners were "beginning to be converted." But the Council's divisions and the "prospect of a new rebellion and treason, aimed principally at the Queen's person" made him apprehensive that the rising in Kent was but the prelude to a worse disaster. He was worried when Mary, who saw her victory as a sign that God approved her marriage, refused to "dissemble" her intentions for reasons of prudence; and he was horrified when she disbanded the troops which had been the instruments of Providence saying that "if God did not watch over her she would fall into hazard every day, even if she took many more precautions."[3] To her more secular-minded adviser, Prudence was the handmaid of Providence. He reminded her that he had been insisting upon the "slackness and negligence" in her government for three months and warned her that Courtenay and Elizabeth, "the two persons most able to cause trouble in the realm," notoriously deserved death. His dispatches to Brussels during February were filled with gloomy forebodings: there

[3] Renard to Charles V, 8 Feb. 1554, P.R.O., Tyler, pp. 127-30 (*Docs. inéds.,* III, 481-6); a second letter of the same date, P.R.O., Tyler, pp. 131-2; Renard to Charles V, 12 Feb. 1554, *ibid.,* pp. 139-42 (*Docs. inéds.,* III, 492-8); same to same, 13 Feb. 1554, P.R.O., Tyler, pp. 143-5; same to same, 17 Feb. 1554, *ibid.,* pp. 155-8 (*Docs. inéds.,* III, 502-8).

was a new and violent rift between Gardiner and Paget, and Gardiner evidently intended to raise explosive religious issues at the coming session of Parliament; the treasury was in a parlous state because the Queen had no one in her Council who looked after her finances; warships were concentrating on the French coast; and there was even a wild report to the effect that Henry II had decided to establish Protestantism in France in order to encourage the English heretics.[4]

Renard's pessimism had little effect upon the Emperor. Charles read his ambassador's dispatches imperturbably, carefully excised all references to the possibility of a fresh insurrection in the copies which were forwarded to Spain, and assured his son that the state of affairs in England was growing "better and better."[5] Wyatt's failure, he wrote Philip, would give Mary a new security from rebellion and French intrigue, and so the Prince should hasten his preparations for sailing. Charles agreed with Mary, in fact, that the psychological moment had come to push through the proxy marriage and to hasten Philip's arrival while the anti-Spanish elements in England were suffering under the stigma of treason. On February 18 he sent Egmont back to London to have the ceremony performed *per verba de praesenti*. Naturally his chief concern was to provide for Philip's safety in England and the burden of his advice to Mary through Egmont was to deal strictly with those actually responsible for the rebellion and to show mercy to the rest. Elizabeth and Courtenay should be "put out of the way" if it could be done with a show of legality, and the French and Venetian ambassadors should be got rid of to stop the danger of foreign intrigue. But there must be no suspicion of dictation to the Council by Renard or Egmont, no hint to the people that the Emperor, not the Queen and her Council, was directing English policy.[6] This insistence upon the danger of ruffling English tempers had been the keynote of Charles's instructions to Renard a month before the rebellion broke out. Perhaps he was moved to repeat

---

[4] P.R.O., Tyler, pp. 139 ff., 145, 156 ff., 176 ff., 196; Tytler, II, 306 ff.

[5] Charles V to Philip, 28 Feb. 1554, P.R.O., Tyler, p. 188. cf. *ibid.*, p. 139, editor's comment.

[6] *Docs. inéds.*, III, 509; Gachard and Piot, IV, 341-7.

himself when he learned that the councillors were treating Renard "as familiarly as if the marriage were already concluded."[7]

Egmont arrived in London on March 2, armed with letters of thanks from the Emperor to those who had stood by the Queen during the rebellion.[8] Before he left for Spain a week later, the marriage had been concluded by proxy, the Council had apparently been galvanized into action, and Renard's whole mood had changed.

At Mary's request Renard had already suggested to her, in the presence of Gardiner, Paget, Rochester, and Petre, that it was time to decide definitely "either to delay, to drop [the marriage], or to proceed"; and he had asked furthermore whether the Council felt able to guarantee Philip's safety. On March 3 he and Egmont asked the same question before the full Council in still more forceful terms, and on the day following they passed on the Emperor's advice to Mary in private. As Renard understood "the indications in the instructions" given to Egmont, "one of the chief points . . . was that neither private persons given as hostages nor the word of the English might be considered as sufficient guarantee unless effective protection were provided" for Philip, in view of the utter faithlessness of the English.[9] So the two envoys implored the Queen to remember that since Philip would not be allowed to land a single Spanish soldier on English shores for his protection, his safety was in her hands: "so let her quite definitely make up her mind on this point . . . , for the success of the marriage depended upon it." She explained that "the law as laid down by the English Parliament did not inflict the capital penalty on those who had consented to treason if they had committed no overt act," but

---

[7] *Span. Cal.*, XI, 455; *Docs. inéds.*, III, 496.

[8] The letters to Pembroke, Clinton, Huntingdon, and Cheyne thanked them for their "valiant service" to the Queen; those to Gardiner, Arundel, and Paget were identical except for the omission of the word "valiant." Others were addressed to Derby, Shrewsbury, Rochester, Petre, and Thirlby; and 22 additional copies were made with the addresses left blank. All the letters hinted at pecuniary reward for the services mentioned. P.R.O., Tyler, pp. 173-5.

[9] For this and following details see the long dispatch of 8 Mar. 1554 from Renard and Egmont to Charles V (P.R.O., Tyler, pp. 204-18), less than half of which is printed by Tytler (II, 315-29). Hostages were nowhere mentioned in Egmont's written instructions (Gachard and Piot, IV, 341-7), and their mention here may have been an invention of Renard's to impress the Queen and Council. For Renard's opinion of English faithlessness, see above, p. 110.

promised to further the Council's efforts to find evidence which would convict Courtenay, Elizabeth, and the other leaders. She assured the ambassadors that she would do her utmost to provide for Philip's safety, "for she would rather never have been born than that any harm should befall him." Renard thought her words "so gracious and convincing that one would be wrong to demand any further proof of her affection for your Majesty and his Highness." Later on in the same day five of the leading councillors waited upon the ambassadors and said "they intended to take measures which would make [Philip] as safe as if he were in his own country." Military and naval forces would be provided and "trustworthy and Catholic men were going to be called to help Parliament not make trouble." The next day Egmont presented the Emperor's letters to seven members of the "inner council" and induced Admiral Howard to accept an Imperial pension. The ambassadors were finally persuaded that, all things considered, it would be "perfectly safe" for Philip to come to England.

The moving scene which took place in the presence-chamber at Whitehall in the afternoon of March 6 has often been described. Egmont and Renard appeared before the Queen and Council, Philip's and Mary's ratifications of the marriage treaty were exchanged, and the necessary oaths were sworn. The Queen then knelt before the Sacrament and "called God to witness . . . that her firm resolve was to keep the marriage and the oath she had made to the Crown." Tears came to the eyes of all those present. Promises per verba de praesenti were solemnly pronounced before Gardiner by Mary and by Egmont, standing as Philip's proctor. Renard had also been named as a proctor but did not participate in the ceremony. "I considered," he explained to the Emperor, "that this act was of too solemn a nature for a man of my degree." Mary, however, did not forget her "spiritual confessor"; a gift of plate was the token of her gratitude to him in her hour of joy.[10]

Egmont left London for Plymouth on March 9 and arrived in Valladolid six weeks later after a series of misfortunes in port and at sea.[11] Renard's optimism lasted barely a week after his col-

[10] Renard and Egmont to Charles V, 8 Mar. 1554, P.R.O., Tyler, pp. 212-13, 217.
[11] Vertot, III, 147; P.R.O., Tyler, pp. 275, 280-1, 399; Gachard and Piot, IV, 379, 381-2, 384-5.

league's departure. On March 13 he wrote Philip a rather frank account of the anti-Spanish feeling among the Councillors and people. Both Queen and Council were sure that he would be safe in England, the ambassador wrote, but others thought he should not make the voyage until September because the passions of the English were apt to "boil" during the summer months; the problem of his security was a "hazardous matter."[12]

Renard betrayed his loss of nerve even more clearly in a long and lugubrious dispatch which he sent off to the Emperor the day after he wrote Philip. "I have lately been turning over in my mind the state of affairs in this kingdom," he wrote; "my charge and responsibility weigh grievously upon me." To trust Philip to the tender mercies of a Council rent by faction and intrigue, and of a people notoriously treacherous and hostile to foreigners even in normal times, was a responsibility which he did not feel able to shoulder alone. He had been nourishing a growing suspicion of Gardiner ever since the latter's cowardly advice to Mary when Wyatt was threatening London, and now he was sure that the Chancellor was at the root of most of the trouble. Gardiner had appointed Southwell, "one of the most ignorant, corrupt, and violent Englishmen alive," to guard and examine the prisoners; Bourne and Waldegrave, two more of the Chancellor's henchmen, were helping Southwell to suppress evidence and to gain Courtenay's acquittal. Gardiner and one or two of his friends had decided by themselves to summon Parliament to Oxford, in order to punish the people of London for their dubious loyalty during the insurrection by depriving them of the profits which the members' presence brought to merchants and innkeepers. The City was in a ferment, relatives of the prisoners were stirring up trouble, and even the loyal and solid citizens were grumbling. When a petition from the Mayor and aldermen, backed by Rochester and others of the Council, induced the Queen to promise that Parliament would be held as usual in London, Gardiner was alone in continuing to insist that it be opened in Oxford. To add to his sins, Gardiner's real interest in the coming Parliament was apparently to see it drop the Queen's title of "Supreme Head" of the Church

12 P.R.O., Tyler, pp. 227-8 (Tytler, II, 333-5).

and revive the heresy statutes, although he had promised the Queen (according to Renard) that ratification of the marriage treaty would be the only measure of importance presented for discussion. To top matters off, reliable reports indicated that a French attack on Guines and the Isle of Wight was apt to take place at any moment. Renard realized that it was too late to ask his master "to reconsider the whole matter," but he intimated clearly that he would like to see the marriage delayed until the fall rather than have Philip arrive during the spring, "when the English are usually of a rebellious temper."[13]

Frightened by the threat of a French attack, Mary sent Paget and Petre to confer with Renard on the evening of March 14, as if he were "one of the Queen's Council." The ambassador told them bluntly that there were three remedies for the danger from abroad: punishment of the prisoners, preparedness, and the curbing of Gardiner's religious zeal. Henry II's main hope, he said, was that the English heretics would rebel once more and help the French set Elizabeth on the throne. The Queen told Renard later in the evening that "she was greatly perplexed as to how she had better behave, and she wished his Highness were already here to take matters in hand." Renard made no reply, afraid for the moment of saying anything to disturb her; but ten days later he repeated to her, point by point, the doubts and misgivings about Philip's safety which he had enlarged upon to the Emperor on the 14th. "With tears in her eyes," Mary repeated her earlier assurance that she would rather never have been born than to have harm come to Philip, and added that there was no reason for him to delay.[14]

Some of Renard's information was faulty and some of his fears were groundless, but he had good reason to be worried about the state of the Council. The immediate result of Wyatt's rebellion had been to discredit Gardiner and his followers in the Council, tainted as they already were by their sympathy for Courtenay.

[13] Renard to Charles V, 14 Mar. 1554, P.R.O., Tyler, pp. 229-37 (cf. *ibid.*, p. 267). About half this dispatch is printed in Tytler, II, 336-41.

[14] Renard to Charles V, 15 Mar. 1554, P.R.O., Tyler, pp. 239-43; same to same, 24 Mar. 1554, *ibid.*, pp. 272-3; same to same, 27 Mar. 1554, *ibid.*, pp. 277-8 (Tytler, II, 349-51).

Gardiner himself had played an unheroic rôle in the crisis, his friends were suspected of being in communication with the rebels, and his enemies—Paget, Pembroke, and Clinton—had raised and led the troops which defeated Wyatt's rabble. The Chancellor's loss had been Paget's gain. The nobles who had saved the Queen from the rebels naturally expected reward, and by the first week of March some of them had been able to insinuate themselves into the "inner council."[15] Gardiner did all he could to prevent the Queen from rewarding Pembroke and Clinton, the men of the hour, but she publicly "caressed" Pembroke and his wife when they returned from the country after Easter and generally did everything possible to show her gratitude.[16]

Stung by the favor being shown to the "heretics" (the new nobility who feared and disliked his religious program), Gardiner began a determined struggle to recapture his lost leadership in the Council. He had certain advantages over his enemies. As Chancellor he was the manager of government measures in Parliament and could claim the right to supervise the all-important examinations of Courtenay, Elizabeth, and the other prisoners; he could count upon the Queen's support for his religious program; and in normal times his administrative talents were more valuable to the government than his opponents' military abilities. But his inconsistent attempt to shield Courtenay and at the same time to send the other leading conspirators to the block, as well as his desire to restore the power of the Church, roused the resentment of Paget and the nobles. Partly from fear of a new rebellion, partly from class interest, and partly from sheer personal hatred of Gardiner, Paget wanted to see as few as possible of the leaders of Wyatt's revolt go to their death; and he owned too much monastic land to relish the Chancellor's religious proposals.

On March 17 Gardiner found himself in a hopeless minority when he proposed to the Council that Elizabeth be transferred

---

[15] When Egmont and Renard consulted the "inner council" on March 5 it consisted of Gardiner, Rochester, Paget, Arundel, Pembroke, Bedford, and Howard (Tytler, II, 324). The last three had had no part in the conduct of affairs before the rebellion. Of those mentioned, only Rochester was inclined to favor the Chancellor.

[16] Renard to Charles V, 14 Mar. 1554, P.R.O., Tyler, p. 231; Gachard and Piot, IV, 376.

from the palace (where she had been confined since shortly after the collapse of the rebellion) to the Tower; but with the Queen's support he managed to gain the victory almost single-handed by suggesting that some member of the Council take the royal prisoner into his custody. When no one was willing to accept this embarrassing responsibility, it was decided that his proposal would have to be followed. On Palm Sunday, March 18, the gates of the Tower closed upon Elizabeth. Since the Queen's marriage was no longer a live issue in the Council, this was the first real test of strength between the rival factions after the rebellion. In the debate Paget's party, swelled by several of Gardiner's own followers, accused the Chancellor of personal animus toward some of the prisoners and charged that he had been examining them on their religious opinions rather than on their treasonable practices.[17] When the Queen rebuked Paget for his conduct, he excused himself by remarking that the nobility had no desire to be ruled by "another Duke of Northumberland, meaning the Chancellor." On Sunday, the 18th, he and a delegation of the majority in the Council surprised the Queen in her oratory after vespers while Gardiner was away from court and persuaded her against her will to pardon eight of the convicted conspirators, arguing that it was a holy day and no time to listen to the advice of "bloodthirsty men."[18]

Renard was in a quandary. Paget's sympathy for Elizabeth and the other prisoners was no less disturbing to him than Gardiner's sympathy for Courtenay. He never altogether trusted Paget after the rebellion, especially in view of the rumor that Croft and Wyatt had insisted upon a private interview with the councillor in the Tower.[19] But by the middle of March his suspicion of Gardiner had outrun his distrust of Paget. Until Paget's tactics in the debate about Elizabeth's imprisonment taught him to appreciate Gardi-

[17] Renard to Charles V, 22 Mar. 1554, P.R.O., Tyler, pp. 261-2; Wiesener, 229. Renard does not say specifically who made the suggestion that one of the councillors take Elizabeth into custody. If it was not Gardiner, as I have assumed, he undoubtedly supported the proposal for strategic reasons. Among those who opposed sending Elizabeth to the Tower were Paget, Sussex, Hastings, Cornwallis, Howard, Pembroke, Arundel, Mason, Petre, Rochester, Gage, Jerningham, and Bourne. The last four were normally supporters of the Chancellor.

[18] Renard to Charles V, 22 and 27 Mar. 1554, P.R.O., Tyler, pp. 263-4, 277; *Chronicle of Queen Jane*, 71. Northampton and Cobham were among those pardoned.

[19] Tytler, II, 310.

ner's genuine efforts to secure convictions of all the prisoners but Courtenay, the ambassador was sorely tempted to take sides in the quarrel against the Chancellor. About March 14 he went to Mary and complained pointedly about the Chancellor's conduct of the prosecutions.[20] For a brief moment his personal animosity toward Gardiner, which dated back to the beginning of the marriage negotiations, had got the better of his judgment, which told him to remain strictly neutral, to back Paget in his opposition to Gardiner's religious policy, and to encourage Gardiner in his severity toward Elizabeth and the leading conspirators.

Once the situation was clear to him, Renard acted with characteristic promptness and diligence. He went to the Queen and gave her a French translation of Thucydides in order that she might ponder the ancient historian's advice upon the subject of rebels. He then went to Gardiner, Paget, and Petre separately and discussed the situation. Out of these conversations there emerged a scheme for remedying what was thought to be the basic trouble— the "multitude of councillors." The informal "inner council" would be officially recognized as a "Council of State" and would handle all important business; Gardiner would give himself to the exacting duties of his own office and attend meetings only when he desired or when his presence was necessary; the great nobles like Howard and Pembroke were to be excluded from regular membership, but they might attend meetings when they were in London. The membership of the new body would consist of Paget, Arundel, Petre, Gardiner, Rochester, and Thomas Thirlby, Bishop of Norwich (who was serving as ambassador to the Emperor). It was hoped that Thirlby, an irenic and tactful diplomat, would help to quiet the factional strife at the council table. The scheme was essentially a bold move by Paget to capture control of the government. He saw that the numerical majority of his party in the full Council counted for little so long as Gardiner was able to do what he liked with the prisoners and draft whatever measures he pleased for Parliament's consideration. Shrewdly he presented the plan as entirely non-partisan in spirit and practice: the principal nobles (who belonged, of course, to his own party) would not like

[20] P.R.O., Tyler, p. 233.

the scheme, he pointed out. But it was Gardiner's supporters, Mary's former household servants, who objected most loudly. Of their number only Rochester was included in the new Council of State; the rest were barred from all business of state in spite of their long-standing loyalty to the Queen, their unquestioned Catholicism, and their constant presence in London. Taken in by Paget's arguments, Renard so far committed himself to support of the plan that he feared a new rising if it should fail. With Gardiner's party in a minority, he wrote, "there is no saying what might not happen." Apparently he thought that Paget's scheme would reconcile the minority to its weakness rather than exasperate it further.[21]

About a week before Parliament opened (on April 2) the Queen summoned Gardiner, Rochester, Paget, Arundel, and Petre, told them that she was entrusting everything to their hands—preparations for Philip's arrival, examination of the prisoners, and management of Parliament—and exhorted them to be worthy of their new responsibility. Renard was elated by the harmony and diligence of the new "Council of State." To all appearances Gardiner and Paget were reconciled, and each tried to outdo the other in protesting his industry and loyalty to Renard in private conversation. Gardiner pleased the ambassador by remarking that there was no hope of tranquillity in the realm so long as Elizabeth remained alive; and Paget confessed to him that he had once been in error on transsubstantiation but that he had seen the light long ago and was really in favor of the reestablishment of Catholicism —so long as it was not done "by fire and sword" as Gardiner wished. Renard attributed the fact that more had been accomplished in one week than during the preceding two months to the efficiency of the new Council of State, and to Paget's diligence. If it had not been for Paget, he wrote Charles, his fears about Philip's safety would not have been set at rest; as it was, he no longer saw any reason why the Prince should delay his voyage.[22]

21 Renard to Charles V, 22 Mar. 1554, P.R.O., Tyler, pp. 265-6 (Tytler, II, 346-7); cf. Tytler, II, 350. In April Gardiner's party included Rochester, Waldegrave, Englefield, Southwell, Gage, Jerningham, and Bourne; Paget's included Arundel, Petre, Pembroke, Howard, Sussex, Hastings, and Cornwallis (Tytler, II, 372).

22 Renard to Charles V, 3 April 1554, P.R.O., Tyler, pp. 318-29 (Gachard and Piot, IV, 371-80).

The plan for reducing the size of the Council was not Renard's only resource in dealing with the chaos and confusion in Mary's government. Months before, he had seen the possibilities which systematic bribery offered of stopping the mouths of Philip's enemies and spurring on the efforts of his friends.

Early in January Egmont had written Philip from London, "More can be done with money in this country than in any other in the world."[23] About the same time Renard had asked Charles for money to be used in small bribes to the humbler members of the government who were opposing the marriage, and had forwarded a list of more important persons who should receive more substantial sums. The Emperor sent 3,000 crowns for the first purpose and by the middle of February Renard had distributed it all. The larger gifts were a more delicate problem. Renard was instructed to consult Mary on the matter, as Charles himself had once consulted her father in a similar situation some years before.[24] When Egmont returned to London at the end of February, he brought an additional 5,000 crowns for small bribes, together with instructions to promise larger rewards to the more important councillors after consultation with Renard and Mary. In order to conciliate the two factions in the Council, Renard asked both Paget and Gardiner to draw up a list of those who should receive gold chains or pensions, and from these two lists he drafted a third which was approved by the Queen, sent to the Emperor, and forwarded to Philip. On the day of the marriage by proxy the Imperial ambassadors distributed the 5,000 crowns in chains and cash. Their largesse made all the stir which they hoped it would make. Noailles heard that they had given out between 7,000 and 8,000 crowns to the courtiers and 4,000 more to the Queen's guards, promising to enrich everyone from high to low.[25]

In spite of Renard's insistence upon the need of advancing something on the pensions, Charles refused to be hurried. He was

[23] *Docs. inéds.,* III, 449-50.

[24] Weiss, IV, 182-3, 187; Gachard and Piot, IV, 306-7, 313, 314; P.R.O., Tyler, pp. 63, 143 ff.

[25] Gachard and Piot, IV, 346; Tytler, II, 324-5; P.R.O., Tyler, pp. 210-11, 225; Noailles to Henry II, 9 Mar. 1554, Aff. Etr., IX, fol. 154. On the subject of Imperial and French bribes in general, see Appendix II, and *Amer. Hist. Rev.,* XLV (April 1940), 546.

determined that his son should reap the credit for granting them and therefore refused to allow Renard to make any advance payments. In vain the ambassador argued his case. Those who had stood by the Queen during the rebellion would expect reward, he pointed out, and those who might cause trouble "because of their position and the numbers of their retainers" must be bought off. The money might be raised by extraordinary taxation in England and payments might be "suppressed" later on, he suggested. Three or four of the prospective recipients already had one foot in the grave, and affairs in England were "always changing." An immediate half-year's advance on all pensions promised was the important thing. The English appetite for bribes, he soon discovered, was more easily whetted than appeased; the only conclusion which the courtiers seemed to draw from the shower of gold on March 6 was that to him that hath shall more be given. At the end of April the beleaguered ambassador remarked ruefully, "The pensions would have been of the greatest service in winning over the great nobles." The Emperor, however, clung to his determination and although Renard made lavish promises to most of the principal nobles and councillors, no pensions were actually paid until Philip was King of England.[26]

On the whole, Renard's conduct after Egmont's departure for Spain had been intelligent and able. If he had given in too far to his temperamental pessimism, it was an honest fear for Philip's safety (as well as for his own reputation) which moved him to do so. If he had come too close to taking sides in the feud between Gardiner and Paget, the temporary success of Paget's plan for expediting the Council's business was some justification. If he had wanted the Imperial pensions to be distributed by himself and not by Philip, he could honestly plead that concern for the Prince's security was his motive. He hardly merited the rebuke which came to him from Brussels early in April—perhaps the severest he received during his residence in England.

His gloomy dispatch of March 14 caused something of a panic at the Imperial court. By a costly bit of negligence, he had sent the

[26] Renard to Charles V, 8 Mar., 22 Mar., 22 Apr. 1554, and Charles V to Renard, 4 May 1554, P.R.O., Tyler, pp. 215-16, 266, 363, 376; Weiss, IV, 226, 232-3; Tytler, II, 351; Gachard and Piot, IV, 376-7.

copy of his dispatch to Philip of the 13th along with the original to Spain instead of to the Emperor, and it was ten days before he discovered his error.[27] One of Charles's most constant concerns, as we have noticed, was to see that no news reached Spain which might delay Philip's preparations for sailing. When he read Renard's thinly veiled advice that Philip postpone his voyage till September, it occurred to him that Renard might have written Philip in such a tone that it would be necessary "to send fresh explanations to the Prince" to keep him from suspending his journey. A special courier was immediately dispatched to London, therefore, to fetch a copy of Renard's letter to Philip. Charles was even more worried by Renard's evident animosity toward Gardiner. He thought the ambassador was meddling too much in the Council's affairs and running the risk of driving Gardiner into "a still worse attitude" by taking Paget's side. If the Chancellor needed a rebuke, it must come from the Queen, not from Renard—when a "reasonable opportunity" occurred, and not "*à propos* of nothing." He was determined not to defer Philip's coming "in spite of all the ambassador said, unless something very serious happened"; and he wrote Philip immediately that affairs were "more settled" in England and that there was no reason for delay.[28]

Until the Emperor, his sister, Mary of Hungary, and Granvelle had thrashed the matter out for a week more, however, no reply was sent to Renard. On April 1 Charles instructed Philip to embark immediately with his personal attendants, without waiting for his full fleet to be ready. "There seems to be no danger threatening your person," he explained, "nor any reason why you should not adhere to your plans. . . . We trust in God, in Whose hands we have left the conduct of this matter." Sooner or later Philip would have to put his trust in the English anyway; to delay or to stop in Flanders before landing in England (as Renard had suggested) would tarnish his prestige, hurt Mary's feelings and encourage both Henry II and the English malcontents.[29] The next

---

[27] Renard to Charles V, 24 Mar. 1554, P.R.O., Tyler, p. 272.

[28] Granvelle to Mary of Hungary, 22 Mar. 1554, P.R.O., Tyler, p. 269 (the frequent underlining in this letter testifies to the depth of Granvelle's agitation); Charles V to Philip, 21 Mar. 1554, *ibid.*, p. 256.

[29] P.R.O., Tyler, pp. 287-94.

day he and Granvelle wrote at length to Renard, explaining in
detail their reasons for hastening Philip's departure for England,
warning the ambassador not to worry Mary or Philip any further
by his doubts, and instructing him to interfere less openly with
the Council's conduct of affairs, to remain strictly neutral in the
quarrel between Gardiner and Paget, and to allow the Queen
herself to bring the Chancellor around, as she had done in November on the question of her marriage. The Emperor tempered his
rebuke by saying that he realized Renard's misgivings were the
result of his sense of duty, and Granvelle added that his master was
"very pleased" by the ambassador's services. But their letters made
it clear enough that they feared Renard was not acting "modestly"
in his dealings with the Council and that the success of the Spanish
match was endangered rather than assured by his pessimism.[30]

Renard had asked his master to send someone to relieve him of
the burden of attending to all the minutiae of Philip's reception in
England, and Charles had already decided to send Courrières for
this purpose, along with a Spaniard, the Licentiate Briviesca de
Muñatones, who was to act as *alcalde,* or justice of the peace, with
civil and criminal jurisdiction over the members of Philip's suite.
The choice of Courrières did not please Renard, and he pointed
out further that the name of *alcalde* was hateful to the English and
that the premature arrival of Courrières and Briviesca would turn
confusion into chaos in the arrangements for Philip's reception.
The fact that the Emperor sent the two men to London on April 2
in spite of his ambassador's warning seems to indicate that he
hoped Courrières's presence would act as a check upon Renard's
pessimism and imprudence. Granvelle explained that Courrières
was coming with the title of ambassador, having refused to accept
any rank inferior to the one he had held on his two previous missions to London, and added a friendly warning. "Try to get on
with him as best you can," he wrote Renard, "and do your best
to please him."[31] In order to remove every chance of friction between the two ambassadors, Granvelle prevented Courrières from
taking Jean Duboys with him to London as his secretary. Duboys

[30] Weiss, IV, 226-38.
[31] *ibid.,* IV, 225, 232, 2367-7; P.R.O., Tyler, pp. 268, 280; Gachard and Piot, IV,
366-7, 369-71, 389.

was loudly voicing his charges that Renard had allowed himself to be bribed during the preceding fall, and Renard was in the embarrassing position of having to defend his past integrity as well as his present good judgment before the Emperor.[32]

When Charles's letter of rebuke reached London, Renard was already so encouraged by the diligence of the new "Council of State" that he saw no further reason himself for delaying Philip's departure from Spain. He immediately dispatched a special courier to Valladolid to tell the Prince that all his doubts had been resolved. On April 11 Wyatt went to the scaffold, and on the following day Parliament ratified the marriage treaty without a dissenting vote.[33] By the middle of April, therefore, there seemed to be no serious obstacle in the way of the Emperor's plans. Renard's insistence that everyone, from Charles V and Philip to Mary and Paget, face the disagreeable elements in the situation frankly and realistically, had on the whole been beneficial rather than detrimental to the Habsburg cause. In enhancing the glory of his final achievement, it had perhaps been beneficial to his own career as well.

*   *   *

While Renard was struggling to make straight the path which would lead Philip to the crown of England, the clouds of war were gathering over the island. For two months after Wyatt's defeat peace between France and England appeared to be at the mercy of an accident. Henry II's tardy decision to send material assistance to the rebels had been based upon the conviction (shared by Noailles) that war was inevitable in any case after the Prince of Spain became Mary's husband, and his determination to do the Queen all the harm in his power was strengthened rather than weakened by the news of Wyatt's disaster. He told Wotton that "he had always detested rebels and conspirators because of the evil example they gave" and vigorously denied the current rumor

---

[32] Weiss, IV, 226, 237, 239; P.R.O., Tyler, pp. 217, 282-6. Briviesca was ordered to investigate Duboys's charges when he reached England, since Renard wished to clear himself immediately.

[33] Gachard and Piot, IV, 380, 387-8, 390; Vertot, III, 169; *Chronicle of Queen Jane,* 72-4; *Machyn Diary,* 59. Strangely enough, there is no reference to Wyatt's execution in Renard's dispatches.

that he had fostered the uprising "by means of his ministers." But Wotton noticed that he looked downcast and that Montmorency was too melancholy to say much of anything except to inquire "who Peter Wyatt was." For a while the burden of every dispatch which arrived at the French court from London and Edinburgh was that all was not yet lost. D'Oysel was particularly bellicose. He and Mary of Loiraine urged Henry to be "mettlesome and bold" since the worst that could happen as a result of his supporting a new rebellion would be war, and this was inevitable in any case. Their injunctions undoubtedly found support at court with the Queen Dowager's brothers, the Guises.[34]

By the middle of February Renard, too, was persuaded that war was the only possible outcome. In fact, he was inclined to view the prospect with equanimity and even advised Charles to hasten the breach.

All I have noticed for some days past [he wrote] confirms my belief that it will be impossible for England to avoid going to war with France and helping your Majesty. It is important to make the most of this, so that if the German princes rise you may be able to use the English support against the French. . . .

Spies from France say that [Henry II] means to do the Queen all the harm he can now he knows his intrigues have been discovered and his ambassador's letters intercepted, hoping to cause fresh revolts, show the English that he keeps his word, and come to the rescue of the prisoners, especially as he hears that the Queen has no money and that her Council is a prey to faction. . . . The time seems to have come for securing English help against France.

No one [he remarked later] could remain at peace longer than his neighbor would let him.[35]

He might have added that when those responsible for the conduct of policy become convinced that the resources of diplomacy are exhausted, war is indeed inevitable. But not everyone in high office wanted war between England and France in the spring of 1554. The Emperor was afraid that the outbreak of hostilities

[34] Renard to Charles V, 1 Mar. 1554, P.R.O., Tyler, pp. 192 ff. (quoting a lost letter of Wotton to Mary of 23 Feb. 1554); Henry II to Noailles, 27 Feb. 1554, Aff. Etr., IX, fol. 141; D'Oysel to Noailles, 2 Mar. 1554, ibid., fols. 143-4.

[35] Renard to Charles V, 12 Feb., 24 Feb., and 15 Mar. 1554, P.R.O., Tyler, pp. 141, 184, 241.

would jeopardize his son's chances of establishing himself on the English throne and warned Renard that the Council must be given no grounds for suspecting that he wished to involve England in his struggle with France. He hinted clearly that he was afraid Renard might touch the English in their most sensitive spot—their dread of being used to further Habsburg ambitions on the continent.[36] Montmorency was as determined as ever to keep the peace, and Noailles was acutely conscious of the personal risk he might incur because of his activities before the rebellion if a breach should occur in Anglo-French relations.[37] The most determined force for peace, however, was the English government. Noailles soon decided that Mary was so short of funds, so conscious of her unpopularity with her subjects, and so fearful for Philip's safety that she and her ministers would suffer almost any affront from France rather than declare war. The French court was easily persuaded that he was right, and the result was that French ministers on both sides of the Channel were quite willing to play with fire in the firm conviction that the English would fight the spread of any conflagration.[38] No statesman, with the possible exception of Renard and the Guises, wanted war; but the French were not afraid to provoke the incidents which might lead to it.

There were many such incidents during February and March. The concentration of French troops near Calais and the gathering of French warships in the Norman harbors caused the English Council considerable anxiety.[39] Clashes at sea between French and English vessels led to diplomatic protests both in London and Paris.[40] The most potent cause of friction, however, was the underhand support which the French government gave to Wyatt's accomplices and followers who had been fortunate enough to

[36] Gachard and Piot, IV, 345.
[37] Noailles to Bourdin, 24 Jan. 1554, Aff. Etr., IX, fol. 126; Vertot, III, 27, 45.
[38] Vertot, III, 75, 100-1, 178; Noailles to Montmorency, 17 Mar., Henry II to Noailles, 21 Mar., and Noailles to Henry II, 31 Mar. 1554, Aff. Etr., IX, fols. 16, 23, 157. Soranzo agreed with Noailles's judgment (Ven. Cal., V, 562-3).
[39] On the Calais incident, see above, p. 124. On Anglo-Imperial concern about control of the Channel, see P.R.O., Tyler, pp. 215, 219; Weiss, IV, 224, 231; Gachard and Piot, IV, 388; For. Cal., Mary, 64, 66.
[40] See e.g. Aff. Etr., IX, fol. 167; Vertot, III, 176-8, 181-2, 191.

escape to France. Carew was rumored to have had a secret noc-
turnal interview with Henry II, and before news of Wyatt's surrender reached him he had gathered together a little band of
his fellow-countrymen at Rouen, got hold of a ship named the
Sacret, and was preparing to make a descent on the English
coast to help the rebels. A month later he and Pickering and
the Killigrew brothers had three ships at sea and were apparently
contemplating an attack on the Isle of Wight. Wotton's spies
kept the English government in touch with the fugitives' activities, and as their money ran short he was able to persuade one
after another of them to sue for pardon. But the threat of invasion
by English exiles backed by French money and supplies hung
over London for many months more and Henry was perfectly
aware that the fugitives were his strongest trump. When Wotton
demanded Carew's extradition as early as February 10, the King
replied blandly that he had never heard of the man. "As I have
ever said to you," he added, "I will keep the peace and amity with
the Queen my good sister, your mistress; nor do I help nor suc-
cour no rebels against her." And until the Guises forced his
hand, he continued to pile negative upon negative in the same
unconvincing and picturesque fashion, in the comfortable conviction that his denials would both exasperate and intimidate his
good sister.[41] War was avoided for the time being largely because
the English government feared an open breach with France more
than it feared an attack by the exiles backed by secret French
support.

In general both sides were quick to listen to protests whenever
the incident obviously had explosive possibilities, but extremely
stubborn whenever the matter seemed to concern individuals
rather than public policy. Gardiner was adamant, for instance,
in his refusal to return Noailles's intercepted correspondence
although Paget advised that it be restored.[42] The Chancellor

---

[41] Tytler, II, 286-91. Also P.R.O., Tyler, pp. 145, 156, 191, 233 ff., 261, 279; Vertot,
III, 57-8, 90, 100, 104-5, 109-18, 136; Aff. Etr., IX, fol. 153; *For. Cal., Mary,* 61, 66-7,
79-80; Weiss, IV, 230. A French agent at Dover was helping to smuggle English refugees
across the Channel in March (Renard to Charles V, 9 Mar. 1554, P.R.O., Tyler, p. 219).
On the subject of the fugitives in general, see C. H. Garrett, *Marian Exiles,* and A. B.
Hinds, *The Making of the England of Elizabeth.*

[42] Tytler, II, 311-12.

stoutly maintained that it was the rebels, not the Queen's men, who had intercepted Noailles's dispatch of January 26, that the document had been lost when the rebels sacked his house in Southwark, and that it had never been given to Renard or to anyone else for decipherment because it was not thought to be "of any suche emportaunce . . . as were worthy the payne of discyphring."[43] Obviously he was sure that Henry II would hardly choose to break the peace over an incident so incriminating to his ambassador.

There was one step short of war which Mary considered taking as a formal token of her indignation at the rapidly accumulating evidence that the rebels had been backed by France. This was to demand Noailles's recall. The day after Wyatt's surrender the Council told Renard that it approved of "reporting to the King of France his ambassador's doings here so that he might send a new one."[44] Blissfully unaware of the Council's decision, Noailles presented himself at court three days later and protested vigorously about the seizure of his dispatches, the arrest of his courier, and the destruction of the French frigate at Margate. Renard heard that he used "audacious and threatening expressions that could only mean a rupture of peaceable relations," but Noailles was delighted with the results of his boldness. "It seems to me, Sire," he wrote Montmorency, "that to give them a ripe one between two green makes them listen more readily to reason and induces them to consider and ponder what may happen."[45]

One of the most striking differences between Renard and Noailles was that when faced with discouraging obstacles, Renard's natural tendency was to turn the matter over in his mind while Noailles's was to find an outlet for his frustrated energies in action. To follow up his advantage, Noailles immediately asked for audience with the Queen in order to remove her suspicion "that the troubles and uprisings with which she is faced daily

[43] Council to Wotton, 22 Feb. 1554, P.R.O., S.P. 69, Vol. III, No. 157 (cf. *For. Cal., Mary*, 60-1). In writing Wotton the Council tried hard to conceal the fact that Gardiner had lied to Noailles for fear it might reach Henry II's ears. The phrase quoted is one of several which were deleted or altered in the original minute, but it undoubtedly represents what Noailles was told.

[44] Renard to Charles V, 8 Feb. 1554, P.R.O., Tyler, p. 129 (*Docs. inéds.*, III, 485).

[45] Renard to Charles V, 12 Feb. 1554, P.R.O., Tyler, p. 142; Vertot, III, 61.

are encouraged and favored by the King." The arrival on February 12 of his brother François, come to serve his diplomatic apprenticeship in London, gave him a good excuse. All was sweetness and light when the two brothers presented themselves at Whitehall on the 16th. The ambassador blandly congratulated the Queen upon her suppression of the rebellion and told her that his brother had been sent over expressly to assure her of Henry II's amiable intentions. He asked to be shown a copy of the article in the marriage treaty guaranteeing peace with France and was told that his request would be granted. He complained again about the interception of his dispatches, but "sugared the bold words" he had used to the Council six days before. The Queen "replied sharply" to his protests by complaining about Carew's activities in France, but Noailles came away with the impression that he and his brother had had a gracious reception, that the Council regretted their mistress' affection for the Prince of Spain, and that everyone was afraid of breaking the peace with France.[46]

For some time Noailles refused to believe that Wyatt's surrender had permanently crippled the forces opposed to the Spanish marriage. Mary pardoned two batches of rebels who were brought to the palace with halters about their necks; but the wholesale execution of scores of others could not but weaken her position and drive the people to vent their fury in a new and more violent uprising, he thought.[47] On February 17 he wrote Montmorency:

> There has never been seen such hanging as has been going on here every day, and mostly of innocent men. The outcry of nobility and people against it is growing hourly; they continue in their obstinate determination to die sooner than endure the domination of a foreign prince in this country. . . . Of the twenty-five or thirty who compose the Queen's Council, there are not three who approve the said marriage, even [including] all those of her own household; and in general, gentlemen as well as others in the land

[46] Renard to Charles V, 17 Feb. 1554, P.R.O., Tyler, p. 157 (*Docs. inéds.,* III, 506-7); *For. Cal., Mary,* 60-1; Vertot, III, 72-5, 123; Noailles to Montmorency, 12 Feb. 1554, Aff. Etr., IX, fol. 135.

[47] Noailles to Montmorency, 12 Feb. 1554, Aff. Etr., IX, fol. 135^v; Vertot, III, 62-3; *Eng. Hist. Rev.,* XXXVIII (1923), 257.

are utterly opposed to it. . . . It seems to me, Sire, that it would be very necessary for the Prince of Spain and the nobles in his Council to be assured of the ill treatment which has been accorded here to his father's ambassadors and which people are determined to accord to his own person if he comes here, because I know that the Queen wishes to keep him from being informed of this in order not to discourage him from sailing. This will be easy to do by not allowing Spaniards passing through France to tarry, and also by writing the news to royal officials on the [Spanish] frontier.[48]

In the same letter Noailles urged that Carew be sent back to England immediately, along with all those who would be "useful for stirring up a rising"; and a little later he advised Henry II to issue a proclamation ordering that *all* Englishmen (including of course the refugees) be welcomed and given every possible favor in France. The King vetoed this last suggestion for fear of provoking Mary too far,[49] but no clear-cut choice was ever made at Paris between conciliating the English government and provoking it to war by further support of its enemies at home and abroad. For two months Henry was content to drift with the tide of events. No instructions of any importance were sent to Noailles until the end of March, the attention of the French government wandered to intrigues in Germany, and the initiative in London was left to Mary and to Charles V.[50]

By the middle of March it had become evident even to Noailles that Mary's victory over Wyatt had so cowed the people that there was little the King of France could do to revive the malcontents' courage short of declaring war—and the immediate effect of such a declaration might well be to drown every Englishman's new-found hostility to Spain in his ancient hatred of France. Noailles was reluctantly convinced that the rebellious elements would not stir unless strongly supported from across the Channel. The English, he decided, were "inclined too lightly to detach themselves from an enterprise and often to leave the road to their liberty to seek a shameful death."[51] Englishmen then and now might have

[48] Noailles to Montmorency, 17 Feb. 1554, Aff. Etr., IX, fols. 137ᵛ-8. cf. Vertot, III, 75.
[49] Vertot, III, 101; Henry II to Noailles, 21 Mar. 1554, Aff. Etr., IX, fol. 22.
[50] Renard to Charles V, 1 Mar. 1554, P.R.O., Tyler, p. 194; Vertot, III, 90, 92, 94.
[51] Noailles to Henry II, 9 Mar. 1554, Aff. Etr., IX, fols. 153-4; Vertot, III, 98.

resented his words, but he was apparently right, and his royal master was just as pessimistic about the possibility of remedying the situation.

I see no way to break off or stop the marriage [he wrote Noailles on March 21] unless those of the country who ought to know the harm which will come to them from it and the slavery to which it will subject them put their hand to the matter; nothing has been or will be left undone on my part to encourage them in this, as I assure myself and as I pray you to believe. . . . You have done me a very welcome service in taking pains to remove the opinion which the Queen and her ministers wish to impress upon the people, that it is I who am encouraging the seditious and favoring the mutinous in her realm, for I know very well that although I wish to benefit the [English] nation, it has such an inveterate hatred for this crown of mine that the common people will find difficulty in accepting any grace or favor from me.[52]

Whether the Council knew what was going on in Noailles's mind or not, it showed itself determined to render him incapable of doing any more harm. The restrictions on his freedom of activity were steadily tightened. An attempt was made to search out his spies, to frighten his agents into inactivity, and to delay his couriers. Before long he was so put to it for reliable information that he was inclined to believe a rumor that Renard had persuaded the Queen to pardon Wyatt in order to make use of the rebel leader's military ability.[53] Although he managed to acquire a new and valuable informer, the news which he sent to France was colored more and more by the bitterness of his own emotions, and for a while he was unable to write anything of importance because he was afraid Renard had found the key to his cipher. At the end of March he was moved from the Charterhouse to Bridewell, a spacious house belonging to the Queen at the western edge of the city which Renard had occupied until then. To his infinite annoyance he found that his rival had removed everything in the house, "even up to the doors, windows, and locks," and that one of Renard's agents was posted on his doorstep to see who went in and out. Even his creditors

[52] Aff. Etr., IX, fol. 22. cf. Vertot, III, 149; P.R.O., Tyler, pp. 233, 239, 260-1.
[53] Vertot, III, 145.

dared not visit him, and by the end of April he was complaining that he was more a prisoner than an ambassador.[54]

As Noailles's temper grew shorter, as the prisoners in the Tower revealed more and more about his part in the conspiracy, and as the Council became more and more disturbed about Carew's activities in France, the complaints and counter-complaints became more acrimonious on both sides of the Channel. A dinner discussion between Wotton and Henry II at Fontainebleau on March 6 degenerated into a futile debate about the harboring of fugitives, the destruction of merchant vessels, and the invasion of diplomatic privilege in both France and England. Two days later Renard reported that the Queen had written to France demanding Noailles's recall. There is no evidence that such a letter was actually sent, but the Venetian government was compelled by Imperial pressure to recall Soranzo about the same time and the rumor soon got about London that Noailles (who was confined to his house by illness) was leaving.[55]

Finally, about the time when Renard was most in despair about Philip's chances of coming to England with safety, Anglo-French relations reached a crisis. On March 15, the day Wyatt was condemned to death in Westminster Hall, Noailles and his brother had a stormy four-hour interview with the Council at Whitehall. The question which hung in the balance, never openly mentioned by either side, was whether it would be war or peace. Noailles spoke first, and at length. He went over his grievances in detail and told his hearers he had "little enough hope" that peace could be preserved after Philip became King of England. After some consultation with his colleagues, Gardiner launched into a caustic rebuttal of the ambassador's "audacious and menacing speech," which he took to be a veiled threat of war. He spoke

[54] Tytler, II, 353-4; Vertot, III, 122-3, 131, 134; Aff. Etr., IX, fols. 138, 140, 157, 192; For. Cal., Mary, 80. Noailles later came to appreciate Bridewell's garden and tennis court and referred to it as the finest house which Philip and Mary owned in London when he was moved again in September 1554, this time to the Deanery of St. Paul's, to make room for some of the nobles in Philip's suite (Aff. Etr., IX, fols. 267, 269, 270, 278; For. Cal., Mary, 85).

[55] Renard to Charles V, 8, 9, and 15 Mar. 1554, P.R.O., Tyler, pp. 214, 220, 241; Vertot, III, 121-2. On Soranzo's recall and its causes, see P.R.O., Tyler, p. 214; Gachard and Piot, IV, 343; Weiss, IV, 219-20; Ven. Cal., V, 448-52, 474-7; Span. Cal., XI, 450, 475.

pointedly about Croft's revelations of D'Oysel's intrigues with
the conspirators. He said Mary was determined to have Carew
extradited; she had no fear of him and his friends, but she was
astounded by the fact that Henry II was sheltering them. Noailles
"was to let the King of France know exactly what they [the
Council] had said, in order that they might see whether he
meant to accept responsibility for his ministers' behavior, and
whether he wanted peace or war, so that the Queen's constant
desire to keep up relations of good neighborhood might not
expose her to a disagreeable surprise." Noailles denied sharply
that his sovereign was supporting Carew, at which Lord Howard
lost his temper, saying that he knew it was true. High words
passed between the two until Noailles said he was sure that if
Howard went to France, the King would give him a commission
to arrest Carew. It was more difficult to seize a criminal in France
than in England, he explained. The country was larger, it had
no "moat" around its borders as England had, the *bans* and
arrière-bans often had to be called out to capture thieves, the
French people were more compassionate than the English toward
fugitives and French princes more merciful by nature. In England
no one condemned to death ever escaped, which proved that the
Council, had they so desired, could have delivered up four fugitives (including Berteville!) whom Noailles had been "demanding" for months past. In conclusion he begged the Council to
believe "that he would do his best to preserve peace."[56]

After sleeping two nights on the results of his interview with
the Council, Noailles began to be afraid that the English meant
what they said and that the question of the English refugees
might actually lead to war.

Since they feel themselves so irritated and outraged by Carew [he wrote
Montmorency], it might be possible as well as beneficial if he [Carew]
would restrain himself a bit more, both in his presence and in his language,
keeping himself concealed and changing his residence until necessity should

---

[56] Renard to Charles V, 22 Mar. 1554, P.R.O., Tyler, pp. 258 *ff.*; Noailles to Montmorency, 16 Mar. 1554, Aff. Etr., IX, fols. 12-15 (wrongly entitled François de Noailles
to Montmorency); Vertot, III, 139. On the date of Wyatt's trial and Noailles's audience,
cf. Journal of François de Noailles, Bib. Nat. f.f., No. 20147, fol. 22; *Chronicle of Queen
Jane,* 68; and *Cobbett's State Trials,* I, 861.

force him to show himself. Meanwhile [it would be well] to offer the Queen's ambassador every means of arresting him in order to amuse his Mistress and to discourage her still further from declaring her ill will. . . . The Imperial ambassador . . . is urging her as strongly as he can to declare herself.[57]

Renard had advised the Council again, in fact, to demand Noailles's recall; and although they were still afraid to take his advice, Wotton was apparently instructed to complain vigorously about Noailles's conduct without explicitly demanding his dismissal. When the English ambassador appeared at Fontainebleau on March 22, Montmorency had not yet received Noailles's account of his stormy interview of the week before. He defended his friend's conduct warmly, however, calling in La Marque to testify to Noailles's integrity and protesting that the ambassador was "of his own bringing up," "honest and gentle," chosen for the London post because he was the best man the Constable knew to preserve friendly relations with England. If he thought Noailles had been guilty of conduct unbecoming an ambassador, Montmorency added, he would recall him instantly. Wotton noted his "very gentle words" at the close of the talk and remarked that he did not seem to take the affair "so hot" as Noailles had taken it. Clearly Montmorency wanted to avoid a breach and was afraid that Noailles had gone too far. In order to preserve both his friend's reputation and his country's peace, he told Wotton in so many words that Henry II would not break with England so long as Noailles's complicity in Wyatt's rebellion was politely ignored, but that a formal demand for the ambassador's recall would be considered as an affront to the honor of the King and himself.[58]

Disturbed by the reports of Wotton's interview, Noailles called upon Gardiner on March 30 in order to defend himself. He let fall the remark, as if in passing, that Elizabeth's letter had fallen into his hands "entirely by chance," "swearing and blaspheming all the oaths in the world" to prove her innocence of any com-

---

[57] Noailles to Montmorency, 17 Mar. 1554, Aff. Etr., IX, fol. 16. cf. *ibid.*, fol. 15.

[58] Renard to Charles V, 22 Mar. 1554, P.R.O., Tyler, p. 260; Tytler, II, 352-9; Gachard and Piot, IV, 382-4.

munication with him.[59] Two days later he approached the Queen with the usual protest about his intercepted dispatches. This time, according to Noailles, Mary lost all "feminine sweetness." When he complained about Wotton's aspersions and said "he desired to leave because he was not acceptable," she replied drily that she had not yet revealed all she knew about his and D'Oysel's activities. Angrily she demanded Carew's extradition and Noailles, unable to decide whether her demand was the result of fear or of a desire to pick a quarrel, advised his master once more to make a show of arresting the rebel leader.[60]

This latest verbal battle in London was echoed as usual across the Channel, but before Wotton saw Montmorency on April 14 the Cardinal of Lorraine had let the cat out of the bag. Either at the King's command or (more likely perhaps) on his own initiative, he had told Cardinal Pole that Henry II had taken Carew and the other fugitives into his service, and that he had no intention of acting as the Queen of England's hangman. Montmorency repeated this defiant admission to Wotton, adding that of course there was no intention of using Carew's services against England, but only against the Emperor. He then proceeded to accuse Wotton of conduct unbecoming an ambassador in spying upon his exiled countrymen in France and attempting to beguile some of them back to loyalty. "Although Embassadours wer privileged," he said, "yet abusing their previleges they didde leese them and might be punisshed for it." In view of Noailles's conduct in London, it was hardly strange that Wotton was astonished at this remark. He decided that further demands for Carew's extradition would be in vain and concluded his report of the interview by remarking, "I cannot see that I shall be able to do your highnesse enye service heere anye longer."[61] Noailles, embarrassed more and more by the necessity of lying about Henry

[59] Gachard and Piot, IV, 373-4; Vertot, III, 131-2.

[60] Gachard and Piot, IV, 377-8; Vertot, III, 132-6; Noailles to D'Oysel, 5 Apr. 1554, Aff. Etr., IX, fol. 409; *For. Cal., Mary,* 72, 77 (the Council's dispatch of Apr. 3 is misdated April c. 27).

[61] Wotton to Mary, 17 Apr. 1554, P.R.O., S.P. 69, Vol. IV, No. 187; Vertot, III, 109-18, 160-6; Renard to Charles V, 22 Apr. 1554, P.R.O., Tyler, pp. 359-61.

II's support of the rebels, was relieved by Montmorency's frankness, but feared its effect on Mary and the Council.[62]

The reader will not have escaped the impression that there was an atmosphere of unreality about these diplomatic debates in London, Paris, and Fontainebleau. They were the aftermath of unsuccessful rebellion, the futile bickerings of statesmen still too resentful to think of conciliation and still too cautious to go to war. The arguments on both sides, particularly the French, were characterized by hypocrisy and bathos; and it is hard to acquit Noailles, whose tactlessness was fast becoming a liability, of bringing England and France closer to war than a more subtle diplomat (such as his brother François later became) would have done. But Noailles was little more than the instrument of a policy which was fundamentally at variance with itself. Since France had neither the naval nor the military resources to be sure of a quick victory over the combined forces of England and Spain, her rulers took refuge in a policy which observers of a later generation would have called "muddling through." The English government was too weak to want war, and this everyone knew. But both Montmorency and Noailles saw that Mary might be provoked beyond endurance and that an Anglo-French war might play directly into Charles V's hands. The Guises were almost certainly ready and willing to run this risk, but they no less than the Constable were caught between two fears: the fear of driving the English into the arms of Spain, and the fear of neglecting any expedient, however dangerous, which might eventually rob the Habsburgs of their English prey. There is the usual indirect evidence of a struggle behind the scenes at the French court, the usual indications of Henry II's stubborn pride, procrastination, and unwillingness to put his full trust in either faction at court. But the dilemma in which the King of France found himself is the fundamental explanation of the compromise policy which his ministers followed for three months after Wyatt's rebellion.

Judged by its fruits, that policy was not altogether so ineffective as it may appear. Noailles himself could find little consolation

[62] Vertot, III, 184; Aff. Etr., IX, fol. 172.

unless it was in the faith of his brother that God was hardening Mary's heart in order some day to visit her with exemplary chastisement.[63] But his presence in London for two more years in the face of Mary's and Renard's protests was a symbol of French strength and English weakness.

[63] François de Noailles to the Cardinal of Châtillon, 12 Apr. 1554, Aff. Etr., IX, fol. 160.

CHAPTER VII

THE COMING OF PHILIP

APRIL TO JULY 1554

ON April 17, hardly a week after Wyatt's execution, a London jury acquitted Sir Nicholas Throckmorton of the charge of high treason and the crowds which thronged about the Guildhall joyfully threw their caps in the air. Renard complained that the jurymen were "heretics to a man," and Gardiner straightway had them imprisoned for "collusion and wickedness." But it was soon clear to everyone that the acquittal had made it virtually impossible for the government to obtain any further convictions of Wyatt's accomplices; apparently Paget would have his way and none of the ringleaders but Wyatt himself would mount the scaffold.[1] The attention of statesmen and people began to turn from the aftermath of rebellion to the coming of the King.

About the same time Noailles's optimism began to revive. "There are many others like Wyatt in this world," he wrote D'Oysel. Half England would like to emigrate to France if it were possible, he thought. Nobility and commons were so thirsty for revolution that they thought Pole was about to make a descent upon England from France—a story which even Noailles noted was hardly in the Cardinal's character—and rumor had it that fifty thousand Englishmen would rise ere midsummer to throw off the Spanish yoke.[2] But so many patriots had been imprisoned

---

[1] *Cobbett's State Trials*, I, 869 *ff.*; *Chronicle of Queen Jane*, 75; Tytler, II, 373-4, 379; Vertot, III, 173-4. Elizabeth was released from the Tower and sent to Woodstock on May 19. A week later Courtenay was sent to Fotheringay. On January 18, 1555, twelve of Wyatt's associates were set free upon payment of fines (*A.P.C.*, V, 90-1, 111; *Chronicle of Queen Jane*, 76).

[2] Vertot, III, 155, 169, 179, 184-5; D'Oysel to Noailles, 20 May 1554, Aff. Etr., IX, fol. 186.

or executed, so many more had fled abroad, and so many of those who still remained had been corrupted by Imperial money that Noailles feared nothing would come of the widespread discontent unless the King of France bestirred himself. On the day of Throck-morton's acquittal he asked Montmorency for 200,000 crowns to "trouble and traverse" Mary's plans.[3] And a week later he sent the Constable a still stronger plea for help:

> I cannot think that popular commotions will be a sufficient obstacle to prevent this marriage unless they are actively supported from abroad, openly and secretly. In which connection I will say to you, my Lord, perhaps more frankly than I should, that delay might bring this affair into a very incon-venient state, while prompt resolution on the other hand might increase the King's prosperity; he might use this situation as a point of departure for greater ventures, especially at this moment when most of the nobility and people of this country are so extremely enraged that they are not afraid to declare aloud that they wish his Majesty [Henry II] were in England, so that each of them might honor and obey him as gladly as if they were all his native subjects.[4]

To D'Oysel he wrote that a large French army would soon be in the field against the Emperor and that it would not be his fault if a part of the troops were not used to give Mary trouble.[5] Henry made no reply to his appeals, however, and as the weather became warm enough for military operations, Montmorency be-came less and less enthusiastic about running the risk of adding one more nation to the list of France's enemies. Noailles might think that April was January come again, but evidently his superiors did not share his belief.

The English were certainly not so enamoured of the King of France as Noailles thought them, but he was not far wrong in his general estimate of the situation in April. Half-way through the short session of Mary's second Parliament (April 2 to May 5) the feud between Gardiner and Paget took a turn for the worse and Renard's new-found satisfaction with the state of the govern-ment was shattered by a fresh wave of despair.

[3] Noailles to Montmorency, 17 Apr. 1554, Aff. Etr., IX, fol. 168.
[4] Noailles to Montmorency, 23 Apr. 1554, Aff. Etr., IX, fol. 170.
[5] Noailles to D'Oysel, 27 Apr. 1554, Aff. Etr., IX, fol. 173. cf. Vertot, III, 224-5.

The chief lesson which both Mary and Gardiner drew from Wyatt's rebellion was (as we have seen) that heresy, not patriotism, was the prime root of sedition in England. Gardiner saw further that unless the old religion were firmly reestablished before the marriage took place, the people would say that Catholicism was being reintroduced in the wake of Spanish domination. He was eager, therefore, to make full use for his purposes of the last Parliament which would meet before Philip became King of England.[6] He had outlined his program to a committee of the Council early in March, but Paget had refused to associate himself with it and soon after Parliament met the Chancellor realized that if he were to push his religious proposals through, he must first challenge Paget's authority in the Council. Accordingly about the middle of April he and his followers raised a storm of objection to the new "Council of State" on the ground that so many of their faction were excluded from its membership, and the Queen was compelled to drop the scheme, barely three weeks after it had gone into effect.[7]

The immediate result was that the quarrel in Council was transferred to Parliament. Checkmated in his attempt to capture control of the machinery of government, Paget carried his feud with Gardiner to the floor of the House of Lords and Parliament immediately became a sounding board for the differences between the Queen's clerical and secular advisers. Both factions had agreed upon ratification of the marriage treaty and upon a bill confirming the full authority of the first woman to wear the English crown (intended to settle any doubts Philip might have about the title of his bride-to-be, and at the same time to block any personal claim to the crown which he might put forth in the future). But there the agreement ended. Gardiner was able to push through a bill restoring the Bishopric of Durham, but only in the face of outspoken opposition. When two bills for the punishment of heretics came up from the lower house, Paget induced the Lords to throw them out on the ground that their passage would enable the bishops to recover ecclesiastical property by prosecuting its holders for heresy; and thanks to his efforts, two more of the

6 Muller, *Gardiner*, 252.   7 Tytler, II, 372-3; Weiss, IV, 340.

Chancellor's proposals—one to drop the Queen's title of "Supreme Head" of the Church, the other to enable her to designate her successor by will (and thus to exclude Elizabeth from the succession)—never reached the floor of either house. As a final gesture of defiance to his rival, Paget even went so far as to kill a bill extending the full protection of the treason laws to Philip.[8]

His motives were obviously so mixed that Renard was considerably embarrassed by his conduct. The ambassador was in thorough sympathy with his friend's attempt to block any religious proposals which might arouse popular opposition and so endanger Philip's safety, but he could not but be suspicious of Paget's factious opposition to the treason bill and his concern about Elizabeth's rights.[9] Sheer personal hatred of Gardiner was apparently driving Paget to oppose Philip's interests as well as the Chancellor's religious program, and the danger was that the Habsburg cause might soon become identified in fact with the cause of religious reaction—a result which both Gardiner and Renard wished to avoid for different reasons. In spite of Charles V's warning about taking sides, Renard could ill afford to stand by and see the leader of the Imperial faction ruin himself with the Queen, as he was rapidly doing. The Emperor's cause seemed to demand that Paget be saved from himself.

About April 21 Renard went to Mary and defended Paget's conduct. Fearing that the upshot of the chaos in Council and Parliament could only be "arms and tumult," he told her it was "no time to feed party quarrels by showing a sour countenance to faithful servants" like Paget. All action on religion should be postponed until the fall, he advised, and every energy devoted meanwhile to the problem of protecting Philip. The Queen replied that she had not been consulted about Gardiner's religious measures beforehand and that she was every whit as worried about the situation as Renard himself; but she hinted that she could not

---

[8] Renard to Charles V, 22 Apr., 27 Apr., and 1 May 1554, P.R.O., Tyler, pp. 355 ff., 368-9, 372-4. See also Muller, *Gardiner*, 252-4; and Pollard, *Pol. Hist.*, 118-21.

[9] Early in April Paget suggested to Renard that if it were impossible to execute Elizabeth, the next best thing would be to marry her to Emmanuel Philibert of Savoy. The proposal found no favor in Brussels and was dropped. (Gachard and Piot, IV, 375, 391; Charles V to Renard, 4 May 1554, P.R.O., Tyler, p. 376; also Vertot, III, 166-7, 262-3.)

stomach Paget's vengeful opposition to the Chancellor's program. While they were conversing a note arrived from Paget addressed to Renard and Renard read its contents to the Queen. Gardiner had just proposed that Elizabeth be disinherited by parliamentary statute and Paget said he had refused his consent "for many reasons"; the storm over the Chancellor's religious proposals, he added, would soon become a serious obstacle to Philip's early arrival. "For the love of God," he concluded, "persuade the Queen to dissolve the Parliament instantly . . . for the times begin to be hot, men's humors are getting inflamed, warmed, fevered." Mary was so impressed that she promised she would "suggest ending the Parliament," but her bewilderment—torn as she was between sympathy with Gardiner's religious objectives and concern over Philip—did little to reassure Renard. He warned Charles that there had been a "change for the worse" and that he was "not at all persuaded that there will be no trouble." In spite of Paget's plea that he hasten Philip's sailing, he hinted once more that it might be dangerous for the Prince to come to England. Perhaps it is unnecessary to add that Charles was no more perturbed by these new counsels of despair than he had been by his ambassador's earlier outbursts.[10]

The truth was that the Tudor system of government by Crown-in-Council had broken down once more under the strain imposed upon it by faction and intrigue. Had Renard persuaded Mary to throw the full weight of her authority upon one side or the other in the quarrel, the storm in Parliament might soon have subsided. But after the Emperor's warning he could hardly do this. "I am doing my best," he wrote, "to remain on good terms with both parties and not to be caught up in their quarrels." When he approached Gardiner and Rochester with advice at the end of April, he was careful to confer also with Paget and Petre. For a while he thought the two antagonists were "half-reconciled," but he soon had to confess that he was having "the greatest difficulty" in deciding how to behave towards each of them. Naturally Mary followed his lead in trying to keep above parties, but her own

10 Tytler, II, 382-3; Renard to Charles V, 22 Apr. 1554, P.R.O., Tyler, pp. 355-63 (extracts in Tytler, II, 371-8); Charles V to Renard, 4 May 1554, P.R.O., Tyler, pp. 375-8; Weiss, IV, 239-40.

religious instincts and Paget's blunders eventually turned the scale. In spite of fresh proof that Gardiner was deliberately suppressing evidence which Renard thought would have convicted both Elizabeth and Courtenay,[11] the Queen's anger with Paget mounted more rapidly than her distrust of Gardiner. Paget's opposition to giving Philip the protection of the treason laws (after he had told her it was a reasonable measure which would pass without difficulty) was the last straw. Since the damage was done and since there was no one near her whom she could trust unreservedly (unless it was Renard himself), there was nothing for her to do but to take Paget's advice and dissolve Parliament.[12]

During the closing days of the session Renard himself began to turn against his most loyal ally in the marriage negotiations. Mary's resentment had some influence on him, but Paget's own conduct was the decisive factor. The ambassador knew it was his duty to oppose trouble makers, whatever their past claims upon his favor, and Paget's activities in Parliament had undeniably stirred up serious trouble. The councillor's enemies were assiduously spreading rumors about his heretical and treasonable connections, and Renard could not but be disturbed by the stories which reached his ears, particularly by a report that there was a plan afoot to marry Elizabeth to the son of Lord Arundel, Paget's closest friend. Renard shrewdly suspected that if Paget lost the Queen's favor he might join the forces opposing the marriage merely to revenge himself upon Gardiner. The day after Parliament rose the ambassador wrote his master, "The outlook is blacker for the Queen than it has ever been."[13]

The embers of the feud smoldered on for two weeks more, ready at any moment to burst into flame. Paget visited Renard to justify his conduct, bewail his plight, and beg the ambassador to intercede for him with the Queen. Renard suspected that he had come to find out "whether there was any intention of shutting him up—a prospect which terrifies him," and replied cautiously that he had better approach the Queen himself. Gardiner

[11] See Renard to Charles V, 1 May 1554, P.R.O., Tyler, pp. 372-4 (Tytler, II, 383-4).
[12] Renard to Charles V, 22 Apr., 27 Apr., 1 May 1554, P.R.O., Tyler, pp. 362, 368-9, 372-4 (extracts in Tytler, II, 371-87).
[13] See note 12.

also came to the Imperial embassy to vent his spleen against Paget and to ask for sympathy; the ambassador told him tactfully but firmly that postponement of the heresy bills could result only in good.[14] A few days later Paget fell on his knees before the Queen on her way from mass and begged her pardon. After scolding him for his conduct she granted him her forgiveness, but she had already told Renard that she could never trust the offender again. Instead of being relieved by Paget's public humiliation, Gardiner and his friends were frightened. They were afraid that the nobles and "heretics" who had backed Paget were plotting more violent measures and that Paget's apology was a mere ruse to cover up their designs. Gardiner himself seems to have thought that there was a plot on foot among some of the nobles to imprison him and "impose their will on the Queen, as was done in England in the reign of King Edward." Paget had lured a friend of the Chancellor's to his house, where he had subjected the man to a two days' cross-examination, and Gardiner was so infuriated by this that he went to the Queen, told her his fears, and asked her to imprison Paget, Arundel, and Pembroke as a precaution. According to Noailles, Mary was so worried that Paget's party might cast Gardiner into the Tower that she ordered the Captain of the Guard not to arrest the Chancellor, and the Lieutenant of the Tower not to receive him, no matter what orders they received from the rest of the Council. But since it was impossible to arrest Paget and his followers on such vague suspicions, it was decided merely to raise a bodyguard for the Queen, to forbid any gentleman's coming to court with more than two servants, and to scatter the suspects by sending them "hither and thither under pretext of some mission or other." If there was to be trouble, it was quite apparent which party would have the support of the Queen.[15]

On May 15 Paget asked Mary for permission to retire to his house in the country, and after a severe verbal lashing the Queen told him "he could come and go as he pleased" so long as he did

[14] Renard to Charles V, 6 May 1554, P.R.O., Tyler, pp. 386-93 (extracts in Tytler, II, 388-91).

[15] Renard to Charles V, 13 May 1554, P.R.O., Tyler, pp. 409-11 (cf. Tytler, II, 392 ff.); Vertot, III, 218-19.

what was right. The unhappy councillor "began to weep, excusing himself as best he could," then went to Renard for comfort, saying it was obvious that the Queen "no longer valued his services." The ambassador did his best to console his friend, "speaking kindly, as he thought the circumstances required," but it was clear that all mutual confidence between the two men was gone. When Paget reached his country seat he had a long talk with Sir Philip Hoby, whom Renard considered "one of the craftiest heretics in England," and this was enough to convince the ambassador that he was "brewing something to the Queen's detriment." The judicious Bishop of Norwich was heard to remark that if Henry VIII were still alive, "he would have had Paget imprisoned and punished."[16]

By the end of May, then, the long quarrel between Gardiner and Paget, between the Catholic patriots and the pro-Habsburg *politiques,* seemed to have been settled in the Chancellor's favor. Paget had not only incurred Mary's undying distrust, he had also lost Renard's confidence. His factious conduct in Parliament had brought about the one result he feared most: Gardiner was once more undisputed "prime minister." Furthermore, by a curious twist of fate, the Chancellor had become the official champion of the Spanish marriage. Philip's cause and the Pope's cause had become entangled with each other in the parliamentary debates, if only because Paget had apparently attacked them both; and Gardiner was now the only person of ability in the Council to whom Renard and Mary could turn for assistance in arranging for Philip's reception. This fact was pregnant with significance for the future. When the Prince of Spain arrived in England, he would find the clerical party in the saddle and the *politiques* overthrown. It might be difficult to oppose any solution to the religious question which the dominant party should offer, and

[16] Renard and Courrières to Charles V, 21 May 1554, P.R.O., Tyler, pp. 423-4; Vertot, III, 225. Renard's two lengthy dispatches of May 21 and May 25 are particularly difficult to piece together, and the solution of the problem at which I have arrived is too complicated to enter into here. Suffice it to say that internal evidence in the fragments at Besançon and Brussels indicates the following dating and division: *Dispatch of May 21:* P.R.O., Tyler, pp. 423-7 (printed with omissions in Weiss, IV, 245-9); *Dispatch of May 25:* P.R.O., Tyler, pp. 428-33 (overlapping parts printed in Weiss, IV, 241-5, and Tytler, II, 398-404). Tyler repeats one passage as belonging to both dispatches; it should be made part of the second.

yet the solution chosen would inevitably appear to bear the stamp of Spanish approval.

Renard's conduct in the crisis was later to be severely criticized by Imperial and Spanish officials, and it is therefore worthwhile to examine the motives which drove him to part with his ablest supporter on the eve of the marriage. Paget had been the only person in England to win his complete confidence. The two men's minds were much alike, their political ideals were much the same, and since Paget was the older and subtler statesman of the two, he had often been able to dominate Renard without the latter's knowing it, and sometimes even to hoodwink him. Paget's opposition to the treason bill opened Renard's eyes, however, and about the same time that the ambassador began to see Paget as he was, Paget became more aware of some of Renard's less admirable traits. Noailles heard that the councillor's friends were intensely jealous of Renard's domination over the Queen and Council, and that Paget had remarked in private that he regretted ever having put his hand to the marriage.[17] Admiral Howard was particularly irritated by the ambassador's dictation, and in English naval quarters it was said "that never an ambassador before had such great credit with the rulers of England as this man."[18] The London political stage was obviously becoming too small for two authors of the Spanish marriage.

Renard's policy was, of course, indefeasible if Mary's and Gardiner's suspicions of Paget's loyalty were correct. The line between opposition and treason was notoriously thin in Mary's reign, and Paget was desperately eager for revenge against his enemy. But he was not a man of any great personal courage or daring, and there was almost certainly a great deal less substance to his plots than Renard supposed. Six months later Paget told the Emperor his own story of the quarrel. The Council had agreed not to propose any controversial religious measures in Parliament, he said, and Gardiner had merely read over the headings of some articles on religion without asking for formal assent. It was "no offense deserving bitter reprimand" for a "straightforward man" to have expressed his dissent in a Council meeting. It was Gardiner who

[17] Vertot, III, 246.   [18] Gachard and Piot, IV, 416.

was responsible for the Queen's displeasure.[19] The thing which rankled most with Paget, in fact, as a friend of Renard's reported during the summer, was that "the very men who tried to prevent the match are now in highest favor" while "others who did not work nearly so hard as he [are] reaping where he sowed."[20] These were hardly the reactions of a desperate conspirator but rather those of a disgruntled place-seeker who had presumed too far upon his sovereign's favor and gratitude.

If Renard had laid aside personal considerations and supported Paget as vigorously in May as he had in preceding months, it is at least arguable that England might never have known the religious persecutions of later years. Even from a purely diplomatic point of view, the ambassador seemed to have lost much and gained little by deserting the leader of the Imperialist faction. But something can be said in favor of his conduct. After April 2 Charles V sent him no instructions of any significance until Philip's arrival—nothing, at any rate, to indicate that Paget's fall had made any impression in Brussels. Presumably the ambassador was still bound, therefore, to remain aloof from party quarrels. Furthermore, if the feud between Gardiner and Paget had to result in victory for one or the other, it was probably less dangerous on the eve of Philip's arrival to have driven Paget and his friends to their country-houses—deeply committed as most of them were to support of the marriage—than to have alienated Courtenay's friends in the Council. Was it mere coincidence that Wyatt's revolt broke out at a time when the Imperialist nobles dominated the government and the Catholic patriots were in eclipse? Gardiner at any rate had a better chance of commanding the confidence of all but the fanatical Protestants among the people than Paget, long noted for his pro-Habsburg prejudices.

There is no evidence, however, that Renard reasoned thus within himself. His handling of the Council's quarrels in the spring of 1554 was more fortunate in its results than wise in its conception.

---

[19] Account of Paget's negotiations at Brussels, 14 Nov. 1554, P.R.O., Tyler, p. 245.
[20] Imperial ambassadors to Charles V, 8 Aug. 1554, P.R.O., Tyler, p. 94.

Meanwhile Noailles was more and more pleased by the news which his informers brought him from Council-chamber and Parliament-house. What he heard convinced him that the government was in no condition to resist the second rebellion which he felt was imminent. Perhaps the moment had come for a final attempt to frighten the Council into a full realization of the disasters which the Spanish marriage was sure to bring upon the realm. A word dropped in the right place—a clear threat that Henry II would never tolerate a Spanish King in England— might terrify the government, weak and divided as it was, and prevent the marriage from ever taking place. It was rather a desperate chance, and Noailles had no instructions to warrant his resorting to any such course; he knew, furthermore, that it might result in war. But he was in a mood to take the bit in his teeth, particularly because he believed that war was inevitable in any case. The result was that two days after Parliament rose, Anglo-French relations reached the breaking-point.

Henry II had made much in his talks with Wotton of Mary's refusal to sign a fresh treaty with France in the preceding December, and on April 14 Montmorency had remarked to the English ambassador that the King of France had no treaty with the Queen of England "except one of amity, so long as she shows amity toward him." As Wotton reported it, King and Constable "seemid to take it ylle . . . that your highnesse refused to entre anye new league with the King or to ratifye the olde treatyes . . . whereby they gather that they cannot so well assure theim selfes of your amitye . . . as they might do elles."[21] After receiving Montmorency's account of this interview, Noailles obtained an audience with the Queen and Council on May 7 to complain about the seizure of a French vessel by some Flemish ships off the Isle of Jersey and to ask whether the Anglo-Flemish fleet which was to convoy Philip through the Channel would respect the neutrality of French shipping.[22] The Council replied that the fleet would fight only if attacked, but the interview had not lasted

[21] Wotton to Mary, 17 Apr. 1554, P.R.O., S.P. 69, Vol. IV, No. 187; Vertot, III, 163-4, 184.

[22] On the Jersey incident see De Langey to ?, n.d., Aff. Etr., IX, fol. 662; Vertot, III, 195, 229, 240-2.

long before the Queen lost her temper. In harboring English traitors, she said, Henry II was clearly breaking the treaties between England and France—and without any shadow of excuse since she had offered him no provocation whatever. Her insistence upon the King's bad faith stung Noailles to fury. He repeated Montmorency's reply to Wotton on the subject of the treaties, but it is clear from the Council's account that he embroidered it considerably in the heat of the moment.

Thambassador being thus often charged with the treaties, at the length sayd playnely that the king his master toke hym selfe not bounde by treaties either to delyver the rebelles or to doo any thing conteyned in the treaties; for seeing the same hath not byn ratefyed sence the quenes highnes' coming to the crowne, he thinketh he is none other wyse bounde to thobservacion of them then of his awne good will and enclinacion, and as her highnes shall by her doynges and shewyng of frendship gyve him cause to do, being neverthelesse for his part mynded by all meanes to entertaine thamitie.[23]

The full significance of Noailles's words escaped the Queen, who had interrupted him constantly, but Gardiner and Paget restrained the torrent of her anger for a moment and asked Noailles either "to hand over a written statement of what he had said, or a copy of the passage of the King's letters in which he said that the old treaties were no longer in force." If the King really felt as Noailles said he did, they pointed out, then the clause in the marriage covenant which bound Philip to observe the existing commitments was "voyd and of no force." The argument was unanswerable and Noailles realized that he had gone too far. He refused to give the Council a written statement of any sort and took refuge in a reference to Mary's mistake in not accepting his suggestion of five months before that she reconfirm the treaties. Paget immediately reminded him that he had made this suggestion unofficially and on his own responsibility; otherwise, he said, the Queen might have given it more serious attention. Completely nonplussed, Noailles "spoke more softly," assured everyone

[23] Council to Wotton, 10 May 1554 (misdated 10 Apr.), P.R.O., S.P. 69, Vol. IV, No. 185. cf. Renard to Charles V, 13 May 1554, P.R.O., Tyler, pp. 411-12; Vertot, III, 195-201, 229-30. In Noailles's account of the interview he claimed that he had stuck closely to the Constable's phraseology, but it is clear from the sequel that the English account of what he said was closer to the truth.

present that Henry had no intention of breaking the treaties unless Mary did, and "departed well satisfyed as yt seemed."

If Noailles had deliberately meant to frighten the English government, he accomplished his purpose. Mary, Renard, and Gardiner were all persuaded that the King of France meant to declare war ere Philip arrived. But no one was more concerned about the possible results of the interview than Noailles himself. He sensed almost immediately that he had blundered. If war resulted from the strong line he had taken and if his government was not ready for it, he would be blamed for the disaster. His account to Henry and Montmorency of what had happened was part justification, part apology. The Council was already more tractable, he reported, thanks to his giving them "one word which touches them to the quick between two soft ones"; the English only wanted to preserve the peace until Philip's arrival gave them the strength to declare war, and if the breach were precipitated, Henry would be free to pounce upon Calais before Spanish troops could succor the garrison. But he warned that he had left Mary "in extreme displeasure and anger" and that Gardiner had asked for an immediate clarification of Henry's attitude; if the King's intention were still "to contain the Queen with honest and soft words," a prompt reply was necessary to preserve the peace.[24]

Meanwhile he set about repairing whatever damage had been done. When the Council sent a messenger to sound him out, he seized upon the opportunity to explain away what he had said to the Queen.

To tell you truth [he said to the messenger] Monsieur le Conestable was he that wrote vnto me of this matter, and in dede touched it sumewhat darkely in his letters, and therefore have I all redy written vnto hym to signify the matter sumewhat playnelyer vnto me, which I doubt not but he will doo, and then shall I be the better hable to satisfy my lorde Chauncellor herein. And (quoth he) what so ever hath byn sayd touching this matter or any other, either by Monsieur le Conestable to the quenes ambassador in Fraunce or by me here to her highnes or her counsell, yet I pray you desyre my lord Chauncellor to think and veryly beleve that the king my master meanith not by any meanes to minister any iust occasion of breache for his

24 This appears to be the most likely interpretation of Noailles's rather confused reasoning. See Vertot, III, 202-3, 211-12. For Renard's conviction that a breach was inevitable, see Renard to Charles V, 27 Apr. 1554, P.R.O., Tyler, p. 369.

part, but by all wayes to intertaine the amitie betwene the quene his good syster and hym.[25]

Noailles's conduct was promptly disavowed at the French court, but unlike Renard he received no personal rebuke for his blunder. In fact, Montmorency's unwavering trust in Noailles, in spite of his many mistakes of judgment, contrasted sharply with the frequent doubts and misgivings about Renard's conduct which assailed both Charles V and Granvelle. The Constable told Wotton on May 16 that either Noailles had made a slip or the Council had misunderstood him; and according to a report which reached Brussels, Henry said that his ambassador "knew not what he was talking about." But Montmorency wrote Noailles that Paget was quibbling when he called the French offer of a new treaty an unofficial proposal, and Henry added that Noailles could not have acted "better nor more prudently" than he had. There is no evidence that the King himself was anything but pleased by what had happened, but the Constable was plainly as concerned as ever to avoid a breach.[26]

In spite of his efforts to soothe the Council, Noailles still clung to his belief that vigorous action on the part of his sovereign might still prevent the marriage. He continued to suggest measures which came dangerously close to war, but which he thought would frighten the English government into tearing up the marriage treaty: support of the English refugees in France, the dispatch of troops to Scotland, the concentration of warships at Brest, and an attempt to suborn the garrison of Calais, whose pay was two years in arrears and whose loyalty was suspected. Above all, he begged Henry II to stop the current rumors that the French government was about to make peace with the Emperor. Early in May Noailles was told that Renard, in the presence of two or three of his most intimate friends, had prayed God to grant peace in Europe so that the Emperor might be free to wreak his vengeance upon the English people, who were crossing his designs so sorely. The story was

---

[25] Mary to Wotton, 29 May 1554, P.R.O., S.P. 69, Vol. IV, No. 212; Vertot, III, 214 ff. ʻoailles's assertion that it was Montmorency, not the King, who had written him of the interview with Wotton was untrue (Vertot, III, 160 ff.).

[26] Weiss, IV, 243; *Ven. Cal.,* V, 502; Montmorency to Noailles, 19 May 1554, Aff. Etr., IX, fol. 182; Vertot, III, 230.

probably apocryphal, but Noailles saw that any settlement of the continental controversy must be avoided at all costs, if the English malcontents were to be encouraged to resist Philip's landing.[27] In order to keep in the good graces of Mary's successor in the event of a successful rebellion, he sent an agent to Richmond to present a gift of some apples to Elizabeth on May 20, the day after her release from the Tower. The agent was caught, searched down to his shirt, and cross-examined by the Council, but managed to conceal the fact that he had come from the French embassy and was released.[28]

About the same time Noailles visited Gardiner. According to the Chancellor, his attitude was "unseemly in one who wished to treat of state affairs," and the interview ended with both statesmen bragging like schoolboys about the relative military strength of their respective nations. Gardiner painted a dashing picture of the war-loving youth of England, so eager for a good fight that they were compelled to seek military service abroad, as Carew and his friends had done; when Philip arrived in England, "young and hot-headed," it would be difficult to restrain his natural desire to draw England into the war. Noailles replied sardonically that he had "never seen an Englishman who wanted to die outside his own country" and added that while he was sure the English were a puissant and bellicose people, never since the age of Charlemagne had France been blessed by a better ruler, a wiser council, more gallant captains and soldiers, stronger foreign allies, and a better-stocked treasury than at present. He noted with satisfaction that this retort made Gardiner change color and shift the conversation to the prospect of European peace.[29]

The climax of the prolonged crisis in Anglo-French relations came during an audience which Noailles had with the Queen on May 27, two days before she left London for Richmond on her way to greet Philip. It was the last time he was to see her before the marriage. His mood was apparently truculent enough when

[27] Advis, 29 Apr. 1554, Aff. Etr., IX, fol. 174; Vertot, III, 188-9, 205-6, 209, 222-5; Weiss, IV, 248.

[28] Vertot, III, 237-8.

[29] Courrières and Renard to Charles V, 21 May 1554, P.R.O., Tyler, pp. 425-6 (see note 16 above); Vertot, III, 240-5.

he arrived at the palace, and the discovery that one of Renard's secretaries was present at the other end of the audience-chamber increased his irritation. He accused the Queen of doing her best to plunge England into war in spite of Henry's honest efforts to preserve the peace, upon which Mary answered tartly that she would not have the burden of Henry's sins and those of "his ministers" upon her own conscience even for the gain of three realms—or of all the kingdoms in the world, as Renard reported it. Noailles was "somewhat warmed" by this direct thrust, and when Mary referred him to Gardiner and the rest of the councillors on some minor complaints, he flew into a petty rage over what he considered an act of personal discourtesy on the part of the Chancellor. When he had returned to the quiet of his house, he wrote Henry his considered opinion that the Queen had made up her mind to declare war and that she was only awaiting the arrival of her husband-to-be to carry out her decision.[30]

The long strain had told heavily upon Noailles's health and spirits, and this final encounter with one as proud and stubborn as himself was the last straw. With the ruin of all his work staring him in the face, he ordered the faithful La Marque to make a firm request at court for his recall. In spite of all his efforts to prevent it, England was to have a Spanish King. His repeated attempts to persuade his government to adopt a more aggressive course had failed, and his own attempt to bluff the English government into accepting diplomatic humiliation in place of war had been disavowed. When war came, he himself would undoubtedly be arrested in revenge for his complicity in Wyatt's rebellion. A great opportunity had been lost, a great mistake made, he wrote D'-Oysel; he could understand Henry's heavy commitments in Italy and elsewhere, he said, but some day the King would regret having allowed the Habsburgs to engulf England. Nostalgia strengthened his conviction that diplomacy, especially in the damp and hostile climate of London, was not his calling. Always more of a soldier than a diplomat at heart, he longed to be back in France where the army was gathering for the summer campaign and

[30] Memoir (Noailles to Henry II), 29 May 1554, Aff. Etr., IX, fol. 192; *For. Cal., Mary*, 87-8; Weiss, IV, 257.

where the issue would be fought out with cannon and sword, not with words.[31]

As the army was assembling, however, both Henry and Montmorency became increasingly apprehensive about the possibility of an attack by the English on their northern flank. Their strategy in the summer of 1554 was to strike down the valley of the Meuse into the heart of the Netherlands before Charles had time to assemble his forces, and they were afraid that any real threat to the integrity of the Low Countries (which were now the stipulated inheritance of the first child born to Philip and Mary) would immediately draw England into the war. The King had lost whatever faith he had had in the English malcontents' ability to stop Philip from landing in England, and he knew that with all his resources absorbed in the campaign on the Flemish border, he could not stop the Prince himself. He assured Wotton once more, therefore, of his desire to preserve the peace with England and instructed Noailles to remain at his post. There must be no breach "this year," he explained.[32] Noailles took his disappointment with bitter resignation, consoling himself with the thought that although the fate of Europe was being decided on the battlefields of Flanders while he was in exile, "affairs over here seem to me just as necessary."[33]

* * *

It was axiomatic with both Noailles and Renard that the warmth of popular passions in England rose and fell with the temperature outdoors, but ironically enough, it was the tempers of the diplomats themselves which had risen with the advent of spring while the common people had remained remarkably placid. In June, however, the attention of embattled ambassadors and jealous councillors turned toward Spain and an ominous calm settled upon London. Noailles relapsed into disheartenment and inactivity,

[31] Noailles to D'Oysel, 5 June 1554, Aff. Etr., IX, fol. 198; Vertot, III, 257-8; Renard to Charles V, 28 June 1554, P.R.O., Tyler, p. 483. Charles V was unwilling to grant Noailles a safe-conduct and ordered Renard to trump up some excuse for delay (Weiss, IV, 257, 259).

[32] Henry II to Noailles, 10 June 1554, Aff. Etr., IX, fols. 203-4; Vertot, III, 259-60; Ven. Cal., V, 511; Renard to Charles V, 20 June 1554, P.R.O., Tyler, p. 468.

[33] Vertot, III, 251, 257-8.

while Renard found that there was little he could do but meet
each problem as it arose and wait—reluctantly convinced that he
was doing everything which could be done to assure Philip of a
favorable reception.

The quarrel in Council was not the only problem—though it
was the thorniest—with which Renard had to deal while Anglo-
French relations were going from bad to worse and Philip's fleet
was slowly gathering at Corunna. Information and advice had to
be sent off to the Prince with every courier who left London or
Brussels. Arrangements had to be made for quartering Philip's
suite and for settling the disputes which were bound to arise between Spaniards and Englishmen. The juncture of the Flemish
and English fleets which were to meet the Spanish flotilla in the
Channel had to be planned and supervised. And last but not least,
the Queen must be comforted and encouraged amid the worries
which were beginning to affect her health.

Perhaps the problem which bothered Charles V most acutely
during the spring was that of making sure that Philip and those he
brought with him to England behaved themselves. "For the love
of God, Duke," he wrote Alva on April 1, "see to it that my son
behaves in the right manner; for otherwise I tell you I would
rather never have taken the matter in hand."[34] When he learned
from Renard that some of the Spanish grandees intended to bring
their wives to England, he wrote Philip that "even soldiers would
be more likely to get on well with the English." Presumably
among the Spaniards the female of the species was more deadly
than the male, but his warning was to go unheeded by five or six
of Philip's followers.[35]

Renard was even more concerned about the problem than his
master, and about the same time he composed a lengthy memorandum for Philip's guidance. The surviving fragment of this paper
in Renard's own hand is interesting evidence of the ambassador's
genius for detail and of his absorbing ambition to make himself
indispensable to the Prince after the latter became King of England. Philip, he wrote, should be gracious to everyone, show him-

[34] P.R.O., Tyler, p. 295.
[35] Charles V to Philip, 9 Apr. 1554, P.R.O., Tyler, p. 345; Tytler, II, 351, 402; Weiss,
IV, 268; For. Cal., Mary, 85; Vertot, III, 298-9.

self often to the people, learn a few words of salutation in the English language, converse with the nobility on every possible occasion, take them hunting, and avoid all semblance of interfering in the Council's conduct of affairs. He should form a private Council of men who had had experience in dealing with foreign nationalities (a subtle recommendation of Renard himself) and put his trust in Paget, "a man of parts." Since it was stipulated that no Spanish soldiers were to set foot on English soil, it would be well for the Prince to have his grandees substitute soldiers for their pages and lackeys, disguising them in their liveries and seeing to it that arquebuses were stowed away in their trunks. Philip himself should be secretly armed when he stepped ashore.[36]

Since Philip was expected to bring about three thousand Spaniards with him to England, the question of how to provide against the almost inevitable disputes between English and Spanish nationals was a serious one. The Emperor's appointment of a Spanish "justice of the peace" was a wise and far-sighted measure, but Renard had difficulty persuading the Council to grant Briviesca the jurisdiction which Charles expected him to have. The English were naturally chary of allowing the *alcalde* to exercise any sort of extraterritorial jurisdiction and insisted that Philip's suite must be subject to English law like any other foreigners who entered the realm. It was finally agreed in the middle of May, however, that Arundel, as Grand Master of the Household to Philip and Mary, should delegate Briviesca and Sir Thomas Holcrofte "to enquire and determyn all comunall causes for all crimes and offenses to be committed by any of the trayne of the quene or prince." This commission satisfied the Council in that it made the *alcalde* technically a law-officer of the Crown. It was therefore easier for them to grant the concession "that in all punisshementes where the same is to be made extraordinarily and by discretion of the judges, consideration

[36] Weiss (IV, 267-8) prints the fragment and dates it June or July 1554; but the reference to Paget as a person to be trusted places it early in April. cf. with it Renard's dispatch to Charles V of April 3 in Gachard and Piot, IV, 371-80. Philip never specifically acknowledged receiving the memorandum, but it was undoubtedly the "longue instruction envoié en Espaigne" to which Renard referred several months later (Weiss, IV, 292). Tyler (P.R.O., Tyler, p. 493) translates "son altèze désembarquant soit armée *acouvertement*" as "openly"; but I believe the force of the "a" is prepositional rather than privative.

be had to the vsage of the nation of thoffendar." Apparently the two judges did their work well, to judge by the swift justice which was later meted out to Spanish roisterers and English thieves; and since Briviesca continued to exercise his functions for over a year, there does not seem to have been any serious objection to the way he fulfilled his duties.[37]

In view of the threat from France, it was obviously desirable for the English and Imperial governments to gain control of the Channel before Philip's fleet rounded Brittany. Early in April Charles had decided to send fourteen Flemish warships to join an English fleet which was being fitted out under Admiral Howard's direction, and at the beginning of May they arrived at Portsmouth.[38] One reason for their dispatch so early in the spring was Renard's conviction that war between France and England was imminent and that Carew might endanger Philip's passage by a sudden descent on the Isle of Wight. The Emperor hoped that the combined Anglo-Imperial fleet would frighten Henry II and the English fugitives into inactivity, but from beginning to end the venture was something of a fiasco. Only a few days after the juncture of the two fleets, three French warships attacked the two English vessels in which Courrières and Briviesca were crossing from Calais to Dover; the ship which was carrying all their horses and some of their baggage was captured and the other reached Dover only with difficulty. "It was an escape in ten thousand, praise be to God," Courrières wrote Renard; "I hope this adventure is the worst I have left to face, for I am an old dog of sixty-seven." It was incredible that the Channel was so poorly guarded, he added.[39]

There were several reasons why the Anglo-Imperial fleet failed to sweep the Channel clear of French marauders. In the first place,

[37] Articles for a Joint Commission to try offenses in Philip's and Mary's household [May 1554], P.R.O., S. P. Dom. 11, Vol. IV, No. 10; Courrières and Renard to Charles V, 21 and 25 May 1554, P.R.O., Tyler, pp. 423, 426, 433 (Weiss, IV, 245-6, and Tytler, II, 403); Muñoz, *Viaje,* 118, 121; Renard to Charles V, 10 July 1555, Antigny, Tyler, p. 196; *A.P.C.,* V, 54, 58, 60.

[38] Weiss, IV, 230-1; Capelle to Renard, 4 May 1554, P.R.O., Tyler, pp. 381-2.

[39] *For. Cal., Mary,* 23, 88; *A.P.C.,* V, 25; Vertot, III, 214, 246-7; Courrières to Renard, Dover, 10 May 1554, P.R.O., Tyler, p. 396; Courrières to Mary of Hungary, 21 May 1554, *ibid.,* pp. 420-1; Renard to Charles V, 28 June 1554, *ibid.,* p. 483.

both the English and Flemish ships had been victualled for only a few weeks in the expectation that Philip would arrive before the end of May. As time went on Capelle, the Flemish commander, was forced to buy more provisions at Portsmouth, and Renard had to finance the purchases with his own funds until the Regent of the Netherlands was able to send money to Courrières, who went to Southampton at the end of May to direct the arrangements for Philip's landing. To make matters worse, the English merchants at Portsmouth combined to raise the prices of the fish and beer which Capelle was forced to purchase.

The English fleet, meanwhile, had troubles of its own. Howard was a typical Admiral of the English navy's early days, which is to say that he disliked the sea. Week after week he waited in vain for word that Philip had set sail, and as his provisions ran low his men became more and more restive. Finally in June they mutinied, complaining that their meat stank, that their ale was sour, and that while they had signed to serve for only a month, they had already served three. Triumphantly they forced Howard to leave shore and go aboard ship by threatening to desert in a body unless he did so, but a quarter of them seem to have deserted in spite of his compliance. Howard blamed it all on Renard, who had sent the fleet to sea, he said, knowing full well that Philip could not set sail for weeks to come.

Perhaps the most serious aspect of the situation was the continued friction between the two admirals and their men. When the Flemish sailors first came ashore, the English "pushed them about" and laughed at the puny size of their "cut-purse" warships. Howard amused himself by referring to the Flemish vessels as "mussel-shells" and did all he could to get them to return to Flanders. Renard had warned Capelle that Howard would bear watching in view of the fact that he was Elizabeth's cousin, and it was not long before Capelle himself was convinced that the English Admiral was encouraging his men to plunder Spanish as well as French merchantmen while waiting for the Prince's arrival. Most of the friction, of course, was not Renard's fault, but by sharing his suspicion of Howard with the Flemish commander he had done much to aggravate the situation. Philip's fleet was strong enough to ward off any attack by the score or so of French vessels which were at sea, and no useful purpose had been accomplished by the Anglo-Imperial fleet when Capelle sailed home in August, "fat and in fine condition and anxious to be at the French."[40]

Renard himself was as worried by Philip's delay as Howard, and Mary was more distraught about it than either. After she left St. James's for Richmond at the close of May, Renard was well-nigh her only source of strength and comfort. In order to have him near her she asked the Duchess of Somerset to move out of her house and leave it for his use. Rumors reached Noailles in London that Mary was so distracted with anxiety about Philip that she sometimes went out of her head. "This poor love-sick woman," wrote François de Noailles, "does nothing but curse and accuse people, the elements, and even her husband." The French envoys were prejudiced and remote from the scene, but as time went on even Renard feared that the Queen's health might break under the strain.[41]

Several incidents which were eloquent of Philip's tactlessness and ignorance of the English scene made Renard's task more difficult. It did not occur to the Prince to write Mary in his own hand until the middle of May, and it was not till June 20 that the Marquis of Las Navas arrived at Guildford to present the letter to her, together with a diamond which the Emperor had once given Philip's mother.[42] Antonio de Guaras, a Spaniard in Mary's service, had brought the Prince word that he had already been proclaimed King of England, and therefore Las Navas had been given a number of letters for members of the English Council signed "Philippus Rex." Naturally Renard saw to it that the Marquis delivered

---

[40] Letters between Renard, Capelle, and the Imperial court, 22 Apr. to 21 Aug. 1554, P.R.O., Tyler, pp. 363, 381-2, 413, 415, 460-1, 472-4; *ibid.*, second half, pp. 21, 43, 116; Weiss, IV, 270, 271, 274-5; Gachard and Piot, IV, 415-17; Vertot, III, 204, 220.

[41] *A.P.C.*, V, 29; François de Noailles to Montmorency, 19 June 1554 (misdated 9 June), Aff. Etr., IX, fol. 202; Renard to Charles V, 4 July 1554, P.R.O., Tyler, p. 14; Vertot, III, 248-9, 252-3.

[42] Philip to Charles V, 11 May 1554, P.R.O., Tyler, pp. 397-8; Molina to Eraso, 16 May 1554, *ibid.*, p. 418; Renard to Charles V, 20 June 1554, *ibid.*, p. 469.

the "King's" messages to the councillors by word of mouth and that the letters with their offensive signatures were suppressed.[43]

Renard's imagination was still haunted at the end of June by the two fears which had been his constant preoccupation since January: the fear of a popular rebellion touched off by a conspiracy at court, and the fear of a sudden blow from France.

Paget's downfall had not healed the split in the Council, which was growing "wider and wider" thanks to a quarrel between Arundel and two of Gardiner's followers. Worse than this, Paget himself was acting suspiciously. Courtenay had confessed that Sir Philip Hoby and Sir Richard Morison (both ambassadors to Charles V during Northumberland's conspiracy) had been Paget's agents seven months before in trying to persuade him to consider a marriage with Elizabeth; and now Hoby was in Brussels consorting with Sir John Mason, the English ambassador there, while Mason was writing to Paget "every day" by private courier. Renard immediately envisaged some deep-laid plot between Hoby and Mason at Brussels, Arundel and Pembroke in the Council, Clinton and Howard in the armed forces, and several lords who had estates and influence in the North—all planned and directed by Paget, who was spending most of his time at his country house five miles outside London. An "astounding amount of intrigue" was going on among the nobility, Renard gathered. Arundel was still anxious to marry his son to Elizabeth, and Paget was even rumored to be ready to avail himself of French help in case of necessity. Both nobility and people were saying that Charles had arranged the marriage to help himself out of a desperate situation on the continent, "wherefore faces are looking glum and the popular temper is uncertain." Renard was told that the malcontents' plan was to wait till Philip arrived, then to pick a quarrel with the Spaniards, upon which the people would rise. He confided his fears to Mary, whose general anxiety was hardly allayed by this fresh cause for worry, and wrote his master that Paget would be in the Tower "were it not that the Queen is afraid to cause a commotion in the kingdom

[43] Philip to members of the Privy Council [c. 12 May 1554], P.R.O., Tyler, p. 407; Philip to Charles V, 15 May 1554, *ibid.*, p. 416a; Renard to Charles V, 9 July 1554, *ibid.*, p. 21.

when his Highness is just about to arrive." There was one ray of hope, however, in the class antagonism which separated nobility and commons.

If the people were as ready to rise as some of the nobility could wish [he wrote on June 28], there would soon be trouble; but the people are more cautious than they have been in the past, for they see that the nobility care more about their own private ambition than about the public welfare.[44]

Although the people did not stir and although Paget's intrigues (whatever their foundation) bore no fruit, the blow from France did fall—albeit in an unexpected quarter. On June 24 the French army fell with overpowering force upon Marienbourg, the gateway to the Netherlands, and two days later the city surrendered. For a moment it seemed as if nothing could prevent Henry II's victorious troops from capturing Brussels and Liège.[45] Noailles joyfully trumpeted the news throughout London. French prestige was immeasurably increased by the victory, he wrote, and the people were looking forward again to delivering themselves from "the miserable servitude in which their Queen wishes to place them" through Henry's assistance.[46] Renard did his best to explain the disaster by attributing it to treachery, but Mary was in despair, largely because she feared Charles would invoke the Anglo-Flemish treaties of mutual assistance in order to bring England to his rescue.[47]

It was to Spain that the Emperor looked for assistance, however, not to England. While French marauding parties were ravaging the countryside up to the very gates of Brussels and his own forces were gathering with painful delay at Namur, he sent an urgent appeal to his son. He asked Philip to take only a few of his servants ashore with him in England, to hurry through the marriage ceremony, and to sail straight for Flanders after spending six or eight days with his bride. The Prince was warned, however, that he must bring no English soldiers with him and make every effort

---

[44] Renard to Charles V, 20 June, 28 June, 4 July, 9 July, 1554, P.R.O., Tyler, pp. 466-8, 483-5, 14-15, 19-22; Imp. ambs. to Charles V, 8 Aug. 1554, *ibid.*, pp. 94-5.
[45] Decrue, *Montmorency*, II, 151 *ff*.
[46] Noailles to Henry II, 3 July 1554, Aff. Etr., IX, fol. 215.
[47] See Vertot, III, 265-6.

"to keep England at peace and avoid any breaches of neutrality."
In order to make sure that the dispatch reached Philip before he
landed in England, one copy was sent to Corunna, one to the Bis-
cayan coast, and one by land to Valladolid.[48]

*   *   *

One face was conspicuously missing from the company of diplomats and courtiers which followed the Queen on her slow progress
from Richmond to Winchester, where she was to meet Philip.
Noailles took a child-like pleasure in scenes of pageantry and
splendor, and he seems to have been prepared to carry off his presence at the marriage ceremony with the same bravado which he
had displayed in appearing at court immediately after Wyatt's
surrender. But the Emperor was afraid that he might claim precedence over Don Pedro Laso, ambassador of the King of the Romans, and so Renard was ordered to see to it that he was not
invited to Winchester. About the middle of July, therefore, he was
informed by Sir Richard Southwell that the Queen desired him
not to attend her marriage because of the scandal which would
result if he raised the precedence issue; she hoped he would not be
bored by remaining in London until her return, which would be
very soon. Noailles answered coldly that he yielded precedence to
no one but the ambassador of the Emperor himself and that he
considered his exclusion from the ceremony an unfriendly act. He
had been prepared to give out that he was confined to his house
"by a nose-bleed or even by illness" in case his rights were not
recognized, but this direct rebuff rendered futile any pretense of
being indisposed.[49]

Noailles had two consolations, however, during his enforced
retirement in London. One was the prospect of "a great rebellion"
which he was told late in July would break out within two weeks

[48] Charles V to Philip, 29 June 1554, P.R.O., Tyler, pp. 486-9. cf. *Ven. Cal.*, V, 527.
[49] Noailles to Montmorency, 26 June 1554, and Noailles to L'Aubespine, 17 July 1554,
Aff. Etr., IX, fols. 212, 228; Renard to Charles V, 20 June 1554, P.R.O., Tyler, p. 468;
Weiss, IV, 253-4, 269; *Docs. inéds.*, III, 524; *For. Cal., Mary*, 107, 114; Vertot, III,
277-9, 280, 292-3, 301, 314.

and which he was zealously encouraging.[50] The other was the birth on July 5 of his first son.[51]

Noailles had rejoiced, much more honestly than Renard, at Mary's restoration of the mass, and it may therefore have been with some sincerity that he decided to ask her to stand godmother to the child. Perhaps he was not unaware, however, that the event offered a golden opportunity to play upon the Queen's ready sympathies at a moment when her thoughts must have been turning to the time when she herself would know the joy of motherhood. With sure instinct he chose his brother to act as his messenger. François had audience with Mary at Bishops Waltham on July 18, the day she heard that Philip's fleet had been sighted in the Channel. His graceful address would have sounded strangely on Antoine's lips. He spoke of his elder brother's joy and of the illness which kept him from coming to court in person—in fact, the illness was the result of "too much happiness," François supposed.

Since the time when the Christian King, your good brother, sent him as ambassador to your Majesty's court [François continued], God has made clear not only to him but to all the world that because of the great care and deep affection which you have devoted to restoring and reestablishing what pertains to His glory, His honor, and His religion in your lands and domains, He has willed to bless and prosper your affairs in unbelievable felicity, in the midst of your greater troubles and adversities and in the face of human expectations, prudence, and violence; this felicity He has so increased in you and in what concerns you that my brother believes firmly that it is out of the fullness of your happiness that he has received what he enjoys at present.[52]

It was striking evidence of the future Bishop of Dax's gift of tact and the warmth of Mary's starved affections that she was touched by his message. She answered that she would have liked

---

[50] Noailles to Montmorency, 27 July 1554, Aff. Etr., IX, fol. 234. Also Noailles to Henry II, 17 July 1554, *ibid.*, fol. 226; and Vertot, III, 273.

[51] Bib. Nat., f.f., No. 32892, fol. 103; *ibid.*, f.f., nouv. acq., No. 328, fol. 53; Journal of François de Noailles, *ibid.*, f.f., No. 20147, fol. 23.

[52] Aff. Etr., IX, fol. 219. This document, written in François de Noailles's hand, was thought by its eighteenth-century editors to be a letter from François to Mary of about July 6, but it is clear from a comparison of it with several other documents of the same sort that it was a draft of the speech which the author meant to deliver to the Queen. Scheyfve had asked Edward VI to stand godfather to his new-born son in October 1552, but the King refused when he learned that the ambassador wanted the ceremony performed by the old rites (*Span. Cal.*, X, pp. lx, 570-3).

to hold the babe at the font herself were she able to go to London. Since this was impossible she named Gardiner and Arundel as godparents and deputed the Countess of Surrey to represent her at the ceremony. On July 22 the child was baptized in London and received the name of Henry in honor of Mary's father, the scourge of the Church.[53] In years to come the name of Henri, Seigneur de Noailles and Comte d'Ayen, recalled a curious and fleeting reconciliation between his father and the bride of Philip of Spain.

Meanwhile Philip had accomplished his voyage. He had set sail from Corunna on July 13, a copy of his father's plea for help reaching him at sea soon afterward. On Thursday, July 19, the anniversary of Mary's proclamation as Queen, his fleet sighted the English coast, and next day it cast anchor off Southampton. Renard was among those who went out by barge to bring the royal bridegroom to shore, but no details are recorded of their meeting.[54] Nor is there any evidence that the ambassador was consulted upon the crucial question of whether the Prince should leave for Flanders directly after the wedding. If he was asked for his opinion on the subject, it is clear from a dispatch which he wrote a week later that he advised against it. Philip immediately wrote his father that he was ready to hurry on to Flanders. But since the French were wasting time and energy in purposeless ravaging expeditions, it soon became clear that the danger was past. Among other things, Charles wanted Philip to win glory and prestige by taking part in a victorious campaign against the French, and since there was little hope of this in the summer of 1554, he soon wrote canceling his earlier instructions. To make all the capital he could out of the incident, he directed Egmont's brother to tell Mary about his son's brave answer and to suggest that she should be grateful to him

[53] Vertot, III, 281-2. Vertot is wrong in asserting that Gardiner, Arundel, and a great company of notables attended Henri de Noailles's baptism (Vertot, I, 293-5). The Countess of Surrey was the Queen's only representative, Gardiner and Arundel being at Southampton with Philip.

[54] Molina to the Princess Regent of Spain, 18 July 1554, P.R.O., Tyler, p. 32; Ruy Gómez to Eraso, 20 July 1554, *ibid.*, p. 38; a Letter relating Philip's voyage, *ibid.*, 68 A *ff.* (Muñoz, *Viaje*, 87 *ff.*); Philip to the Princess Regent, 2 Sept. 1554, *ibid.*, p. 138; Gachard and Piot, IV, 15 *ff.*; *Docs. inéds.*, III, 519. Philip had originally directed Renard to meet him at sea (Renard to Charles V, 28 June 1554, P.R.O., Tyler, p. 485).

for refusing to allow Philip to hasten to his side. The Queen thanked her cousin humbly "for having so far spared the person of the King."[55]

No word of the Emperor's appeal was allowed to reach the Queen, however, while Philip was resting from his voyage at Southampton over the weekend. On Monday the 23rd he set out for Winchester in a driving rainstorm and that evening he met his bride. Two days later Gardiner performed the momentous rites which Renard had all but perjured himself to bring about and which Noailles had all but disgraced himself to prevent. Mary's eyes never left the Sacrament during the whole ceremony, which lasted an hour. "She is a saintly woman," wrote a Spanish observer. Whether Renard was as deeply moved by the spectacle as others present, we do not know. "The love and devotion toward their majesties," he wrote, "is such that one may expect only a good and perfect union from the alliance." That evening Don Pedro Laso led the ball which inaugurated a week of "such triumphing, banqueting, singing, masking, and dancing as was never in England heretofore," while Noailles watched the bonfires in the streets from his window in London. "God grant," he had written shortly before, "that it may be to the benefit and common weal of the whole of Christendom."[56]

[55] Renard to Charles V, 29 July 1554, P.R.O., Tyler, p. 59 (Weiss, IV, 294-5); Charles V to Philip, 2 Aug. 1554, P.R.O., Tyler, p. 69; Charles V's instructions to M. de Humbermont, 4 Aug. 1554, ibid., pp. 80-3; Mary to Charles V, 15 Aug. 1554, ibid., p. 105.

[56] A Letter relating Philip's voyage, P.R.O., Tyler, pp. 68 A ff. (Muñoz, Viaje, 93-5); Chronicle of Queen Jane, Appendix X; Weiss, IV, 295; Noailles to Bochetel, 16 July 1554, Aff. Etr., IX, fol. 225.

CHAPTER VIII

THE ROAD TO ROME

S INCE our mission is completed," Renard wrote Charles the day after the marriage on behalf of himself and Courrières, "we await your Majesty's good will and pleasure in the matter of our recall." It was as if he were writing *finis* to a fairy tale. Now that the Prince and Princess were safely married, they would of course live happily ever after. But no one, not even Mary herself and certainly not her more prosaic cousin in Brussels, really thought that the tale was ended. The Emperor's reply was that although Courrières might return, Renard must stay on for a time to give Philip the benefit of his "considerable knowledge of affairs and persons" derived from his "long residence and incessant activity in England." Renard protested that he had already given the King all the advice he was able to offer, but it was to no avail. To Charles the work of establishing Habsburg influence in England was not ended, it was just beginning.[1]

Perhaps, as one writer suggests, Renard realized that his work was but half accomplished and that there were fertile opportunities ahead to make himself indispensable both to Philip and to the Emperor in harvesting the fruits expected from the alliance. In this case his request for recall was intended simply to strengthen his hand for the task.[2] Charles was a sick man, and rumor had it that he intended soon to abdicate in favor of his son and finish out his days in retirement. The question which haunted all his Flemish and Franc-Comtois servants, Granvelle no less than Renard, was what would happen to them when Philip became King of Spain,

---

[1] Weiss, IV, 279, 284-6 (this document is overlooked in P.R.O., Tyler), 290, 292; Charles V to his ambassadors, 4 Aug. 1554, P.R.O., Tyler, pp. 78-9.
[2] Tridon, "Renard," 215-16.

Lord of the Netherlands, and ruler of half Italy, as well as King of England. Philip was notoriously Spanish in his feelings and sympathies, and some of his countrymen already resented the prominent part taken by non-Spaniards in negotiating the match with Mary. But Renard considered that he had a better claim to the King's gratitude than almost anyone else in the Imperial service, and the meticulous attention which he had devoted to every detail of Philip's reception in England was evidence of how eagerly he turned to greet the rising sun.

Renard had been too long in England, however, to have any illusions about the thorny path which lay ahead of Philip. He may have realized that the marriage marked the climax of his career and that anything he might accomplish afterward in England would be an anticlimax. Perhaps he already sensed the futility of ever trying to win Philip's favor: if the marriage were a failure— as it might well be—the King would almost surely turn against those who had had a hand in its making. There is no real reason, in fact, to think that Renard's request for recall was anything but sincere.

Renard's fears did not overcome his hopes, however, for some time. During the first few months after the marriage ceremony, Habsburg influence reached its highwater mark in England. Philip had brought enough money with him to buy the temporary favor of councillors and courtiers, and the first impression which he made upon the people was unexpectedly favorable, thanks to the careful coaching of his father and of Renard. He made an honest and pathetic effort to adopt English customs, even to dining in public and drinking beer; and personally he was not altogether unpopular.[3] The fact remained, however, that he was almost as unfitted for the task of governing England as his wife. His stiff dignity, his notorious linguistic limitations, his preference for the written over the spoken word in dealing with subordinates, his distaste for the physical sports so dear to the English, and his narrow Spanish patriotism made it impossible that he should ever win the

[3] Constant, "Mariage," 261-4; *Docs. inéds.,* III, 530-1; Courrières to Charles V, 11 Aug. 1554, P.R.O., Tyler, p. 97; *Eng. Hist. Rev.,* VII (1892), 267 *ff.* See also Appendix II.

hearts of the people, far less the confidence of the ruling class.[4] It was impossible for him to conceal from others his feeling that his presence in England was a distasteful and fruitless exile; and it is significant that all the various plans for making his marriage a political success came from others—from his father, from Renard, or from Paget—not from himself or even from his Spanish favorites.

The inescapable fact which weighed upon the spirits of Englishmen high and low was the presence of the Spaniard in their midst. Just as Charles V and Renard had feared, there were innumerable bloody affrays and "incidents," particularly during the first three months after the marriage. One gains the impression that the aggressors were generally Englishmen, but the Spaniards were not entirely innocent victims of the hatred of their hosts.[5] None of the outbreaks had serious results, but two plots which reached Noailles's ears came perilously close to demonstrating that Habsburg hopes in England were built on sand.

On September 2 a conspiracy was discovered which, had it ripened, might have been associated forever with the event of St. Bartholomew's Eve, 1572. Some hardy spirits planned to surround Hampton Court (where the King and Queen were staying) by night—"contrary to the custom of the English," Noailles remarked —and to slaughter all the Spaniards they found in the palace. Every Londoner who was playing host to a Spaniard was to murder his guest at the same time. Noailles added that Philip, Mary, and their councillors would hardly have escaped the same fate.[6] How much truth there was in the report and how far it spread we do not know, but a month later (October 1) a false rumor that there was a design on foot in London to assassinate all the priests and foreigners threw two thousand Spaniards at Westminster into a panic.[7] A second plot which might have had incalculable results was only revealed a year and a half later. On Sunday, No-

[4] On Philip's character, see Merriman, *Rise of the Spanish Empire*, IV, 19 *ff.*; also *Ven. Cal.*, VI, Part II, 1061 *ff.*

[5] References to such incidents are legion in the diplomatic correspondence of the autumn of 1554. For examples see Constant, "Mariage," 264-71, and Stone, *Mary*, 343.

[6] Advis, 5 Sept. 1554, Aff. Etr., IX, fols. 261ᵛ-262.

[7] Advis, 4 Oct. 1554, Aff. Etr., IX, fol. 275; Stroppiana to Granvelle, 6 Oct. 1554, P.R.O., Tyler, p. 186.

vember 25, a cane spree was staged at Whitehall by the Spaniards
for the delectation of Queen and people. The sport lasted three-
quarters of an hour and Philip pleased his wife by taking part in
it, but "it left the spectators cold . . . and the English made fun
of it." If his own confession many months later can be believed, a
man named Lewkner, who supplied the court with cards and dice
for gambling purposes, had arranged with Sir Francis Verney and
Captain Edward Turner to kill Philip and all his Spanish attendants during the contest. Over three hundred persons, he claimed,
were in the plot, which was to have been executed at the third
round of the game; but only two rounds were run off, so the design was never attempted. The conspirators seem to have lost their
nerve at the last moment.[8] The existing documents afford only
glimpses of these hare-brained conspiracies; but even if we allow
for Noailles's eagerness to believe any tale of sedition which came
to his ears, it is obvious that as the people in general became more
hopeless of avoiding the Spanish yoke, the resolute few were becoming more desperate.

Imperial diplomacy in England was concerned with many
problems in the autumn of 1554—how to seat Philip firmly upon
his new throne, how to persuade the English to allow him to be
crowned (a ceremony of considerable symbolic, if not legal significance), how to reconcile the factions among the councillors, how
to restore the government's finances, reform the administration of
law, and increase the navy. But none was more important now
than that of formally restoring England to the Roman communion.

For a year Charles V had consistently opposed every move of
Mary's and Gardiner's which looked toward the renewal of England's obedience to the Pope, on the ground that the Queen's
marriage and the settlement of the realm were the indispensable
preliminaries. Mary had been assured over and over that her cousin

[8] Advis, 18 June 1556, Aff. Etr., XIII, fol. 20ᵛ. On Lewkner see *Machyn Diary*, 108;
Ven. Cal., VI, Part I, 475, 484; *For. Cal., Mary*, 231. On the cane spree, see *Machyn
Diary*, 76; Relation du jeu de cannes, by Durand, Aff. Etr., IX, fol. 291 (misdated 26
Oct. 1554—see Durand to François de Noailles, 30 Nov. 1554, Aff. Etr., IX, fol. 309);
Langosco to Granvelle, 25 Nov. 1554, P.R.O., Tyler, p. 282; Renard to Charles V, 30
Nov. 1554, *ibid.*, p. 289; Muñoz, *Viaje*, 118, 128.

had only the religious and political good of England in mind in proposing the Spanish match, but it often required all of Renard's tact to explain why the Emperor refused so long to allow Cardinal Reginald Pole, the Papal Legate, to set foot in England. Now that the marriage ceremony was over, there were no plausible arguments for further delay and several strong reasons for hastening the reconciliation. The return of England to the Roman obedience would strengthen Charles's hand in Germany and the Netherlands; it would add to Philip's personal prestige; and above all it might increase Philip's power in England by removing the prevailing uncertainty about the fate of the ecclesiastical lands. Paget had taught Renard the importance of the church land question in the fall of 1553, and the ambassador hardly needed to impress it upon Charles, who knew its history well. Long before the marriage, the nobles knew that they could count upon the Emperor's support if Mary and the bishops should try to make them disgorge the lands which they had acquired when the monasteries fell in Henry VIII's reign. But like later American businessmen who argued in a crisis that their fear was not of "regimentation" but of "uncertainty," the English gentry by the summer of 1554 were showing symptoms of a case of nerves over the vague threat of confiscation which hung over them. All the materials for a serious conflagration were present. Mary's conscience was known to everyone; Philip's devotion to the Church was notorious; Pole made no attempt to conceal his opposition to Henry VIII's alienations; Gardiner was in the saddle and Paget in disgrace. Unless the new nobility were confirmed in their possessions, the road to Rome would be rough indeed and the alliance of Tudor and Habsburg short-lived.

* * *

The Spanish marriage was like some fateful poison which threatened to destroy everyone whose lips it touched—first Paget, then Renard, and finally Mary herself. The rift between Philip and his father's Franc-Comtois ambassador, which began shortly after the marriage and which had widened to a gulf before the latter's tragic death, foreshadowed the process by which the King of England was soon to hispanicize his father's whole administration.[9]

It was natural that the Spanish lords who accompanied Philip to England should be jealous of Renard as soon as they discovered how commanding his influence was with English statesmen and particularly with the Queen. The most outspoken of them was the King's favorite and closest personal adviser, Ruy Gómez da Silva. About a month after the marriage Gómez unburdened himself to Eraso, the Emperor's Spanish secretary, in terms which probably reflected the feelings of most of Philip's followers.

I do not want to injure anyone, but I fear our ambassador's attitude has not always been wise, for from what we have been able to make out, he has taken sides for one of the parties here; and as his influence with the Queen is great, he is able to be of use to some and do serious harm to others. The result is that those who are out of favor are resentful, and one of them is Paget, who, as the ambassador himself confesses, helped him more than anyone else during the marriage negotiations. The King has already done much to remedy this. . . . The Queen is a good soul, but not so able as we were led to suppose—I mean as a stateswoman. The ambassador, far from succeeding in affairs here, gets everything into a muddle, and whereas he ought to be lighting us on our way, he has plunged us into darkness. However, I do not blame him, but rather the person who sent a man of his small attainments to conduct so capital an affair as this match, instead of entrusting it to a Spaniard.[10]

The Emperor's sister, Mary of Hungary, had already criticized Renard's alienation of Paget in a letter to Granvelle; and whether her views were inspired by Eraso or not, Gómez's innuendoes soon reached the Emperor's ears through the Spanish secretary. Granvelle, the "person" referred to, was cut to the quick and found himself reduced to writing his master a labored defense of Renard's and his own conduct.[11]

As time went on, the Spaniards blamed Renard for all the inconveniences incident to their residence in England and even for the national quarrels which were the expected result of the mar-

[9] See L. Febvre, *Philippe II et la Franche-Comté*, 133-5, 157.
[10] Ruy Gómez to Eraso, 23 Aug. 1554, P.R.O., Tyler, p. 118.
[11] Gachard and Piot, IV, 430-2; Weiss, IV, 298-300. Febvre (*op. cit.*, 144) did not see Gómez's letter quoted above and so concluded wrongly that it was Renard, not Eraso and Gómez, who started the slander against Granvelle.

riage. With London landlords merrily raising rents, a serious lodging problem arose which had to be ironed out by conferences between the Duke of Alva, Ruy Gómez, Briviesca, and the English Council.[12] A still more serious difficulty was laid directly at Renard's door. The Council had insisted (and the Emperor had consented) that Philip should be served exclusively by Englishmen, and a list of household and personal servants had been handed to the Prince on his arrival. Since all of them were to be paid by Philip, the scheme was simply one more method of buying the support of some of the nobles and their sons. Naturally Philip and his Spanish servants resented the plan deeply. The English officials chosen behaved rather badly, Sir Anthony Browne having to be removed from the important post of Master of Philip's Horse early in September. The Emperor did all he could to mollify his son's anger and Philip finally consented to keep a few English gentlemen to wait upon his table, but he stuck to it that those appointed to serve his bed-chamber were not "good enough Catholics" to be constantly around his person. Ruy Gómez blamed Renard for the whole incident and persuaded Philip that during the spring while the Emperor was ill, "others" (Granvelle and Renard) had "solicited" Mary and the Council in the matter. At any rate, it was to Eraso, not to Renard, that the King confided his irritations, and it was Eraso who was given the task of solving the difficulty.[13]

The Emperor's Spanish secretary, in fact, almost usurped Renard's position as official Imperial representative in England during the fall of 1554. He had handled the correspondence between Brussels and Spain during the preceding year, and it was natural that Philip and Ruy Gómez should continue to keep in touch with the Emperor's wishes through him rather than through Renard after the marriage. He seems to have persuaded Charles for a time that

---

[12] *A.P.C.*, V, 61-2; Weiss, IV, 317; Renard to Charles V, 3 Sept. 1554, P.R.O., Tyler, p. 142.

[13] See the provision about English servants in the marriage treaty, above, p. 101. *Docs. inéds.*, III, 526-7, 529; Vertot, III, 296; Muñoz, *op. cit.*, 96; Renard to Charles V, 18 Sept. 1554, P.R.O., Tyler, pp. 152 *ff.*; Charles V's Instructions to Eraso [1 Oct. 1554], *ibid.*, pp. 170 *ff.*; Charles V to Eraso, 20 Oct. 1554, *ibid.*, p. 212; Philip to Eraso [14 or 15 Nov. 1554], *ibid.*, p. 259; Advis, 5 Sept. 1554, Aff. Etr., IX, fol. 261. Lists of those appointed to serve Philip in Gachard and Piot, IV, 442-7 (see corrections in P.R.O., Tyler, pp. 495 *ff.*).

neither Granvelle nor Renard were to be trusted, and so when the Emperor decided to take the religious question in hand, it was Eraso himself who went to London with full instructions for Philip. The secretary was told to remind Philip of his father's intention to abdicate as soon as Philip was settled upon the English throne; the Emperor expected that his son would cross to Flanders during the coming winter to discuss all the necessary details. There was no mention of Renard in the instructions. Obviously it was not Charles's intention to take the ambassador into his confidence in the matter of his abdication, however necessary he thought it was to keep Renard in England.[14]

Eraso's talks with Philip are not recorded, but a month later (October 1) he was sent once more from Brussels to London with instructions on the religious problem. By this time, however, Renard had been able to prove his usefulness. The Emperor wrote him that he might be required to assist Eraso and made a few flattering references to his recent dispatches and to his experience of English affairs.[15] In answer to the ambassador's reiterated request for recall, Charles instructed Eraso:

> You will speak to the King about my ambassador in England, and say that I think he ought to give him a pension as a reward for the good service he rendered in the marriage negotiations. The King will think over whether he had better be kept there, and if so in what capacity. . . .[16]

The last phrase suggested the crux of the question. The post of ambassador from a father to his son was an anomaly. Communications between Brussels and London—till now a matter of diplomacy—would obviously become increasingly a family matter and could be handled by secretaries and couriers. Renard probably hoped that he would be called to serve on the Emperor's Council, or perhaps formally admitted to Philip's inner circle of advisers; but Charles left the decision in Philip's hands and the King refused either to dismiss him or to reward him for his diplomatic services by giving him a post of responsibility. For some time to come

---

[14] Charles V's Instructions to Eraso, 1 Sept. 1554, P.R.O., Tyler, pp. 128-33. cf. Weiss, IV, 295-8.
[15] Charles V to Renard, 1 Oct. 1554, P.R.O., Tyler, p. 169.
[16] Charles V's Instructions to Eraso [1 Oct. 1554], P.R.O., Tyler, p. 176.

Renard was to endure the humiliation of serving as adviser to a master who turned elsewhere for counsel whenever possible.

In depending upon Ruy Gómez rather than upon Renard for guidance, Philip made a natural but serious mistake. Within a month after the marriage, Gómez was so angry about the way Philip was being treated by the Council and so worried about his safety that he was making arrangements (perhaps behind his master's back) to spirit the King out of the country in case the situation did not improve. He told the Admiral of Castile that Philip felt "oppressed" and that means ought to be devised for getting him out of England and "setting him at liberty." When the fleet returned to Spain, the Admiral suggested to the Spanish Council that some ships be sent to England on the pretext of transporting troops to Flanders; Philip could go aboard on the excuse of reviewing the fleet, then either sail for Flanders or stay aboard until the English consented to let him live "as befits their King and sovereign Lord."[17] The favorite talked so freely at court about Philip's displeasure and resentment that his words reached Noailles and probably many others outside the palace as well.[18] Renard's one concern, on the other hand, was to keep Philip in England and to make his stay a success. In spite of his pessimism about the state of public opinion, he never tired of pointing out to the Emperor that unless Philip stayed in England at least until the religious question was settled and perhaps until he was crowned, the diplomatic efforts of the past year would prove to have been wasted.[19]

In a word, the undercurrent of tension after the marriage between Philip's Spaniards and his father's French-speaking servants did much to destroy the unity and singleness of purpose which normally characterized Habsburg diplomacy.

[17] Molina to Philip, Valladolid, 13 Sept. 1554, P.R.O., Tyler, pp. 148-9. On August 27 Pedro de Hoyo wrote Molina from Hampton Court, "Ruy Gómez tells me that his Majesty wishes you to have a boat placed at his disposal so that he may return without delay" (ibid., pp. 123-4).
[18] Noailles to Henry II, and Advis, 5 Sept. 1554, Aff. Etr., IX, fols. 260, 262.
[19] Weiss, IV, 294-5, 319, 320.

The negotiations between Rome, Brussels, and London which led to England's reconciliation with the Papacy have attracted the attention of many writers and need not be detailed here.[20] Since Julius III, Charles V, and even Pole himself realized that the recognition of Henry VIII's land settlement was a political necessity, the diplomatic problem really reduced itself to the question of modifying the brief which the Pope had sent Pole on June 28, 1554, empowering the latter to absolve England from schism and to confirm the lay owners under certain conditions.[21] The English Council offered three objections to the brief when its contents became known: (1) the document was dated before the marriage and yet referred to Philip as King; (2) the authority granted to Pole was not explicit enough; and (3) cases of particular gravity could be referred upon Pole's initiative to Rome. Renard noted these deficiencies with his usual perspicacity the moment he received a copy of the brief from Pole late in August. He saw that it was the Pope's intention to have Pole consider each case of alienated property separately and on its own merits, granting dispensations to those holders for whom Philip and Mary interceded, and reserving for papal decision all "important" cases. He pointed out that the Catholics in England held more church property than the heretics and that they would never consent to the reconciliation unless they obtained a general dispensation. He said he sympathized with the Pope's fear that England's return to the fold might appear to be purchased at a price, but remarked, cynically perhaps, that "the loftiest issues of religion ought to be considered in preference to a mere question of church property."[22]

The situation was critical enough to give point to Renard's warnings. During August the friction between the two factions in the Council was as bad as ever, Paget was still reported to be hatching conspiracies at his country house, agitators were attempting to rouse the people of London against the Spaniards, and wild rumors were flying about the city. It was said that thousands of

[20] See in particular, L. Pastor, *History of the Popes*, XIII, 270-89; and *Ven. Cal.*, V, Preface.

[21] Copy of the brief in Weiss, IV, 264-6.

[22] Renard to Charles V, 3 Sept. 1554, P.R.O., Tyler, pp. 144-6. The Papal Nuncio at Brussels shared Renard's sentiments (*Ven. Cal.*, V, 589).

Spanish troops had landed in the South, that the monasteries were to be restored, and that the clergy were about to take their revenge on the heretics, backed by Spanish steel. The landed gentry were openly threatening trouble if Pole entered the realm without a clear guarantee that no church lands in private hands would be restored; and when the writs went out in September for a new Parliament, it was felt necessary to send letters to the sheriffs and lords-lieutenant ordering them to assure everyone that the Queen intended no "alteration of any particular man's possessions, as among other false rumors is spread abroad." In the face of all these dangers, Pole was pressing the Emperor for permission to cross the Channel as Papal Legate, and Gardiner was trying to persuade Philip that it would be perfectly safe to admit the Cardinal "when the hot weather was over." "Neither the Council nor the Parliament ought to be allowed to dictate in this matter," Gardiner argued, "for they would never consent to his coming at all." "The Chancellor is very hot and wants to settle the matter at once," Renard complained; "the truth is I do not see how it can be done."[23]

The issue was drawn clearly enough. The lay nobility were determined that the reconciliation should be a business bargain between Parliament and Pope; the clerical party was equally determined that it should be the work of ecclesiastical authority alone, in form at least. There could be no doubt about where the Emperor stood on the issue, and scarcely less doubt about the need for utilizing Renard's experience in dealing with it. The efforts of Pole and Gardiner to save the Pope's face were doomed from the start, and the earliest signs of their defeat were Renard's presence at practically all the important conferences on religion and (even more significant) Paget's return to the political arena.

When the King and Queen made their formal entry into London on August 18 Paget was present; and when it came time for the lords and councillors to retire to the country after the festivities, he went to the Queen and apologized humbly for the error of his

---

[23] Renard and Courrières to Charles V, 8 Aug. 1554, P.R.O., Tyler, pp. 92-5; Renard to Charles V, 3 Sept. 1554, *ibid.,* pp. 142-6; Weiss, IV, 281-4, 286-8, 325-8 (this last document should be dated August, not October 1554).

ways. After a brief retirement he was back at court early in October taking a prominent part in the religious negotiations; a month later Renard was reminding the Emperor of how much Paget had done for the marriage and remarking that he was "a man of great experience."[24] It was certainly not Mary or Renard, distrustful as they were of his loyalty, who helped the chief promoter of the marriage to climb back into favor. Probably it was Arundel and his other friends in the government who suggested that he swallow his pride and return to his place at the council-table, where his leadership was needed if the clergy's zeal were to be curbed. But his strongest boost came from the Emperor's sister and from Ruy Gómez, as we have seen. Charles shared his sister's views about Paget's ability, and Eraso may have had something to do with the fact that Philip admitted the fallen councillor to the conferences on religion soon after the secretary's second trip to London.[25] Within a short while Paget and Renard were once more working in harmony upon a problem in which their views were in exact agreement.

In all the letters which passed between London and Brussels, there was never any reference to the Queen's wishes on the subject of the reconciliation, the matter above all others closest to her heart, but in a sense she was the most important person in England during the fall of 1554. If she could but conceive a child, Philip's position would be immensely strengthened, Parliament might be persuaded to consent to his coronation, and the religious settlement might be put through on the inevitable wave of sympathy for a Queen who was to become a mother. Renard saw all this clearly enough, and when one of Mary's physicians told him about the middle of September that the Queen was "very probably with child," he was quick to spread the rumor and wrote the Emperor,

---

[24] Renard to Charles V, 3 Sept., 18 Sept., and 6 Nov. 1554, P.R.O., Tyler, pp. 142, 157, 222; Weiss, IV, 320, 331.

[25] In the original minute of Mary of Hungary's letter to Granvelle of 14 Aug. 1554 (P.R.O., Tyler, p. 103), the following phrase was crossed out: "especially as I remember hearing his Majesty [Charles] say that he would be very sorry were Paget to allow himself to be seduced, and that he thought this expedient [winning Paget back by reward] ought to be tried without delay." On October 20 Charles wrote Eraso that he was pleased to hear Philip was "making ready for treating the religious question with the assistance of Paget, who has returned; he is the right man . . ." (P.R.O., Tyler, p. 212).

"If it is true everything will calm down." The doctor assured Emmanuel Philibert's ambassador that "if it were not true all the signs described by physicians would prove to be fallacious." Two weeks later Philip confirmed the news to his father, and Ruy Gómez wrote, "All is on the right road . . . ; this pregnancy will put a stop to every difficulty."[26] The word soon spread through the city and there were those who laughed at it, saying the rumor was a calculated device of the government to facilitate Philip's coronation. But even Noailles, who agreed with the scoffers, had to admit that by the middle of October a curious calm had settled upon London. The rumor of Mary's condition had done its work, aided by the advent of "cooler weather." The English were speaking more softly of their unwelcome guests, the Spaniards were holding their heads higher, Spanish gold and social festivities at court were helping to cool the tempers of the English nobles as they returned from the country, and Renard was more optimistic than he had been for months.[27]

Coincident with this change for the better and with Paget's return to the council-board, Renard was suddenly entrusted with a mission of the highest importance. Philip and his father had agreed in September that Pole should not cross the Channel until "more of the leading men of the country and a larger section of public opinion" had been won over, and until the Pope had been induced to grant a new brief "in precisely the form we have submitted to him." By mid-October the first condition seemed to have been met, and Philip had dispatched a messenger to Rome to aid his father's ambassador there in bringing Julius III to terms. Charles was determined that nothing should be left to Pole's discretion when he arrived in England; the Cardinal was only "to confirm the agreements already arrived at."[28] But Philip thought it would be well in the interim to make sure that Pole himself understood exactly what was expected of him. On October 12 he decided to send Renard to Brussels, probably at the ambassador's own sugges-

---

[26] Renard to Charles V, 18 Sept. 1554, P.R.O., Tyler, p. 157; Langosco to Granvelle, 19 Sept. 1554, *ibid.*, p. 158; Ruy Gómez to Eraso, 2 Oct. 1554, *ibid.*, p. 181.

[27] Advis, 22 Sept. 1554, Aff. Etr., IX, fol. 264; Noailles to Vendôme, 20 Oct. 1554, *ibid.*, fol. 287; Weiss, IV, 317 *ff.*; *Docs. inéds.*, III, 532.

[28] Charles V's Instructions to Eraso [1 Oct. 1554], P.R.O., Tyler, pp. 170 *ff.*

tion. Suffering from gout, anxious to present his request for recall
to the Emperor in person, and confident of his ability to persuade
the unworldly Cardinal of the importance of worldly matters,
Renard set out in haste a few days later and arrived at the Emperor's court on the 20th, just after Philip's courier to Rome had
passed through.[29]

It was a busy and profitable week which Renard spent in Brussels. His two conferences with Charles V, followed in each case by
a conversation with Pole, cleared the way for the formal invitation
from Philip and Mary which opened the gates of England to the
Cardinal. Granvelle had already told Pole the exact changes in
the original papal brief which the English demanded, and Renard
(who had undoubtedly helped in drafting the Council's terms)
explained their significance in "a long and apposite discourse." He
enlarged upon the history of Mary's difficulties since her accession,
the stiff-neckedness of the lay landholders, and the need for
worldly compromise. He drew from Pole a promise that he would
not enter England as Legate and that he would follow the advice
of Philip and Mary in everything. It was hard for the Cardinal to
renounce his convictions about the land question, but Renard had
already learned the art of soothing tender consciences in his long
association with Mary. He pointed out that the present landowners
were protected by the Statute of Praemunire in any case, and that
Mary intended at least to restore the church lands held by the
crown; the reconciliation might appear to be "bought," but unless
England returned to the Roman fold, "King Philip and Queen
Mary could not long hold the Crown." When Pole said that Renard had brought him hope, Renard replied that he had brought
certainty—and Pole, his "oil of patience" almost exhausted, was
pathetically grateful.[30]

Philip was not entirely satisfied by the report which Renard
sent to London of these conversations. Pole had assured the ambassador that even if the new brief did not reach England in time,
the Pope had promised to confirm everything his Legate did in

[29] Philip to Eraso [12 Oct. 1554], P.R.O., Tyler, p. 188; Mary to Charles V, 16 Oct.
1554, ibid., p. 204; Charles V to Manrique de Lara, 18 Oct. 1554, ibid., pp. 206 ff.;
Charles V to Philip, 20 Oct. 1554, ibid., p. 211.
[30] Ven. Cal., V, 581-90.

a brief of the year before, a copy of which had been sent to Mary. Philip immediately referred the whole question to "competent persons," who agreed that Pole's powers were still not "explicit" enough and that the Pope's intentions appeared to be "fluctuating." There was no time to lose. Parliament, summoned for November 11, could not be postponed until the arrival of the new brief, if only because Pole's attainder had to be reversed at the earliest opportunity. So the King summoned some Spanish friars and some members of "both councils" (the phrase is significant) to meet with him and the Queen, and presented the difficulty to them. In view of Pole's assurance to Renard that Julius III would certainly grant the new brief, it was agreed that Philip "might without conscientious scruple take the matter into his own hands," i.e. pledge the Pope's indulgence to the lay landholders in advance.[31]

As soon as Renard returned to London and gave his verbal report, the English Council consented (on November 3) to summon Pole, and four days later Paget and Sir Edward Hastings were sent to escort the Cardinal across the water. Arundel, Pembroke, and some others whose attitude was "dubious" had previously been won over, and Renard was so encouraged by the political atmosphere—and by the fact that Mary's dresses no longer fitted her—that he suggested to the Queen that she have the matter of Philip's coronation proposed to Parliament. Philip wrote Eraso that in his "toilsome negotiations with the interested parties great and small," he had been only "the instrument"; "the guiding impulse" had come from his father—and from God.[32]

On Saturday, November 24, Pole's barge made its way up the Thames to the steps of Westminster Palace and there the Cardinal was greeted by Philip and Mary. "Both," wrote an observer, "shed tears and the Queen felt her child move, so it may well be said, 'exultavit infans in utero pius.' "[33] In private conversation Philip made clear to Pole what was expected of him and on the following Wednesday the Cardinal addressed the members of Parliament

[31] Philip to Eraso [14 or 15 Nov. 1554], P.R.O., Tyler, pp. 256 ff.
[32] Philip to Eraso (above); and Renard to Charles V, 6 Nov. 1554, P.R.O., Tyler, pp. 222-3.
[33] Langosco to Granvelle, 25 Nov. 1554, P.R.O., Tyler, p. 282.

assembled at the Palace for almost an hour. He praised the Queen and gave "still higher praise," said Renard, to the King; he referred to the marriage (which had troubled him so deeply) as "a miracle and the work of God"; and he assured the members that his powers were "so ample that Parliament would be well-satisfied." The courier from Rome bringing the corrected papal brief had, in fact, arrived just an hour before the Cardinal faced his audience.[34] Te Deums were sung in every London church for the Queen's pregnancy, and the next day Parliament passed a petition for reconciliation with Rome. On St. Andrew's Day, the 30th, Pole formally absolved the realm from schism in an elaborate and colorful ceremony. Catholics the world over rejoiced that England, in the words of Gardiner's text the following Sunday, had awakened from her slumber.

*   *   *

During the "toilsome negotiations" which led to the reconciliation, Paget, Renard, and the Emperor were giving a great deal of thought to the political problem.

When Paget was in Brussels waiting to conduct Pole to London, the Emperor invited him to a long conversation à deux on the state of England (November 12). The two had met before, but there was some embarrassment on both sides while the Englishman was explaining his recent disgrace. Finally Paget launched into a lengthy analysis of what was wrong with the English government and how Philip could remedy it. He had always been convinced that the Spanish alliance alone could save his country from internal disorder and French aggression, and now he had a heaven-sent opportunity to tell the Emperor himself how he thought the alliance might be made a benefit to both nations. When the Queen came to the throne, he said, she had been forced to reward many of her personal followers with appointments to the Council, as well as to retain many of her brother's appointees; "the result was

---

[34] Renard to Charles V, 30 Nov. 1554, P.R.O., Tyler, pp. 287 ff. The brief was dispatched from Rome on Nov. 7 (Julius III to Charles V, 7 Nov. 1554, ibid., p. 226), and Philip remarked that it was "even ampler in form than we had asked for" (Philip to Manrique de Lara, 6 Dec. 1554, ibid., p. 306).

that England, which had always been a monarchy, was now governed by such a crowd that it was much more like a republic." The only remedy, "given the Queen's gentle character and inexperience in governing," was for Philip to take over the task of ruling, with the assistance of a small Privy Council made up exclusively of Englishmen. Those best qualified to sit on this reduced Council, he suggested, were himself, Arundel, Clinton, Admiral Howard, the Bishop of Norwich, and above all Petre, "who was as good as a Council register and reminded the members of everything that had occurred in the past"; Gardiner, "a better hand at stopping up a dangerous hole than at preventing the hole from being pierced," had best be excluded. In exercising its judicial powers, this Council should "deal mildly with the nobility and use, if necessary, a certain amount of severity with the common people, whose nature it was to be rebellious." In religion, all would be well if only the nobles were not disturbed in their possessions and if Pole played no favorites. With proper care the financial chaos could be set right in eighteen months: the trouble was "lack of method." Now that the Queen was with child, there was no reason to keep Elizabeth and Courtenay in confinement any longer since their influence would soon disappear; Elizabeth could be married off to "some poor German prince" and Courtenay could be sent off to Rome to present England's submission to the Pope. Finally, it was high time, he said, for Philip "to take his sword in hand, grow hardened to the heat and cold of campaigning, defend his subjects, and strike terror into his foes," with the help of English volunteers. When Charles protested that he had been very careful not to drag England into the war, Paget replied that "the scruple was most praiseworthy," but that "English troops would certainly strengthen his forces" and that the Anglo-Flemish treaties allowed him to call upon England for help.

In sending Renard an account of Paget's suggestions Charles took serious exception to some of the Englishman's points, but he agreed heartily with his main thesis—that Philip must make the task of governing England his own personal and special care— "for the object of the marriage is that he should do so." The best example which Philip could follow, Charles thought, was that of his great-grandfather Ferdinand of Aragon, the husband of Isabella of Castile: Philip's aim "should be so to act that while he in reality does everything, the initiative should always seem to proceed from the Queen and her Council." Reduction of the Council's membership was "a somewhat invidious, though necessary step"; certainly no Spaniards should be included in the new body, but Gardiner was too important to be dropped. Paget's advice on the administration of justice was obviously "meant to bolster up the nobility" and care must be taken not to alienate the people, who seemed to be devoted to Philip and Mary. But Paget was right on the religious question, Charles thought: it was well to remember how the apostles bore with the weaker brethren until they grew firm in the faith, and how Ferdinand and Isabella went about the reduction of the Moors in Granada. To marry Elizabeth to a German prince whose estates were near the sea would be dangerous, but to send Courtenay to Rome on such a mission as Paget suggested would be a good way to discredit him with the Protestants. Finally, it was too early, Charles warned, to launch England upon rearmament; a full treasury was the primary need.[35]

Renard was still suspicious of Paget's motives, especially with regard to Elizabeth and Courtenay; and in discussing the Emperor's account with Philip (as he was ordered to do), he was severely critical of the proposal to reduce the Council's membership. He pointed out that the scheme had been tried six months before and that it had had to be abandoned because of the resentment of Gardiner's friends.[36] To raise the issue now would be to invite serious trouble since Paget's trip to Brussels had reawakened Gardiner's jealousy; Paget openly coveted Gardiner's seals, Arundel had his eye upon the Treasurership, and the Catholics in the Council were in enough of a panic as it was. Renard was in hearty accord with Paget's remaining suggestions, however, and reminded Charles that he had already mentioned many of them himself.[37]

[35] An account of the negotiations at Brussels of Lord Paget, 14 Nov. 1554, P.R.O., Tyler, pp. 243-55. A copy of this document was sent immediately to Renard; another went to Philip by Paget himself (Weiss, IV, 334).

[36] See pp. 147-8, 169.   [37] Weiss, IV, 340.

THE ROAD TO ROME

Sometime in December Renard drew up a comprehensive memorandum of his own on the subject of England's place in Habsburg *Weltpolitik* and submitted it to Philip. The burden of it was that since God had brought affairs in England to such a happy issue—true religion restored and the Queen with child— Philip should turn his attention to his wider responsibilities as Charles V's prospective heir. The Emperor's health was failing rapidly, the resources of all the Habsburg dominions (with the possible exception of Spain) were nearing exhaustion, and there was no immediate prospect that the King of France would offer honorable terms of peace. So Philip must somehow make use of England's resources to restore his family fortunes. He must call upon English troops and ships to help him redress the balance on the continent, with or without a declaration of war. But only an England well-governed, prosperous, and devoted to its King would be of any use to him in such a venture. Therefore he must arm himself with the two necessities of war, "good counsel and money." The present Lord Treasurer, Winchester, was capable of straightening out Mary's finances (Renard confessed that finance was "not part of his profession," but he knew a good business head when he saw one).[38] Good counsel, however, was even more important than a well-stocked treasury. Philip must have counsellors who were "prudent, tried, sedate, mature, and loyal"; and before leaving England he must appoint a man of credit and authority to represent him during his absence and to serve as *liaison* between the Queen and her Council—a delicate hint, perhaps, that Renard himself was the right man. The King should join his father in the Netherlands as soon as possible, but not before the close of Parliament and not until both Queen and people thoroughly understood why it was necessary for him to leave England.[39]

[38] On the work of "this extraordinarily able administrator" as Treasurer, see F. C. Dietz, *English Public Finance, 1558-1641* (New York, 1932), 6, 19-21, 30-2.

[39] Weiss, IV, 359-67. The document was written some time before Parliament definitely rejected the proposal to crown Philip about January 9, 1555 (Vertot, IV, 137). Although unrelated to the English problem, Renard's efforts to induce Philip to settle the differences between the German and Spanish branches of the Habsburg family are worthy of note (Weiss, IV, 322-3, 343-5).

Obviously Philip had no lack of "good counsel," even if his counsellors had some difficulty in agreeing among themselves. Perhaps Charles V, Paget, and Renard all had a premonition that once the religious problem was settled, Philip would lose what little interest he had in governing England. If so, the premonition was correct. Eraso, who trumpeted Philip's wisdom and virtues in Brussels upon his return from London in November, was convinced that "in truth the King had greatly changed."[40] But the King's inmost feelings about England and the English had not changed. Even before Pole arrived in England Philip's attention had begun to turn across the Channel, to Flanders, Germany, and Naples. He wrote Eraso that he wanted to see his father by January at the latest and remarked that it would be easier for him to leave Mary now that she was with child. He wanted the Flemish to get to know him before his father left the country and hoped Charles would see to it that there were no unpleasant incidents upon his arrival, as there had been the last time he visited Brussels. He confessed that for some years past he had wanted to lead a campaign and hoped his chance would come as soon as possible, provided the Emperor made sure that his first military adventure would be a success.[41] In 1554 the "Prudent King" of later years was a young man eager to find a more fertile field than England could offer for his political and military talents; and Renard had some reason to remark eight years later that England would never have fallen to such low estate (from the Habsburg point of view) if Philip had followed the advice offered him.[42] The closing months of the year were the turning-point of his career as King of England. Up to the reconciliation his prestige rose fairly steadily, but after that it began to sink.

* * *

In spite of Spanish enmity, Renard had managed to make himself indispensable to Philip in the matter of religion, if not in that of political counsel. Before he was definitely relegated to idleness

[40] Eraso to Ruy Gómez, 29 Nov. 1554, P.R.O., Tyler, p. 286.
[41] Philip to Eraso [14 or 15 Nov. 1554], P.R.O., Tyler, pp. 258 ff.
[42] Renard to Philip [1562], Weiss, V, 22.

and futility, he served the King well in one more sphere—in Parliament.

While he was in Brussels at the end of October, he had begged the Emperor once more to allow him to leave his post in England. Charles had consented subject to Philip's approval, but had written his son that it would be well to keep Renard in London until Parliament finished its work.[43] It was fortunate that Philip followed his father's advice. Mary's third Parliament has been called the "least unsatisfactory" of all her parliaments. The sheriffs had been enjoined to return members of the "wise, grave, and Catholic sort," and as Paget remarked to the Emperor in Brussels, the "right men" had been called up. But when the "right men" reached Westminster, the government had considerable difficulty in inducing them to vote the right way.[44]

It was of the highest importance to Philip's European prestige that his first Parliament should pass all the measures proposed to it. Renard therefore advised him strongly not to propose any bills which might arouse serious opposition. In a further attempt to be useful, the ambassador sketched out what he thought should be the main points of the speech from the throne. He advised Philip to say that he intended to prove to the members that he was "not only the husband of the Queen but the spouse of their republic" by following their advice in everything. He should add that he meant not only to observe the marriage treaty "but also to ward off all innovations likely to menace the ancient customs and liberties of the land." The members would repeat his words throughout the country and the good impressions thus created would be lasting. Apparently Gardiner gave the speech on November 15 in much the form which Renard had suggested and the ambassador was pleased with the results.[45]

In spite of, or perhaps because of his desire to get to Flanders as quickly as possible, Philip gave parliamentary affairs almost as

[43] Charles V to Philip [25 Oct. 1554], P.R.O., Tyler, p. 215; Renard to Charles V, 14 Nov. 1554, *ibid.*, p. 238.

[44] Weiss, IV, 324; Vertot, III, 348-9; Account of Paget's Negotiation, 14 Nov. 1554, P.R.O., Tyler, p. 249. See the general accounts in Pollard, *Pol. Hist.*, 126-31, and in R. W. Dixon, *History of the Church of England*, IV, 287 *ff*.

[45] Renard to Charles V, 23 Nov. 1554, Weiss, IV, 341-2; and inclosure, Renard to Philip, c. 12 Nov. 1554, P.R.O., Tyler, p. 277.

close attention as he had given the arrangements for the reconciliation. He seems to have followed Renard's advice that he attend all Council meetings at which any important bill was discussed, "to keep the requisite hold on so large, turbulent, and discordant" a body.[46] At any rate, he did his best to obviate some of the difficulties connected with translating the religious agreement into law. But in spite of Renard's warning, there was too much "must" legislation in the government's program, and the result was a confused and complicated series of parliamentary maneuvers which are still difficult to understand, despite the new light cast on them by Renard's unpublished dispatches.

Gardiner's party in the Council wanted to revive the heresy statutes, recover as much land as possible for the Church, exclude Elizabeth from the succession, and keep England out of the continental war in order to facilitate the restoration of the Church at home. Their strength in Parliament lay among the "wise, grave, and Catholic sort" in the lower house. Paget's party, on the other hand, feared the revival of clerical power and the loss of their abbey lands. Some of them were attracted by the glory and reward which a war with France would bring them, and a few (including Paget himself) foresaw that a foreign war would take the clergy's minds off the abbey lands. Since most of them were peers, their strength lay in the House of Lords. The result was a twofold struggle: an open difference of opinion between Lords and Commons, embittered by class feeling; and a more subtle conflict within the lower house itself between those who put their religion first and those who thought in purely secular and national terms.

The bill which revived the fifteenth-century statutes against heresy passed both houses before Christmas without much difficulty, although Renard reported that there was some grumbling in the upper house.[47] But there was more difficulty over the famous bill "repealing all statutes, articles, and provisions against the See Apostolic of Rome . . . *and also* for the establishment of all spiritual and ecclesiastical possessions and hereditaments conveyed to the laity." The landholders in both houses wanted the papal dispensation included in the statute itself. Pole threatened to return

---

[46] Renard to Philip, c. 12 Nov. 1554, P.R.O., Tyler, p. 277.   [47] Weiss, IV, 347.

to Rome if this were done, and some members of the Commons who owned no abbey lands moved that no dispensation whatever should be granted to the lay holders. The clerical party found lawyers to argue that there was no need to mention the land settlement at all in the act because the kings of England had always had jurisdiction over ecclesiastical lands since time immemorial. Philip tried in vain to persuade the leaders to compromise the matter by passing two separate acts, but the nobles and gentry eventually had their way. The bill passed during the second week of January, "not without great difficulty," Renard reported.[48]

During the third week in December while the debates on this bill were in progress, the Lords sent down to the Commons a bill (defeated in the previous Parliament) which extended the protection of the treason laws to Philip.[49] The Commons immediately rejected it on the ground that it did not give the King all the protection he deserved, and proceeded to write one of their own. The new bill gave Philip the guardianship of Mary's children in case the Queen died leaving issue under age, in addition to granting him in more explicit form the same protection which the Lord's bill gave him. At one point it was even moved to give Philip the crown if Mary died without issue.

This uprising in the Commons in favor of Philip's rights was led, strangely enough, by Sir John Pollard, who had presented the petition against a foreign marriage as Speaker of Mary's first Parliament, and by a lawyer named Brown.[50] Curiously diverse motives inspired these leaders and the majority which

---

[48] Weiss, IV, 346-7; Renard to Charles V, 12 Jan. 1555, Antigny, Tyler, p. 3; Vertot, IV, 36.

[49] Summary of the bill as rejected by the Commons, enclosed in Renard's dispatch of 21 Dec. 1554 to Charles V, P.R.O., Tyler, p. 329.

[50] There were four members of this name: Sir Anthony Brown, the Queen's Master of Horse, whom Philip removed from the same office in his own service; Robert Brown, alderman (Colchester); Robert Brown (Nuportburgh in Cornwall), possibly the same person; and Ralph Brown (Warwick borough). A Robert Brown was one of the thirty-seven members who withdrew from Parliament on January 12 (see below, p. 221), and I think it likely that he was the person mentioned. It may, however, have been Sir John Brown, a resident of Oxfordshire like Pollard and apparently a friend of the latter's; there is no record of his being a member of this Parliament, but the returns for Banbury in Oxfordshire are lost. (*Official Return of Members*, Part I, 389-91; *A.P.C.*, V, 146.)

rose to back them. The Commons themselves told Philip that they had been influenced by his gracious conduct as King and particularly by his speech from the throne.[51] But Renard heard that the Catholic knights and burgesses who had no church plunder in their possession were nettled by their failure to make the nobles disgorge their abbey lands and seized upon this opportunity to retaliate upon the House of Lords. Whether Gardiner backed the movement in order to get revenge on the "heretics" is not clear. He knew about the Commons' bill and resented the fact that Philip communicated affairs of state to him only after they had already been settled; like those in the lower house who were afraid that certain peers were trying "to get the government into their hands," the Chancellor feared that Paget was trying to take the seals away from him. There were indications, however, that the Commons liked Gardiner's leadership as little as they liked the Lords'. Renard heard a rumor that "certain intriguers," "rather French partisans than Imperialists," had drafted the new bill with the object of splitting opinion and thereby of defeating Gardiner's proposal that Elizabeth be declared a bastard.[52]

When the Commons referred its bill to a committee a reaction began. During the holidays Petre, Rochester, and Englefield went to Renard at Mary's request and read him a copy of the committee's draft. Evidently Gardiner's friends had been at pains to conciliate national sentiment because the new draft provided for a sort of regency council consisting of six earls, six barons, and six bishops; Philip was to have the guardianship of his children after Mary's death, but he could not convoke Parliament, declare war, or arrange a marriage for his heir or heirs without the consent of these eighteen peers. Renard objected tactfully but firmly to several features of the amended bill. To designate Philip

---

[51] Address to Philip and Mary, in Petre's hand, n.d., P.R.O., S.P.Dom. 11, Vol. V, No. 2 (together with a draft of the Commons' bill in Latin, *ibid.*, no. 1).

[52] Renard to Charles V, 21 Dec. 1554, and Renard to Philip [end of Dec. 1554], P.R.O., Tyler, pp. 326-8, 335-40. Weiss (IV, 345-9, 357-9) prints most of the first dispatch, but only an insignificant fragment of the second. These two letters constitute the only contemporary account which we have of the incident. They throw a flood of light upon the attitude of both houses, but they leave many questions still unanswered because Renard, intelligent though he was, never thoroughly understood the issues himself.

as guardian of the heirs was more of "a declaratory act than anything necessary" since all law recognized that the proper guardian of a child was its father. It would be more to the point to give the father the management of the child's property, i.e. to give Philip the government of the realm during a minority. The regency council was a dangerous scheme, he intimated. Before the peers could be called together to consent to a declaration of war, the kingdom might be invaded, "wherefore such a condition might serve to encourage the enemies of the realm to attack it"; Philip meant to consult the leading men of the country in any case, and the marriage treaty already contained every necessary safeguard. Every attempt Renard made to discover "who was responsible for the bill, who drafted it, in what mood it was conceived, and whether it contained anything else" was frustrated; and Petre burned a Latin summary of it which he had begun to write out but refused to leave with the ambassador.

If Renard can be believed, the situation was serious. Alva and Ruy Gómez liked the Commons' bill less than the Lords'. The Lords were determined to throw out the new bill partly to prevent the lower house from usurping what they considered to be a function of the Privy Council, partly to keep several of their own number from being nominated to the proposed regency council. Members were forming sides in anticipation of trouble and people were arming.[53]

Two other questions added considerably to the heat of the controversy: the question of Philip's coronation, and the perennial problem of Anglo-French relations. Although Renard did not think it absolutely necessary, a proposal that Philip be crowned had been submitted to Parliament at his own suggestion. About January 9 it was unanimously rejected in the Commons.[54] The members were ready enough to give Philip the future shadow of a crown in the shape of a regent's rights, if only to guard against any recurrence of the feudal violence which characterized the reign of Edward VI; but they were unwilling to give him its

[53] Renard to Philip [end of Dec. 1554], P.R.O., Tyler, pp. 335-40.
[54] Weiss, IV, 341; Vertot, IV, 136-7; Ven. Cal., VI, Part I, p. xxxv.

present substance for fear he might use it as an excuse to drag
England into war with France.

The Commons had good reason to fear that the government,
or at least some of its members, wanted war. When Paget and
Sir Edward Hastings returned from Brussels with Pole, they told
a friend of Noailles's (without a shadow of truth) that the Emperor had urged them to draw England into the war. Perhaps
to frighten the French ambassador, they added that they thought
Mary would agree.[55] Noailles refused to be frightened—a quick
thrust from Scotland would keep the English from doing any
harm on the continent, he thought, and an open breach would
clear the atmosphere—but he was nevertheless concerned by the
reports which an anonymous English informer was sending him
from Parliament.

A request has been made to them in Parliament [this informer wrote on
December 16] to wage war against the King of France in favor of the
Emperor, their ancient friend and ally. This has been absolutely refused
by a great number of the members, both lords and commons (*commun
poeuple*). But the Queen and her Council, seeing that they cannot persuade
the people to do this, have stirred up a great number of men who share
their opinion and bear them favor, and have had them come into the
presence of the Houses, [where] they have cried out and asked the Queen
and her Council to provide them redress for the fact that during recent
years they have been pillaged and robbed at sea of all their goods by the
French and can get no justice or recompence from the King of France,
praying and desiring permission and leave, in the form of letters of marque,
to take their recompence from these subjects of the King of France.[56]

The letters requested had been secretly granted, the writer continued, "in order to envenom and inflame the hearts of the English people against the French." A little later a peer introduced
a bill in the lower house proposing that it was "reasonable for
the son to succor his father," but the Commons promptly rejected
it as a step toward war and a violation of the marriage treaty.[57]

[55] Noailles to Henry II, 30 Nov. 1554, Aff. Etr., IX, fol. 308 (cf. Vertot, IV, 26-8).
[56] Mémoire d'Angleterre, 16 Dec. 1554, Aff. Etr., IX, fol. 327. The author of this
communication may have been either Edward Randall or Sir John Leigh. cf. Vertot,
IV, 113.
[57] Vertot, IV, 76.

During the fall the English government had been officially posing as "honest broker" between France and Spain in an attempt to arrange a peace settlement on the continent, and there is no indication that either Philip or Renard gave any official encouragement to the warmongers. But Paget apparently wanted war, and the King's Spanish advisers may have thought that a threat from England might help bring the French to terms. In any case the agitation for war was not spontaneous, it was staged. True, hatred of the foreigner was stronger among the middle classes than among the nobility, as Soranzo noticed;[58] and Philip was more popular in the Commons than he was in the Lords, partly because the middle classes were traditional supporters of the monarchy against the feudal nobility. But the middle classes feared the effect which war would have upon trade, and the knights and burgesses had come to hate the Spaniard in their midst more heartily than the Frenchman across the sea.

The crisis reached its climax during the second week of January. Several of the principal nobles (including Arundel, Pembroke, and several peers from the North of England) had absented themselves from the House of Lords on various pretexts. Renard heard that they had dodged voting on the regency bill in order not to prejudice the lords' right to appoint a Protector in case of need, but Noailles may have had something to do with the action of the northern peers.[59] On January 12 thirty-seven members of the lower house took the unprecedented course of returning to their homes before the end of the session in protest against the government's policies.[60]

The storm finally blew over, but Philip's prestige had suffered a severe blow. The treason and regency bill was altered to meet Renard's objections by a committee of both houses and passed in the closing days of the session. Philip was given the government of the realm as well as the guardianship of his children during their minority, the regency council was dropped, and a

[58] *Ven. Cal.*, V, 544. cf. the remarks of Ruy Gómez (*Docs. inéds.*, III, 531) and of Paget (Account . . . , 14 Nov. 1554, P.R.O., Tyler, p. 249).

[59] Renard to Charles V, 17 Jan. 1555, Antigny, Tyler, p. 6; *Amer. Hist. Rev.*, XLV (April 1940), 549-50.

[60] Edward Coke, *Fourth Part of the Institutes* (London, 1669), 17-21.

clause was added reaffirming the articles of the marriage treaty.[61] An attempt by Gardiner to induce the members to agree to a benevolence and a final attempt by Secretary Bourne to get a declaration of war both failed, and on January 16 Philip and Mary went down by water to dissolve the Parliament. According to Noailles, they made no attempt to conceal their displeasure about the results of the session.[62]

Mary's third Parliament is of interest to the historian for two reasons. By restoring the papal jurisdiction and the statutes against heresy without restoring the church lands, by providing against feudal anarchy in case of a future minority and yet refusing to crown Philip, and by resolutely refusing to go to war in the Habsburg interest, it mirrored the opinions of the average middle-class Englishman of Tudor times, his interest in matters of the purse and his lack of interest in religious doctrine, his distaste for a war which would disrupt trade and his faith in monarchy as the only stable form of government. It also proved that the Tudor constitution was unworkable and that packing the House of Commons was a futile expedient when Crown and Council had not one, but many conflicting objectives to pursue. If Philip and Mary, Gardiner and Paget, Renard and Ruy Gómez had all thought alike, the initiative displayed by Sir John Pollard and his followers would have been unthinkable.

* * *

The most important effect of the reconciliation with Rome was the triumph of clerical reaction. Events of the previous spring had shown that Gardiner's party had a way of thriving upon parliamentary defeat, and in January 1555 the substance of victory went once more to the Chancellor, in spite of the parliamentary triumph of his enemies in the matter of the church lands. Stung by the Lords' refusal to disgorge their possessions, Mary was all the more determined to restore the ecclesiastical property which had remained in the hands of the Crown as an example to the lay owners. Furthermore both she and her Chancellor were convinced that firm enforcement of Parliament's permissive leg-

[61] *Statutes of the Realm,* 1 and 2 Philip and Mary c. 10; Vertot, IV, 153-4; Renard to Charles V, 12 and 17 Jan. 1555, Antigny, Tyler, pp. 3, 6-7.
[62] Vertot, IV, 149, 154-5; Advis, 8 Feb. 1555, Aff. Etr., IX, fol. 365.

islation against heretics would remove the chief source of sedition in the realm. Since only the Catholics in the Council could be trusted to carry out these two objectives, Gardiner and his followers were finally in a position to carry out the policy of political conciliation and religious severity which they had long been advocating in opposition to Renard and Paget.

On January 18, two days after Parliament rose, the Council met in the Tower and released a dozen prisoners who had been implicated in Wyatt's rebellion, among them Sir James Croft, Sir Edward Rogers, and Sir Edward Warner. They were told that they owed their freedom to Philip and his father, and undoubtedly Philip had a hand in the affair. But among the councillors present at the meeting not one was of the "Imperialist" faction, and there is no indication that either Renard (who made no mention of the incident) or Charles V had anything to do with their action.[63] When a committee of the Council was appointed a short while later to supervise the restoration of the church property held by the crown, only friends of the Chancellor's were appointed, in spite of an attempt by some of Paget's party to gain membership and sabotage the whole transaction.[64] Shortly after the release of the political prisoners, Gardiner summoned a group of Edwardine divines to his house for examination, and on February 4 the first Protestant martyr went to the stake. The spectacle of notorious traitors like Croft gaining their liberty while popular preachers like John Rogers were wending their way to Smithfield was naturally one which troubled Renard as much as it pleased Noailles.[65]

After the dissolution of Parliament, in fact, Renard felt more keenly than ever that he must shake the dust of England from his feet if he were to preserve his reputation—if not even his life. Gouty and utterly dejected, he composed a lugubrious letter to Charles V asking again that he be recalled. The heretics hated him for bringing the papists into the realm, he wrote, and Elizabeth's friends hated him for introducing the Spaniards. Paget had told him that some of the Duke of Northumberland's relatives

[63] *A.P.C.*, V, 90-1; Vertot, IV, 146-7; *Machyn Diary*, 80; Wiesener, 305-6.
[64] *Ven. Cal.*, VI, Part I, 11, 27.   [65] Weiss, IV, 399-400; Vertot, IV, 173, 177-8.

and friends had hired four assassins to kill him at his own dinner-table, and he was convinced that he would not live long after Philip left England. With some exaggeration he claimed that he had been excluded from all affairs of state except the religious question "for the past six months," and added a jealous refer-ence to Ruy Gómez (who had made two trips to Brussels during the parliamentary crisis). Before he sent the dispatch off, however, he toned down his complaints, omitted the names of his enemies, and suppressed the reference to his banishment from Philip's counsels.[66] Granvelle had tried in vain to get him appointed to the Privy Council of the Netherlands—the objections were his gout and his ignorance of Flemish—but did manage to get him a second promise of recall.[67]

Meanwhile the ambassador did everything he could to stop the religious persecutions. The day after Rogers "broke the ice" Renard wrote Philip a vigorous letter urging that the bishops' zeal for heresy-hunting be curbed. Judging by the demonstration of popular sympathy at Rogers's execution, he said, England would soon be in the throes of rebellion unless the bishops were told that there were more politic ways of dealing with here-tics—such as imprisonment, banishment, or "secret executions." Philip seems to have acted immediately upon the ambassador's advice. On February 10 one of the King's Spanish monks in-veighed against the use of force in dealing with heretics in a vigorous sermon at court, and for a few weeks afterward the executions ceased. After presiding at the trials of the first few victims, Gardiner himself took no further part in the prosecu-tions.[68] But within a month the fires were lighted once more,

[66] Renard to Charles V, 10 Feb. 1555 (minute in Weiss, IV, 399-402; original dis-patch in Antigny, Tyler, pp. 22-3). Also Renard to Charles V, 19 Jan. and 3 Feb. 1555, Antigny, Tyler, pp. 9, 21.

[67] Weiss, IV, 369, 406.

[68] Renard to Philip [5 Feb. 1555], Antigny, Tyler, p. 24; Wiesener, 324-5. cf. J. M. Stone, Mary, 364-5, and see below, p. 258. On Feb. 10 Renard wrote Charles V, "Mes lettres escriptes, l'on a remonstré aux évesques qu'il ne convenoit précipiter les choses de la religion; et selon ce j'entens qu'ilz ne procederont plus oultre." (Antigny, Tyler, p. 23.) On Gardiner's part in the trials, see Muller, Gardiner, 269, 284.

to continue sporadically during the rest of the spring in spite of repeated objections from Renard.[69]

Neither Renard nor Noailles ever showed the slightest sympathy for the martyrs' cause. Noailles often seems to have pitied the victims as human beings, but he was "a very good Christian," as Henry II once remarked to the Count of Lalaing, and he could never condone the error of heresy itself. Once he prayed God to show Mary "the true way" of saving heretics—by persuasion rather than by force—but in the last analysis he considered questions of "celestial and temporal sovereignty" beyond his concern and ken. To him as to Renard, the victims of the Catholic reaction were pawns in a political chess game in which the stake was foreign domination of England.[70]

As spring succeeded winter, the religious persecutions engendered a series of local risings in the southern and eastern counties, and Renard believed that another major rebellion in favor of Elizabeth and Courtenay was imminent.[71] For the moment, concern about the future of Habsburg interests in England overcame his worry about his own health and safety, and in spite of his longing to return to Brussels he even considered offering to stay on at his post because of the seriousness of the situation.[72] Sometime in March he composed another of his long memorials on the state of the realm for Philip's perusal. Since the King was to leave England soon, he wrote, every effort must be made immediately to reform the administration, quiet the people, and settle the question of the succession. Otherwise every advantage originally expected from the marriage would be irretrievably lost.

[69] On March 27 Renard wrote Charles V that he had already sent Philip "several memoirs" about the burnings (Antigny, Tyler, p. 37; Weiss, IV, 402-6 prints most of this dispatch under the date, February 1555). See also Weiss, IV, 395, 397.

[70] Vertot, IV, 177-8; Advis, 1 June 1555, Aff. Etr., IX, fol. 453; Noailles to D'Oysel, 3 July 1555, ibid., fol. 464; Noailles to Bassefontaine, 7 Apr. 1556, ibid., fol. 615; Advis, 22 May 1556, ibid., fol. 643; Lalaing to Philip, 11 Apr. 1556, Antigny, Tyler, p. 255.

[71] See the references in Pollard, Pol. Hist., 142, note 6. Also Renard to Charles V, 13 Mar. 1555, Antigny, Tyler, pp. 31-2; and Weiss, IV, 402-3, 422-3.

[72] On March 27, 1555, after Ruy Gómez had brought the long-sought order for his recall, Renard drafted a postscript to his dispatch of that date saying that he did not wish to shirk his duty and would stay on in England if requested (Weiss, IV, 406). But the postscript was omitted from the dispatch as it was sent to Brussels (Antigny, Tyler). The interpretation put upon the dispatch by Tridon ("Renard," pp. 232-3) is therefore untenable.

Renard realized clearly that good government in Tudor England
depended upon the harmony and loyalty of the Privy Council,
and once more he urged that the Council's membership be reduced to about seven in the interests of efficiency. Again he
suggested that the heretics be treated with the mercy "which
the Church has always used," and again he pointed out the importance of restoring the government's finances. But his most
interesting suggestion was that in case Mary bore no heir the
succession should be settled upon Elizabeth, on condition that
she marry Emmanuel Philibert of Savoy. The Duke would be
popular in England as no Spaniard, Frenchman, or German
could be; he would curb Elizabeth's heretical tendencies; and
his lost estates in Savoy would offer England an excuse to declare
war on France. Only thus could Mary Stuart be excluded from
the succession and the English people made to forget their heresy
and disloyalty.[73]

We do not know how much attention Philip paid to Renard's
advice, but the fact was that few of the ambassador's suggestions
bore any fruit. As the belief grew that Mary would soon become
the mother of an heir to the throne, the government's policy of
clemency to political offenders reached its climax. Early in April
Courtenay was released and sent to Brussels; shortly after his
departure Elizabeth was brought from Woodstock to the palace
at Westminster. Renard openly regretted the almost simultaneous release of the two most dangerous persons in the land and
hinted plainly to Charles V that the Council's action was the
result of logrolling between the rival factions and of Philip's
intervention. When Gardiner urged Courtenay's release, Howard
argued that as much should be done for Elizabeth; when Courtenay was sent abroad, Gardiner argued that Elizabeth too should
be got out of the realm. After Gardiner, accompanied by Shrewsbury, Arundel, and Petre, had tried to induce the Princess to
withdraw to Flanders voluntarily, Philip seems to have settled
the matter by advising that she be allowed to remain until after

[73] Weiss, IV, 393-9. Internal evidence indicates that the document was written about
the same time as Renard's letter to Charles V of 27 Mar. 1555 (Weiss, IV, 402-6; and
Antigny, Tyler).

the Queen's lying-in. A rumor even reached Noailles that the King was planning to preserve Habsburg control in England by marrying Elizabeth himself in case Mary died in childbirth.[74]

One thing at least was clear by the end of April: Renard's usefulness in England was at an end. The gulf between his and Philip's views was now too wide to be bridged. On some matters such as the heresy trials and the importance of making sure of Elizabeth in case the Queen should die, the two were in fair agreement. But there was a certain inflexibility in Renard's thinking, which was increased by his exclusion from Philip's inner counsels; furthermore, all of his proposals—the imposition of a strong hand upon the Council, Elizabeth's marriage to a disinherited prince whose loyalty to Habsburg interests was not yet proved, and breaking the marriage treaty by drawing England into the war—presupposed a monarch less governed by caution than Philip. Discouraged by the King's indifference to his advice and disheartened by the growing conflict between Flemish and Spanish interests within the Habsburg Empire, Renard apparently decided that since the Spanish marriage had profited Charles V's cause so little, it would be best to take advantage of the current peace negotiations and to come to terms with France while yet there was time.[75]

England was once more a member of what Sir Thomas More had called "the common corps of Christendom," and her statesmen were already engaged in the task of restoring peace among the disjointed members of the European body politic.

[74] Renard to Charles V, 13 Mar., 21 April, and 6 May 1555, Antigny, Tyler, pp. 33, 67-9, 74-5; Weiss, IV, 405; Instructions to La Marque, 7 May 1555, Aff. Etr., IX, fol. 445; Wiesener, 305-16.

[75] See Renard to Charles V, 21 April 1555, Antigny, Tyler, p. 68; and Vertot, IV, 312-13.

CHAPTER IX

THE QUEST FOR EUROPEAN PEACE

AUGUST 1554 TO JUNE 1555

*W*HILE England was on the road to Rome under Spanish guidance, French diplomats had not been idle. Philip's trials and tribulations after his marriage did not obscure the fact that French diplomacy had suffered a major defeat when he became King of England. The King of France, it is true, still retained the military advantage which he gained by the capture of Metz, Toul, and Verdun two years before, but the future was not bright. The threat of English intervention was a danger which Henry II might belittle but could hardly ignore, especially after his army began to fritter away its advantages during the latter part of August 1554. A few months or a year hence Philip might be able to throw the resources of his new kingdom into the war and France might lose everything she had gained. It was not the first or last time that the European balance of power seemed to depend upon England's decision.

If he were to capitalize upon his temporary military superiority when Philip landed in England, Henry II had two courses open to him: the execution of a swift and determined blow at Philip's position supported by English malcontents on both sides of the Channel, or the negotiation of a peace treaty consolidating the gains France had already made. Either course, consistently followed, bade fair to remove the future threat from England. Noailles, sanguine as ever about the malcontents' strength, was strongly in favor of the first; Montmorency inclined to the second; but Henry II, encamped with his army and still hopeful of winning a decisive victory on the Flemish frontier, was unwilling to give all his attention to the English problem and to stake everything upon its solution. The result was a compromise. France, it was decided, was not so strong that she could risk a preventive war against England, nor so weak that she must come to terms with the Emperor in fear of future English intervention. There was a good chance of French victory on the continent if only England could be kept out the war for the time being, and this could be done by curbing Noailles's zeal for intrigue, by encouraging Mary and her Council to resist any Spanish attempt to break the marriage treaty, and above all, by talking peace. Neither Mary nor her people wanted war, but they could not refuse to help Philip forever; a proposal from France, however insincere, that England assume the rôle of peacemaker would offer English statesmen a way out of their dilemma.

After the marriage Noailles was so strongly convinced that immediate solution of the English problem was the *sine qua non* of French triumph in Europe that he could see no advantage in a policy of compromise. He wanted Henry to turn his attention from the "east" to the "west," from Italy, Germany, and the Levant to England, the real key to French hegemony in Europe as he saw it.[1] He begged Montmorency to take advantage of the rising English hatred of the Spaniard, to invite Sir Peter Carew back from Venice, where he and other English refugees had fled, and to support a descent by the survivors of Wyatt's rebellion upon the English coast. The English were a changeable people who loved revolution, he wrote; the most discredited exiles had often returned to England's shores in triumph "with very little aid and help from the foreigner, even the French"; the only stimulus which the people now needed to put Courtenay and Elizabeth upon the throne was the leadership of Carew "or some other person of quality."[2] All the "valiant men" of the country were ready to rise against Philip, he added, but they would not stir without leadership and help from abroad. Hence it was important to thwart the efforts which Wotton was making to win back the English fugitives in France by offers of pardon.[3]

[1] Vertot, III, 317-18.
[2] Noailles to Montmorency, 10 Aug. 1554, Aff. Etr., IX, fol. 247.
[3] Noailles to Montmorency, 26 Aug. 1554, Aff. Etr., IX, fol. 256.

For the most part, Noailles's entreaties fell upon deaf ears. Montmorency ordered Odet de Selve, French ambassador in Venice, to keep Carew in good humor and wrote Noailles to watch out for an English refugee named Edward Randall who was returning to England on the strength of a general pardon in order to stir up what trouble he could in the French interest.[4] But both Montmorency and Henry II were too busy campaigning in August to pay much attention to Noailles's suggestions.

Randall arrived in London on August 17 with letters of recommendation from Wotton to Philip and Mary.[5] About a month later he sent an anonymous letter to Noailles saying that the discontented nobles and commoners were confidently expecting the aid of their friend, the King of France, in expelling the Spaniard from England. A few days afterward he went to Noailles's house and presented his case in person, with "vehemence and ardor." If Henry II would only take Carew into his service, put him at the head of fifteen hundred English refugees and Gascon musketeers, fit them out with three or four ships, and send them across the Channel, Randall was sure they could rouse the whole country to revolt and pack Philip and his Spaniards out of England. Noailles replied cautiously. He reminded his enthusiastic informer that the leaders of Wyatt's rebellion had proved an untrustworthy lot: Pickering had gone to Wotton after his flight to France and Croft had betrayed to the Council the fact that D'Oysel and Noailles had promised him French support. But Randall's "ardor" was apparently contagious. Noailles wrote Montmorency that the patriots in England were helpless without support from France, but if they were "led, supported, and strengthened a very little by the King's prudence and forces," they could easily send Philip back across the sea in shame and confusion.[6] We have already seen that a curious calm settled upon London about the middle of October, and one of the first effects which Noailles noticed was that Randall, who

---

[4] Montmorency to Noailles, 17 Aug. 1554, Aff. Etr., IX, fol. 248.

[5] Vertot, III, 306-7; *For. Cal., Mary*, 113.

[6] Noailles to Montmorency, 4 Oct. 1554, Aff. Etr., IX, fols. 273-4. Randall's letter to Noailles is enclosed in Noailles's dispatch to Montmorency of 22 Sept. 1554, *ibid.*, fol. 271. See also *Amer. Hist. Rev.*, XLV (April 1940), 549 ff.

had moved into the house next door to his, dared not communicate with him any longer. A dispatch soon came from Montmorency warning the ambassador that there was no apparent "firmness and resolution" in Randall's scheme and ordering him not to commit himself any further.[7] Reluctantly, Noailles turned from thoughts of intrigue to thoughts of peace.

* * *

The peace negotiations which began in London in the fall of 1554 and which eventually resulted in a short-lived truce between the warring continental powers have little intrinsic interest for the modern reader. As often in the history of diplomacy, the human energy expended seemed entirely out of proportion to the results—a brief suspension of hostilities in a war which did little to change the course of history. But the long and tiresome quest for European peace was an important phase of the struggle between Habsburg and Valois to dominate England during Mary's reign. Like Americans faced with war in Europe, Englishmen prayed for peace or for continuation of the war across the sea depending upon their personal interests and their conception of the nation's good; and like the belligerents of 1914 or 1939, France and Spain adapted their diplomacy so far as possible to the aim of winning over or of neutralizing the power which might turn the balance.

Broadly speaking, the English government wished to see peace restored on the Continent, while the English people had no such desire—a fact which Noailles had noticed before and which he reported again in September.[8] Mary, Gardiner, and Paget honestly wanted peace. War was as hateful to Mary's deeply religious nature as it was to Cardinal Pole's, and she sensed clearly enough that the war on the Continent would eventually rob her of her husband's presence, draw England into hostilities with France, and perhaps destroy the religious restoration which she had begun. Gardiner and Paget both hated the French, but each of them knew England's need for internal recovery; settlement of the

[7] Montmorency to Noailles, 17 Oct. 1554, Aff. Etr., IX, fol. 286; Noailles to Montmorency, 20 Oct. 1554, *ibid.*, fol. 288.

[8] Advis, 22 Sept. 1554, Aff. Etr., IX, fol. 264.

quarrel on the Continent would give Gardiner the chance to reorganize the nation's religion and Paget the opportunity to reorganize its government. But many an Englishman, especially those who hated the Pope and the Spaniard, believed that England would suffer if the Emperor and the King of France ceased cutting each other's throats across the Channel. Many of Noailles's friends expressed the fear that, once Charles V's hands were free, he would turn upon England with irresistible force and fasten the Habsburg yoke upon the island kingdom for generations to come.

The English government had already made several unsuccessful attempts to bring the belligerents together. A few weeks after her accession Mary had sounded out both sides and in September 1553 Gardiner had formally proposed English mediation. Two months later after the Chancellor had lost his influence with the Queen, Paget revived the proposal, mainly to quiet the fears of those who predicted that Mary's marriage to Philip would drag England into war. The failure of these efforts was understandable. The King of France was not unnaturally suspicious, as both Montmorency and Noailles pointed out, of a mediatrix who was half-Spanish by birth and wholly Spanish in her sympathies. Early in 1554 the Pope had tried his hand at negotiating a settlement through Cardinal Pole, who was eager to make himself useful while waiting for Charles V's permission to enter England. Here, however, the shoe was on the other foot. Pole's frank dislike of the Spanish marriage blinded Charles and Granvelle to the sincerity of his motives, and the terms which he brought from Paris to Brussels in April were contemptuously rejected. On the whole, the Imperial government was just as suspicious of papal mediation as the French government was of English; and the fact that both Pole and Mary were notoriously innocent of the world and its ways did little to inspire confidence on either side in the possibility of a settlement.[9]

Papal and English efforts to effect a settlement were brought closer together in the summer of 1554 when Pole, recognizing

[9] The history of these efforts at mediation may be followed in *Span. Cal.,* Vol. XI; *Ven. Cal.,* Vol. V; *For. Cal., Mary;* and Vertot, Vols. II and III.

his own failure, asked Mary to renew her earlier offer of mediation. For a short while after the French capture of Marienbourg in June and before Philip's arrival in England there seemed to be a real likelihood that Charles V would sue for peace. During the year past it had been a regular part of both Renard's and Noailles's strategy to spread reports of the enemy's exhaustion and desire for peace, and Noailles was particularly active in trumpeting the Emperor's weakness in London during July. But when Pole's messengers reached Mary at Farnham, Renard effectually discouraged her from making any move, and a few weeks later he persuaded Philip himself to block an attempt of the Cardinal to write Montmorency on the subject of peace. Renard's advice, combined with a turn for the better in the Imperial army's position in the Netherlands, induced Charles V to play a waiting game and to leave the next move to the French.[10]

It was Noailles, in fact, who was responsible for the next overtures, although his part in their inception was quite accidental. On August 21, three days after Philip and Mary made their formal entry into London, he went to pay his respects to the royal bride and groom. After a few words with Mary, he was presented to Philip by Gardiner. It was an embarrassing moment. Philip had granted the ambassador audience not as the son of Henry II's archfoe but as King of England, and Noailles had come upon his own responsibility without letters from his sovereign. An unfriendly observer reported that he stumbled for words, and the cold formality of his address was indistinguishable from sarcasm to the King, who understood French but could not speak it. Noailles expressed the hope that Philip would keep England at peace with France and that the marriage would lead to a settlement of the war on the Continent, as the Queen had often assured him it would. In replying for the King, Gardiner passed over the ambassador's reference to English mediation and said that Philip would keep his new kingdom out of the war "so long as it was to England's advantage and benefit." Noailles was not

[10] See *Ven. Cal.*, V, 505-7, 569; *For. Cal., Mary,* 92-3; Vertot, IV, 42; Weiss, IV, 275-6 (should be dated 9 June 1554), and 288; Renard to Charles V, 9 July 1554, P.R.O., Tyler, pp. 18 *ff.*; Pole to Montmorency, 24 July 1554, *ibid.,* p. 41 (the letter which Philip vetoed).

encouraged by this phrase, but he gathered that the English would resist any attempt to drag them into an open declaration of war for at least a year.[11]

On the last day of August François de Noailles left London to report the results of this interview to Henry II. When he reached Compiègne a week later, he found King and Constable in a far less bellicose frame of mind than they had been a few months before. The French campaign in the North had been disappointing, the cold weather was coming on, and Protestant revolts had broken out in three French towns. Montmorency, supported by François's account of the state of affairs in England, seems to have persuaded Henry that it was an auspicious moment to open negotiations for peace in London. Mary and her Council could be counted upon to bring pressure on Philip, and Philip might be able to persuade his father that the interests of England and the Netherlands required peace. Henry might thus gain better terms than if he waited until Philip had established his power in England, and even if the negotiations failed, England would be kept out of the war so long as her King and Queen were officially acting as mediators. François was instructed, therefore, to return to London and to open the subject to Gardiner in private. He was to suggest that if Gardiner would persuade Philip and Mary to offer their mediation, Montmorency, who admired Gardiner as a fellow-lover of peace, would persuade Henry to accept their good offices.[12]

When François reached London on October 6, however, he discovered that his brother was in no mood to talk peace. About a week before, the ambassador had been forced to move house for the fifth time since his arrival in England, this time from Bridewell to the Deanery of St. Paul's. He had made it clear to the Council that he considered the order for his removal an imposition; his winter provisions had already been stored in Bridewell, and he resented the "pain, inconvenience, expense, and humiliation" of moving. He was convinced that the Council

[11] Vertot, III, 305-6, 308-11; Weiss, IV, 296; Renard to Charles V, 3 Sept. 1554, P.R.O., Tyler, pp. 143 ff.

[12] Journal of François de Noailles, Bib. Nat., f.f., No. 20417, fol. 23ᵛ; Vertot, III, 331-7.

intended to fill Bridewell with Spanish troops and munitions in order to overawe the City.[13] His temper had been further ruffled by a quarrel with Admiral Howard over the fact that some French warships were prowling about the Dover-Calais passage in the hope of capturing some of the numerous Spanish and Imperial dignitaries who were continually crossing the Channel. Knowing Howard's temper, he had been outwardly conciliatory, but privately he had rejoiced that the incident seemed likely either to provoke England to a declaration of war or to force Philip to sue for peace. The captains of the French vessels soon apologized, but not before Henry II had rebuked Noailles for his bellicose feelings; Montmorency's letter ordering him to drop his dealings with Randall was in the same packet.[14] Convinced that neither the English nor the Spaniards were ready to talk peace and that François's mission had little hope of success if the Emperor got the impression that the French were suing for terms, he refused to allow his brother to approach Gardiner and asked Henry to send letters of credence addressed directly to the Queen, whom he considered to be more sincerely interested in peace than the Chancellor. Until the letters arrived almost a month after François returned to London, the ambassador kept his brother confined to his house under excuse of illness.[15]

On Sunday, November 4, the two brothers finally presented their letters to Mary and Gardiner. François supplied the tact and finesse which his elder brother always lacked in dealing with the Queen, and Antoine remarked naïvely upon how pleased she was when François told her that Henry II sympathized with her joy in the presence of "the one you love." Gardiner, too, was unusually gracious and promised that Mary would do all she could to bring the belligerents to an agreement. Next day he invited both brothers to dinner and François acted out his rôle

[13] Antoine to François de Noailles, 21 Sept. 1554, Aff. Etr., IX, fol. 267; Noailles to Henry II, 22 Sept. 1554, ibid., fol. 269; Noailles to Montmorency, 22 Sept. 1554, ibid., fol. 270; Antoine to François de Noailles, 6 Oct. 1554, ibid., fol. 278.

[14] Vertot, III, 337-45; IV, 2; Weiss, IV, 321; Montmorency to Noailles, 17 Oct. 1554, Aff. Etr., IX, fol. 286.

[15] Noailles to Montmorency, 6 and 20 Oct. 1554, Aff. Etr., IX, fols. 279, 288. It was probably a remark of Mary's to Howard during a dance which suggested to Noailles that she would be a better instrument of peace than Gardiner (Vertot, III, 339).

of personal emissary from one peace-lover to another. The Constable, he said, had opposed the war from the start; it was "sundry young lords" at the French court who had persuaded Henry II to break with the Emperor; if Gardiner would persuade Philip and Mary to act as mediators, Montmorency would come to London in person to forward the negotiations.[16]

Gardiner was obviously impressed by these proposals, but they had almost exactly the effect which Antoine de Noailles feared they would have upon the enemies of France. Philip and Renard thought that they were either a cloak for French intrigue or part of an attempt to discover whether England meant to declare war, while others of the King's advisers inferred that the French were suing for peace through dire necessity. Renard was given the task of drafting Gardiner's reply. He advised the Chancellor to remind François de Noailles of Montmorency's caustic remarks in the past about Mary's prejudice as a mediator, and to point out that since the marriage, the Queen of England was vitally interested in any territorial settlement on the Continent which might prejudice the rights of her heirs. Gardiner followed out Renard's advice almost to the letter, but he left the way open to further conversations by suggesting to François that Pole would be the ideal mediator after his arrival in England, especially if the French still suspected Mary's motives. When François left London on November 18, both he and his brother were sure that they could at least count upon Mary and Gardiner, if not upon Philip, to further the cause of peace.[17] Meanwhile an unofficial French agent had gone to Brussels and begun direct conversations with the Emperor, but the talks served only to prove that neither side was yet willing to come to terms and that London was still the logical place for exploratory negotiations.[18]

[16] Vertot, III, 353-8; Speech of François de Noailles to Mary, 4 Nov. 1554, Aff. Etr., IX, fol. 293; Journal of François de Noailles, Bib. Nat., f.f., No. 20417, fol. 25; Renard to Charles V, 14 Nov. 1554, P.R.O., Tyler, pp. 234 ff.

[17] Vertot, IV, 4-13; Renard to Charles V, 14 Nov. 1554, and Renard's draft of a reply to François de Noailles, P.R.O., Tyler, pp. 234-9.

[18] The agent was Nicholas de Vaudemont, Governor of Lorraine. On his mission see For. Cal., Mary, 132-5; Weiss, IV, 344, 370; Vertot, IV, 12, 43, 67-8, 89-90; Renard to Charles V, 30 Nov. 1554, P.R.O., Tyler, p. 287; Charles V to Philip, 7 Dec. 1554, ibid., p. 309.

QUEST FOR EUROPEAN PEACE

When Parliament met on November 11 the peace talks languished and Noailles relapsed into his earlier mood of cynical disillusionment about the possibility of a settlement. Everything he heard convinced him that there was a determined campaign afoot to drive England into war with France, a prospect which he considered with some equanimity, as we have seen. Once more he was turning to intrigue; once more he advised Henry to reenforce the French garrison in Scotland; and once more he expressed his belief that an open breach would clear the air.[19] But his government emphatically refused to share this belief. Henry wrote bluntly that war must be avoided at all costs and Montmorency told him to employ "all the five natural senses" to defeat the warmongers. Both agreed with an earlier suggestion of Noailles himself that the best way to keep England neutral was to pursue with Pole the conversations already begun with Gardiner.[20]

Noailles had, in fact, approached Pole on the subject of peace the day before the ceremony of reconciliation, but the results had been discouraging. The Cardinal still felt the sting of Charles V's rebuff six months before and Noailles remarked that he seemed timid and reserved, "as if he were afraid of being overheard by one of his own company." Three days later the ambassador was refused permission to attend the mass at St. Paul's (just in front of his house) at which Philip, Pole, Gardiner, and a great company of notables celebrated England's return to the Roman obedience. He interpreted this affront as simply one more straw in the wind which was driving England and France into war. With his wife and his brother in France, the usually sanguine ambassador gave himself up to despair and wrote asking for instructions about how he should act in "such an obscure and difficult position."[21]

[19] See above, p. 220. French reenforcements were sent to Scotland in the following February and Noailles was pleased with the results. Vertot, IV, 13-14, 50, 91, 110, 166, 176-7, 185-6, 199, 252; D'Oysel to Noailles, 23 Feb. 1555, Aff. Etr., IX, fol. 373.

[20] Vertot, IV, 49-50; Montmorency to Noailles, 12 Dec. 1554, Aff. Etr., IX, fol. 322; François to Antoine de Noailles, 13 Dec. 1554, ibid., fols. 323-4.

[21] Vertot, IV, 31-4, 37-9, 60-3; Antoine to François de Noailles, 17 Dec. 1554, Aff. Etr., IX, fol. 326.

Out of discouragement, however, came a spark of hope which was fanned into flame by an energetic, loquacious, and likable member of the Cardinal's suite named Vincenzo Parpaglia. Parpaglia, Abbot of San Salutore, a small abbey near Turin, had already made the task of bringing peace to a war-torn Europe his chief concern,[22] and for two years more he was to travel all over the face of Europe as professional peacemaker. He was tactful, indefatigable, and transparently honest, but he was not entirely disinterested. His sovereign, Emmanuel Philibert of Savoy, was an exile from his estates, which were occupied by French troops; and Parpaglia believed (unlike Emmanuel Philibert himself, who had gone over to the Emperor) that a peace settlement which favored France was the only practical way of restoring the Duke to his estates—and incidentally of regaining the revenues of his own abbey. It was he who introduced Noailles to Pole at their first conference, and for over a year he and the ambassador were to work in the closest harmony. It was a strange partnership, but Parpaglia's sincerity and naïveté were congenial to a man like Noailles who was an intriguer by necessity, not by nature, and who could admire such qualities in others at the very moment he was taking advantage of them.

It was Parpaglia who persuaded both Pole and Noailles that there was real hope of a settlement if the Cardinal would take up the work of mediation where Gardiner had left it. At Noailles's suggestion, Pole discussed the matter in private with Philip and Mary and out of their conferences during the second week of December came the first concrete suggestion as to how a settlement might be reached, namely, that French and Imperial delegates should meet and discuss peace terms on neutral English territory near Calais. Dispatched in haste to the French court, La Marque presented this proposal to Henry II the day before Christmas. Within a week François de Noailles was on his way back to London with instructions to tell Pole that the King of France would agree to send delegates to a conference provided the agenda were agreed upon beforehand.[23]

---

[22] See *Ven. Cal.*, V, 415, note, and 441-2.

[23] Vertot, III, 324-7; IV, 41-7, 54-63, 84-92; Montmorency to Noailles, 24 Dec. 1554, Aff. Etr., IX, fol. 334.

Before François reached London on January 6, new difficulties had developed. News of French successes in Italy had reached England during the Christmas holidays and made a considerable impression. Gardiner and Pole were more desirous than ever to stop the war before further victories made Henry II intractable, but the news angered Philip and stiffened his attitude. François de Noailles found London swarming with Flemish and Italian nobles, all asking the King for money or for protection of their estates from the French, "so that one need only come to London to see all of Europe."[24] Typical of these embittered suitors was Emmanuel Philibert of Savoy, who spent a month in England after Christmas angling for the hand of the Princess Elizabeth, and who spoiled many a social gathering by his whining about French successes in Piedmont.[25]

The chief difficulty, however, was the growing friction between Gardiner and Pole. Convinced of Pole's ineptitude and eager to keep the negotiations in his own hands, Gardiner persuaded Philip that it would be better to hold the proposed peace conference in London rather than in the Calais Pale—a suggestion which naturally found but cold welcome at the French embassy.[26] The truth was that there were too many mediators and too little mediation. Gardiner, Pole, and Parpaglia each had his own axe to grind. Gardiner angrily regretted having cast suspicion upon Mary's impartiality as a peacemaker (a tack which he had taken at Renard's advice), but the damage was done and he could only wince when François de Noailles reminded him that it was he himself who had suggested Pole as the ideal mediator.[27] Pole in turn (as Antoine de Noailles was quick to point out) had hurt his own reputation for impartiality by writing the King of France without formally approaching the Emperor at the same time.[28]

[24] François de Noailles to Cardinal of Châtillon, 11 Jan. 1555, Aff. Etr., IX, fol. 352; Vertot, IV, 151-2.

[25] Vertot, IV, 96-7, 172-3; Emmanuel Philibert to Langosco, 19 Nov. 1554, P.R.O., Tyler, p. 282, note; Weiss, IV, 349-51, 398.

[26] Vertot, IV, 96-8, 104-10, 119, 167-8; speech of François de Noailles to Mary, 9 Jan. 1554, Aff. Etr., IX, fols. 348-9.

[27] Vertot, IV, 120-3, and 130, note; also ibid., 140-1.

[28] Vertot, IV, 106, 144.

And Parpaglia's concern for the interests of Emmanuel Philibert made both Noailles and Montmorency suspicious of him.[29]

During the closing days of Parliament Noailles realized that something had to be done to "warm up" the peacemakers so he sent word to Gardiner that his brother François, who had only just arrived in London, intended to return to France immediately unless the English had further proposals to make. The result was a series of dinners and conferences between Gardiner, Pole, Renard, and the French envoys. Eventually Philip decided that something might be gained by consulting his father, and since the French refused to suggest terms until the Emperor had approved the conference plan in principle, Parpaglia was finally sent off on January 19 to give Charles a first-hand account of the negotiations and to ask him whether he would agree to send commissioners to the Calais Pale. After Parliament rose, therefore, the attention of the diplomats turned from London to Brussels, and Noailles, jubilant over the failure of the campaign to draw England into the war, decided that his King would have "a very honorable peace in a few days."[30]

* * *

For a month and a half after Parpaglia reached Brussels there was an embarrassing lull in the negotiations. Week after week the Abbot was refused audience with the Emperor, who was stricken by a peculiarly severe attack of gout. Granvelle was busy stamping out the embers of a recent rebellion in Antwerp; and even Ruy Gómez, whom Philip sent to Brussels ten days after Parpaglia, was unable to get any official answer to the conference proposal for several weeks.[31] The Emperor's gout was not the only cause of the hesitation at the Imperial court. In spite of the French government's financial difficulties, Henry II still had the upper hand. Early in March his army won a second victory in Piedmont; meanwhile his Protestant and infidel allies were giving the Emperor's brother considerable trouble in Germany. Except

---

[29] Vertot, IV, 108-9; Montmorency to Noailles, 13 Jan. 1555, Aff. Etr., IX, fol. 355.
[30] Vertot, IV, 119, 124-5, 133-46, 150-2; Renard to Charles V, 12, 17, and 19 Jan. 1555, Antigny, Tyler, pp. 3, 6-7, 9.
[31] For. Cal., Mary, 149, 154-6, 157, 158-9; Vertot, IV, 207-8, 247-50, 252-3.

for the shadowy hope of assistance from England, there was hardly a bright spot on the Imperial horizon, unless it was Siena. There the gallant courage of a French garrison was expected to succumb soon to a superior investing force, an event which would provide Charles with a much-needed bargaining point. But the Emperor knew that what was being proposed to him in February was essentially a peace of capitulation, and he was naturally loathe to agree to any kind of conference, even to one presided over by the English.

Eventually it was pressure from Philip and Mary which induced him to agree, a fact which paid tribute to Montmorency's sagacity in opening the negotiations in England and to François de Noailles's skill in carrying them out. The delays at Brussels had worried the English and Antoine de Noailles had been quick to take advantage of the fact. He took pains to impress upon the Council that France was under no necessity of suing for peace; he wrote D'Oysel suggesting that Dunbar be fortified so that Scotland might become "the real scourge of England"; he took care to contradict all reports that Siena was in danger of capture; and twice he announced that his brother would be compelled to leave London unless word came soon from Brussels.[32] His activities, combined with the popular discontent occasioned by the heresy prosecutions, had their effect upon Philip. Some weeks later Parpaglia confided to Noailles "in great secrecy" that Philip and Mary had sent "strong persuasions" to Brussels; and still later he told Montmorency that any success in the negotiations should be attributed to the Prince of Spain, who "had entreated the Emperor to yield in the matter of peace, going so far as to give him to understand that if he refused to treat, he [Philip] would treat without him."[33] The enthusiastic Abbot was undoubtedly guilty of some exaggeration and he failed to mention one important factor in the Emperor's decision, the financial straits of the Im-

[32] Vertot, IV, 180, 185-6, 199-200, 217-18, 252; Noailles to Montmorency, 27 Jan. 1555, Aff. Etr., IX, fol. 358; Noailles to D'Oysel, 17 Feb. 1555, *ibid.,* fol. 370; D'Oysel to Noailles, 30 Mar. 1555, *ibid.,* fols. 398ᵛ-9.

[33] Instructions to La Marque, 7 May 1555, Aff. Etr., IX, fol. 445ᵛ; Procès verbal de la conférence tenue à Marc, Bib. Nat., f.f., No. 704, fol. 205. See also Vertot, IV, 218-19, 247-52, 311-12, 332-3.

perial government;[34] but he was on the spot when Charles was making up his mind and there is no reason to doubt his testimony that Philip's persuasions turned the scale at the Imperial court.

On March 1 Ruy Gómez left Brussels with the Emperor's verbal consent to the conference. Shortly after he reached London a week later Parpaglia arrived with belated confirmation of his report.[35] François de Noailles immediately set out for France, and within twenty-four hours of his arrival at Montereau, Florimond Robertet de Fresnes, Henry II's financial secretary, was on his way to London in order to fix upon a date for the parley. The secretary arrived on March 29 and conferred immediately with Pole, Gardiner, and Mary. Once again the next move was up to Charles.[36]

So far English mediation had been remarkably successful, and Noailles reported that Mary's health was noticeably improved by her joy in the prospect of European peace.[37] On the surface, it seemed to be a tribute to English impartiality that the stronger power had shown more alacrity than the weaker in agreeing to treat. But the realities of the situation remained unchanged. Sincere as Pole, Gardiner, Mary, and even Philip were in their desire for peace, there was no real basis for an understanding—a fact which became abundantly evident when the news of Pope Julius III's death (on March 23) reached Paris. Since the French had been anything but sincere from the beginning, any event which tended to strengthen Henry II's position—such as the election of a French Pope or the disappointment of Mary's hope for an heir— would destroy what little desire there was among French statesmen for a settlement. As soon as he heard of the Pope's illness, Montmorency ordered Noailles to flatter Pole with the assurance

---

[34] For a gloomy picture of the state of the Habsburg treasury see Eraso to Molina, 12 Apr. 1555, Antigny, Tyler, pp. 54-6. On the French side, see George Duruy, *De Pactis Anno 1556 apud Valcellas Indutiis* (Paris, 1883), pp. 17-18.

[35] Weiss, IV, 407; *Ven. Cal.,* VI, Part I, 20, 24-5; Vertot, IV, 230-2, 235-41; Noailles to Montmorency, 10 Mar. 1555, Aff. Etr., IX, fol. 379; Noailles to D'Oysel, 17 Mar. 1555, *ibid.,* fol. 389.

[36] Vertot, IV, 254-9, 260-1 (the author of this dispatch was Antoine de Noailles, not François); Mary to Charles V, 28 March 1555, Antigny, Tyler; *For. Cal., Mary,* 162; *Ven. Cal.,* VI, Part I, 33-6.

[37] Advis, 22 Mar. 1555, and Noailles to Montmorency, 2 Apr. 1555, Aff. Etr., IX, fols. 394, 404-5.

that he would receive French support in the conclave. Parpaglia hastily pointed out to Noailles that such support would ruin Pole's chances since it would lose him the Emperor's backing. As a matter of fact, since both Henry II and Charles V wanted a Pope who would be more manageable than the incorruptible Cardinal, neither made any serious efforts in Pole's behalf. The election of Marcellus II early in April merely postponed the issue since the new Pope lived only a few weeks, but meanwhile Henry's appetite for a fresh diplomatic victory had been whetted and the cause of peace had suffered proportionately.[38]

Day after day passed after the French secretary's arrival in London, and still no word came from Brussels as to whom the Emperor intended to send to the parley and when they would be ready. Charles V was still confined to his bed, it is true, but the French suspected that he was deliberately procrastinating in the hope that Siena would fall and that Mary's child would be born before the conference met. Noailles's pessimistic dispatches, together with news that an Imperial army was gathering at Namur, convinced Henry that the Emperor had drawn back; and on April 17 an order was dispatched from Fontainebleau recalling the secretary. On the same day in London, however, Noailles learned that Charles had finally appointed an Imperial delegation of six headed by Granvelle, and within a week both sides had agreed to send their representatives to Marcq, a little village in the Calais Pale equidistant from the French and Imperial frontiers, during the third week of May. "Here," Noailles wrote D'Oysel, "is the consummation of the work of God and of one of your most faithful and devoted friends."[39]

Noailles unquestionably overestimated his own part in the success of the negotiations. He had been lukewarm at the start about Montmorency's request for English mediation; he had regretted Henry's readiness to agree to every successive proposal which

[38] Montmorency to Noailles, 31 March 1555, Aff. Etr., IX, fol. 401; Noailles to Montmorency, 2 and 6 April 1555, *ibid.*, fols. 404, 412; Vertot, IV, 262-3, 264-6, 268-9, 281-2, 284, 287-8, 303-4; Philip to Charles V and to Juan Manrique, 8 April 1555, Antigny, Tyler, pp. 48-50.

[39] Vertot, IV, 263, 270, 272-6, 277-82, 292; *For. Cal., Mary,* 162; *Ven. Cal.,* VI, Part I, 47; Noailles and de Fresnes to Montmorency, 12 and 23 April 1555, Aff. Etr., IX, fols. 413, 434.

came from Pole and Gardiner; and he had consistently advised the use of force, veiled or otherwise, in preference to the way of conciliation.[40] But it is at least doubtful whether the English government would have taken the cause of peace so closely to heart if Noailles had not publicized his country's prestige and strength so shrewdly. The difference of opinion between the factions of Guise and Montmorency at the French court was reflected (unconsciously, of course) in the truculence of Antoine de Noailles and the tact of his younger brother in London. It was because one brother was the complement of the other that Mary, Pole, and Gardiner were kept impressed but not discouraged by French self-confidence.

In a different sense, Pole and Gardiner were the complement of each other. Pole's idealism and devotion to a cause which transcended national boundaries were the necessary counterpart of Gardiner's patriotism and hard practical sense. The fact that there were two mediators, not one, helps to explain why Henry II and Charles V, neither of whom was really willing to make sacrifices for peace, were induced to send delegates to a parley. The French, who distrusted Gardiner, could assume (as they did) that Pole was the real mediator. The Emperor, who never thoroughly trusted Pole, could ignore Parpaglia, the Cardinal's emissary, and negotiate directly with Mary and Gardiner through Philip's envoys and couriers. In a sense, the parley at Marcq was made possible by the fact that English and papal mediation had never wholly fused.[41]

* * *

Hopes were high in London early in May as the delegates made ready to attend the conference. Noailles was sure that the Emperor was too ill and too eager to lay aside his political burdens to haggle long over terms; the last excuse for delay was removed, he thought, when news arrived that Siena had finally surrendered

---

[40] See e.g. his letters to Montmorency and to L'Aubespine of 12 April 1555, Aff. Etr., IX, fols. 413, 415.

[41] See in particular Renard to Charles V, 21 Apr. 1555, Antigny, Tyler, p. 69; Montmorency to Noailles, 17 Apr. 1555, Aff. Etr., IX, fol. 430; Noailles to Montmorency, 27 Apr. 1555, *ibid.*, fol. 438; and Vertot, IV, 256, 263, 267-8, 275-6, 286, 296-7.

on April 21.[42] Renard, on the other hand, was equally sure that Henry II wanted peace at almost any price.

According to what I understand from the advices of some friends [he wrote Charles], the election of the new Pope, the surrender of Siena, the poverty of the French people, the progress of affairs in this kingdom [England], and the difficulty of obtaining money are spurring and even compelling the French to make peace.[43]

These oversanguine dispatches from both ambassadors had the effect of persuading both the French and the Imperial governments to expect too much. There was no need for either Henry or Charles to send delegations empowered to make important concessions if what their envoys in London said was true. Neither side had reached the point of preferring a compromise peace to continuation of the war; but each was persuaded—thanks to the pressure of exhausted resources, of public opinion, and of Anglo-papal mediation—that peace was worth discussing in the hope that the other side would yield.

Three weeks before the parley was scheduled to begin, the French delegates decided that they would not consent to any territorial restitutions nor discuss the grievances of outsiders such as the English, the Duke of Savoy, or other "allies" of the Emperor.[44] This meant in effect that Charles V would be offered the choice of accepting the *status quo* as the basis of a settlement or of continuing the war. Needless to say, there was nothing in the dispatches from London to prepare Charles for the complete intransigence of the French. He and Granvelle apparently hoped much from their one trump card—the possibility that Mary might bear a child before the parley began—but their hope was cruelly deceived. On the last day of April a report reached London from Hampton Court that the Queen had been brought to bed and all the medieval pageantry of rejoicing began.[45] But the bells were soon silenced and the bonfires soon extinguished. Noailles's

---

[42] Vertot, IV, 225, 288, 307, 312-13; Advis, 2 April 1555, Aff. Etr., IX, fol. 406; Instructions to La Marque, 7 May 1555, *ibid.*, fols. 444-5.

[43] Renard to Charles V, 6 May 1555, Antigny, Tyler, p. 74.

[44] Procès verbal, Bib. Nat., f.f., No. 704, fol. 203ᵛ. See also *Ven. Cal.*, VI, Part I, 59-60.

[45] *Ven. Cal.*, VI, Part I, 60-1; *Machyn Diary*, 86; Renard to Charles V, 6 May 1555, Antigny, Tyler, p. 74; *For. Cal., Mary*, 165-6.

earlier suspicions that Mary's "pregnancy" was merely a patholog-
ical condition were soon confirmed by one of his informers, and
before long the French had lost their fear, and the Emperor had
almost lost his hope that the Queen would become a mother.[46]
In spite of his lack of bargaining-power, however, Charles hoped
that the alacrity of the French in agreeing to the conference
meant that they were willing to renounce some of their conquests at least in return for a lasting peace. He instructed his delegates, therefore, to work for a restoration of the *status quo ante
bellum* as the basis of any agreement. This was asking much in
return for very little; but if the French proved to be unyielding,
the Imperial representatives were directed not to let the parley
break up without some arrangement for continuing the negotiations. The blame for refusing to come to terms must at all costs
be put upon the French in order to win public opinion in England.[47]

Since the Emperor was resolved to continue fighting unless
the French offered to make territorial restitutions, and since the
French were determined not to give up an inch of territory, the
conference was doomed to failure from the start. But none of the
delegates were fully aware of the hopelessness of their task before they met. One can hardly blame the mediators—Pole, Gardiner, and Paget—for being even more blindly optimistic than the
belligerents. The arrangement of the parley was the most notable
attempt made by English statesmen during Mary's reign to relieve their nation of the incubus of foreign intervention and to
recover some of the prestige which English diplomacy had possessed under Henry VIII. A settlement of the continental war
under English auspices would not only strengthen the reputation
of Mary's government at home and abroad; it would also obviate
the disaster of England's being drawn into hostilities with France
in Philip's interest. "The eagle and the cock would sing in harmony while the lion looked on," as one of Gardiner's servants put

---

[46] Vertot, IV, 227, 290-1, 334, 342; Instructions to La Marque, 7 May 1555, Aff. Etr.,
Vol. IX, fol. 445; Advis, 1 and 6 June 1555, *ibid.*, fols. 453, 454. For evidence that Sir
John Leigh was Noailles's informer, see *Amer. Hist. Rev.*, XLV (April 1940), 544.

[47] The Emperor's instructions to his commissioners may be reconstructed from the
dispatches which they sent him during the parley. See note 50.

it; and all those who had helped stake English prestige upon the success of the parley echoed his hope.[48]

The English delegates struggled under two serious difficulties, however. In the first place, Noailles's dispatches betrayed to the French deputation the fact that many of Gardiner's countrymen hoped he would fail. The average Englishman, in fact, was afraid that the Habsburg eagle would turn to rend the British lion once its quarrel with the cock was settled.[49] In the second place, the English representatives went to Marcq without having obtained the previous understandings which the French had originally demanded—understandings which appear to be necessary to the success of international conferences in all ages. There were no agenda, no written statements of minimum demands, only voluminous dossiers on each side to prove the justice of its claims. Because of this the English insisted that there be no direct conversations between the rival deputations; the mediators were to serve as the only channel of communication until some concrete basis for agreement was found. The French objected strongly to this plan on the ground that it made the English "judges" of the dispute instead of "witnesses" to a settlement, but Gardiner was adamant and the disputants did not confer face-to-face until half-way through the parley.[50]

For over two weeks (May 23 to June 7) the conferees haggled and quarreled over their claims and counterclaims, pausing occasionally to deliver themselves of elegant orations on peace. After the third meeting it was clear that there could be no agreement. Granvelle insisted on restitutions; the French replied by demand-

[48] Procès verbal, Bib. Nat., f.f., No. 704, fols. 201[v] and 203[v]; Vertot, IV, 286, 296-7, 326, 335-6.

[49] Vertot, IV, 328, 332, 335-6.

[50] The foregoing details, together with those which follow, are drawn from two first-hand accounts of the parley at Marcq: "Procès verbal de la conférence tenue à Marc" by Charles de Marillac, one of the French delegates (Bib. Nat., f.f., No. 704, fols. 199-226); and seven letters of the Imperial Peace Commissioners to Charles V, 20 May to 8 June 1555 (Antigny, Tyler). The second-hand accounts of the Venetian ambassadors (*Ven. Cal.,* VI, Part I, 80 *ff.*) are also useful. Montmorency and the Cardinal of Lorraine were the co-leaders of the French deputation, while Granvelle was the undisputed head of the Imperial delegation. Pole was technically the presiding officer of the conference; Gardiner, Paget, and Arundel, the mediators. Others present whom we have already met were L'Aubespine, Boisdauphin, François de Noailles, La Marque, and Parpaglia.

ing Milan in addition to their conquests. Once Montmorency seemed upon the point of making important concessions after Granvelle had appealed to him personally as a lover of peace, but a frown from the Cardinal of Lorraine brought the color to his cheeks and made him change the tone of his "very fine and honest" speech.[51] Gardiner, the leading figure at the parley, did his best in the early stages of the talks to play the part of an honest broker by inducing both sides to moderate their demands. He told the French their claim to Milan was unreasonable, and he told the Imperialists they must offer something tangible if they expected to recover their lost territories. The Emperor, he suggested, should take compassion on "the infirmity of the French," in imitation of the compassion which St. Paul said man should have for the frailty of woman; Charles, he added, "in this was the man." Granvelle, however, was not at all sympathetic about what he referred to as "the infirmity of the French about Milan." As time wore on, the Chancellor lost something of his impartiality. He asked Granvelle to confide in the English "not as mediators but as negotiators of our common affairs"; he indulged in sarcastic comments on French generosity to the Imperial delegates; he presented Granvelle's proposals to the French as if they were his own; and he finally became involved in an angry altercation with Montmorency which scandalized his English colleagues, "because it seemed to them that he was exceeding the terms suitable to a mediator." Paget took even less pains to conceal his prejudice. Even before the opening meeting he told Granvelle he was acting not as a mediator but as an "affectionate servant" of the Emperor, "as all the English were obliged to be"; and throughout the parley he served the Imperial delegation as a kind of unofficial adviser and agent.[52]

Pole was the only one among the mediators whose impartiality was above question. It was a tribute to his integrity if not to his

---

[51] Imperial Commissioners to Charles V, 30 May 1555, Antigny, Tyler.

[52] Imperial Commissioners to Charles V, 20 May to 8 June 1555, Antigny, Tyler. J. A. Muller's suspicion (*Stephen Gardiner,* 283) that Paget "played for the approval of Charles and Philip by siding with the Imperialists against Gardiner's moderate proposals for compromise," is partly borne out by this new evidence; but Gardiner's proposals were by no means so impartial as Muller implies. Paget's efforts did not win him the Emperor's confidence (*Ven. Cal.,* VI, Part I, 146).

tact that he won the resentment of the Imperialists, the contempt of the French, and the jealousy of his compatriots. In the silence which followed Montmorency's conciliatory speech Pole rose, addressed the Cardinal of Lorraine as one clergyman to another, and suggested naïvely that both sides submit their disputes to "some judge," such as the Pope or a General Council. The French jumped at the suggestion, aware that such judgment would take months or years and that meanwhile the *status quo* would remain undisturbed. The Imperial commissioners were faced with the unpleasant choice of rejecting arbitration point-blank or of consenting (against their instructions) to a truce without restitutions. The equivocations to which Granvelle was forced to resort gave the French a much-needed pretext for blaming the failure of the conference on their enemies; and as a result the Imperial delegation left the parley well-nigh as contemptuous of English mediators as the French themselves.[53]

To initiated observers, however, it was perfectly clear where responsibility for the parley's failure lay. While the delegates were sitting, the wheel of fortune turned definitely in favor of France. The Lutheran princes were standing firm for their rights in the Diet which was to result four months later in the Peace of Augsburg, and a Turkish fleet was on its way to cooperate with the French in the western Mediterranean. By the end of May the French delegates knew from Noailles's dispatches that there was little danger of the birth of a child who would inherit both England and the Netherlands; and on June 2 news reached Marcq that the French faction in the Cardinal college had managed to elect a fiery, seventy-nine-year-old Neapolitan who hated the Habsburgs and all their works, Giovanni Pietro Caraffa. With such tempting prospects of further triumphs for French arms and French diplomacy throughout Europe, it is no wonder that Henry II's delegates decided as early as the third meeting to break up the parley unless their enemies capitulated to every demand made upon them.[54]

---

[53] Imperial Commissioners to Charles V, 30 May and 2 June 1555, Antigny, Tyler; *Ven. Cal.*, VI, Part I, 103-4.

[54] Decrue, *Montmorency*, II, 169; *Ven. Cal.*, VI, Part I, 95, 98, 117.

Toward the close of the conference the Cardinal of Lorraine drew Granvelle aside and asked genially whether an exchange of prisoners could not be arranged even if the peace negotiations fell through. "I answered him in the same spirit," Granvelle wrote, "that they were dreadful and wanted things their own way." The Cardinal only smiled and replied, "Rendez vous donc." Pole told him roundly that no matter what the French might say, all Christendom would lay the blame for the parley's failure at their door; but the French delegates contented themselves by remarking to the English as they left Marcq that "the thing was not yet ripe."[55] As the belligerents and mediators wended their way homeward, it seemed more than likely to any thoughtful observer that when the fruit of peace finally ripened, the English would not be invited to help in the plucking.

[55] Imperial Commissioners to Charles V, 2 and 8 June 1555, Antigny, Tyler, pp. 165 ff., 177.

CHAPTER X

TRUCE WITHOUT PEACE

JUNE 1555 TO FEBRUARY 1556

EWS of the failure of English mediation at Marcq was variously received in the different capitals of Europe. As soon as word reached the French court, orders to raise troops were sent out, "after which the Most Christian King went out hunting." Granvelle was genuinely disappointed but persuaded himself that in the eyes of the English the blame had been placed where it belonged. In London Renard took a characteristically gloomy view of the situation; the breakdown of negotiations, he thought, would encourage the malcontents and inspire the French to renewed intrigue in England. Noailles feared a sudden English declaration of war, but soon concluded that domestic difficulties would force the Council to hold its hand throughout the coming winter. He felt the conference had at least shown the Emperor that recognition of French conquests must be the basis of any future settlement. If the Venetian ambassador in London is to be believed, Philip realized that such recognition would have to come sooner or later and blamed his father for being so stubborn.[1]

The greatest disappointment, however, was felt by those who had staked the English government's prestige upon the parley's success—by Mary, Pole and Gardiner. Gardiner openly blamed the French for the rupture of negotiations and Pole cautiously echoed his opinion, but both were hopeful about the possibility of continuing negotiations through the ordinary diplomatic channels.[2] The Queen resented the intransigence of the French even

[1] *Ven. Cal.*, VI, Part I, 103, 106-7; Part II, 1064; Weiss, IV, 433-4, 439-40; Vertot, IV, 355-7, 360; V, 5-6.
[2] *Ven. Cal.*, VI, Part I, 112; Vertot, IV, 359-60; V, 2-3; Imperial Commissioners to Charles V, 8 June 1555, Antigny, Tyler, pp. 179-80.

more bitterly than did those who had been present at the conference, but neither she nor they could forget that every consideration which had originally induced her to offer her services as mediator had gained rather than lost force. The Protestant *carbonnades,* as Noailles somewhat gleefully reported, were becoming the occasion of increasingly serious local disturbances, and it was apparent that the show of French strength at Marcq might encourage a serious rebellion in England.[3] Unless the Queen swallowed her pride, unless she accepted the French rebuff with patience, England might yet be cast into the throes of foreign or civil war.

It was Parpaglia and Noailles who gathered up the broken threads of the conference and offered the English a second opportunity to settle the peace of Europe. Just before the French commissioners left the scene of the parley, the indefatigable Abbot had visited them at Ardres and urged that they agree to a truce so that discussion of peace terms might continue. The French refused, but admitted that a truce would eventually be necessary and that when the "right time" came they would listen to further proposals, "especially" if they came from Mary and Pole. The promise was not put into writing, but Parpaglia was allowed to take it down by dictation.[4] Meanwhile Noailles had suggested that his brother be sent back to London, in order to offer the English an opportunity to renew the negotiations if they wished.[5]

When François de Noailles reached London at the end of June, he found his elder brother in an optimistic mood. For the first time since Wyatt's rebellion the ambassador had been invited to a public ceremony—the obsequies at St. Paul's for the mad Joanna, Charles V's mother. Spaniards present were courteous to him; Admiral Howard (who had had a falling-out with Philip) ostentatiously invited himself to dinner at the French embassy; and during the week following, Gardiner and the Council went out of their way to be pleasant to him. Noailles concluded that

[3] Noailles to Montmorency, 30 June 1555, Aff. Etr., IX, fol. 463.

[4] Procès verbal, Bib. Nat., f.f., No. 704, fol. 226ᵛ. This was probably the mysterious paper which Michiele thought Montmorency had handed to Parpaglia at the close of the parley (*Ven. Cal.,* VI, Part I, 159).

[5] Vertot, IV, 352; V, 1. It was already settled that François would succeed his brother as ambassador and the latter was looking for an opportunity to press for his recall. Noailles to M. de Noaillac, 9 July 1555, Aff. Etr., IX, fol. 474.

both Philip and Mary wanted a settlement more keenly than ever, and remarked to an Englishman that it would not be long before peace came, "from England."[6]

François's interviews with Mary, Gardiner, and Pole only partially justified his elder brother's optimism. François was surprised at the unanimity with which the mediators blamed Henry II for the parley's failure. The Queen gave him to understand that her patience could not last forever. She was Philip's wife; she could not preserve her neutrality much longer; if Henry II desired it, she was willing to offer her services once more as mediator, but this would be the last time. Even though the French knew how to discount it, the threat of war was clear enough, and it sufficed to set the peacemakers busily to work during the first week of July. The French envoys talked with Pole and Pole conferred with Philip and Mary; Parpaglia worked out terms for a truce with Gutierre López de Padilla, one-time Spanish ambassador to Savoy and now Philip's *maître d'hôtel*; and on July 9 a long conference was held at Richmond between the Cardinal, Parpaglia, López, Gardiner, Arundel, and Paget. Parpaglia was the moving spirit throughout, shuttling almost daily between Noailles and Renard in London, Pole at Richmond, and Philip at Hampton Court.[7]

The Emperor rose cautiously to the French bait. He interpreted François de Noailles's return to London correctly as another disingenuous attempt of Henry II to keep England out of the war by talking peace. But he reminded Philip "how convenient and necessary peace would be to us in view of the state of affairs," and advised him to encourage the negotiations if there seemed to be any chance whatever of a fair offer from the French.[8] Philip was in perfect agreement with his father. Even before Secretary Eraso arrived in London with these instructions, the King had decided to test Henry II's sincerity by following a suggestion which probably emanated from Paget or Gardiner. This was to ask that

---

[6] Vertot, IV, 358; V, 6, 15-17; Renard to Charles V, 29 June and 10 July 1555, Antigny, Tyler, pp. 186, 192-5. cf. Weiss, IV, 442 *ff.*

[7] Vertot, V, 24-34; François de Noailles to Montmorency, 12 July 1555, Aff. Etr., IX, fol. 483; Renard to Charles V, 10 July 1555, Antigny, Tyler, pp. 192 *ff.* (incomplete copy in Weiss, IV, 442-8); *Ven. Cal.*, VI, Part I, 130-4, 136-7, 142-3.

[8] Charles V to Philip, 16 July 1555, Antigny, Tyler, pp. 199-202.

Antoine or François de Noailles be given full powers to negotiate peace in London, if necessary with the help of other commissioners.

The proposal caught the French ambassador offguard. Early in July he had confessed that he was "very confused." Was the Council really preparing for war? Were the new and circumstantial rumors true that Mary's pregnancy had not "gone up in smoke" after all? Had Philip finally decided to leave for Flanders? He did not know. Furthermore, François's instructions were so vague that he had no means of knowing whether Henry II really wanted peace or not.[9] Apparently François persuaded him that Montmorency wanted a settlement, but both brothers forgot that the breakdown of negotiations at Marcq would inevitably discredit the Constable and strengthen the Guise faction at the French court. The ambassador was divided in his own mind about whether the peace-talks ought to be pursued seriously. He was once more in close touch with a group of irresponsible conspirators and was expecting a popular revolt by September. He was afraid that open talk of peace in London would discourage the plotters and advised Montmorency to think twice before appointing commissioners. But at the same time he realized that a blunt refusal of Philip's suggestion would strain Anglo-French relations to the breaking-point. He therefore encouraged Parpaglia to believe that Henry II would agree to the suggestion, and when François left London on August 14 he carried letters from the ambassador urging Montmorency to suggest peace terms secretly to Pole or Gardiner in order to keep the English in hopes.[10]

Hardly had François started on his journey, however, when a dispatch arrived from Montmorency rebuking Noailles for going so far. Henry II would never consent to negotiate in London, the Constable wrote, nor (by implication) would he suggest terms. Noailles was hurt and angry. If only he were in France, he wrote François, he was sure he would be able to defend his conduct

[9] Noailles to Montmorency, 30 June 1555, Aff. Etr., IX, fol. 463; Noailles to Henry II, 15 and 21 July 1555, ibid., fols. 488, 490; François de Noailles to Montmorency, 21 July 1555, ibid., fol. 494. For Henry II's ambiguous instructions to the two brothers, see Vertot, V, 35-8.

[10] Vertot, V, 39-41, 43-4, 46-7, 57-8, 67, 70-1, 73-4; Ven. Cal., VI, Part I, 142-3, 144, 152. Noailles's intrigues are discussed in the succeeding chapter.

and to persuade Montmorency and the Cardinal of Lorraine how badly this curt rebuff would be received in London.[11]

Fortunately he was spared the embarrassment of having to make explanations to the English. On August 3 the pretense of Mary's pregnancy was formally dropped when what Noailles called the "seraglio" at Hampton Court was broken up and the court removed to Oatlands.[12] Soon afterward the foreign diplomats learned that Philip was leaving England to join his father, and for two months the peace negotiations languished. What effect would the King's departure have upon internal affairs in England? How would the Emperor's coming abdication of his sovereignty in the Low Countries affect the international situation? Would Philip listen more readily than his father to overtures of peace? Such questions as these had first to be answered before the peace of Europe could be settled; and once Philip was across the Channel, London would lose its importance in the diplomatic scene.

While Philip was making ready for his journey, Noailles returned to the congenial task of maintaining the "grandeur and reputation" of the King of France. He took a strong line with the Council on the subject of recent disturbances along the Scottish border; he protested vigorously about the arrest of a French frigate which carried his dispatches from Dover to Calais; and when Gardiner warned him that control of the Channel belonged by right to England and that Admiral Howard had been given orders to fire upon any French ships which attempted to interfere with Philip's passage, Noailles replied that the sea was broad and common to all, that no one could call himself its master without the force to back up his words, and that no Christian prince could muster the sea power necessary to control the Channel, "as anyone who understands naval affairs knows well enough." Apparently the English Council had less understanding of maritime affairs than the ex-Admiral of France. A few days after Philip's departure—partly perhaps as a result of Noailles's bluster—they gave

---

[11] Cardinal de Châtillon to François de Noailles, 8 Aug. 1555, and Antoine to François de Noailles, 14 Aug. 1555, Aff. Etr., IX, fols. 508, 513; Vertot, V, 77; *Ven. Cal.*, VI, Part I, 168-9, 179.

[12] Noailles to Henry II, 15 July 1555, Aff. Etr., IX, fol. 488; *Ven. Cal.*, VI, Part I, 147.

orders to repair the ships which were unfit for service, with the express purpose of establishing control over the Channel crossing.[13]

* * *

Meanwhile the Emperor, sick in body and weary in spirit, was absorbed in plans for his abdication. Even the prospect of finally finding rest from his labors could not dull the habits of a lifetime, however. To preserve the Habsburg heritage was his aim in abdication as it had been in active government. Austria had already gone to his brother Ferdinand, and in spite of all his efforts to gain the Imperial crown for Philip, it too seemed destined to fall to the King of the Romans. Since the inheritance must be divided, there were those who thought that the Netherlands should go to the Austrian branch of the family—and the bloodshed of the next half-century proved them right. But Philip had been made King of England to protect Spain's money-markets in the North, and it could now be argued that he must have the Netherlands to protect England. England, as Charles saw it, would replace the Empire as the indispensable nexus between Spain and the Low Countries, and a new Spanish Empire would replace the old.

Whether Philip was ever stirred by his father's dream it is hard to say. He knew that he was unpopular in England; he knew that the Netherlands would probably prefer German to Spanish rule; and he longed to return to his beloved Spain. He pled with his father through Ruy Gómez to be allowed to go to Spain after the abdication ceremonies, but Charles pointed out what a disastrous effect this might have upon Habsburg rule in England and the Low Countries, especially while the war with France lasted. Dutifully Philip resigned himself to his father's will and set about establishing his position in England as best he could before leaving for Brussels, "so as not to have thrown away so much money, time, toil, and repute."[14]

During the last month before his departure Philip took a more active part in affairs of state than ever before, as the Venetian

---

[13] Vertot, V, 98, 101-7, 112-13, 115 ff.; For. Cal., Mary, 182-4; P.R.O., S.P.Dom. 11, Vol. VI, No. 17.

[14] Ven. Cal., VI, Part I, 140-1, 145, 152; Vertot, V, 131.

ambassador had predicted he might.[15] The situation was certainly serious enough to challenge his abilities as a statesman. The Council was still torn by faction, the heretics were still untamed, the country was more unsettled than ever, the navy was in a perilous state of disrepair, the borders were in no condition to resist attack, and the problem of what to do with Elizabeth was still unsolved. Once his decision to leave England was announced, Philip was able to galvanize the Council into action. Orders were given to strengthen the country's defenses; it was decided to summon Parliament for the purpose of granting a subsidy; and affairs of state were finally committed to a select council of eight members— a reform which Renard had advocated in vain for almost two years. Philip was no more successful than Renard, however, in disposing of Elizabeth. His suggestion that she be sent to Brussels (where she might be used to the Habsburg advantage should Mary die) found no favor.[16]

The part which Philip himself played in shaping these decisions may perhaps be gathered from the one bit of direct evidence which we possess. At the beginning of August the councillors who were in attendance at Hampton Court—members of Gardiner's faction almost without exception—were meeting almost daily;[17] and about August 2 Philip wrote a hasty and somewhat cryptic account of one of these meetings to a member of his circle of advisers:

We have spent many hours today upon the matter of the reprehensions (*las correciones*) in order to finish them up, since I should like to finish the elections (*las eleciones*) and the question of the government (*lo de la orden*) tomorrow and to be free for the other affairs. Today I have proposed several articles to them which the Chancellor had drawn up comprising three points: first, that they elect none but Catholics and none who are suspect; second, that they take great care to lay down the law on religion (*castigar lo de la religion*) in their districts—and this to the limit of their ability from now on; and third, that they say mass every day provided there be no notable obstacle. And although I have sworn to keep it secret, inasmuch as it becomes the manifest service of God to know your opinion, and knowing that you will keep it secret as I charge you, I beg you earnestly to send me

---

[15] *Ven. Cal.*, VI, Part I, 107.

[16] *ibid.*, 152, 178, 183, 211-12; Memorials of Council proceedings after Philip's departure, P.R.O., S.P.Dom. 11, Vol. VI, Nos. 16-21.

[17] See *A.P.C.*, V, 170 *ff*.

your opinion about what I should do tomorrow on the matter here stated. Of these three points which I have mentioned, the first was accepted by almost all; many stick at the second, saying that they are already obliged to it by the proclamations (*placartes*) under pain of losing their property and everything else, and that since they have this obligation it would not be right to impose another upon them; still more oppose the third, saying that as Christians they already have that obligation and that harm would be done them, for if they should sin by not fulfilling it, they would sin doubly in breaking the oath which they would be obliged to make upon it. I am afraid that some of them, although few, are not acting with good intention, and that the rest do not fall in with this—whether because it seems to place too large an obligation upon them I know not, though in fact it will be only a very small one. Seeing this, and since it was already very late, I chose not to make up my mind but to put the matter off until tomorrow, and I would like much to have your opinion immediately about what it seems to you that I can do tomorrow which will not bring difficulty. . . .[18]

The letter suggests how Philip might have dealt with the problem of heresy in England if left to himself and not subjected to the counsels of prudence which came from his father and from Renard; furthermore it suggests how cautiously one must ascribe to the King himself any consistent or effective opposition to the prosecution of heresy.[19] Although Gardiner's proposals were eventually put into effect,[20] even the Catholic laymen in the Council

[18] Philip to ? [2 Aug. 1555], Besançon, Bibliothèque publique, Fonds Granvelle, Vol. V, fol. 58; transcript in Antigny, Tyler, pp. 206-7. The original letter, a rough draft in Philip's own hand, is without date, place, or address; but I follow Tyler in assuming that the date noted (written in by another hand and crossed out) is probably accurate. Other details in the letter—Philip's hope of speaking soon to Egmont and Horn, and his request for advice about what to do with the cantors whom he cannot take with him—indicate that the document was written some time shortly before his departure for Brussels. The fact that the letter eventually ended up among Granvelle's papers suggests, but does not prove, that it was originally addressed to Renard (as Tyler guesses), or perhaps to Eraso (who was in London at the end of July). But the tone of familiarity and trust in the person addressed suggests that it may have been meant for Ruy Gómez, who was upon the point of leaving London for Brussels about this time (*Ven. Cal.*, VI, Part I, 144, 152; Vertot, V, 49; Weiss, IV, 450).

[19] See above, p. 224.

[20] See Froude, VI, 465-6; and cf. Noailles's Advis of 22 May 1556, Aff. Étr., IX, fol. 643: "Au jugement desquels heretiques l'on y procede et regarde maintenant de plus pres que l'on a faict par cy devant, ayant ceste Royne mis personnaiges en chacune parroise de son royaulme qui rendent compte de tous ceux qui ne se trouvent aux dymanches et festes au service de l'église, et jusques à ceux la qui par mespris ou oubly ne preignent du pain et eau béniste."

were apparently unwilling to approve his religious program in the summer of 1555; and although Philip was obviously acting with considerable caution, it is clear that the Chancellor's proposals had his personal sympathy and approval. In sponsoring Gardiner's suggestions, however, the King was perhaps influenced in part by an important political consideration. In setting up a council of state to manage affairs after his departure, it was important for him to win the confidence of the clerical party and thus to prevent any repetition of the storm of opposition with which the Chancellor and his friends had greeted Mary's abortive reduction of the Privy Council's active membership sixteen months before. If such was his aim, the stratagem was successful. Just before his departure he appointed a select council composed of Pole, Gardiner, Thirlby, Paget, Arundel, Pembroke, Winchester, and Petre. In spite of the predominance of Imperialist nobles and lay administrators, there was no outcry from the Chancellor's followers and everyone was impressed by the King's tact and judgment.[21]

One is left with the impression that, given the will, Philip had the ability to govern England. But as he looked back upon his year's experience, he complained to Mary that he had been excluded from the government in a way "unbecoming to his dignity" and threatened never to return "without sharing the government with her."[22]

On August 29 the King's barge dropped down the Thames, leaving two heartbroken figures behind. In a way the measure of their grief was the measure of the Spanish marriage. Mary, sensing the disappointment of all her hopes as woman and Queen, kept back her tears only until she was alone in an upper room of the palace at Greenwich. Her "spiritual confessor" of former days, perhaps not even present at the scene, gave way to a more unlovely manifestation of personal tragedy. Bitter and unresigned, chagrined at his failure to win Philip's confidence, Renard publicly complained about the King's lack of gratitude. If his secretary can be believed, he even contemplated writing a book which would paint Philip and Mary "in their true colors" in return for their disappointment of his ambition. About two weeks after the

21 *Ven. Cal.*, VI, Part I, 178, 183. cf. Weiss, IV, 396. 22 *Ven. Cal.*, VI, Part I, 212.

King's departure Renard himself left England. Like some haughty rebellious sinner of Dante's *Inferno,* he seemed to incur the wrath of the very elements themselves as he crossed the Channel. A storm destroyed all his possessions but "one cape," "200,000 crowns' worth" in all. Small wonder that seven years later he thought that he had stayed three and a half, not two years, in England. Mary, in her letter of commendation to the Emperor, spoke not only of the ambassador's diligence and wisdom in a time of great danger but also of "the desire he had to serve us and the affection he bore to my affairs." But Renard himself knew better how to sum up the significance of his work in England. "If everything did not succeed as was expected," he wrote to Philip seven years later, "the fault cannot be attributed to me; I did what I was ordered."[23]

* * *

For a time after Philip's departure it seemed as if the two-year struggle between Habsburg and Valois to dominate England had lost its *raison d'être.* Neither Spain nor France had won a decisive victory. Philip was thoroughly disillusioned about the possibilities of turning his newest possession into a servile instrument of his will, and Henry II had learned that the English would tolerate French intrigue only so long as the threat from Spain endured. But even while Renard was crossing the Channel and Noailles was enjoying his new-found leisure by indulging his taste for the chase, a storm was brewing in Italy which threatened to sweep England once more into the main stream of continental affairs. Just at the moment when the island kingdom seemed to lose most of its significance in European diplomacy, the King of France made the fateful mistake which his ancestors had so often made of plunging himself into the maelstrom of Italian politics.

In September 1555 the new Pope, Paul IV, made dramatic demonstration of his implacable hatred of the Habsburgs by imprisoning several cardinals and Roman nobles of Imperialist leanings. The Guises immediately saw their chance. They argued with some show of reason that a Franco-Papal alliance would

23 Weiss, V, 11. Also *ibid.,* 22, 42; Vertot, V, 133-4; *Ven. Cal.,* VI, Part I, 193; Mary to Charles V [Sept. 1555], Antigny, Tyler, p. 205 (misdated "July" by Tyler).

bring the Emperor to his knees more quickly than would further military campaigns in the north. Charles's power was waning; his control over Germany was seriously crippled by the religious Peace of Augsburg (September 25), and one primary aim of French policy would be attained when the Habsburg inheritance was divided between Philip and Ferdinand after the Emperor's abdication. But there was still need of a final blow which would force the tottering Habsburgs to their knees, and to the Guises, the actions of the impetuous pontiff offered a heaven-sent opportunity to advance their family interest and their nation's prestige at one and the same time.

Immediately the question of England's attitude became of importance. An offensive alliance between France and the Papacy might exasperate English public opinion and goad English statesmen into war—especially if French troops were withdrawn to Italy in any great numbers leaving the French border open to attack from Calais or the Netherlands. Mary might be compelled to consent to war against her will and Philip might acquire the popularity (and the coronation) which he had sought in vain once he became the leader of a crusade against France and the Papacy, both anathema to many of the English middle classes. Montmorency, fighting a losing battle against the Guises at court, was particularly worried by these considerations during the latter part of September. Shortly before the Cardinal of Lorraine left for Rome (October 1) to negotiate the papal alliance, the Constable confessed his worries in private to François de Noailles. While they were talking, the King, the Dauphin, the Cardinal, and the Duke of Guise entered the room and asked François whether there was any assurance that England would remain neutral. The latter replied in the negative and wrote gloomily to his brother in London, "instead of a good peace we may enter on a great war."[24]

Perhaps the "good peace" and the "great war" were not altogether incompatible, however, especially if the threat of a Franco-papal alliance should induce Philip to negotiate a truce in the North. The threat implicit in the Cardinal of Lorraine's journey

[24] Vertot, V, 152-5. Also *ibid.*, 188-9, 199; *Ven. Cal.*, VI, Part I, 227; *For. Cal., Mary*, 185-6, 188.

to Rome was felt almost immediately in Brussels, and even before the Emperor's formal abdication Philip turned his attention toward reviving the peace negotiations. Renard, quick to see an opportunity of making himself useful once more, threw himself into the work with characteristic energy. Before leaving London he had promised Parpaglia to use what influence he had with Charles and Philip, and on October 12 he wrote the Abbot from Brussels that he had persuaded them to make new overtures. Philip wrote Mary at the same time asking her to "mediate vigorously" by threatening war in case the French still refused fair terms. Parpaglia, who had already tried to transfer the negotiations from London to Brussels, took new hope from Philip's unwonted energy. Apparently the King was even willing to agree to a temporary truce in case a definitive peace were still impossible.[25]

In spite of his fear of English intervention, Montmorency was in no hurry to take advantage of Philip's overtures, and Noailles was even less eager than the Constable. The ambassador now felt that his brother's mission to England during the summer had been a mistake. In renewing the peace talks Henry II had admitted by implication that the Spanish marriage was a success instead of a failure; Europe and especially England had drawn the conclusion that France was weakening in the face of the Anglo-Spanish alliance. Apologizing for the unscrupulousness of the suggestion, he urged Montmorency to continue the war until the hollowness of Philip's position in England became apparent to all. When he first heard that Henry II was considering an offensive alliance with the Pope, he rejoiced. Like François he was afraid that Paul IV could not be trusted, but unlike his brother he thought that the new departure would strengthen rather than weaken the French position. He was glad that the immediate effect of the Cardinal's trip to Rome was to discourage the peace party in France and to stimulate new offers from Brussels and London. Henry II could now dictate his own terms; the quarry had been brought to bay and the bellicose ambassador wanted to be in at the kill. If the King meant to take immediate advantage of the opportunity, Noailles naturally desired to share in the glory of negotiating the

[25] Vertot, V, 162-6; *Ven. Cal.*, VI, Part I, 159, 208, 215, 227, 230, 259.

peace, as he confided to L'Aubespine; but the prospect soon appeared to be so dim that he wrote asking for his recall without waiting for further word from the French court.[26]

By the middle of November it had become clear, in fact, that peace would not come either from London or from Rome. The honest brokers of the year before had either lost their enthusiasm or passed from the stage. During the moving ceremony on October 25 in which the Emperor had abdicated his lordship of the Netherlands, Philip had formally inherited his father's quarrel with France; Mary was apparently disillusioned about the efficacy of peace talks and conferences; Pole no longer represented either the curia or the English government in any real sense; and the irenic Julius III was dead. An offer from the embattled Paul IV to act the part of peacemaker had already reduced the profession of mediation to an absurdity, and on November 12 Gardiner succumbed to the illness which had stricken him shortly after his return from the parley at Marcq. Noailles greeted the Chancellor's death with unabashed joy. Relations between the two had been unusually cordial after Philip's departure—Madame de Noailles had sent *confitures,* her husband white wine, to cheer the invalid—but the French ambassador could not but rejoice that the strong hand which had brought some order out of chaos in Mary's government was finally removed. Noailles could forgive Paget, the author of the Spanish marriage, before he could forgive Gardiner, the convert.[27]

By the end of the month another and more direct road to peace had been found. It had been agreed at Marcq that commissioners from both sides should meet on the frontier to arrange an exchange of prisoners and a French agent had been sent to the border in September, but it was not until after the Emperor's abdication that Philip sent an Imperial trumpet to agree to a conference. Since the French had far more to gain from such an exchange than their enemies, Philip's move was a clear invitation to discuss peace terms

[26] Vertot, V, 130-2, 141, 175-6, 180, 188-9; Montmorency to Noailles, 6 and 16 Oct. 1555, Aff. Etr., IX, fols. 539, 546; Noailles to D'Oysel, 20 Oct. 1555, *ibid.,* fol. 550; Antoine to François de Noailles, 10 Nov. 1555, *ibid.,* fol. 559.

[27] Antoine to François de Noailles, 6 Oct. 1555, Aff. Etr., IX, fol. 540ᵛ; Vertot, V, 127, 205. On the results of Gardiner's death, see *Ven. Cal.,* VI, Part I, 251-2.

directly, without English mediation. But the two roads to peace
did not diverge immediately. Philip had no intention of short-
circuiting the route through London, and it was Pole himself
who first formally suggested to Noailles that terms might profit-
ably be discussed at the conference on prisoners.[28]

The suggestion aroused Noailles's flagging interest in the negotiations. Gradually he realized that he might yet be able to leave
London as the most successful diplomat of his day, destroyer of
Habsburg influence in England and author of a European peace
settlement. His agents were once more meddling successfully in
parliamentary affairs and Montmorency had given him a task
calculated to appeal to his patriotism and diplomatic skill, namely
to "cover up, deny, conceal, and contradict" the Franco-papal
understanding, in order to keep England out of the war. On November 26 he sent L'Aubespine a long and statesmanlike appeal
for peace, adding that he was ready to remain at his post two
months longer. The substance of victory was already Henry's, he
wrote; to presume any further upon God's favor, as Charles the
Bold and the Emperor himself had done, would be to invite divine
retribution; peace with honor would profit the King, restore the
nobles to their meadows and mills, and give the *bon homme* back
his slice of bread. Philip was naturally peace-loving, extravagant,
and fond of display. Why teach him to be economical and conscious of his grievances? To continue fighting now would be to
make of a Philip "mild and gracious" another Charles, "shrewd,
calculating, and malicious, the most dangerous enemy which ever
our land had." How much influence these arguments had at the
French court we do not know, but perhaps they helped strengthen
Montmorency's case for peace. Later, when Henry II came to
explain to his ally the Sultan why he had concluded a truce, his
letter (probably drafted by L'Aubespine) mentioned the danger
of English intervention and repeated the substance, and even the
phraseology, of Noailles's argument anent Philip.[29]

28 *Ven. Cal.*, VI, Part I, 191, 238; Vertot, V, 225-6, 230.

29 Vertot, V, 219-22; G. Ribier, *Lettres et mémoires d'estat*, II, 659; George Duruy,
De pactis . . . apud Valcellas indutiis, 62-5. On Noailles's intrigues in Parliament, see
below, pp. 275 *ff*.

During December Parpaglia made a final and futile effort to gain a permanent settlement through Pole's mediation. No one, not even Parpaglia himself, had much respect for Pole's ability; Noailles had strict orders to avoid giving any impression that the French wanted peace; and Philip had no intention of putting the negotiations in Pole's or Mary's hands, though he was willing to use the cloak of English mediation for what it was worth. A week before Christmas Parpaglia was sent by Pole and Mary to Brussels, only to discover that third parties were now no more welcome in the Netherlands than they were in France.[30]

Meanwhile Renard had once more become the central figure in the diplomatic scene. Once back at the Imperial court he was able to recover something of his earlier prestige and on November 17 Philip was induced to appoint him a member of the Privy Council of Flanders.[31] Soon afterward he was chosen as the actual head (under the titular leadership of the Count of Lalaing) of the Imperial commission sent to negotiate an exchange of prisoners with Admiral Coligny at the abbey of Vaucelles. The line which he took during the discussions which followed was largely determined by his personal ambition. He seems to have decided that Philip and his Spanish advisers, unlike Charles and Granvelle, would welcome a truce at almost any price, and he set himself to gain a quick settlement. Since the French made it clear from the outset that they would not tolerate even the formality of mediation, Renard publicly advocated exclusion of the English as the only way to reach an agreement. Careful as he was to follow instructions when he found that Granvelle was determined to have Pole and Mary included in the discussions if at all possible, he never wavered in his determination to get a cessation of hostilities, on the French terms if necessary.[32]

Underlying Renard's calculations was a confused conflict of opinion at the Imperial court. Philip's Spanish followers (especially Ruy Gómez) wanted a quick agreement. They cared little about the immediate war issues and still less about English feel-

---

[30] Vertot, V, 249-50, 260, 262, 289; *Ven. Cal.*, VI, Part I, 288, 293, 297-8, 301-3, 310.
[31] Besançon, Fonds Granvelle, Vol. LXXV, fol. 207; Vertot, V, 239-40.
[32] Weiss, IV, 515-19, 522-31; also Vertot, V, 316.

ings. Granvelle and the Emperor's French-speaking counsellors were more stubborn about submitting to French demands and more concerned about how Mary and Pole would feel if a truce were negotiated behind their backs. By throwing his influence on the side of the Spaniards, Renard of course hoped to gain Philip's favor. Unfortunately he aroused Granvelle's enmity and Mary's suspicion without winning the King's confidence. Granvelle was apparently able to persuade Philip that Renard had exceeded his instructions in making concessions to the French, some color being given to his accusations by a concurrent investigation into the treasonable activities of Etienne Quiclet, Renard's *maître d'hôtel* in England.[33]

Meanwhile a struggle parallel to that between the Spaniards and Franc-Comtois at Brussels was being waged between Montmorency and the Duke of Guise within the *conseil des affaires* at Blois. The Franco-papal alliance, formally signed by the Cardinal of Lorraine at Rome on December 15, was the best lever the French possessed to bring Philip to terms. Coligny was therefore careful to let news of it leak out at Vaucelles early in January. But everyone "in the know" (as Noailles put it) was aware that Philip might well discount the immediate threat from an aged and none-too-wealthy pontiff. The Cardinal's absence in Rome had temporarily given Montmorency the upper hand over Guise, but the Constable was forced to fight every step of his way in persuading Henry II to agree to a truce—and the Cardinal was already hurrying back to Blois in the hope of blocking a settlement. Like Renard, Coligny (who was the Constable's nephew) was working against time in order to outwit a rival faction of warmongers at home.[34]

[33] On the conflict between Granvelle and the Spaniards, see *Ven. Cal.*, VI, Part I, 289, 302, 326, 339, 341, 369, 382; Part II, 992. On Granvelle's and Philip's suspicions of Renard after the truce, see "Vunière," *Etude historique sur Simon Renard*, 103-5; Tridon, "Renard," 243; L. Febvre, *Philippe II et la Franche-Comté*, 156-8; *For. Cal., Mary,* 211; Vertot, V, 316.

[34] Noailles to Montmorency, 27 Dec. 1555, Aff. Etr., IX, fol. 577; *Ven. Cal.*, VI, Part I, 314, 324, 329, 335; Weiss, IV, 594. On June 13, 1556, Renard wrote Philip from Paris, "la tresve qu'ilz ont traicté ayt esté par necessité et par le seul conseil du connestable pour traverser les actions du cardinal de Loreyne, et d'Italye, et pour retirer les prisonniers qu'ilz luy tient" (Antigny, Tyler, p. 267).

These considerations help to explain the fact that the Truce of Vaucelles, signed by the commissioners on February 5, 1556, was hardly a truce at all. Rather it was a document marking a certain stage in the long quarrel between Habsburg and Valois and in the political evolution of the French, Spanish, and English monarchies. Both in Brussels and in Blois there was a faction in favor of war and a faction in favor of peace. (If diplomatic observers can be believed, the advocates of peace had the support of the mass of the common people on both sides.) For a moment, financial need, diplomatic circumstances, and domestic rivalries conspired to produce an agreement to suspend hostilities for five years, without settlement of the outstanding issues; and since the French remained in possession of more conquered territory than their enemies, the agreement was naturally interpreted as a signal diplomatic victory for Henry II. But at any moment the balance of forces which had produced the armistice might shift, plunging Europe once more into war.

The truce had significant bearing upon Anglo-French and Anglo-Spanish relations. The long and toilsome negotiations which led up to it began, as we have seen, in England, but they did not end there. Gardiner's and Paget's attempt to make their nation's voice count again in European affairs had failed, and the failure could not but reflect upon what little prestige Mary's government still possessed. The English middle classes, who disliked their government's attempt to stop the continental war, could rejoice that the agreement had been concluded behind the Queen's back. It was to be expected that the French, remembering their experience at Marcq, should flatly reject English mediation at Vaucelles; but Mary, Pole, and the English Council saved their bitterest resentment for Philip—and for each other. Never before in Mary's reign had the court rung with such recrimination and abuse as it did in January 1556. The Queen could not forgive her husband and Renard for their callous disregard of English prestige at Vaucelles. Pole was characteristically cautious in expressing his feelings, but he was angered by Philip's treatment of Parpaglia at Brussels. Parpaglia himself was hurt that others had reaped where he had sown and said some ungracious things about Pole's "negligence and timidity." Paget, Arundel, and their fellow councillors blamed the Cardinal and the Abbot for monopolizing—and botching—the negotiations. The Truce of Vaucelles discredited the English government at home and abroad, deepened the animosity of Englishmen for their Spanish King, and all but extinguished any lingering hope which Philip's few friends in England may have had that the Spanish marriage would yet prove to be a blessing to the realm.[35]

If the tiresome negotiations which have formed the burden of the preceding pages be considered as part of the long effort of French diplomats to immobilize England and to ward off the threat implicit in the Spanish marriage, then Antoine de Noailles deserved much of the credit which his devoted younger brother insisted upon giving him. François had protested to Antoine at the end of December that Coligny was stealing the honor which belonged to the ambassador himself.

> However [he wrote], from whatever quarter this greatly desired good may result, you will have the part in it and the honor which has been given to those who have successfully carried a heavy burden nine hundred and ninety paces and have put it down momentarily in order to breathe—only to have someone who would not have dared undertake to remove it at the beginning of the course steal possession of it and carry it to the goal. So in truth every one of good judgment and good sense considered the trip to Ardres [the parley at Marcq] so fruitful for the good of the King's affairs that, wherever the peace or the truce may be born, all my life I shall think that it was conceived there—and we are almost at the ninth month of gestation.[36]

Whether Antoine de Noailles felt so keenly about the matter as his more voluble brother we do not know. In any case, he consoled himself with the thought that there were others in England who were even more chagrined than he at being relegated to the outer darkness. He was tired of "this nasty island" that was England, tired of explaining to English critics why his

[35] Vertot, V, 235-6, 274, 285-7, 289-90, 304; Ven. Cal., VI, Part I, 327-8; François de Noailles to Montmorency, 3 Feb. 1557, Aff. Etr., XIII, fol. 150; Montmorency to Noailles, 20 Feb. 1556, Aff. Etr., IX, fol. 586.

[36] François to Antoine de Noailles, 27 Dec. 1555, Aff. Etr., IX, fol. 578.

Most Christian King felt it necessary to ally himself with the Turk, and glad to see peace come, from whatever quarter. The day the truce was signed at Vaucelles he was out hunting in the royal park of Nonesuch—with such zest that his greyhounds brought down two more deer than the Queen's patent had allowed him.[37]

[37] Vertot, V, 269 *ff.*; A. J. Kempe, *Loseley Manuscripts,* 155-6.

CHAPTER XI

DUDLEY'S CONSPIRACY

JULY 1555 TO JUNE 1556

ON March 1556, hardly more than a month after the diplomats signed the Truce of Vaucelles, the people of London were startled to learn that a desperate and widespread conspiracy against the Queen had been discovered. "The stout and dyvellyshe hartes of the people of England" were once more ready "to worke treason and make insurrections,"[1] but the stoutest hearts had been at the preparation of their deviltry since the previous July. Like the Truce itself, which François de Noailles pictured as conceived at Marcq and brought forth at Vaucelles, the plot which bears the name of Sir Henry Dudley was nine months in the womb.

Mention has already been made in the preceding chapter of the wave of popular restlessness which troubled the Council and rejoiced the French ambassador during the summer of 1555. There was an ugly temper in the crowds which came to witness the suffering of heretics, and several outbreaks of popular resentment were recorded in the Council's minute-book. The strong stand taken by the French at Marcq encouraged those who feared that peace on the continent might enable Philip to destroy the liberties of Englishmen. There were serious affrays between Englishmen and Spaniards in June and hatred of the foreigner seemed to grind deeper than ever in the hearts of the people. Once again the diplomats were musing upon the relation between summer weather and popular sedition.[2]

---

[1] The phrases quoted are from John Bradford's Letter in Strype, *Memorials* (ed. 1816), VII, 186.

[2] Vertot, V, 12-13; *Ven. Cal.,* VI, Part I, 85, 126; Pollard, *Pol. Hist.,* 142-3.

Early in July while Philip and Mary were at Hampton Court, Pole at Richmond, and most of the courtiers at their country houses to avoid the London heat, a group of ex-rebels were meeting at Paul's and other places in the city. Renard reported that all of them were heretics, many of them associates of Wyatt who had been released from the Tower six months before, and some of them relatives or followers of Elizabeth. Michiele noted that among them were "the Dudleys," "sons of the late Duke of Northumberland." "Their intentions not being considered good," Gardiner ordered them to disperse to their country houses. The suspects protested vigorously that they were "honest men," not traitors, but the Council was firm. It was not enough not to be traitors, they were told; they must keep themselves above every suspicion of sedition.[3]

From these vague data it is impossible to reconstruct a list of those who aroused the government's suspicion. But it is not impossible that among "the Dudleys" was Sir Henry Dudley, a distant cousin of Northumberland's whom we have already met as the Duke's agent in France during July 1553.[4] And it seems beyond doubt that one of the number was Edward Randall of Kent.

On July 15 Randall visited Noailles and told him that "fifty gentlemen" of his acquaintance had formed a conspiracy "to recover their liberties" before the end of August or to die in the attempt. The plot, said Randall, was different from the one he had outlined to the ambassador eleven months before, but like the first, its success would depend upon persuading Sir Peter Carew to return to France from Germany so that he and the English exiles abroad might support the efforts of the conspirators at home. Noailles, absorbed in peace negotiations, made no promises, and two weeks later Montmorency vetoed any support of the scheme. Carew's presence in France, he thought, would

---

[3] Renard to Charles V, 10 July 1555, Weiss, IV, 447-8 (lacunae supplied in Antigny, Tyler); *Ven. Cal.*, VI, Part I, 137; Wiesener, 323. cf. the list of those released from the Tower on Jan. 18, 1555 (*A.P.C.*, V, 90-1).

[4] See above, pp. 50 ff. Also *D.N.B.*, s.v. Henry Dudley; *Span. Cal.*, X and XI, index; Garrett, *Marian Exiles*, 147-9.

only irritate Mary without accomplishing anything for the French cause, and he saw little "resolution" in what the plotters proposed.[5]

About the same time that Randall was conferring with Noailles, one Edward Horsey (later an accomplice in Dudley's conspiracy) was taking advantage of a commission to carry up letters from Dorset to the Council to spread rumors of a "commocion" in his home county. The Council had to warn the sheriffs of nine counties to punish those who were spreading the report.[6] In September an obscure conspirator named Bowes crossed to France, got into touch with Boisdauphin ("the gret and thick embasitor that wase here in Kyng Edwardes time"), and obtained permission from Henry II "to uuse and occupye a mint ther for the ayd of his contrymen against the Spanerdes."[7]

François de Noailles thought that only the unusually heavy summer rains had prevented a general rising,[8] but it was more probably the government's alertness, Noailles's refusal to commit himself, and Philip's departure for Brussels which sapped whatever "resolution" the rebellious spirits of the realm may have had. Between the King's departure and the opening of Parliament on October 21 there were only the vaguest rumors of sedition, but the government was not happy about the state of the kingdom. On August 31, two days after Philip left Greenwich, the select council approved Mary's decision to summon Parliament in order to approve the restoration to the church of the ecclesiastical revenues in possession of the Crown and to obtain a subsidy. Neither proposal would be popular, and many might grumble about granting money to a government which seemed to be deliberately diminishing the Crown's revenue. In order to quiet the fears of the lay owners of monastic property—or as the Council put it, to "better admonish the people" and to stamp out "seditious rumors"—a bull of Paul IV confirming Julius III's dispensation

---

[5] Noailles to Montmorency, 15 July 1555, Aff. Etr., IX, fol. 489; Montmorency to Noailles, 27 July 1555, ibid., fols. 498ᵛ-9.

[6] A.P.C., V, 168-70; Ven. Cal., VI, Part I, 144.

[7] Examination of William Hinnes, 28 Mar. 1556, P.R.O., S.P.Dom. 11, Vol. VII, No. 39.

[8] Vertot, V, 73. See also ibid., 44, 50.

was published from Paul's Cross on September 1 and ordered to be printed in Latin and English.[9]

There were good reasons why Mary's fourth Parliament proved to be the most unruly and obstructive of her reign. Economic distress was aggravating the religious and political unrest. The summer's harvest had been poor and the cost of food and fuel was rising sharply. The fateful association in the popular mind of religious persecution and Spanish tyranny had been nourished by nine months of *carbonnades* and Anglo-Spanish affrays. Persistent rumors that Mary meant to have Philip crowned (so that he might prolong his reign in England after her death) stiffened the resolution of many who came up to Westminster determined to preserve English freedom. The Venetian ambassador, Michiele, has left a celebrated description of the membership of this most interesting of Mary's parliaments:

The present House of Commons, whether by accident or from design, a thing not seen for many years in any Parliament, is quite full of gentry and nobility (for the most part suspected in the matter of religion), and therefore more daring and licentious than former houses, which consisted of burgesses and plebeians, by nature timid and respectful, who easily inclined towards the will of the sovereign.[10]

The temper of some of the more "daring and licentious" members may be gauged by the fact that perhaps a dozen of them were later guilty, or strongly suspected of being guilty of treason: Sir John Pollard (the Speaker), Sir Nicholas Arnold, Sir Anthony Kingston, Sir William Courtenay, Sir John Perrot, Sir Giles Strangways, Edmund and Francis Verney, Henry Peckham, and possibly John Throckmorton, Thomas White, and John Philips.[11] Was it "by accident" that Gloucester, Devon, and Bucks returned

---

[9] Memorials of Council proceedings, P.R.O., S.P.Dom. 11, Vol. VI, Nos. 16, 18. One of Paul IV's first acts had been to issue a bull condemning the alienation of ecclesiastical property in general. See Haile, *Pole*, 468.

[10] *Ven. Cal.*, VI, Part I, 251; Pollard, *Pol. Hist.*, 143.

[11] cf. *Official Return of Members*, I, 392-5, with the lists of conspirators and suspects in P.R.O., S.P.Dom. 11, Vol. VII, Nos. 23-5; *Machyn Diary*, 103, 104; *Ven. Cal.*, VI, Part I, 439-40, 446-7; and *Verney Papers*, 58-76. The identification of Thomas White and John Philips, members for Downton and Poole respectively, with Dudley's accomplices of the same names seems reasonably certain. But it is not so clear that the John Throckmorton who sat for Coventry was the conspirator of the same name (see *A.P.C.*, IV, 324, 388; V, 70; VI, 75, 124; and Pollard, *Pol. Hist.*, 144).

a group of gentry determined (as later events proved) to risk their very lives to overthrow Mary? Or was it "from design"? Were the meetings at Paul's in July the prelude to other gatherings at the country houses of the south and west? Did Randall's "fifty gentlemen" decide in September to use constitutional means to thwart Philip's coronation before they turned again to rebellion? If so, the elections of 1555 witnessed the earliest concerted attempt of an opposition group to capture control of Parliament in Tudor history. But in the absence of evidence all that can be said is that, for its time, the opposition of some hundred members formed a remarkably well disciplined and suspiciously well organized parliamentary faction, possessed of unusually shrewd leadership.[12]

The departure of Philip and Renard, together with Gardiner's death (November 12), left the government without a leader capable of planning and executing a parliamentary policy. The Council's Secretary, Petre, might have filled the rôle, but one of Noailles's informers, a "gentleman servant" of the Queen, had heard him complain bitterly about the baneful results of the Spanish marriage only two weeks before Parliament met. One who hated the Spaniards as heartily as Petre said he did was no man to direct a program which (in the Queen's mind at least) included Philip's coronation.[13] Noailles heard that after the Chancellor's death Mary remarked to Pole that there was no one about her whom she could trust except the Cardinal himself.[14] Seven of Gardiner's party in the Council had seats in the House of Commons, but not one of them proved capable of leadership. In fact, during the debate on a bill which proposed to confiscate the property of refugees who remained abroad, Sir Edward Hastings, who was managing the bill for the government along with Sir Robert Rochester, almost came to blows with Sir George Howard, an outspoken member of the opposition; and Pembroke

[12] One illustration of the shrewdness of the opposition leaders is to be found in the way they defeated the government's proposal to abolish the election of nonresident members —by introducing a Place Bill (Pollard, *Pol. Hist.*, 148; *Ven. Cal.*, VI, Part I, 252).

[13] Vertot, V, 167-8. The informer cannot be identified, but it may have been either Sir John Leigh or Sir George Howard. See below.

[14] *ibid.*, V, 205, 206-7; *Ven. Cal.*, VI, Part I, 299.

had an unseemly quarrel with Sir John Perrot over the same issue.[15] It is significant that in its extremity the government had recourse to the expert services of Sir William Cecil, hitherto excluded from the Queen's circle of advisers, in managing several of its bills.[16]

The French ambassador would have been blind indeed not to have taken advantage of such an unexampled opportunity for intrigue. Seditious pamphlets, written by English refugees in the Rhine valley and filled with harrowing pictures of Habsburg tyranny in Naples and Milan were circulating about the streets of London and even in the chambers of Parliament.[17] Petre feared a rising in the North, where some of the local gentry were supposed to have been bribed by French money, and the Council was frightened enough to treat Noailles unusually well during October and November. About the middle of November the Queen graciously informed him through Parpaglia that "she wanted her godson [Henri de Noailles] to be well-lodged, and his father also"; in order to allow the ambassador to be near Pole during the peace negotiations, she again offered him a comfortable house in Southwark which he seems to have occupied for a while during the summer.[18] There was no longer any necessity (as there had been two years before) for conspirators and members of the parliamentary opposition to visit the French ambassador by a postern gate and under cover of darkness.

Naturally the question which interested Noailles most was that of Philip's coronation—or, as he now put it, the plan of excluding the "rightful heirs" to the crown, meaning Elizabeth. A year before he had ignored all parliamentary issues, such as

[15] Vertot, V, 253; *Ven. Cal.,* VI, Part I, 283.

[16] Pollard, *Pol. Hist.,* 144, and references there given.

[17] Vertot, V, 241, 254; *Ven. Cal.,* VI, Part I, 269-70; Noailles to Montmorency, 22 Dec. 1555, Aff. Etr., IX, fol. 576. Froude (VI, 365-7) thinks that John Bradford's Letter to Arundel was one of these pamphlets, but its reference to "this time of peace" would seem to date it after the Truce of Vaucelles (Feb. 5, 1556) and before Bradford was arrested in Dudley's plot (March 1556). Bradford refers to books he has heard of, but not seen—"The Lamentation of Napelles" and "The Mourning of Mylayne"—which were undoubtedly two of the pamphlets in question. See Strype, *Memorials* (ed. 1816), VII, 183-99; and Garrett, *Marian Exiles,* 96-7.

[18] Vertot, V, 164, 168, 181. On Noailles's removal to Southwark, see Vertot, V, 195, 218; and Antoine to François de Noailles, 31 Oct., 10 Nov., and 20 Nov. 1555, Aff. Etr., XVIII, fol. 13; IX, fols. 559, 575.

the religious question, which did not directly concern Anglo-French relations. But now everything was grist to his mill. Through his agents and friends he interested himself in every bill which encountered opposition: the subsidy, the refugees' bill, and a bill renouncing the Crown's share in annates.

Early in the session there was so much opposition to the subsidy bill that Noailles was sure the Queen would not get all the money she wanted—"and if my intrigues and spies prove of service, she will get nothing." "Four good heads" (Sir Anthony Kingston, Sir Nicholas Arnold, Sir William Courtenay, and Sir John Perrot?) among the members had individually promised him to oppose any grant, but this first skirmish resulted in defeat for the opposition. The Queen gave up her demand for an additional fifteenth, which would have borne heavily upon the poor in view of the bad harvest, and the subsidy alone passed the Commons on October 31. "In such a body the majority vote prevails," Noailles wrote the same day, "and the dissenting opinions of a hundred gentlemen were useless in a body of three hundred persons." Perhaps not all the hundred were "gentlemen," but the word confirms Michiele's description of the character of the opposition.[19]

In the debates over the annates bill the opposition came closer to victory. The expected objections were raised as soon as the bill was introduced. Two days after the opening session Gardiner had attempted to reassure the lay owners of church property by stating that the proposal was not aimed at them, but neither Lords nor Commons were satisfied. The Queen "determined to use her personal authority in the form adopted by former sovereigns when apprehensive of any of their proposals encountering any repulse or contradiction." She summoned sixty members of the Commons and many of the Lords to the palace on November 19 and explained forcefully that her conscience demanded the bill. A private member had the temerity to launch into a reply but he was silenced by his fellow-members. Six days later, after the bill had passed the Lords, eight members accompanied by four other men "of substance" went secretly to dine with Noailles.

[19] Vertot, V, 171, 184-5, 187, 190; *Ven. Cal.,* VI, Part I, 229, 238-9, 243.

Among them was a Courtenay, probably Sir William. They said they had come on the suggestion of Don Diego de Azevedo, Philip's steward, to pump the ambassador, but they stayed to discuss the opposition which the bill had encountered—and perhaps to concert measures for its defeat. The chief talking-point of the parliamentary opposition was that the Queen had no legal or moral right to alienate crown property, and Noailles indulged in the luxury of irony on the subject with his guests. He told them

that they should not be so obstinate about doing her will to the diminution of her revenues, since they had so readily accorded her such a great sum of money [in the subsidy], which they well knew was destined to be used for the aid and succor of him [Philip] whose only aim in the world is to oppress them and put them in perpetual servitude.[20]

His sarcasm must have cut deep with members who were attempting to base their arguments on broad patriotic grounds, but again their efforts were in vain. The bill was committed to a joint committee (of which Cecil was a member), and on December 3 it was pushed through the Commons in amended form—but only after the doors had been locked on the members for most of the day.[21]

Naturally the opposition was in an ugly mood when the refugees bill reached its final stages of debate. Whether the exiles abroad were heretics or patriots did not greatly matter; they found numerous friends in Parliament. The members by now were afraid that the government was conducting a subtle attack upon property rights and upon the national honor; both the Henrician land settlement and the rights of Elizabeth were in danger. Gardiner had promised in a roundabout way at the opening session that the question of Philip's coronation would not be broached, but some of the members knew that while they were sitting at Westminster Philip was playing shamelessly upon his wife's devotion to force her to do his will in the matter. At any rate rumors of the King's letters and of Mary's piteous replies

---

[20] Advis, 26 Nov. 1555, Aff. Etr., IX, fol. 565. Noailles says simply that he spoke thus "à quelques uns qui m'en parloient," but it is clear from his letter to Montmorency of the same date (Vertot, V, 224-5) that his argument must have been used at the dinner mentioned.

[21] Ven. Cal., VI, Part I, 217, 251, 259-60, 268, 270.

reached Noailles, and they must also have reached the ears of his associates.[22] The Commons were more than ready to throw out the bill against the fugitives in revenge for earlier defeats. All that was needed was a leader, and the rôle was soon filled by Sir Anthony Kingston of Gloucestershire. Fearing the government meant to win over the "noes" by playing for time, as it had done with the annates bill, he posted himself at the door of the House with several friends to prevent anyone leaving and announced "in a loud voice" that the present bill would not be passed against the consciences of many as the other had. The bill was defeated, the Parliament dissolved, and Sir Anthony clapped in the Tower with one or two of his friends.[23]

There is reason to believe that Kingston was inspired by something more than factious motives in blocking the government's move against the refugees abroad. The mere presence in France and Germany of several hundred English exiles was a constant source of anxiety to Mary and the Council, particularly in November and December 1555. A recent writer finds evidence of a well-organized propaganda campaign conceived and directed by Sir John Cheke and John Ponet, the leaders of the English colony at Strasbourg. The seditious pamphlets which appeared in London while Parliament was sitting were written by Englishmen abroad, printed at Emden, and disseminated through the eastern counties by agents of the exiles. No clear evidence has yet been found of any direct connection between the religious exiles in the Rhineland and their more treasonably minded countrymen in France, but the difference between religion and politics in the mentality of the Marian exiles was indeed "but a hair's breadth." Carew, ex-leader of the fugitives in France, had made a furtive visit to England during the previous spring, and in December he was in Brussels suing Philip for his pardon, but also in close touch with Cheke's propaganda campaign. Sir Henry Dudley had relatives in the Rhine colonies, and the little group at Wesel were

[22] *Ven. Cal.,* VI, Part I, 218, 227, 229, 281, 299; Vertot, V, 172, 175, 185, 190, 246.
[23] *Ven. Cal.,* VI, Part I, 243-4, 251, 275, 283; *Verney Papers,* 66. Noailles entrusted the story of Kingston's "merveilleuse bravade" to La Marque, to be passed on to the French court by word of mouth. Noailles to Montmorency, 12 Dec. 1555, Aff. Etr., IX, fol. 570.

suspected of having been privy to his plot.[24] Propaganda from Germany and the threat of invasion (led by Englishmen) from France were trump cards in the hands of English trouble-makers at home, and Kingston must have been fully aware of how disastrous a law confiscating their property at home would be to his allies abroad.

Even before the dissolution of Parliament (December 9) the thoughts of the opposition leaders were turning to treason. Many of them—Kingston, Pollard, Perrot, Courtenay, Chichester, Dudley, Ashton, Henry Peckham, and the Tremayne brothers—met regularly during the session at a tavern called Arundel's to concert their resistance to "such matters as should be spoken of in the Parliament House other than liked them."[25] Some of them had undoubtedly been among the "fifty gentlemen" who were ready for rebellion in July. It will be remembered that Wyatt's accomplices turned to treason shortly after Mary's sharp speech to the Commons' delegation which petitioned her to marry an Englishman. There is reason to believe that Dudley's friends turned definitely to plans of violence about the time that the Queen addressed the members on the annates bill (November 19). It was probably sometime during that week that a French intriguer named Berteville, who had been in Noailles's pay for two years,[26] wrote Montmorency that "le sieur DuDelay" had a mind to do Henry II some service. The letter is lost, but it seems to have contained hints about a conspiracy. The Constable thought the plot was "not something to be disdained if our affairs should require it and should change for the worse." But he warned Noailles to step warily.

Since we must be discreet, you will take care to hear on oath from Berteville when, how, and from whom he heard this, and if you see and

---

[24] Garrett, *Marian Exiles,* 14, 27-8, 32-3, 50-1, 104-8, 114-17, 147-9. I cannot feel that Miss Garrett has proved the "particular connection between rebels in France and refugees in Germany which makes of the Dudley conspiracy one of the most far-reaching events of the Tudor period" (p. 148). Dudley's practical calculations were based first and foremost on help from France; perhaps he counted upon the pens of the refugees in Germany, but there is no evidence that he counted upon their swords.

[25] Examination of John Daniel, P.R.O., S.P.Dom. 11, Vol. VIII, No. 35; Froude, VI, 434-5.

[26] On Berteville, see *Amer. Hist. Rev.,* XLV (April 1940), 540 *ff.*

recognize plausibility, dig deeper into the affair with the individual himself
[Dudley?] to whom, if he be wise and prudent, the king will not refuse
his good graces; and meanwhile, awaiting a good opportunity, we could
spare him some good pension. . . .[27]

Noailles was at first inclined to be skeptical about Berteville's
information. When Montmorency's letter reached him, his agents
were out of favor and he could see little "foundation" in their
designs. But after he had spoken to Berteville during the second
week in December, he decided that the plot deserved "greater consideration" than he had thought.[28] On the 16th he sent his most
trusted servant, La Marque, to France with letters from both
Berteville and Dudley to the Constable. Dudley's letter is lost,
but Berteville's has survived. Written before Kingston was imprisoned in the Tower it illustrates how far the conspirators'
plans had advanced before the dissolution of Parliament.[29]

Milord, I wrote you in my last letter that Dudley had begged me to
advise you of the good intention he has to do his Majesty the King [of
France] a service. I promised him to do so. Since then he has asked me
for a reply, which I told him I had not received. He has got into touch
with one [Randall][30] whom the Prince of Spain has taken into his service
as a colonel of infantry[31] so long as he will serve, and with four captains
to whom he is giving two hundred crowns in wages for life, who are so
well attached that they have offered and sworn and promised to Dudley
that if he goes to serve his Majesty [Henry II], they will turn French
whenever he pleases and tells them to, being ready to do so in the presence
of whomever you care to send. I know they are good captains and in good
repute with the soldiers. Whether one should put any faith in this I leave
to your discretion.

Moreover, I have in my presence a knight named Anthony Kingston
(*Quinston*) who lives on the western coast; he can assuredly raise more
than six thousand men in his district and more than sixty of the most
important knights of the district. In talking with Dudley as one who relies
much on him and who hates the Spaniards mightily, [Kingston] said to

---

[27] Montmorency to Noailles, 26 Nov. 1555, Aff. Etr., XVII, fols. 212-14 (original
minute). This passage is omitted from Vertot's published version of the dispatch. See
Vertot, V, 230; and Note on the Sources, p. 347.

[28] Vertot, V, 234, 256.

[29] Kingston was imprisoned from Dec. 10 to Dec. 24 (*A.P.C.*, V, 202, 207, 208). On
Dudley's letter, see below, note 37.

[30] See *Amer. Hist. Rev.*, XLV (April 1940), 551.

[31] "Craint" (undeciphered). The context later shows that the word means "soldiers"
or "infantry." See the last sentence quoted of the letter.

him, "If you go into the service of the King [of France], and land in my county, I will go to meet you with all my forces to chase these tyrants from our country. This I say to you in the presence of this gentleman [Berteville]."

Moreover Dudley told me he has an agreement with the Captain [Richard Uvedale] of the fort of the Isle of Wight (*Huit*) that whenever the King pleases he will surrender it into his hands. Also, if war starts between France and England, he [Dudley] knows a way to take Hammes and Guines, where he has been and where he has had [the captaincy of] the guard.[32]

You may think about all these things and let me know your pleasure. In my opinion and on my life, Dudley carries out a task faithfully, and that, I assure you, you may hear and count on; the result can only be the employment of a gentleman who is certainly most valiant. What I write you is the result of my desire to be the means of his [doing] some good service for his Majesty, and for that I would willingly risk my life. I know for sure that if Dudley once came into England with a thousand soldiers to deliver the country from servitude, he would quickly have twenty thousand men, and the best.[33]

La Marque was well received at Blois. Noailles had asked his brother François to request that the courier be made a royal *valet de chambre* as a reward for his services in England. The request was immediately granted, and François attributed Henry II's alacrity to the "influence and reputation" which the ambassador had at court.[34] Noailles's recommendation that Dudley be given a pension was likewise approved. "I shall be very glad," Henry wrote, "if you will keep him alert and in such a position that you may get as much use as may be hoped out of him."[35]

Berteville had said early in December that he wanted to introduce Dudley to Noailles, but Noailles seems to have held off until he received permission from Henry. It is not altogether clear what Dudley asked of the ambassador and how far Noailles committed himself. Shortly afterward, Dudley said to one of his accomplices,

[32] Sir Henry Dudley's brother, Lord Edmund Dudley, was Lieutenant of Hammes in 1556. Henry himself had been Captain of the Guard at Guines in 1551, and in the following year he supervised the fortification of Portsmouth. (*D.N.B.*, s.v. Henry Dudley; and Garrett, *Marian Exiles*, 147.)

[33] Berteville to Montmorency, n.d., Aff. Etr., IX, fol. 660. Original (*ibid.*, XI, fol. 353) unsigned and in Noailles's cipher.

[34] Antoine to François de Noailles, 15 Dec. 1555, Aff. Etr., IX, fol. 572; François to Antoine de Noailles, 27 Dec. 1555, *ibid.*, fol. 578.

[35] Vertot, V, 262.

here is the Frenche kinges Imbassatour who seeth what estate I lyve in and howe my lyvinge is gone and myne offices taken from me, and he hath offered me that if I will goe over and serve the Frenche kinge, he will not only warraunt that I shall have veraye good enterteynement for my self, but that I shall also be of the kinges previe chambre, and will also warraunt me to have IIIIC crownes a yere for IIII or V gentlemen which I shall bringe with me.[36]

There was undoubtedly more to the conversation, however. Some of Noailles's erstwhile enthusiasm for fostering sedition had been fired anew. To encourage the conspirators he pictured the favor shown to La Marque as the result of Henry II's pleasure with Dudley's letter;[37] and the sequel proved that the ambassador must have satisfied all the "conditions" which Dudley had previously laid down through Berteville.[38]

When war finally broke out between France and England eighteen months later, the English government accused Noailles of having offered the conspirators his house as a place for their meetings.[39] It is not impossible that after Dudley left London some time in January Noailles kept in touch with them through the intrepid "Long John" Throckmorton, although Throckmorton steadfastly denied it later under torture.[40] But after the first conferences with Berteville and Dudley, we know little of Noailles's activities—mainly because at least seven of his most important dispatches during the first four months of 1556 are lost or destroyed.

[36] Confession of John Daniel, 11 Apr. 1556, P.R.O., S.P.Dom. 11, Vol. VIII, No. 6.

[37] Early in February Dudley and Throckmorton were staying at Richard Uvedale's house near Portsmouth. Uvedale later confessed that he had overheard a conversation in French which he pictured as not meant for his ears. The record of this conversation as it exists today is almost illegible, but I believe the meaning is clear if the passage is compared with what has been said above. Dudley said to Throckmorton, "Jeo Balle vn lettre al monsieur Embassator, Et le dit Ambassetor anuoiet par son vierlet [La Marque, on December 16] à le Roye de Faunce le dit lettre, le quel le Roye luy preist [three words crossed out] anvoie [?] bone part que le dit Ambassator dist à moy quell le Roy prist et fait [?] dit vierlet [word crossed out] un de son prevy chambre." Confession of Richard Uvedale, 23 Apr. 1556, P.R.O., S.P.Dom. 11, Vol. VIII, No. 24.

[38] Vertot, V, 256.

[39] Proclamation of war, 7 June 1557, *Tudor and Stuart Proclamations,* ed. Steele, No. 474; copy in French, Aff. Etr., XIII, fols. 225-7.

[40] *Ven. Cal.,* VI, Part I, 423; Confession of John Throckmorton, 18 Apr. 1556, P.R.O., S.P.Dom. 11, Vol. VIII, No. 14.

January and February were troubled months in England. Soon after Parliament was dissolved the fires were lighted anew at Smithfield and elsewhere; a rebellion broke out in Ireland; a pamphlet appeared proclaiming that Edward VI was "still alive and well and in France," awaiting only a popular rebellion to cross the Channel and recover his crown; and the people, particularly in London were grumbling ominously about paying the subsidy, which many were convinced would be used to finance Philip's wars rather than to pay the Queen's debts.[41] In this fevered atmosphere the plot expanded steadily, both in personnel and objectives. The rumors that Mary was pressing for Philip's coronation had focused popular attention once again upon Elizabeth, the legitimate heir, and the conspirators planned to win national support by proclaiming at the right moment that their aim was to pack Mary out of the realm and to put her sister and Courtenay on the throne. "Ower swett Lady Elyzabethe," they were sure, was a "lyberall Dame, and nothing so unthankfull as her syster ys."[42] Their most pressing problem was money. If Henry II would not finance the invasion from abroad which was to support the rising at home, there was another way. Fifty thousand pounds in Spanish silver was reposing in the Exchequer. The Keeper of the Star Chamber was bribed and plans laid to spirit the treasure down to a boat on the Thames, to be carried to France and coined there, probably in the mint which Bowes had got permission to set up.[43]

Noailles's knottiest problem was how to keep the greater part of the conspirators from crossing to France as a result of his promises of French favor to Dudley. The plot was not scheduled to break until late in the spring and many of the plotters apparently felt that the invasion from France was the more romantic—and safer—part of the scheme. Berteville crossed the Channel on January 25 with Jean Ribaut, the navigator, who appears to have been his associate in dealing with Dudley. On February 8 Dudley took

---

[41] Advis, 14 Jan. 1556, Aff. Etr., IX, fol. 583; Vertot, V, 305-7; Pollard, *Pol. Hist.*, 150.

[42] Declaration of Henry Peckham [May 1556], P.R.O., S.P.Dom. 11, Vol. VIII, No. 52.

[43] *Verney Papers*, 61-5.

ship, after making final arrangements with Uvedale to have the guns in the fortress pegged when the exiles landed at Portsmouth; he would return, he said, with ten or twelve good sail and three thousand men, "and by godes bloude I will dryve oute theise Spanyardes or I will dye for it." About March 1 Christopher Ashton went to join his "sonne Dudley," and by the middle of the month sixteen of the conspirators were across the sea. Throckmorton and Bedell were left in charge at home.[44]

Henry II's promises to Dudley through Noailles were closely related to the current peace negotiations at Vaucelles. The two factions at the French court were agreed upon one thing: if an agreement was reached, it must include solid diplomatic advantages. Montmorency was determined that any settlement must include the ransoming of his son and the other French captives in Flanders, and even the Guises could profit by a truce if it constituted a clear diplomatic triumph. In an ironic sense, therefore, *si vis pacem, para bellum* was the guiding principle of French diplomacy in December and January.[45] The offensive alliance with the Pope and the negotiations with Dudley were part and parcel of the same policy. Both could be used to bring pressure to bear on Philip so long as the peace talks continued, and both could be turned to advantage if the parley at Vaucelles came to naught. The news that a truce had been signed on February 5 made little immediate difference at the French court. The Emperor might yet refuse to ratify it and arrangements for ransoming the prisoners were not yet definitely concluded; intrigues which might frighten Philip into ratification were still useful. Hence although Montmorency was embarrassed and angered by Dudley's crossing the Channel, he had no intention of repudiating

---

[44] Confessions of Uvedale, Peckham, and Peter Killigrew, P.R.O., S.P.Dom. 11, Vol. VII, No. 32; Vol. VIII, No. 52; Vol. IX, No. 24. Vertot, V, 298-9; *Verney Papers,* 61-5; Froude, VI, 438 *ff.* The reference to "my sonne Dudley" (in S.P.Dom. 11, Vol. VII, No. 32) proves, I think, that Garrett (*op. cit.,* 149) is wrong in saying that Dudley was son-in-law to Lord Audley, not to Ashton, in 1556. The chronology of the conspirators' movements as given in Baga de Secretis, *4th Report of the Deputy Keeper of the Public Records,* 253-5, does not agree with the sources above and should not be trusted.

[45] See e.g. Vertot, V, 276-8.

the conspirators simply because a truce had been negotiated with the King of England. But he warned Noailles on February 7 to be particularly cautious. Elizabeth, he wrote, must be prevented at any cost "from making any move whatever to undertake what you write." The conspirators were to be kept in leash, but they were not to get the impression that Henry "wished them well any less than he had always done," especially since it was rumored that Philip meant to subdue England by force now that his troops were no longer needed to defend the Netherlands. Some additional excuse for this breach of the spirit of the truce could be found in Noailles's recent discovery of a nebulous Anglo-Spanish plot to seize Havre.[46]

When the first of the rebels arrived at Blois, they were ordered to stay ten or twelve leagues away from the court in order to avoid suspicion.[47] But some time later Berteville and Ribaut were allowed to bring Dudley to see the King, secretly and at night. In view of the truce, it was dangerous to promise too much. Henry gave Dudley a thousand crowns with lesser gifts for the others, but he limited himself pretty much to "faire woordes and great promisses." He "willed them to go through with their enterprise" and promised that if Philip sent the bulk of his troops east to make war on the Turk, he would aid them with "men, money, and other thinges necessary."[48] After the interview Berteville and Ribaut told Dudley and his friends "to go into Normandy and ther lye tell thay were sent for, for so it was the kynges pleswer."[49] This of course was tantamount to a rebuff, as Dudley realized later, but for the moment he tried to make all the capital he could out of the interview by exaggerating the assurance of French support among his accomplices in France and England. Perhaps it was Henry's refusal of immediate financial and military as-

[46] Vertot, V, 298-9; also *ibid.*, 309-10. On the plot to seize Havre, see *ibid.*, 291-6, 302.

[47] Vertot, V, 302-3.

[48] Wotton to Mary, 12 Apr. 1556, P.R.O., S.P. 69, Vol. VIII, No. 496 (*For. Cal., Mary*, 222-3); Weiss, IV, 566 (this dispatch should be dated April 25 instead of May 25). See also note 49. The accounts vary on the amount of Henry's gift to Dudley.

[49] Examination of Peter Killigrew, 21? Aug. 1556, P.R.O., S.P.Dom. 11, Vol. IX, No. 25.

sistance which induced those at home to fall back on the plan of robbing the Exchequer.[50]

On March 11 Montmorency wrote Noailles that since the Truce was not yet ratified nor the prisoners ransomed, Henry was determined to support Dudley, "discreetly and secretly." Noailles was to assure the conspirators in England that the King would allow them to keep in touch with their brethren abroad. Mary and the Council were to be told that Henry meant to keep the peace with England, but that they must not count too blindly upon his friendship. The very next day, however, the Emperor's ratification (signed two weeks before) arrived at court, along with an agreement about the prisoners. Noailles's courier had been delayed, and a second dispatch jubilantly announcing this news and omitting all reference to Dudley was sent along with the first.[51]

What Noailles made of these two letters did not greatly matter. The plot had already been betrayed ere they reached him. Thomas White, who had helped hire the vessel which was to carry the stolen treasure abroad, had lost his nerve and gone to Pole sometime during the first week of March. Possibly Sir Peter Carew, who was in Antwerp suing for his pardon, had betrayed what he knew of the plot to Philip about the same time.[52] The government held its hand for two weeks. Some hint of White's treachery may have leaked out to the conspirators since several of them pled with Noailles for permission to cross to France, and

[50] As the editor of the *Verney Papers* suggests (p. 64). The indictment of Dethick, Bedell, and Rosey alleged that they broke into the Exchequer, weighed one of the chests of silver, and settled upon the plan of spiriting the treasure to France on March 6 (*4th Report of the Deputy Keeper*, 255-6). This sudden activity may have been the result of news from abroad, but it is impossible to date Dudley's interview with the King accurately. It probably took place late in February, but it may have been as late as the end of March (see note 60 below).

[51] Vertot, V, 308-11, 314-17.

[52] On White see *Verney Papers*, 65; and *Ven. Cal.*, VI, Part I, 384. On Carew see *Ven. Cal.*, VI, Part I, 447, 454, 475, 526; Weiss, IV, 588; Philip to Mary, 16 Mar. 1556, P.R.O., S.P.Dom. 11, Vol. VII, No. 20. It is impossible to say exactly how the plot was revealed. The evidence seems to suggest that the first arrests were made on the basis of White's revelations to Pole, whereupon Carew saw his chance to curry favor with Philip by revealing the names of his Devonshire friends whom he knew were implicated. This information, given to Paget sometime after his arrival in Brussels on April 13, led to the arrest of the five ex-members of Parliament on April 29 (see below). Miss Garrett (*op. cit.*, 106-7, 147-8) thinks Carew bought his pardon by revealing the whole plot to Philip long before Paget's arrival in Flanders.

when he refused, asked him at least to get them "a little bolster-ing" from Henry. The Council probably had no proof yet of Noailles's part in the plot, but they had been worried by Dudley's flight to France and it was not hard to put two and two together. It was not surprising, then, that when Noailles presented himself at court on Sunday, March 8, to thank Mary and Pole for their efforts in behalf of peace, Mary spoke pointedly about her hope that the truce would allow Philip and Henry II to turn their attention to the infidels abroad and "the rebels" at home. Noailles knew what she meant. Unaware that the game was up, he ad-vised Montmorency to send Dudley to Italy for a while.[53]

On the 18th the government struck. About twenty of the con-spirators were seized and sent to the Tower. The examinations began immediately, more suspects were arrested, and on April 4 Dudley and most of his fellow-fugitives abroad were proclaimed traitors. Sir Anthony Kingston was summoned, but died of the stone on his way up to London.[54] Details of the plot came out bit by bit—first the design of robbing the Exchequer, next the con-nection with the fugitives in France, and finally the amazing ramifications among the gentry of Devonshire and among public officials all the way from Cornwall and Portsmouth to Dover, Gravesend, and London. It was even rumored that some Privy Councillors were in the know.[55] How many persons in England were privy to some part of the plot no one will ever know, but if one may judge by the terror which seized the Council imme-diately after the examinations began, their number was legion. Not all of the prisoners were so steadfast as Throckmorton on the rack, and each new confession seemed to point the finger of suspicion at someone still at large. The Queen could trust no one

[53] Vertot, V, 311-13, 321. It is quite possible, of course, that Mary had not yet been told about what had been discovered, but Noailles's account of the interview makes one suspect that she had.

[54] *Tudor and Stuart Proclamations*, No. 466; *Machyn Diary*, 102-3; *Ven. Cal.*, VI, Part I, 385, 398, 417.

[55] *For. Cal., Mary*, 222. Michiele's reports (*Ven. Cal.*, VI, Part I, 383 *ff.*) are the best guide to the gradual unraveling of the plot since it is difficult to date many of the prisoners' confessions. Some time soon after the examinations began, the Select Council wrote Philip, "those traitors meaninges semeth to be tattempt some enterprise in the cowntes of Cornwale, Devonshire, Dorsett, Hampshyre, Norfolk, or some one of these" (P.R.O., S.P.Dom. 11, Vol. IX, No. 15).

but her most devoted and Catholic councillors to sit on the commission to examine the culprits: Rochester, Englefield, Waldegrave, Jerningham, and Hastings. "As for all other noble men," Shrewsbury was informed, "they meddle nothing; and if any suitors speak unto them, they wish them good speed . . . and will them to resort unto the Commissioners."[56]

Perhaps the Council's fright helps to explain the fact that Noailles was not very worried about his position for almost a month after the first arrests. The passages had been closed for a time after March 18, but none of his dispatches had been intercepted. He knew that Mary was even more afraid of breaking the peace with France than she had been after Wyatt's failure, and he had already learned how to put a bold face on such matters. Early in April the Council decided to send Lord Clinton to France to demand the extradition of Dudley and the fugitives, but Noailles was told that it would be done "modestly." A Frenchman had been arrested on suspicion of treason in Sussex on March 11,[57] but there was no persecution of other French residents in England.

The ambassador took what precautions he could, however. He entrusted his report of the first arrests (the dispatch is lost) to La Marque. He sent a letter to the Abbé de Bassefontaine, the new French ambassador at Brussels, which would edify the English government if it were intercepted.[58] And he sent the Council an innocuous dispatch from Henry II of March 31 to prove that the King meant never to be "outdone in honesty" by Mary.[59] Another dispatch of the same date from Montmorency he wisely kept to himself. The Constable, still ignorant of the plot's disclosure, had written that "Dudley and the six English gentlemen who are here with him" were being ordered to keep away from court and to scatter themselves throughout the country as if they

---

[56] Lodge, *Illustrations,* I, 268. Noailles heard that Mary felt she could trust only Montague and Hastings among all those around her (Vertot, V, 362).

[57] *A.P.C.,* V, 246.

[58] The Queen, he wrote, "se conduit fort dextrement et prudemment comme elle fait en toutes ses actions, estant tres vertueuse et catholique, et faisant paroistre au surplus par tous ses effets vouloir inviolablement entretenir l'amitié et bonne intelligence qui est si bien establie d'entre le Roy son bon frere et sa Majesté" (Noailles to Bassefontaine, 7 Apr. 1556, Aff. Etr., IX, fol. 615).

[59] Vertot, V, 324-5, 331-2.

were fleeing from their creditors. They had not been sent to Italy as Noailles advised because Dudley had objected that this would cripple their ability to support a rising in England and cool the enthusiasm of their accomplices there. The plot was not to be "neglected," Montmorency added, but Noailles must prevent any more conspirators from crossing to France.[60]

There was no more vivid illustration of the weakness of Mary's government two and a half years after her accession than the way it handled the clear evidence which it had acquired by the middle of April that Noailles was deeply implicated in the conspiracy. By the end of March, the rumor was current in London that there had been "an understanding with some foreign prince or potentate"; two weeks later the newsmongers were talking openly of "a special understanding with the King of France."[61] A dozen years before, such rumors would have started an anti-French riot in the city, but now the people feared the Spaniard more than the Frenchman. Dislike of the Spanish match had driven hundreds to sympathize with Wyatt, and now fear of Philip's coronation drove hundreds more to listen eagerly to the anti-Spanish whispering campaign which was sedulously fostered by the French embassy. While the conspirators' trials were proceeding, the government and its enemies engaged in a bitter struggle to sway English public opinion. Information reached Noailles from Luxembourg that Philip intended to land in England with ten companies of German and Flemish soldiers. The ambassador himself thought there was little in the report, but he did his best to spread it. He passed the story on to Pole through an agent, and Pole was considerably impressed, thanks to the agent's being able to conceal the fact that his sources were French.[62] The people of London were already persuaded that Philip meant to have himself crowned, if necessary by force. A bricklayer expressed the unspoken thoughts of perhaps a majority of his coun-

[60] Montmorency to Noailles, 31 Mar. 1556, Aff. Etr., IX, fols. 609-10. The words directly quoted would seem to indicate that Dudley was once more at the French court (Amboise).

[61] Ven. Cal., VI, Part I, 392, 411.

[62] This appears to be the most likely interpretation of Michiele's report on the subject. See Ven. Cal., VI, Part I, 411-12; and cf. Vertot, V, 342-3, and Montmorency to Noailles, 7 May 1556, Aff. Etr., IX, fol. 625.

trymen when he told a friend that he and five hundred men "woold spend their lyves in kepyng the crowne in Inglishe mens handes and that the strangers shoold never have yt."[63] It mattered little that many of the rumors which inflamed the people had no foundation. It was a fact that Philip wanted to be crowned and that Mary was leaving no stone unturned to gratify his wish. This was all the Queen's enemies needed to make Dudley's plot appear as patriotic self-defense. The situation was so serious by May that several members of the Council had to announce publicly that Philip had never desired such a breach of the marriage treaty, and that even if he had, the crown would never be given to a foreigner.[64]

The fear that Philip would take the crown by force was coupled with the rumor that the rightful heir was to be packed off to Spain or Flanders. Whether or not Elizabeth herself was privy to the plot (as the government feared), some of her household seem to have known too much for their own good about the conspirators' plans. She was the natural focus of all disaffection, she had powerful friends in the Council, and Mary was convinced that she had an understanding with "some foreign prince." Naturally Noailles did all he could through Parpaglia to prevent her being taken abroad, and thanks to help from an unexpected quarter, his efforts were successful. Elizabeth's biographer offers convincing evidence that it was Philip who saved the princess from imprisonment or banishment. The King knew that Parliament would never consent to his coronation if Elizabeth were abroad. He knew further that if Mary should die suddenly, it would be well to have the good will of her successor. But ultimately it was the fear of a popular insurrection which induced both Philip and the Council to treat Elizabeth with deference during the crisis. When a message was sent to her that the Queen refused to believe

---

[63] Examination of William Crowe, 11 May 1556, P.R.O., S.P.Dom. 11, Vol. VIII, No. 70.

[64] Vertot, V, 365. William Crowe (above) heard that Pembroke was going "to fetche the crowne from the Earle of Shrewsbery to crowne the Kyng withal." This rumor seems to have been based on the fact that Mary, following Philip's advice to Paget in Brussels, was attempting to win the individual consent of Shrewsbury, Derby, Westmoreland, and others to the coronation (*Ven. Cal.*, VI, Part I, 415-16; Advis, 31 May and 11 June 1556, Aff. Etr., IX, fol. 645, and XIII, fol. 15ᵛ).

the stories of her complicity in the plot, she sensed the strength of her position and haughtily refused even to come to court as Mary requested.[65]

In such an atmosphere, the French ambassador seemed to hold most of the trumps, and the Council hardly dared to proceed against him directly. On April 12, however, at the trial of Throckmorton and Uvedale, the government launched its counterattack against the French propaganda campaign. The public prosecutor, basing himself largely on information received from Wotton in France, plainly accused the prisoners of having had dealings with Noailles through Berteville. Apparently no reference was made to Dudley's secret interview with Henry II, and the prosecutor spoke throughout with "due reverence and honor" of the King himself. But no doubt was left in the courtroom about the government's suspicion of Noailles's integrity.[66]

A week later Throckmorton and Uvedale were hanged and quartered at Tyburn. Information from Carew in Flanders had cast suspicion upon the leaders of the parliamentary opposition, and when five of them—Pollard, Perrot, Arnold, Chichester, and Sir William Courtenay—were bold enough to show their sympathy with the "poor wretches" suffering execution, they were hustled off to the Fleet, then to the Tower. They were doubtless asked some embarrassing questions about their relations with the French ambassador, but no charge could be found against them and they were all eventually released.[67] It was otherwise with Captain William Stanton, an associate of Wyatt's who had had treasonable dealings with Noailles three years before. Imprisoned on April 29 with the ex-members of Parliament, he was convicted and executed within three weeks. The populace accompanied both

[65] Wiesener, 340-4, and references there given.
[66] Henry II to Noailles, 7 May 1556, Aff. Etr., IX, fol. 628. See also *Ven. Cal.*, VI, Part I, 422-3; *For. Cal., Mary,* 222; and Renard to Philip, 13 June 1556, Antigny, Tyler, p. 268. Renard reported that it was Wotton who had warned Mary of "les prattiques de Noailles," but the prisoners' depositions furnished the government with plenty of indirect evidence.
[67] Vertot, V, 351; *Ven. Cal.,* VI, Part I, 439-40; *Machyn Diary,* 104; List of suspects in P.R.O., S.P.Dom 11, Vol. VII, No. 24. See note 52 above. Perrot and Chichester were released before the end of May (Advis, 31 May 1556, Aff. Etr., IX, fol. 645); Pollard, Courtenay, and Arnold were released in the following December (Advis, 15 Dec. 1556, *ibid.,* XIII, fol. 122).

him and his fellow-conspirator, Daniel, to and from their trials in tears, "a demonstration rarely or never made in favor of persons condemned for high treason," as Michiele remarked.[68] Randall was more fortunate than his friend Stanton. Throckmorton steadfastly refused to implicate him, and he was apparently able to cover up his connections with the French embassy; by July he was at liberty.[69]

As the lightning thus struck closer and closer—as the commissioners continued to interrogate everyone from members of Parliament and servants of Elizabeth to officials of the mint and military commanders on how well they knew the French ambassador[70]— Noailles's confidence began to disappear. He had come to England on the understanding that he would be replaced within a year. He had begged for his recall on several occasions, and it was already understood that his brother François would take his place as soon as possible.[71] But François was in Rome trying to explain to Paul IV why Henry II had signed a truce with Philip, the Pope's enemy, behind the papal back—a task which was as futile as it was tedious.[72] By the time François got back to Paris, his elder brother might conceivably be in irons. Michiele heard that the Council had debated the question whether they could proceed against the ambassador "as a plotter and contriver against the state and person of the sovereign with whom he resides" without violating the *jus gentium*. To avoid war with France, it was decided not to put the legal niceties of the case to a test.[73] When the debate was held and whether Noailles got wind of it, we do not know. But on the day Throckmorton went to the scaffold (April 28) the ambassador realized that the game was up and that the

[68] *Ven. Cal.,* VI, Part I, 447; *Machyn Diary,* 105-6.

[69] Confession of Throckmorton, 18 Apr. 1556, P.R.O., S.P.Dom. 11, Vol. VIII, No. 14. On May 31, 1556, Noailles reported that Captain "Wouldal" had been released (Advis, Aff. Etr., IX, fol. 645). On July 8 Gilles de Noailles wrote that Randall had "recently" been released (Advis, *ibid.,* XIII, fol. 27).

[70] See e.g. the examination of Battista Castiglione, Elizabeth's Italian master, in P.R.O., S.P.Dom. 11, Vol. VIII, No. 80.

[71] Vertot, V, 300, 351, 363; Weiss, IV, 566-7 (should be dated April 25, 1556).

[72] François left Blois for Rome about February 18 and was back at Fontainebleau by June 11 (Montmorency to Noailles, 20 Feb. 1556, and François de Noailles to Cardinal of Tournon, 18 June 1556, Aff. Etr., IX, fol. 586, and XIII, fols. 84-5).

[73] *Ven. Cal.,* VI, Part I, 460.

sooner he put the Channel between himself and England the better. The fact that his wife was pregnant and that he himself was
suffering from colic added to his anxiety and haste. He sent Henry
II a copy of the prosecutor's speech at Throckmorton's trial and
asked that he be recalled immediately. He suggested that his
youngest brother Gilles, who fortunately happened to be in Paris
at the time, he sent over to "keep the place warm" for François.
His letters to Henry II, Gilles, and François are lost, but the replies leave no doubt of his trepidation.

> M. de Noailles [Gilles wrote François] has so great a desire to get out
> of there, and says he is under such constraint and pressure to do so, that in
> my opinion, he will sojourn there as briefly as possible ere I arrive.

Diffident of his own qualifications and almost totally unprepared
for the position as he was, Gilles was immediately appointed
French *agent* in London and dispatched from Paris in haste. The
official excuse given (even in a letter to François) was Antoine's
illness.[74]

Noailles's last audience with the Queen and her Council before
he took his leave was a fitting epilogue to his three years' embassy
in England. Little of importance was said on either side, but it
was as if all Mary's frustrated hopes and longings, all Noailles's
bitter hatred of her public policies and half-ironic pity for her
person were compressed into the diplomatic understatements of
the occasion. Noailles thanked the Queen for sending Clinton to
France, and the Queen thanked Noailles for the hospitality accorded her ambassador. Three times she called loudly upon Clinton, who was just back from his trip, to confirm the fact that
the King of France had promised to give up Dudley and his
fellow-traitors, and Clinton answered yes—if Henry "were able
to recover them." When Noailles referred to them as "refugees,"
she asked him sharply to call them "abominable heretics and
traitors, and worse still, if possible." Noailles restrained the retort

---

[74] Noailles to L'Aubespine, 29 Apr. 1556, Aff. Etr., IX, fol. 620; Henry II and Montmorency to Noailles, 7 May 1556, *ibid.*, IX, fols. 625, 628; Gilles to François de Noailles,
9 May 1556, *ibid.*, XIII, fols. 12-13 (quotation above); Montmorency to François de
Noailles, 26 May 1556, *ibid.*, XIII, fol. 84; Gilles to François de Noailles, 11 June 1556,
ibid., XVIII, fol. 84; Antoine to François de Noailles, Paris, 16 June 1556, *ibid.*, IX,
fol. 650.

which was on his lips for fear of driving her into a rage—and for fear she might think he was trying to excuse himself before being accused. Perhaps he was more truly sorry than ever before for this tragic Queen who had tried to win the love of a husband and the love of her people and lost both because she had listened to evil counsel. "For that reason one must excuse her," he wrote.[75]

On May 25, three weeks after this audience, Antoine and Gilles de Noailles went to court together, the one to take his leave, the other to present his credentials. Mary made no attempt to conceal her pleasure. She was as happy in welcoming the younger brother, Antoine wrote, as she was in dismissing the elder—but no happier than he himself would be when he set foot again on French soil.[76] On June 4 he left London and within ten days he was in Paris, where his doctors ordered a purge—"to rid me," he wrote François, "of all the evil humors which have so long possessed me in this unhappy island Kingdom."[77] François soon rejoined him in the capital, and after two weeks of rest the ex-ambassador journeyed on to the court at Fontainebleau. There he made his report.[78] Characteristically, its burden was the need for action, for intrigue, for confidence in the eventual triumph of Mary's enemies. The Queen was so ill, so distraught by Philip's treatment of her that she could not last long. Meanwhile, as Henry himself had put it, she was dealing with a Hydra, "which when it loses one or two heads, gives birth overnight to an infinity of others."[79] True, the plot had been nipped in the bud, Dudley was helpless for lack of funds, and Carew, the most prominent survivor of Wyatt's rebellion, had again played traitor to his friends by aiding the kidnapping of Sir John Cheke on Flemish soil.[80] Before Noailles left London he had warned Montmorency that Courtenay must be kept from sharing Cheke's fate since every hope of

[75] Vertot, V, 352-8.   [76] *ibid.*, 372.
[77] Antoine to François de Noailles, 16 June 1556, Aff. Etr., IX, fol. 650.
[78] The nature of Noailles's report can be gathered from scattered bits of indirect evidence: Noailles to the King of Navarre, 30 June 1556, Aff. Etr., IX, fol. 654; Gilles to Antoine de Noailles, 8 July 1556, *ibid.*, fol. 653; Weiss, IV, 605.
[79] Henry II to Noailles, 7 May 1556, Aff. Etr., IX, fol. 628.
[80] On May 13, 1556 (*Ven. Cal.*, VI, Part I, 452). Miss Garrett offers convincing defense of the thesis that one price which Carew paid for his pardon was the betrayal of Cheke (*op. cit.*, 106-7).

English liberty rested "in him alone." Randall's friend, Henry Killigrew, was actually sent to Ferrara with the French government's blessing, but he was apparently unable to persuade Courtenay to come to France.[81]

The truth was that in spite of Noailles's warm reception at Fontainebleau the policy which he represented was already thoroughly discredited by Dudley's failure. When he arrived at court, the most prominent figure there was the Pope's sinister and choleric nephew, Cardinal Caraffa. Everyone knew that he had come not to bring peace (as the Pope proclaimed) but a sword. He was urging the French to break the truce and to throw their whole military weight against the Spanish in Italy. The Guises were backing him strongly, arguing that a quick offensive in Italy was the only way to prevent Philip from crushing his Lutheran enemies in Germany and "establishing" himself in England. Once more all eyes at court were turned toward the "opportunity" in Italy, and England was again on the periphery of French diplomatic calculations. Montmorency was fighting a losing battle to preserve the truce. Apparently he would soon be doomed to his familiar task of holding the diplomatic ring in the North while the French troops marched south across the Alps. Further intrigue in England meant war, and war on two fronts might mean disaster.

Renard, who had been appointed Imperial ambassador to France for the second time after the Truce of Vaucelles, saw the situation clearly.

They well know [he wrote from Paris] that they cannot in any way favor the rebels without getting into a war with England, far less shelter Courtenay without risking this extremity of war.[82]

There can be no question about where Antoine and François de Noailles stood on the issue being debated at court. Personally,

[81] Noailles to Montmorency, 29 Apr. 1556, Aff. Etr., IX, fol. 621; For. Cal., Mary, 229, 238; Weiss, IV, 587-8, 605. How much Courtenay knew of Dudley's conspiracy remains a mystery since the French ambassador at Venice apparently persuaded the Venetian authorities to remove many incriminating letters to and from France when Courtenay's correspondence was handed over to the English ambassador after his death (Sept. 18, 1556). Ven. Cal., VI, Part II, 818, note.

[82] Renard to Philip, 13 June 1556, Antigny, Tyler, p. 268.

both were on good terms with the Cardinal of Lorraine, and Antoine was charmed by his introduction to Mary of Lorraine's famous daughter, Mary Stuart.[83] But neither brother had any stomach for the Guises' policy of adventure in Italy. François's trip to Rome had filled him with contempt for Paul IV and Caraffa. He could see nothing but disaster in the Franco-papal alliance, and he was saddened by the ease with which second-rate Italian princes were able to persuade Henry II to expend French blood and treasure in the settlement of their selfish quarrels. When he said so in no uncertain terms on his return from Italy, he undoubtedly had the support of his elder brother and of Montmorency, but he lost the favor of the whole Guise faction.[84]

Three years before, the rulers of France and Spain both seemed convinced that the hegemony of Europe would be decided in London rather than in the Italian peninsula. In the summer of 1556, Antoine de Noailles and Simon Renard still shared this conviction, but events had moved beyond them. On July 5 they were both present at Fontainebleau when Caraffa delivered a violent and unseemly Philippic against the Habsburgs in the presence of all the foreign ambassadors. Apparently Noailles was as shocked as Renard. He whispered to his erstwhile opponent that the Pope would disavow the tirade.[85] Even if the wish proved father to the thought, the two rival ambassadors were enlisted for the moment in a common cause, that of keeping France out of an Italian war.

[83] Noailles to Mary of Lorraine, 4 Aug. 1556, Aff. Etr., IX, fol. 655.

[84] See the interesting memoranda of his mission in Aff. Etr., XIII, fols. 77-83; also François de Noailles to Cardinal of Tournon, 3 July 1556, ibid., XIII, fols. 87-8.

[85] Weiss, IV, 627-31; Ven. Cal., VI, Part I, 507-9; Wotton to Council, 13 July 1556, P.R.O., S.P. 69, Vol. IX, No. 520 (For. Cal., Mary, 240).

CHAPTER XII

THE EVE OF CONFLICT

JUNE 1556 TO JUNE 1557

*W*AR between France and England was the logical, but not the inevitable outcome of the Spanish marriage. When Antoine de Noailles left England, it was over two years since Philip had promised to see the peace between France and England observed and to give "no cause of any breach." The King had not kept his promise, nor had he ever meant to. But the fact was that after three years of Spanish influence and French intrigue, England was still nominally at peace with her ancient enemy and English statesmen had even helped reconcile the quarrel of France and Spain on the Continent.

Peace was a relative term in the sixteenth century, no less than it is now. The distinction between civil strife and international war was never clear, and the troubled relations between Mary's government and its enemies at home and abroad from 1553 to 1557 are perhaps best described as undeclared warfare. But it is nonetheless significant of the strength of English public opinion and the weakness of the English government that Noailles's connection with three major conspiracies in as many years did not result in a formal declaration of war. It was eventually Spanish pressure as much as French provocation which drew England into her most humiliating war of the century. How that pressure was exercised, how it was resisted, and how it triumphed in the very moment of defeat is a story which has never been told in all its fullness.

To the common people who had greeted the Truce of Vaucelles with joy, hardly a cloud appeared in the diplomatic sky as summer came on; but already the storm which had threatened to engulf all Europe a year ago was lowering again over Rome. No more heart-rending news ever reached Mary the Catholic from abroad than the report in July that her husband was drifting into war with the Pope. For almost a year the Guises, backed by Cardinal Caraffa and all the Italian *fuorusciti* who hated the Spanish rule in Italy, had been pushing Paul IV on to a breach with the Habsburgs. The truce was an intolerable blow to their ambitions and from the moment of its conclusion the Cardinal of Lorraine had set himself to break it. Caraffa's presence at the French court gave the Guise faction the support it needed to launch a vigorous attack on Montmorency's peace policy. In order to force Henry II's hand, the Pope had dispossessed and ex-communicated the leading members of the Imperialist Colonna family in May. Caraffa brazenly pictured this lively action of his uncle as evidence of Habsburg tyranny and demanded that Henry II consider it a *casus belli* under the terms of the secret Franco-papal treaty of December 1555. Specifically he demanded the immediate dispatch of French troops under the Duke of Guise to save the Pope from the Spaniards. For a moment even Montmorency wavered. The rumor leaked out that the French Council had decided on war at a secret meeting on July 31 and the King gave Caraffa the impression that the Holy Father need have no fear of desertion in his hour of need. In reality, however, the Cardinal started back to Rome on August 11 almost empty handed. The Constable was able to convince his master that France was too exhausted to risk breaking the truce before spring, and orders were sent to the French ambassador at Rome to avoid an open breach.[1]

In Brussels Charles V and Granvelle were playing the Guises' part by taking a serious view of the troubles at Rome, while Philip and Ruy Gómez were making desperate efforts to preserve the peace at almost any price.[2] Henry II soon made it clear that he would consider an Imperial attack on the Pope as a breach of the truce, which meant that war would be renewed in the North as well as the South. This Philip particularly wanted to avoid.

---

[1] Romier, *Origines,* II, 44-74 (particularly 73-4). Older accounts of Caraffa's mission maintain that it was unqualifiedly successful. See Decrue, *Montmorency,* II, 190-1; Charrière, *Négociations de la France dans le Levant,* II, 371-2. See also *Ven. Cal.,* VI, Part I, 548, 563, 576.

[2] *Ven. Cal.,* VI, Part I, 498, 532, 537, 599-600.

The Netherlands treasury was hardly less exhausted than that of France; the Emperor was on the point of embarking for Spain; and the liquidation of Dudley's conspiracy had reawakened hope in Brussels that the Spanish yoke might now be finally imposed on England, a task which would obviously be impossible if the truce were broken. A last-minute attempt to get Philip's claim to the Empire approved by the electors had failed in July and the Emperor's original idea of "compensation in England" was once more uppermost in the minds of Imperial courtiers, although they were forbidden to talk about it. "I assure you," Bassefontaine wrote Gilles de Noailles from Brussels, "that their whole aim, counsel, and plan has no other end but to occupy this kingdom [England] and so install themselves there that they may use it against us."[3] As Henry II's attention turned toward Italy, Philip's turned toward the Flemish frontier and England. While Ruy Gómez talked peace, Granvelle made difficulties about the ransoming of the French prisoners. Philip seems to have hoped that this combination of blandishments and threats would give pause to the warmongers in both France and Italy.[4]

Everyone knew, however, that peace was at the mercy of the irascible Pontiff, and no one in Brussels was more bitter about the Guises' open plot "to unleash the Pope and his friends" than François de Noailles. "That is the way they make a monkey out of our truce," he wrote as he watched the plot unfold at Fontainebleau.[5] By the end of August, both Renard in Paris and Bassefontaine in Brussels were sure the truce was doomed, and on September 1 the blow fell. Provoked beyond endurance by Paul's actions, Alva crossed the frontier of the Papal States.

While all Europe waited to see whether the conflict would spread northward from Rome, Anglo-French relations were left to take care of themselves. After the last of the conspirators went to the gallows in July, English affairs roused hardly a flicker of interest at Fontainebleau. Gilles de Noailles was left almost entirely to his own devices. Young and inexperienced, aware of

[3] Bassefontaine to Gilles de Noailles, 17 July and 2 Aug. 1556, Aff. Etr., XIII, fols. 28-9, 35. (Quotation from latter dispatch.)
[4] Ven. Cal., VI, Part I, 665, 690.
[5] François de Noailles to Cardinal of Tournon, 8 Aug. 1556, Aff. Etr., XIII, fols. 89-91.

his own limitations, and acutely lonely after his elder brother left London, the Councillor of Bordeaux remained dutifully at his post for five months as a symbol of the lull in Anglo-French diplomacy. As a mere *agent* he commanded little respect in London, and it was natural that both Montmorency and Mary preferred to transact what business there was through Wotton at Paris. His lengthy news dispatches were fairly well-informed (thanks to Antoine's staff of spies) and unusually objective, but they went unanswered as often as not. François de Noailles, when he returned from Rome, was naturally not anxious to take up his charge as ambassador. The London post had become of second-rate importance; Montmorency needed his help in combatting the Cardinal of Lorraine's influence at court; and his stay in France was rewarded when he was appointed Bishop of Dax in August. It was understood that as soon as "the many affairs and schemes" which Henry II had in England became of pressing importance, the ablest of the three brothers would be sent over to manage them.[6]

Meanwhile few of the King's schemes were of importance except the perennial one of preserving what Antoine de Noailles called "the existing amity" between France and England. This was not difficult. The morale of the Queen and her advisers reached a new low as summer came on. Dudley's conspiracy had left its aftermath of fear, suspicion, and discontent. English pirates based on French ports were scouring the Channel and the rumor was that Dudley himself was still planning a desperate descent on the English coast. The government was in worse financial straits than ever and the political atmosphere was no less oppressive than the weather, which was ruining the crops by drought. In view of the domestic situation, no one at court could contemplate a breach with France without a thrill of anxiety.

Since Gardiner's death there had been no guiding hand in the Council, no strong will to make the Tudor system of conciliar

[6] On Gilles's position in England, see *Ven. Cal.*, VI, Part II, 769; Gilles to François de Noailles, 11 and [?] June 1556, Aff. Etr., XVIII, fols. 84, 92. On François's delay, *Ven. Cal.*, VI, Part I, 544; *For. Cal., Mary,* 239; L'Aubespine to Gilles de Noailles, 28 Aug. 1556, Aff. Etr., XIII, fol. 44.

government work even tolerably well. The contemporary documents contain few hints as to who was really directing the conduct of affairs in 1556. Certainly the Queen was more than ever incapable of giving the lead. The long strain of ill-health and emotional frustration was beginning to take severe toll. When Don Francisco de Mendoza came in July to say that Philip would be in England within six weeks, Mary lost her temper. "It was nothing but mere promises and ineffective words," she told him with the resentment born of despair. Never again would she plead with Philip to return, as she had been doing. In a trembling hand she wrote the Emperor:

> Since it has pleased your Majesty to break your promise in this matter, as you have done before concerning the return of my lord the King and good husband, I am constrained to be content, although it is to my inexpressible regret.[7]

Gilles de Noailles heard from some of her intimates "that she has been seen scratching the portraits of her husband the King of Spain which she keeps in her room."[8]

Pole was hardly more capable of directing the Council's activities than the Queen. François de Noailles wrote later that the Cardinal seemed to be as frightened of the lowliest member of the Council as he would be of Henry VIII if the latter were alive. What influence he had as Mary's most trusted adviser in religious affairs was seriously impaired when reports of the Pope's quarrel with Philip began to reach England. If the King drew the realm into war with the Papacy, if the Catholics had to choose definitely between their religion and their patriotism, it might go hard with the cause closest to the hearts of both Queen and Cardinal. When Pole proposed to send someone to point out to Paul IV what disastrous effects a Papal-Imperial war would have on the cause of Rome in England, the scheme was vetoed by the Emperor, who feared it might only make matters worse. The suspicion that Pole's efforts in behalf of peace were being hampered by political

[7] Mary to Charles V, 15 July 1556, Antigny, Tyler, p. 271 ("most unsteadily and irregularly written"—Tyler); Advis, 19 July 1556, Aff. Etr., XIII, fol. 33.
[8] Gilles de Noailles to Montmorency, 30 June 1556, Aff. Etr., XIII, fol. 24. See also *ibid.*, fols. 16-17, 19-20, 33; Vertot, V, 361-2, 370.

considerations in Brussels must have helped reduce his prestige in the Council to a minimum.[9]

Paget was undoubtedly the leading figure in the government, but he dared not try to fill Gardiner's shoes. His party had incurred Mary's suspicion by washing their hands of the business of examining Dudley's confederates, as we have seen; and it was too dangerous for him openly to join Elizabeth's increasing company of supporters. The old factional quarrels in Council were stilled, and the moderates (like Heath, the new Chancellor; Thirlby, Bishop of Ely; and Sir John Mason, who returned from his post at Brussels early in the fall) were beginning to take a more prominent part in affairs. War would immediately put the nobles' party in the saddle, but for many months the Council offered the curious spectacle (for Mary's reign) of a group of Imperial pensioners and Catholic patriots working in harmony to keep their prostrate nation out of war. For the first time since the Queen's accession, the diplomatic reports speak more often of the policy of "the Council" as a whole than of the aims of individual councillors, a fact which is eloquent of the stiffening national resistance to Mary's rule.[10]

During most of the summer domestic problems monopolized the Council's attention. In June a rumor was going the rounds in London that Courtenay had been kidnapped by Imperial agents, had escaped to France, and was plotting with the exiles there. In July an English youth tried to impersonate him in Sussex, and about the same time a rising broke out at Ipswich in favor of Courtenay and Elizabeth, fomented by a romantic agent of the exiles in Germany called "Trudgeover." The ringleaders were easily apprehended, but one of them frightened the government before his execution by sending the Queen a sealed letter containing a fantastic list of his alleged accomplices in England and abroad—perhaps not so fantastic as the Queen officially regarded

[9] Gilles de Noailles to Montmorency, 30 June and 19 July 1556, Aff. Etr., XIII, fols. 24, 35; Bassefontaine to G. de N., 17 July 1556, *ibid.*, fols. 28-9; François de Noailles to Henry II, 9 Nov. 1556, *ibid.*, fol. 97^v; *Ven. Cal.*, VI, Part I, 495, 599-600. Philip favored Pole's efforts, but wanted to control them through Brussels.

[10] See *A.P.C.*, VI, pp. xxiii ff., and the references below to the Council's disputes with Mary and Philip over the issue of war.

it. Three months later London was buzzing with the report of a plot to set up "one supposed to be the late King Edward," backed by several nobles and city merchants. In November Mary besought the Emperor to send Philip back to save the realm.

If his presence will not help it [she wrote], not only I, but also those wiser fear that it will be in very grave danger for lack of good order; we see the danger before our own eyes.[11]

In December the government resorted to measures to preserve public order which would have horrified the first two Tudors. Gentlemen who had dismissed their retainers because of the burden of royal exactions were ordered by proclamation to rehire those who had been dismissed.[12] It began to look as if Henry II's prophecy that the Queen would find herself dealing with a Hydra was coming true.

The middle classes were exacerbated beyond measure in July by the imposition of a forced loan. Letters were sent to a thousand selected individuals demanding £60 from each. The success of this expedient induced the Council a month later to demand £100 from every gentleman or cleric who had £20 in annual revenue. Immediately the cry went up that the Queen's purpose was "to weaken and humiliate her people and to favor the foreigner." Alternate threats and grants of special privileges were used to squeeze loans out of the Merchant Adventurers, and by December the government was able to send Philip 150,000 ducats secretly for the pay of his garrisons. Meanwhile the merchant class in the city was frightened by the fear of inflation through depreciation of the currency. There was some justice in the current accusation that Mary was bleeding her wealthier subjects to pay for her husband's wars abroad and to build up a "rebellion fund" at home. In August (a bitter commentary on the third anniversary of her accession to the throne), copies of an indescribably foul lampoon

[11] Mary to Charles V, 10 Nov. 1556, Antigny, Tyler, p. 294. Mary was worried perhaps by reports of the plot to seize Calais (see below). On the incident in Sussex, see *Ven. Cal.*, VI, Part I, 571; and Advis, 11 June 1556, Aff. Etr., XIII, fol. 17. On the rising at Ipswich, Advis, 3 and 16 Aug. 1556, and Gilles de Noailles to Montmorency, 30 Aug. 1556, *ibid.*, fols. 38, 42ᵛ, 46ᵛ; *Ven. Cal.*, VI, Part I, 578-9; *A.P.C.*, V, 310, 312. (Gilles heard that the leader of the rising was an agent of Dudley's.) On the plot in London, Advis, 18 Oct. 1556, Aff. Etr., XIII, fol. 60.

[12] Advis, 15 Dec. 1556, Aff. Etr., XIII, fol. 121.

were found scattered through her chambers at Croydon. Its title was *Maria Ruyna Angliae,* and its text consisted of a detailed account of the money she had sent under cover to Flanders— how it was raised, who transported it, and to whom it was delivered. It was illustrated by a picture of a nude Queen giving suck to hosts of Spaniards.[13]

In such an atmosphere there was a certain unreality about the incidents which continued to trouble Anglo-French relations. During the summer and fall there were disturbances in each of the three areas where the two nations had what amounted to a common frontier—the Tweed, the Calais Pale, and the Channel. All three Noailles brothers complained frequently about the time and energy which a French representative in London was compelled to devote to Scottish affairs, but the burden was heaviest on Gilles. Border raids were endemic, and there was nothing very unusual about the marauding expeditions of the Grahams which were beginning to exasperate Mary of Lorraine's government in Scotland. Gilles protested dutifully and regularly to the English Council, and the dispute was finally patched up by a Border Commission. The only significant element in the situation was that after the Truce of Vaucelles, Henry II had ordered the withdrawal of most of his military forces from Scotland. This meant that when Philip later needed arguments to persuade the English to break with France, an attack upon the comparatively defenseless Scots was the most attractive inducement he could offer.[14]

A dispute in the Calais Pale which dragged on from June to December likewise embittered Mary's relations with France although it never at any time threatened to result in a breach. The English disputed French possession of a wealthy monastic establishment on the border variously known as St. Inglevert and Sandingfield. Gilles de Noailles was provoked that the dispute

---

[13] Gilles de Noailles to Montmorency, 30 Aug. 1556, Aff. Etr., XIII, fol. 46. On the government's loans and exactions, see Advis, 19 July, 16 Aug., 5 Oct., 18 Oct., 15 Dec., 25 Dec. 1556, Aff. Etr., XIII, fols. 33ᵛ-34, 42, 57, 60, 121ᵛ, 129ᵛ; Bassefontaine to François de Noailles, 13 Dec. 1556, *ibid.*, fol. 110ᵛ; *A.P.C.*, VI, 5, 8, 19-20, 25, 45; *Ven. Cal.*, VI, Part II, 862, 868, 879, 880.

[14] The French troops embarked in June (D'Oysel to Gilles de Noailles, 11 June 1556, Aff. Etr., XIII, fols. 17-18). The result seems to have been that the English immediately took the offensive on the border (G. de N. to Montmorency, 16 Aug. 1556, *ibid.*, fol. 41).

was referred to Wotton in Paris when it might have been more easily settled in London, but the English (who seem to have been the aggressors) eventually obtained a meeting of commissioners on the border in November. Appeals to local inhabitants, to old maps, and even to Froissart's *Chronicles* proved fruitless. The meetings broke up in December, and the question remained unsettled until the Duke of Guise captured Calais the following year.[15]

A more serious question was the activity of Anglo-French pirates in the Channel. Most of the little band of fugitives in France were by now reduced to penury, but a few of them like the Killigrews had acquired some ships from the French authorities and were engaged in the profitable and patriotic business of preying on English commerce. Occasionally they were injudicious enough to attack a French vessel, and Montmorency was not sorry when an English vice-admiral captured Peter Killigrew off Plymouth in July. But the English considered it sheer effrontery when the Constable demanded that the pirates' best ship, the *Sacret,* be returned to Henry II on the ground that it had been lent to Killigrew only for the duration of the Franco-Imperial War. Reference of the dispute to the Sandingfield commissioners accomplished nothing, but the French were so insistent that the English Council considered returning the vessel simply to avoid any excuse for a breach. The undeclared war on the seas continued to try the patience of the diplomats in London and Paris until the question was absorbed in wider issues the following spring.[16]

The brunt of settling these minor disputes had fallen on Wotton, who was also doing invaluable service in ferreting out the exiles' plots. The Council was stunned, therefore, when Mary proposed in September that Wotton be recalled and that English affairs at Paris

---

[15] The most important unpublished documents on the dispute are as follows: Montmorency to Noailles, 31 May 1556, Aff. Etr., IX, fol. 644; Gilles de Noailles to Montmorency, 30 June, 8 July, 21 Oct. 1556, *ibid.,* XIII, fols. 25, 26, 62; Montmorency to François de Noailles, 5 Dec. 1556, *ibid.,* fol. 109; Report of the Commissioners' Conference, Dec. 1556, *ibid.,* fols. 115-18; Instructions to Cassaigne, 10 Apr. 1557, *ibid.,* fol. 189. See also *For. Cal., Mary, passim.*

[16] See Garrett, *Marian Exiles,* 205-7, and references there given. Also Peter Killigrew's confessions, P.R.O., S.P.Dom. 11, Vol. IX, Nos. 25, 26; Council to Philip, [22] Nov. 1556, *ibid.,* No. 50; Montmorency to Gilles de Noailles, 28 Aug. 1556, Aff. Etr., XIII, fol. 45; G. de N. to Montmorency, 10 Sept. 1556, *ibid.,* fols. 48, 50-1; Instructions to Durand, 19 Sept. 1556, *ibid.,* fol. 52.

be left in Renard's hands, on the ground that it was illogical and unnecessary to maintain ambassadors from both husband and wife at the same court. The councillors were already oversensitive about Mary's attempts to subordinate English to Spanish interests. They resolutely rejected the proposal:

because they wished in no wise to run the risk of pooling their quarrels by such a consolidation nor to confuse such different and separate negotiations, which they need to keep distinct, in order not to see friendships altered by such a mistake in response to the passions of a foreigner.[17]

Four months before, Renard had advised Philip that Wotton be recalled because his loyalty was suspect, but the King backed the Council and a dangerous step toward war was averted.[18]

The Council had good reason to take the stand it did. Until the middle of September Montmorency had been able to keep the Guises in check, but about the 23rd word reached the French court that Alva was only a dozen miles from Rome, and a letter arrived from Caraffa saying that French prestige in Italy would soon vanish unless troops were sent immediately to save the Pope. Henry II's Council met almost daily for two weeks. The Constable struggled manfully to preserve the peace against the united forces of Guise, the Cardinal of Lorraine, Catherine de' Medici, and the King himself; and Renard went to the length of exceeding his instructions to keep Henry from committing himself to war. But it was all in vain. The King hinted clearly to Renard that he considered the truce broken, and by the second week in October the Duke of Guise had obtained his long-coveted commission to march to Rome. The news reached London a week later.[19]

While the younger nobility were flocking to join Guise's expedition in hope of fame and glory, the Constable gloomily applied himself to the familiar task of keeping England out of the conflict. The moment he recognized that his master was determined to prosecute the war in Italy to a finish, he had François de Noailles

[17] Advis, 5 Oct. 1556, Aff. Etr., XIII, fol. 58.

[18] Weiss, IV, 563-4; Council to Philip, 16 Sept. 1556, and Philip to Council, 30 Sept. 1556, P.R.O., S.P.Dom. 11, Vol. IX, Nos. 31, 34; Advis, 18 Oct. 1556, Aff. Etr., XIII, fol. 60.

[19] Romier, Origines, II, 97-100; Ven. Cal., VI, Part I, 640-1, 649, 651-2, 658, 681, 708; Advis, 21 Oct. 1556, Aff. Etr., XIII, fol. 61.

ordered to London. To checkmate Philip's inevitable attempts to draw England in would require the best talents available. The new Bishop of Dax had the ability, and furthermore he was *persona grata* with Mary in a way that neither of his brothers ever became. On November 6 he arrived in London with a large retinue, the object of which was to impress the English with the grandeur of their potential enemy. Two days later he presented his credentials at court while Gilles took his leave. The Queen received the new ambassador with obvious pleasure, "telling me several times," he wrote, "with an open and laughing countenance, that I was most welcome." With the touch his elder brother always lacked, he referred gracefully to "the sincere love" which Henry bore Mary and to the high opinion the King had of her "rare virtues"—phrases which would have stuck in Antoine's throat.[20]

On November 9 he wrote Henry II the first of an interesting series of periodic analyses of the state of the realm, modelled (consciously perhaps) on the reports which contemporary Venetian ambassadors made to their government upon returning from a foreign embassy.[21] "Everyone knows, Sire," he began, with the flair for facile generalization characteristic of Renaissance historians, "that England, more than any other province of Christendom, has always received and borne intercourse with all foreign nations with very bad grace." Like Machiavelli, he went on to illustrate his general proposition by a rapid survey of the facts, drawn in this case from Mary's reign. Beginning by remonstrances against the Spanish marriage based on Henry VIII's Will and on the law of the land, and passing on to libels and caricatures, the English people had ended in open rebellion and secret conspiracies. Yet Mary had kept her crown and the popular opposition to Spanish

[20] Montmorency to Gilles de Noailles, 13 and 24 Oct. 1556, Aff. Etr., XVIII, fols. 187, 196; G. de N. to Montmorency, 6 Nov. 1556, *ibid.*, fols. 217-18; François de Noailles to Montmorency, 9 Nov. 1556, *ibid.*, XIII, fols. 97-8. François was ordered to take up his post on Oct. 13, his credentials were dated Oct. 20, and he left court on Oct. 22. His retinue numbered over a score of persons. (Passports of 19 June 1557, *ibid.*, XVIII, fols. 459, 460.)

[21] Aff. Etr., XIII, fols. 95-7. The original minute of this dispatch, unlike those of many of François's others, has been preserved (*ibid.*, XIX, fols. 207-9). The dispatch was "merveilleusement bien receue" at the French court (Cyrault to Fr. de N., 22 Nov. 1556, *ibid.*, XVIII, fol. 243).

rule had come to naught. Why? The ambassador's answer was as penetrating as it was unconventional. It was because her realm was divided in religion, because the Queen had been able to follow the ancient maxim, *divide et impera*. If all Englishmen had been of one religion in 1553, particularly if that religion had been the Queen's, she would never have been able to win Parliament's grudging consent to her marriage. With two warring factions in the realm, however, the plots of one were discovered and blocked by the other; an excuse was provided for wholesale executions of opposition leaders; and Mary was able to terrorize her people into submission. But the cost had been great. In spite of the average Englishman's hatred of the Pope's spiritual authority, Paul IV had recently become something of a popular hero with the people. "Their final and only hope of liberty is now founded solely on the wars between Your Majesty and their King, in which they wish you so much fortune and success that your forces may come over here." The Queen hated the French for keeping her husband away from England and would do everything to revenge herself on them, but she would hesitate to put arms in the hands of subjects who might turn them against the Spaniard and even against her own person.

François de Noailles saw more clearly than anyone of his day how religious division hampered the effective expression of English national sentiment during Mary's reign, but he overestimated the people's love for his own nation. The English exiles in France and the French government itself made the same mistake. Although the main theme of every dispatch which the ambassador received from Paris was the necessity of preserving the peace with England, Henry II apparently saw no danger in approving a plot of the exiles to seize Calais in the late fall. Wotton got wind of the scheme a few days before the Bishop of Dax left France, but the latter knew nothing of it until he heard of it a month later through English sources. Dudley was at the French court at the end of October planning the *coup*. Agents were sent to suborn the garrisons of Guines and Hammes while French troops were quietly concentrated near the Pale. The dispatch of reenforcements and munitions from England under Pembroke frightened

M.^{RE} FRANÇOIS DE NOAILLES EVESQUE D'ACQS CON.^{BR}
D'ESTAT, AMBASSADEUR POUR SA MAJESTÉ EN
ANGLÆTERRE, A VENISE, A ROME, ET A CONSTANTINOPLE,
MORT LE XIX. SEPTEMBRE M. D. LXXXV. AGÉ DE LXV. ANS.

François de Noailles

the French out of making an attack, but Wotton heard later that "it lacked but little that Calais was not delivered up to the French King."[22]

The incident was perfectly typical of the dualism in French policy which was eventually to wreck the English Council's efforts to keep their country out of war. But the recovery of Calais was always Henry II's most cherished dream, and if the plot had succeeded, war with England would have been a cheap price indeed to pay for the victory. In fact, several ambiguous phrases in the King's letters to François de Noailles suggest that the French plan in November was to strike two swift, simultaneous blows— one directed at Milan, the other at Calais—while Philip was still off his guard. Henry wrote that he did not want Mary and her Council to suspect that his military preparations were so advanced as they were and directed François to say that he was anxious to listen to peace terms, so that his designs would be "less impeded." "If everyone else had proceeded with the same despatch, we would not be so far ahead," he added.[23]

As soon as Wotton had definite information about the Calais plot he sent off one of his secretaries with the news (November 15). The man accomplished the trip from Paris to London in the incredible time of twenty-five hours. Two days later a courier arrived from Brussels (having made the round trip from London in five days), with a demand from Philip that the English fulfil their treaties with the Netherlands by sending money and troops as soon as the truce was broken in the north.[24] In order to bring pressure to bear upon Henry II and the Pope, Philip wanted Mary formally to renew the treaties in question and to announce publicly that England would defend the Low Countries. Figueroa as his master's personal representative presented the demands at a series of secret and extraordinary meetings of the Council held

[22] Wotton's dispatches (*For. Cal., Mary,* 267-82), and Council to Philip, [22] Nov. 1556 (P.R.O., S.P.Dom. 11, Vol. IX, No. 50) are practically the only primary sources for the plot. But see Strype, *Memorials* (ed. 1816), V, 95-9; and Romier, *Origines,* I, 30.

[23] Henry II to François de Noailles, 11 Nov. 1556, Aff. Etr., XIII, fols. 98ᵛ-99. cf. same to same, 29 Nov. and 15 Dec. 1556, *ibid.,* fols. 104, 123.

[24] *For. Cal., Mary,* 276; *Ven. Cal.,* VI, Part II, 808-9, 835; François de Noailles to Montmorency, 24 Nov. 1556, Aff. Etr., XIII, fol. 102.

in the Queen's chambers at St. James's (November 19-23). The issue was finally drawn between war and peace, between a Queen whose only desire was to satisfy her husband and a Council which was still unanimously opposed to any measure which would compromise English neutrality.

The councillors approved sending financial and naval support to the King, but they refused to promise troops or to renew the Anglo-Flemish treaties. Three years ago, they pointed out, Mary had refused to renew the Anglo-French treaties under similar circumstances; Henry II might be provoked to war if the Flemish engagements were now reaffirmed at Philip's behest. England could not risk war with France, they insisted, in view of the popular temper and the scarcity of food. The issue was debated almost daily until Mary left Westminster for Greenwich on December 22, and the Queen had perforce to submit to her advisers. But she reiterated angrily that she meant to assist her husband with every resource at her command once war broke out on the Continent. Meanwhile, as a desperate expedient to extinguish the flames in Italy, the Council persuaded Philip to allow Pole to send his servant Rich to remonstrate with the Pope. An armistice had been concluded between Alva and Paul IV on November 19, which naturally led the English to hope that argument might yet save the peace of Europe. At the end of December François de Noailles gloomily concluded that although the Council might keep England out of war till spring, the Queen would eventually have her way.[25]

The Council's resistance infuriated Philip's agents and sympathizers in London. While the debates continued at Westminster behind half-closed doors, the Spaniards formed a lobby in favor of war and literally besieged the court and the city with their arguments. "The Imperialists are losing no day nor hour in schooling this people," François reported. Their arguments were on every man's lips, "as much in the houses of lords and merchants as on street corners and in all the taverns." To anyone of the

[25] François de Noailles to Montmorency, 24 Nov. and 8 Dec. 1556, Aff. Etr., XIII, fols. 102, 107-8; Fr. de N. to Henry II, 15 Dec. 1556, ibid., fol. 112; Advis, 25 Dec. 1556 and 8 Jan. 1557, ibid., fols. 129, 133; Fr. de N. to Bassefontaine, 29 Dec. 1556, ibid., fol. 127.

twentieth century transported back into the London of 1556, their propaganda would have had a strangely familiar ring. The King of France was attacking the King of England now (they told anyone who would listen), but he would end by attacking England itself. The Calais plot (François was sure it had been invented by Renard in Paris for propaganda purposes) proved as much. The English could not afford to let Henry II upset the balance of power: "If they do not take care of their affairs in good time it will be too late to run for remedies when there is no longer any power in Europe which can equal yours [Henry II's]." Furthermore, the English had an unexampled opportunity to attack Scotland while the garrisons were weak and the French were busy in Italy. Both self-defense and self-interest, in other words, required that the aggressor be curbed—especially if profit and honor could be combined in counter-aggression of the right sort. There was no hint of offering the one bait which the English merchant classes would presumably have swallowed at a gulp—opening the Spanish-American trade to Mary's subjects.[26]

Mary did her best to second the Spaniards' efforts. At the end of the legal term in December, the Chancellor addressed the assembled judges before they went down to the country and told them that never since the time of William the Conqueror had England been in greater danger from her "ancient enemies."[27] To win the trading classes, the Queen issued a proclamation compelling all foreign cloth exporters in England to land their goods in Flanders, thus putting the whole cloth trade temporarily in the hands of English and Flemish merchants. A proclamation of December 23 did something to allay the fear of inflation.[28]

François de Noailles labored night and day to counteract the efforts of the Spaniards, but it was disheartening business at best. After Guise left Paris for Italy on November 18, the ambassador was told that he must "cover up" the King's intention of breaking the truce the moment the Duke reached Italy in about a month. François was justifiably irritated by his master's naïveté. To say

---

[26] François de Noailles to Henry II, 15 Dec. 1556, Aff. Etr., XIII, fols. 111-13.
[27] Advis, 15 Dec. 1556, ibid., XIII, fol. 120ᵛ.
[28] Advis, 8 Jan. and 26 Mar. 1557, ibid., XIII, fols. 133, 175; Ven. Cal., VI, Part II, 889.

that Henry was making no preparations for war in Italy, when Renard must have seen Guise's gallant company of nobility leave Paris with his own eyes and when the news was on everyone's lips in London,—"to feed the people with this sort of thing would make them out to be very barbarous and badly informed." "I know," he complained to L'Aubespine, "that for the first of my duties you wish me to learn to lie. I see well that it is a quality which belongs to an ambassador, and I hope that in this favorable atmosphere I shall learn many others."[29] To "lie abroad for his country" was all the more difficult for him because of his profound contempt for the whole policy which Guise's expedition represented, and because he knew that not only Montmorency and Coligny, but even Bassefontaine at Brussels and D'Oysel at Edinburgh agreed with him.[30]

The French ambassador's problem was to find means of influencing the English Council without antagonizing them. He realized that his elder brother's method of diplomatic threats combined with the encouragement of treason was no longer applicable. Once only was he tempted to adopt Antoine's technique. Elizabeth was in London for a week at the beginning of December and François knew that Mary was moving heaven and earth to persuade her to marry Emmanuel Philibert of Savoy, as Philip wished. When Henry II heard that the project was being renewed, he threatened to have Elizabeth declared a bastard by the Pope and to raise Mary Stuart's claim to the throne if the marriage took place. Ironically enough, the Queen used the same threats to gain her sister's consent, but without success. François saw the possibilities in the situation and intended to speak to the Princess while she was at court, "to ascertain the state of her patience and whether she is nourishing any design for next summer." But he decided the attempt would be too dangerous: if he were discovered, his position would be hopelessly compromised. However, it would appear that he had an important visitor from the Princess's house-

---

[29] François de Noailles to L'Aubespine, 1 Dec. 1556, Aff. Etr., XIII, fols. 105-6.

[30] Bassefontaine to François de Noailles, 13 Dec. 1556, ibid., XIII, fol. 110; Fr. de N. to D'Oysel, 6 Dec. 1556, ibid., fol. 106; Coligny to Fr. de N., 31 Mar. 1557, ibid., XVIII, fol. 380.

hold. Twice the Countess of Sussex called upon him in disguise to say that Elizabeth's servants were urging her to extricate herself from her difficulties by fleeing to France. She asked the ambassador if he could arrange the escape. François advised strongly against the venture and later boasted that if Elizabeth had not heeded his warning, she would not have become Queen. The Countess, however, was undaunted. Accompanied by three of her ladies and three servants, she crossed to France to study the possibilities. On their return the following April they were all clapped in the Fleet and questioned closely about the persons they had talked to in France and in England after their return.[31]

One way to bring pressure to bear on the Council, François thought, was to reenforce the French garrison in Scotland. He remembered that the dispatch of troops to Edinburgh on Antoine's advice two years before had spurred Gardiner to talk peace, and he hoped it would now have the effect of destroying the Spaniards' argument that Scotland was an easy prey to English attack. Henry II approved the plan, but it was not till the following April that the troops left France and even then the King could spare only five hundred Gascons, which François magnified to fifteen hundred in spreading the news in London. D'Oysel had never been very sanguine about the results and the actual effect was to exasperate rather than to mollify the English government.[32]

In the last analysis, the ambassador's only resort was to make use of his own gifts of tact and personal charm. This he did like a master, relying upon the genuine pleasure which Mary and Pole found in his company. The Cardinal had told him to feel free to visit the court as often as he chose and to talk "privately and intimately" with himself, the Queen, and the Council.[33]

[31] François de Noailles to Henry II, 15 Dec. 1555, Aff. Etr., XIII, fol. 112ᵛ; Renard to Philip, 12 Jan. 1557, Antigny, Tyler, p. 297 (cf. Tridon, "Renard," 266); Wiesener, 350-3; A.P.C., VI, 76-7. I have been unable to discover the original of François's letter of Dec. 2, 1570, quoted by Vertot (I, 334), which is the basis for the story of Elizabeth's intended flight.

[32] François de Noailles to D'Oysel, 6 and 21 Dec. 1556, Aff. Etr., XIII, fols. 107, 125-6; Fr. de N. to Montmorency, 8 Dec. 1556, ibid., fol. 108; Montmorency to Fr. de N., 24 Dec. 1556, ibid., fol. 131; D'Oysel to Fr. de N., 25 Jan. 1557, ibid., fol. 145; Fr. de N. to Montmorency, 17 May 1557, ibid., fol. 217; Ven. Cal., VI, Part II, 1017, 1028.

[33] François de Noailles to Henry II, 1 Dec. 1556, Aff. Etr., XIII, fol. 105.

François soon took advantage of the invitation by attending mass regularly on Sundays with the Queen and by dining afterward with Pole. He presented Mary with editions of Justin Martyr and Ronsard, and gave Pole Godfrey of Bouillon's history of the First Crusade, together with some treatises on fish and human anatomy.[34] Gilles had taken a portrait of the Queen to Catherine de' Medici when he left London on December 2 and Mary was delighted with the portrait of Catherine which was soon sent in return.[35] By Christmas François had moved the Queen to laughter on her way to and from chapel and drawn tears from the Cardinal's eyes as the two of them conversed in private about the war clouds threatening Europe. Until the opening of the new year, Henry II's case was sure of a fairly sympathetic hearing at court.[36]

* * *

Suddenly and almost without warning, all of the ambassador's good work was undone by an act of signal stupidity on the part of his King. Worried by reports that Paul IV was discussing peace with Alva, Henry decided to break the truce in the North in order to stiffen the Pope's backbone. On the night of January 5-6, 1557, Coligny tried to surprise the town of Douai on the Flemish frontier. The attempt was a rather ludicrous failure and the French did their best to conceal it by stopping all couriers at the borders for several days. But the news was all over London by the 9th. Philip deliberately tried to minimize the incident at first, but Henry had left him almost no choice. Within three weeks Bassefontaine in Brussels and Renard in Paris were under arrest, and on the 31st war was formally declared between France and Spain.[37]

---

[34] Durand to Antoine de Noailles, 6 Jan. 1557, in Vertot's manuscript account of François de Noailles's career (omitted from the first volume of his published work), Bib. Nat., f.f., nouv. acq., no. 9520, pp. 119-20.

[35] François de Noailles to Catherine de' Medici, 1 Dec. 1556 and 22 Feb. 1557, Aff. Etr., XIII, fols. 105, 160ᵛ-161.

[36] François de Noailles to Henry II and to Montmorency, 15 Dec. 1556, ibid., fols. 113-14; Fr. de N. to Montmorency, 25 Dec. 1556, ibid., fol. 128ᵛ.

[37] Montmorency to François de Noailles [8 Jan. 1557], Aff. Etr., XIII, fols. 139-40; Instructions, Fr. de N. to Boudeville, [22] Jan. 1557, ibid., fol. 138; Montmorency to Fr. de N., 26 Jan. 1557, ibid., fols. 141-2; Ven. Cal., VI, Part II, 902, 907, 916.

The result in England was a second and more severe crisis in the debate between Queen and Council. Although there was obviously no immediate danger to England, Mary began to prepare the country for war. The sheriffs of several eastern and midland counties were summoned to report on how many troops could be mustered and what were the religious and military records of those who had fought in previous wars. The royal pensioners were equipped with new standards bearing the arms of both Philip and Mary, "with a great eagle above." Ships were ordered refitted and further reenforcements were sent to Calais. Plans were laid to collect the remaining £150,000 of the subsidy granted by the last Parliament. Spies were set to watch the French ambassador at Figueroa's request. So far as the royal prerogative could do it, the nation was made ready to come to the aid of its Spanish King.[38]

The Council, however, was still a stumbling-block. In reply to renewed pressure from Mary and Figueroa, they grudgingly approved the preparedness measures and even consented to raise the six thousand foot and six hundred horse which they were bound by treaty to send to Philip if the Netherlands were attacked. But they were still stubbornly opposed to a declaration of war.[39] They were caught, as the Bishop of Dax remarked, in an unpleasant dilemma: if Philip won the war, the English would be the first to feel the "insolence" of his victory, whether they had been his allies or not; if he lost, Mary's government would never survive the burden of war expenditures and the inevitable aftermath of popular risings.[40] The ambassador was now convinced that war would result in Mary's losing her crown.

I do not know [he wrote] whether, if she tries to bend the bow still further, the wood and the string may not fly into fragments. She is on the eve of bankrupting either her own mind or her kingdom. . . . It is impossible that the crown will not fall from her head and roll so far that some one else may pick it up before she has wept for her sins.

Hence he concluded that if Mary should openly declare war on France, it would "not be the worst thing" which could happen

[38] Instructions, [22] Jan. 1557, Aff. Etr., XIII, fols. 137, 139; Advis, 3 Feb. 1537, ibid., fol. 151ᵛ.
[39] François de Noailles to Henry II, 16 Feb. 1557, ibid., XIII, fol. 155ᵛ.
[40] Same to same, [22] Jan. 1557, ibid., XIII, fol. 135.

to Henry II. If the King made a descent on the English coast, he would find "enough people to take him by the hand and pull him to shore, provided the thing were done under the mask of the Lady Elizabeth."[41]

Perhaps François was trying to make the best out of the inevitable. As early as the end of January the ranks of the peace-party in the Council were beginning to break. The Catholics, led by Pole, Petre, and Sir John Mason, still clung to non-intervention; and they were still in a large majority. But the nobles were becoming restless. They were the only class which profited by war in the sixteenth century, the only class in France, for instance, which consistently backed the Valois's adventures in Italy. The English upper classes differed in degree, but not in kind from their French brethren. When Mary cashiered a number of court pensioners and members of her guard during the preceding October, there was such a fearful outcry against her "avarice" that she was forced to rehire some and to send others to Calais with Pembroke.[42] As the prospect of war with the ancient enemy roused tempting visions of plunder, lucrative military offices, and martial glory, a strange company of Imperial pensioners and ex-conspirators began to drift over to the Queen's side. Paget came out openly for war. The Spaniards were making tempting offers to Pembroke and Clinton, and the French ambassador was told that both were so anxious to dip their fingers in the Queen's purse that they were ready to break the peace at her personal command and thus to present the Council with a *fait accompli*.[43] When war came, the list of military and naval officers included a revealing number of once-disaffected nobles, ex-traitors, and pirates: Lords Pembroke, Clinton, Robert and Ambrose Dudley; Sir James Croft, Sir Peter Carew, Sir Gawain Carew, Sir William Courtenay; Peter Killigrew (of the *Sacret*), Strangways, and Stukeley.[44]

[41] François de Noailles to Bourdin, 22 Jan. 1557, *ibid.*, XIII, fols. 135ᵛ-136; Wiesener, 353.

[42] Advis, 5 Oct. 1556, Aff. Etr., XIII, fol. 57; Gilles de Noailles to Montmorency, 6 Nov. 1556, *ibid.*, XVIII, fol. 218; François de Noailles to Montmorency, 24 Nov. 1556, *ibid.*, XIII, fol. 102.

[43] François de Noailles to Montmorency, 29 Jan. 1557, *ibid.*, XIII, fol. 140. On Paget, see Pollard, *Pol. Hist.*, 163.

[44] List of Officers of the Queen's Army and Navy, in Advis [8 May 1557], Aff. Etr.,

Once more François de Noailles was hard put to do his part in keeping England out of war. He knew that his master would probably not agree with him that an open breach would be a blessing in disguise, and in February Henry made his position clear in no uncertain terms:

The principal thing that I desire from you . . . is that you take pains to keep me on friendly terms with the Queen of England . . . so that in that direction, if possible, nothing should happen to thwart me, and so that during these wars I may not have them [the English] for open and declared enemies.[45]

The ambassador, on his own initiative, had already carried off a clever ruse calculated to strengthen the pacifists in the Council. He had acquired an important new informer in George Brooke, son of Lord Cobham and cousin of Wyatt, who seems to have held a position of trust in the Council as a sort of under-secretary. Brooke informed him that orders had been sent out in January to seize one of the ambassador's packets on its way to France. François took advantage of the opportunity to write several unciphered dispatches which would supply the peace-party with arguments when they reached the Council. In them he pretended that L'Aubespine's secretary had betrayed his cipher and that he was forced therefore to write in plain language (a statement which caused an amusing flurry of uneasiness at the French court when L'Aubespine took a copy of the dispatch seriously after it reached him). The Queen, he wrote, would never think of declaring war. She knew England's weakness and France's strength too well for that. She was devoutly religious and it would hurt her conscience to break her word. Furthermore, she knew that if her people kept out of war, they would grow fat on the trade which was now impossible for merchants of the belligerent nations.[46]

There seems every reason to believe that these edifying arguments reached the Council because the ambassador received a most

XIII, fol. 211. cf. *Verney Papers*, 75; *A.P.C.*, VI, p. xx; Instructions, 10 Apr. 1557, Aff. Etr., XIII, fol. 189.

[45] Henry II to François de Noailles, 16 Feb. 1557, Aff. Etr., XIII, fol. 157ᵛ.

[46] Instructions, [22] Jan. 1557, Aff. Etr., XIII, fol. 138; L'Aubespine to François de Noailles, 4 Feb. 1557, *ibid.*, XVIII, fol. 310. The bogus dispatches (of Jan. 18, 1557) are in Aff. Etr., XVIII, fols. 300-2.

cordial reception when he journeyed out to Greenwich on January 31 to attend mass with the Queen. Everyone listened eagerly while he explained that Henry had not meant to break the truce by attacking Douai; in fact, the King was actually seeking peace terms from Philip. Even Figueroa, who had never spoken to François before, came up to congratulate him. The next day a courier brought the news that the King of France had declared war on Spain the very same day his ambassador was telling stories at Greenwich. Undaunted François returned to court on February 2, in order "not to appear a liar." Pole greeted him with "infinite sighs," but it was a commentary on the Cardinal's naïveté and the ambassador's persuasiveness that when the conversation was over, Pole was excited again about the prospect of peace through English mediation and François was proud that he had supplied the Council with one more argument against English intervention.[47]

The incident at Greenwich, however, proved to be the turning-point in the Bishop of Dax's career in England. Unlike Pole, the Queen never forgave his falsehood and usually averted her eyes from him whenever they met thereafter. About the middle of February he reached the depths of discouragement. His usefulness was gone, he complained to one of Henry's secretaries. To argue the French case at court now was well-nigh impossible. If he spoke firmly, he would only irritate the Queen further; if he spoke apologetically, the Council would think France was no longer to be feared. The King should replace him with someone who was wiser and abler.

It is true that a scheming ambassador might well irritate and provoke those with whom he has to negotiate, to the point of giving them an occasion to break relations; but I cannot believe that the most prudent man in the world can say anything, or effect any miracle, whereby those who wish to enter upon a war may be restrained and diverted from their intention.[48]

Montmorency did his best to cheer the ambassador up and ordered him by no means to discontinue his visits to court, as he threatened to do. On February 21 François presented Catherine de'

[47] François de Noailles to Montmorency, 3 Feb. 1557, Aff. Etr., XIII, fols. 148-51.
[48] François de Noailles to Bourdin, 16 Feb. 1557, ibid., fols. 156-7. On Mary's attitude, see also Ven. Cal., VI, Part II, 1074.

Medici's portrait to Mary, taking care not to irritate her by any appearance of ostentation. The Queen's starved affections were always readily moved by personal tokens of this sort and she was unexpectedly amiable. But after dinner the Council went to the mat with him over some recent French depredations on English shipping, and his victory of tact turned as usual to ashes.[49]

The same discouraging results attended a second attempt which he made two weeks later to regain the court's confidence. Several copies of a *Discours* justifying Henry II's breach of the truce had been sent on to him for distribution where they would do most good. When he showed one of them to Pole, the Cardinal was so shocked by its bitterness that he begged the ambassador not to circulate them for fear the Queen would be angered. Montmorency agreed that Pole was probably right, and when an Italian translation of the pamphlet reached England in May, it seems to have had the effect which the Cardinal anticipated.[50]

As François de Noailles saw the situation early in March on the eve of Philip's rumored departure for England, there were only a few rays of light in the darkness. Mason had told him he would rather die than counsel war, adding that he had said as much in a meeting of the full Council. And two other leading members of the Council (perhaps Mason was one of them) had dared confide to him "that their intention and their duty was to have no respect either for King or for Queen, but solely for the public good of the kingdom"—rather significant words in the mouths of Tudor Privy Councillors. Pole was a rock of defense to the peace-party, and the Spaniards openly blamed him for Mary's failure thus far to win over the Council. But once Philip was in England—particularly once he threatened to desert his wife a second time—François knew she would "try to force not only men, but also the elements themselves, to consent to her will."[51]

[49] François de Noailles to Catherine de' Medici and to Montmorency, 22 Feb. 1557, Aff. Etr., XIII, fols. 160-2.

[50] François de Noailles to Montmorency, 8 Mar. 1557, *ibid.*, XIII, fols. 167-8; Montmorency to Fr. de N., 20 Mar. 1557, *ibid.*, fol. 176; Advis, 6 May 1557, *ibid.*, fol. 205.

[51] François de Noailles to Montmorency, 27 Feb. 1557, *ibid.*, XIII, fol. 162ᵛ; Fr. de N. to Henry II and to Montmorency, 8 Mar. 1557, *ibid.*, fols. 166-8.

Immediately after the French broke the truce in the North Philip began to think of making his long-delayed trip to England. His plan of campaign against France was determined by the circumstances. He meant to relieve the pressure in Italy by striking hard at the weakest link in Henry's armor, the Franco-Flemish frontier. The first desideratum was money, the next was men. Spain could be expected to supply both, but if the blow were to be effective, active English support was absolutely necessary. For almost two centuries a close Anglo-Burgundian alliance had always spelled disaster for France on the northern border and now such an alliance was doubly necessary in view of the economic ties between Spain and the Netherlands. England's friendly neutrality would help protect the Netherlands from attack (as it had for three years), but only an English declaration of war could assure the success of the offensive campaign which military considerations now demanded.[52]

Philip did not relish returning to England. Perhaps he knew that in January Wotton had discovered a plot of some of the "best" men in England to depose Mary and to treat her as she had treated Lady Jane Grey. The plot (if it ever existed) was more dangerous perhaps than any other of the reign in that the conspirators patriotically refused to rely on help from Henry II or from the English exiles. Wotton's informer made a pointed contrast between his duty to "the realm" and his duty to the Queen in much the same way that the two councillors did in speaking to the Bishop of Dax.[53]

Apart from the possible danger to his person, Philip could not afford to cross the Channel unless he were sure of success. If the English refused him support to his face his prestige would be ruined. Ruy Gómez was dispatched from Brussels on February 2, therefore, to prepare the way. He was instructed to broach the question of English intervention to no one but Paget, who was to suggest it in Council on his own responsibility. Afterward he

[52] See Kervyn de Lettenhove, *Relations politiques*, I, 70 *ff.*

[53] *For. Cal., Mary,* 285-6. See above, p. 319. Wotton's dispatch was deciphered by George Brooke, who passed its contents on to François de Noailles. Montmorency denied that the plot was a propaganda trick of the French to frighten Mary. Advis, 3 Feb. 1557, Aff. Etr., XIII, fol. 152; Montmorency to Fr. de N., 16 Feb. 1557, *ibid.,* fol. 158.

was to go to Spain to raise the money, the troops, and the ships which were so desperately needed in Flanders.[54]

Gómez exceeded his instructions by frankly demanding of the Queen a promise of English participation in the war in return for Philip's coming to England. For such a blessing as her husband's presence Mary was ready to promise anything. On February 21 she sent a courier to Philip "to beg him not to be afraid to come, assuring him that his presence here will enable him to obtain what he wants." She promised that ere he arrived the most important nobles and a majority of the Council would be persuaded to do his will.[55] There seems to be little doubt, therefore, that Philip left Brussels on March 8 in the assurance that his trip would not be in vain. But any confidence he had in Mary's ability to fulfil her promise was misplaced. Early in March Pole still hoped much from the King's "benign nature." Once in England and away from his bellicose Spanish advisers, Philip might be persuaded to make peace with France, he thought, and the hope was undoubtedly shared by many in the Council.[56] Ruy Gómez's visit had done nothing to lessen the unpopularity of Spaniards in English court circles. He was forced to wait two weeks at Falmouth for a ship to take him to Spain, and when he complained to Figueroa, Mary sent an angry rebuke to the Lord Treasurer, who was responsible for supplying the vessel. Winchester replied to the Queen's messenger, in the presence of others,

You will say to her Majesty that she may say what she likes and fly into a rage when she wishes, for she is Queen; but she must also remember that she is a woman, and consequently she does not know how to measure her wishes by the convenience of time and money.[57]

The atmosphere at court was so hostile to Philip that his friends felt it necessary to spread the report that he was coming "more to satisfy the Queen and to remove from her and from her supporters the feeling about his long absence and about the love which he is

[54] Kervyn de Lettenhove, op. cit., I, 54-9.

[55] François de Noailles to Henry II, 22 Feb. and 5 Apr. 1557, Aff. Etr., XIII, fols. 160, 181; Ven. Cal., VI, Part II, 956.

[56] François de Noailles to Montmorency, 8 Mar. 1557, Aff. Etr., XIII, fol. 168.

[57] François de Noailles to Henry II, 8 Mar. 1557, ibid., XIII, fol. 166[v].

said to have been making to the ladies in Flanders, than for any other reason."[58]

According to the French ambassador, the English were as sorry to see Philip when he arrived at Greenwich on March 20 as the Flemish were glad to get rid of him—and Philip was just as sorry to be in England again. The person most embarrassed by his arrival was Pole. As Legate of Philip's enemy, the Pope, he could have no official dealings with the King, and just before Philip landed at Greenwich, the Cardinal left by barge for Lambeth. When the King and Queen removed to Westminster three days later, Pole crossed the river three times to visit them in secret at their urgent request, but he found Philip's nature a good deal less "benign" than he had expected and on March 29 at dawn he left Lambeth for Canterbury. Rumors soon reached him there that Paul IV had decided to revoke his commission as *legatus a latere* the moment Philip arrived—an event which marked the tragic end of Mary's dream that marriage with a Habsburg would aid the reestablishment of Roman Catholicism in England. The moral leader of the peace-party—and the only member of the government who had any real personal influence with the Queen—was thus eliminated before the third and final crisis opened in the Council's debates.[59]

Between April 1 and May 1, the most dramatic Council meetings of the reign took place at Westminster and Greenwich. Thanks to the fact that George Brooke, the French ambassador's informer, was present at all the meetings, we know more about the discussions than we do about any parallel series between the death of Edward VI and the accession of Elizabeth.

Philip had arranged to present his case before the Select Council which had officially been in charge of affairs since the fall of 1555. Since Gardiner was dead, Pole absent in Canterbury, and Pembroke at Calais, this group probably comprised Paget, Arundel, Heath, Thirlby, Winchester, Mason, and Petre.[60] There was a

[58] Advis, 8 Mar. 1557, *ibid.*, XIII, fol. 169.
[59] François de Noailles to Montmorency, 21, 26, and 29 Mar. 1557, *ibid.*, XIII, fols. 174-5, 179ᵛ-181; Instructions to Cassaigne, 10 Apr. 1557, *ibid.*, fol. 187ᵛ.
[60] *Ven. Cal.*, VI, Part II, 1004. The evidence for the Select Council's membership is based on widely scattered references in the diplomatic reports to ministers who seem to

certain historical fitness in the fact that Simon Renard, negotiator of the Spanish marriage, had come to England with his master to preside over what D'Oysel called the "warmed-over honeymoon" and to serve as the King's chief intermediary in dealing with the councillors.

There was no mob outside the windows as the ministers argued the question of war, but there could be no mistaking the temper of the people. A proclamation limiting the length of rapiers which might be worn in London was openly laughed at. Rumors flew about that the troops Gómez was sending from Spain were destined for England. Pamphlets appeared saying that Philip was not legally married to Mary because of his pre-contract with the Princess of Portugal, and ugly stories were circulated about his relations with his cousin, the Duchess of Lorraine, who had come along in his train from Flanders. A second forced loan of £60,000 was boldly resisted because of the suspicion that the money would be spent on Philip's entertainment. François de Noailles remarked sagely that the English never loved the French except (as at present) when the French could do them no harm. At any rate, not a voice was raised in favor of war outside the court.[61]

On April 1 Mary summoned the Select Council to her room and in the presence of her husband gave them a learned lecture on the coincidence of Divine Law and the Balance of Power:

She expounded to them the obedience which she owed her husband and the power which he had over her as much by divine as by human law, citing to them many examples from the Old and New Testament, and begged them to consider the greatness and prosperity of the kingdom of France, which was already menacing the whole world. So that if they did not decide to aid her husband, who was beginning to be the weaker party (because of the recent misfortunes of the Emperor his father), they might be sure that the King of France, having driven the King her husband from Italy, as he was about to do through lack of help, would soon afterward turn to them and drive them out of their own house. Therefore, they should decide not to allow a power which has always been so suspect and hostile to them to grow beyond measure.

have been taking a prominent part in affairs. Note the final elimination of Mary's former household servants, so prominent at the beginning of the reign.

[61] Advis, 26 Mar. 1557, Aff. Etr., XIII, fol. 176; François de Noailles to Montmorency, 29 Mar. and 5 Apr. 1557, ibid., fols. 180, 182; Instructions, 10 Apr. 1557, ibid., fol. 188.

George Brooke, who was present, remarked that the argument could not possibly have been better presented.[62]

The councillors asked for twenty-four hours to deliberate, but their differences were so violent that it was not till the 3rd that they reached a decision, namely that they "ought not and could not declare war." The memoir containing their arguments was drafted in Latin by Brooke (who gave a copy of it to the French ambassador) in order that Philip might be able to read it. Their case was well-nigh unanswerable. The realm, they maintained, was in no condition to wage a war, what with the scarcity of food, the government's financial straits, and the restlessness of the people. It would be disastrous to cut off England's trade with France because neither Spain nor Flanders could supply her with the grain, the wine, the salt, and the woad which were now so scarce. The marriage treaty expressly forbade Philip to draw England into his quarrel with France, and Henry II had offered Mary no provocation whatever. To declare war and then be unable to carry it through to a finish would ruin English prestige and prove to the French that Philip alone was responsible for the declaration.[63]

The Queen was exasperated. Angrily she ordered the ministers to meet again and draft a reply "which would satisfy her and her husband." For two more days the harassed councillors met and wrangled while Philip had numbers of English treaties with foreign countries translated into Latin or Spanish for his perusal and Renard plied back and forth between the King and the council-chamber ("flattering and lying," François was sure).[64] The Quartermaster General of the Navy testified that it was difficult to find the food needed for his ships, and the French ambassador apparently helped impress the Council with the seriousness of the scarcity by threatening to stop an impending shipment of wine and grain from France which his elder brother had arranged.[65] At the height of the debate, Philip made a desperate

---

[62] François de Noailles to Montmorency, 5 Apr. 1557, *ibid.*, XIII, fol. 182ᵛ.

[63] *ibid.*, XIII, fols. 182ᵛ-183; Froude, VI, 474. On Brooke's part, see Advis, 5 April 1557, and Instructions, 10 Apr. 1557, Aff. Etr., XIII, fols. 184, 187.

[64] François de Noailles to Montmorency, 5 Apr. 1557, Aff. Etr., XIII, fol. 183.

[65] Instructions, 10 Apr. 1557, *ibid.*, XIII, fol. 188ᵛ.

reply to the argument that England could not risk a stoppage of trade with France. Brooke told François de Noailles of "the offers which the King has made to the English through his minister Renard to draw them to his side and turn them from traffic with France, promising them in addition permission to trade with Peru, and the Scottish enterprise."[66] Well might the ambassador observe, "it seems to the Spaniards that the mere wind of this declaration [of war] will serve them more than all the gold of the Indies."[67] Probably no one will ever know how much sincerity accompanied this offer to open the Spanish-American trade to Englishmen, but it is certain that it was actually made. If the Council had accepted the promise at its face value, as apparently they did not, the course of Elizabethan history might well have been profoundly changed.

For three days after April 5 all London thought the Council had capitulated, but in reality Philip was as far as ever from getting what he wanted. The ministers refused to declare war until the following fall, after the harvest was in. François de Noailles knew that "what is postponed is not yet refused," but he was confident that the danger was over for the summer at least. Renard, who had little stomach for the whole affair, gave vent to some of his most picturesque expletives in blaming Philip's Spanish advisers for the King's plight. "They didn't know how to do the job either of war or of peace," he remarked; they were too proud and ignorant to negotiate the peace which Philip's territories needed so badly, and none of them knew how to plan and conduct a military campaign; worst of all (to Renard), they could not tolerate "the former counsellors and servants of the Emperor." The *impasse* in which Philip found himself was a good example, he thought, of what came of their advice.[68]

On the 13th the court removed to Greenwich for the Easter holidays and Mary took up where Renard had left off. It was not the first time that she had stood fast when her "spiritual con-

66 ". . . La permission du commerce du Peru et l'entreprinse d'Ecosse." Instructions, *ibid.*
67 François de Noailles to Montmorency, 28 Apr. 1557, *ibid.*, XIII, fol. 193.
68 François de Noailles to Henry II and to Montmorency, 10 Apr. 1557, *ibid.*, XIII, fol. 186; Advis, [c. 20] Apr. 1557, *ibid.*, fols. 191-2.

fessor" of other days had given way to ill-tempered despair. She threatened publicly to dismiss two-thirds of her councillors unless they did her will. One by one she summoned them privately to her room and threatened them, "some with death, some with the loss of their goods and estates, if they did not consent to the will of her husband." As a result, they assembled on the 20th and offered the King 800,000 crowns and the assistance of six thousand foot and one thousand horse, but Philip refused to be satisfied with anything less than an open declaration of war. "He much preferred to have the whole world know that they were willing to share his fortune than he did to have all their goods and riches." Reassembled on the 24th at Westminster, they added twenty ships and four thousand more men, together with a promise to pay the troops for three months; but they still refused the open breach which Philip's military plans required, and so the Queen ordered them to meet once more on the 29th. Apparently the Council had at last given an answer to the old riddle of what happens when an irresistible force meets an immovable object.[69]

Suddenly victory came to Philip like manna from heaven. Late in the evening of April 28 a courier arrived at court with the news that Thomas Stafford had swooped down upon the Yorkshire coast with a handful of English exiles and French sailors and had seized the castle of Scarborough. When the Council met the following morning, their will to resist was finally broken. French arrogance had accomplished what the glitter of Spanish gold had failed to achieve, the victory of English patriotism over English prudence.[70]

It was in vain that François de Noailles argued to Paget on May 1 that to impute support of Stafford's expedition to Henry II was to slander a great and virtuous prince; if the King of France meant

---

[69] Advis, [c. 20] Apr. 1557, *ibid.*, XIII, fol. 191ᵛ; François de Noailles to Montmorency and to Bourdin, 28 Apr. 1557, *ibid.*, fols. 193, 194; Advis, 28 Apr. 1557, *ibid.*, fol. 195. See also Weiss, V, 63, 71; Kervyn de Lettenhove, *Relations politiques*, I, 66; *Ven. Cal.*, VI, Part II, 1018, 1019.

[70] There is no direct evidence that the Council decided in favor of war on April 29, but the circumstantial evidence is strong that the decision was made by May 1 at least. See Advis, 6 and 8 May 1557, Aff. Etr., XIII, fols. 204, 207ᵛ; François de Noailles to Henry II, 8 May 1557, *ibid.*, fols. 205ᵛ-206. As late as May 17 François thought the Council was still undecided (Fr. de N. to Henry II, *ibid.*, fol. 217).

to attack England, he would have done more than send over thirty rascals under a hare-brained exile who was laughed at even by his other compatriots in France. It was in vain that Stafford maintained (at his trial) that the French government had given him little or no support, and (on the scaffold) that he died a good Englishman. The people might laugh at Mary for having the traitor's remains taken from the Tower Chapel and desecrated on the spot of his execution when she heard that he had died impenitent. Many might think secretly that he was a martyr in the cause of English liberty. But it was finally clear that the monarch of France had no more real respect for that liberty than the King of Spain.[71]

Henry II's underhanded and halfhearted support of Stafford's expedition was the result of a strange and almost willful blindness to the danger in the North which dominated the French court throughout the spring. François de Noailles had correctly diagnosed Philip's military strategy as early as February, but Montmorency was unconvinced.[72] Even Coligny, who firmly believed that the issue between Habsburg and Valois would be settled not in Italy but in the North, thought that there was no serious danger of an attack from Flanders on the frontier he was defending.[73] Some of the ambassador's dispatches from London were delayed in April, but the Constable was unmoved by the threat of English intervention until François's letter of April 28 arrived about May 6. The court was apparently stunned to learn that a breach might be imminent, but as late as May 29 Montmorency was so ignorant of the true state of affairs that he sent off a special

---

[71] Discours, 1 May 1557, ibid., XIII, fols. 212-14; Advis, 23 and 31 May 1557, ibid., fols. 221, 223. Stafford was beheaded on May 28. On the question how far Henry II committed himself to Stafford's support, Wotton's warning before the event is significant: "It is thought that the French King will not sturre in anye of these matters till he may perceyve some lykelihode of breache, which is now verie much suspected, specially seing the King's Majestie [Philip] is come over. And then, suspectinge anye such thinge he will not faill (according to his olde wont) to see whether he can be before hande with their Majesties." Note by Wotton, before 14 April 1557, P.R.O., S.P. 69, Vol. X, no. 587 (For. Cal., Mary, 293). cf. Ven. Cal., VI, Part II, 1106-7.

[72] Advis, 3 Feb. 1557, Aff. Etr., XIII, fol. 151; Instructions, Henry II to François de Noailles, 7 Feb. 1557, ibid., fol. 154; Fr. de N. to Henry II, 16 Feb. 1557, ibid., fol. 155.

[73] Coligny to François de Noailles, 31 Mar. and 23 Apr. 1557, Aff. Etr., XVIII, fols. 380, 413.

envoy to protest to Mary about some minor English depredations in the Channel.[74] The final comment on Henry's all-absorbing interest in Italian affairs was written in blood on August 10 when Philip's army annihilated an opposing French force near St. Quentin and captured the Constable himself.

* * *

François de Noailles's last few weeks in England were naturally unhappy ones. Naval and military leaders had been summoned from Calais, the Scottish border, and the fleet, and on May 3 there was a council of war in Pembroke's house. Rumors soon got about that the English meant to surprise Havre or Boulogne, but the Council wanted to hold its hand until the fleet which Philip had ordered from Spain arrived in the Channel.[75]

As he watched the preparations for war, the Bishop of Dax once more persuaded himself that an open breach was after all the better way, especially since Henry II (thanks to the ambassador's own efforts), was still free to make a descent on England "under the mask of Elizabeth." The second of Philip's main aims in coming to England had been to make sure of Mary's successor by marrying her to the Prince of Savoy and taking her across to Flanders. François had warned her of the scheme through the Marchioness of Northampton as soon as he got wind of it at the end of April, and Elizabeth had replied that she would die rather than bend to the King's will. The ambassador could leave England in the confidence that his King "never had a finer opportunity in this country than at present."[76]

At the end of May Renard crossed to Flanders and a herald was sent to declare war at Reims. On June 7, as soon as Wotton (with tears in his eyes) had taken leave of Henry II, the herald did his duty. Simultaneously war was declared in London by

[74] Montmorency to François de Noailles, 8 Apr., 13 May, 29 May 1557, Aff. Etr., XIII, fol. 185, XVIII, fol. 437, XIII, fol. 228; *Ven. Cal.*, VI, Part II, 1034-5, 1042, 1149.

[75] Advis, 6 May 1557, Aff. Etr., XIII, fol. 204; François de Noailles to Montmorency, 31 May 1557, *ibid.*, fol. 222.

[76] Advis, [c. 20] Apr. 1557, Aff. Etr., XIII, fol. 191; François de Noailles to Montmorency, 28 Apr. 1557, *ibid.*, fol. 193; Fr. de N. to Henry II, 8 May 1557, *ibid.*, fol. 206; *Ven. Cal.*, VI, Part II, 1015; Wiesener, 354-8.

proclamation. François de Noailles left London on June 21, Philip ten days later. In spite of vigorous appeals to public sentiment by both governments, the outbreak of war aroused little enthusiasm on either side of the Channel.[77]

The drama of intrigue and diplomacy was ended and the stage left to the men-at-arms.

[77] Advis, 31 May 1557, Aff. Etr., XIII, fol. 223ᵛ; Montmorency to François de Noailles, 7 June 1557, *ibid.*, XVIII, fol. 457; Fr. de N. to D'Oysel, 13 and 21 June 1557, *ibid.*, XIII, fols. 228ᵛ-229, 230-1; Mary's Proclamation of War, 7 June 1557, *ibid.*, fols. 225-7; Henry II's Manifesto, June 1557, *ibid.*, fols. 232-6.

CONCLUSION

AFTER almost four centuries of historical writing, the Spanish marriage still awaits an apologist. Catholics and Protestants alike have condemned it, Spaniards and Frenchmen have deplored it, and Englishmen of all shades of opinion look back upon it as one of the more regrettable incidents of their national history.

It is not difficult to argue, as does one of Renard's biographers, that the Emperor's objective, difficult as it was of attainment, was not a chimera. If Mary had worked to reestablish national unity and national self-respect after the troubles of her brother's reign instead of exasperating her subjects by religious persecution; if she had taken an early and resolute part in her husband's war against France; above all, if a child had been born of the marriage—then the destiny of all Europe would have been changed.[1] One might add that if Philip had been other than the person he was, if he had accepted his anomalous position as graciously as Prince Albert of Saxe-Coburg-Gotha three centuries later, if he had tactfully applied his undoubted abilities to the problem of reorganizing and revitalizing his wife's government, then Renard's work might not have been in vain.

Speculation about what might have been is at best, however, the periphery of sober history. It can illuminate, but it cannot explain. To understand the actions and motives of diplomats long since dead it is necessary to take into account the possibilities which they themselves saw in any given situation, but it is a rash historian indeed who thinks he can estimate exactly how narrowly each of these possibilities failed of realization.

The four troubled years between the accession of Mary and the outbreak of war between France and England marked the beginning of that subtle psychological revolution which finally substi-

[1] Tridon, "Renard," 236.

tuted Spain for France as the national enemy in the minds of most Englishmen. The Anglo-French peace-treaty signed at Cateau-Cambrésis in 1559, the "Diplomatic Revolution" of 1569-1572, and the Anglo-Spanish War of Elizabeth's later years had their dress rehearsal in the aftermath of Mary's marriage. More important, the fusion of Protestantism and nationalism which has left its mark even on the England of today can be dated from the years when the nation was subjected against its will to one who was both a Catholic and a foreigner.

This is the broad significance of that rivalry between French and Spanish ambassadors at the court of Mary Tudor which has been the theme of the preceding pages. Any attempt to summarize the part played in the final result by personalities, by blind historical forces, and by that ultimate mystery called chance would exhaust the writer's powers and the reader's patience. To recall the title of a book written a generation ago,[2] Simon Renard and Antoine de Noailles contributed much to "The Making of the England of Elizabeth." Together they temporarily made of England a battle-ground where Habsburg and Valois fought for European hegemony. After their work was done, it was obviously impossible for Elizabeth to continue her sister's foreign policy, as the dean of Tudor historians has remarked.[3] The spirit of the new reign was to be isolationist and nationalistic, largely because its leaders had reached maturity in a reign which was neither. In a superficial sense, Renard was on the side of the past, Noailles of the future: the one was forced by circumstances to play the dynastic game of an age which was rapidly passing, the other was compelled to ally himself with that growing "consciousness-of-kind" which, under the name of nationalism, was later to dominate the modern world. But neither really understood English national consciousness, though both learned to respect and to manipulate it. Sixteenth-century diplomats lived in a world of dispatches and audiences, of paper treaties and hypocritical altercations, of subtle plot and counterplot to vindicate things called personal honor and

---

[2] A. B. Hinds, *The Making of the England of Elizabeth* (New York, 1895).
[3] Pollard, *Pol. Hist.*, 171.

dynastic prestige—a world which often had only the most tenuous connection with the real world of expanding commerce and industry, of ordinary social relationships, of religious and spiritual aspirations, and of scientific and intellectual achievement. The dominant note of Mary's reign was undoubtedly sterility, and the foreign intrigue of the reign is simply one more proof of the fact; but (if one may be permitted to resort to paradox) it was a sterility which was pregnant with growth and change.

* * *

The later destinies of the leading characters in the story were in some ways closely related to their careers in England.

The marriage of Philip and Mary marked the high-point of Renard's career. The very faults of character which helped him climb to the dizzy heights of success—lack of scruples and incorrigible personal ambition—eventually led to his downfall. Failing to win Philip's favor by demonstrating his abilities, he made the mistake of trying to win it by force. After the King left the Netherlands for Spain in 1559, a struggle to the death began in Brussels between the ex-ambassador and Granvelle for control of the Council of State. Renard allied himself with William of Orange and the others who were later to lead the Dutch in their struggle for freedom from Spanish rule, while Granvelle cast in his lot with the Spanish party. But the issue was primarily a personal one, perfectly symbolized by a masquerade produced before some of Renard's friends in 1564 which represented a Cardinal (Granvelle was elevated to the purple in 1561) hounded by a pack of devils decked with foxes' tails. The obvious pun on Renard's name delighted the company as much as it irritated the Cardinal. The quarrel eventually resulted in victory for Granvelle, thanks to the vindictive use he made of Etienne Quiclet's vague charges of treason against the ambassador. In spite of heroic but tactless efforts over the course of many years, Renard was never able to clear himself of the suspicion that he had betrayed his master in the very moment of his triumph in England. One of his biographers remarks that by his devoted efforts in London he had failed to add a great realm to Philip's dominions, while by his factious intrigues in the Netherlands he helped lose Philip the richest of his provinces. He died in disgrace at Madrid on August 8, 1573.[4]

Antoine de Noailles's few remaining years of life were spent, as his whole life had been spent, in the service of his King. The three years in London remained a distasteful memory in his mind, and the hatred he had developed for England and things English never left him. England's shadow seemed to follow him even after he had exchanged diplomacy for administrative and military pursuits. After the disaster at St. Quentin (in which English troops played a minor part) he was one of those who were called on to command a garrison on the threatened frontier, a position which he fulfilled with dash and vigor. Soon afterward he was sent to his native province as Governor of Bordeaux. There his chief business was to defend the district against a possible Anglo-Spanish attack. The news of Guise's capture of Calais in January 1558 gave him a thrill of vindictive pleasure. The achievement of "chasing these biting flies of Englishmen across the sea" was indeed a fitting capstone to his work in London. The opening of the religious troubles in 1560 saddened him deeply. The Calvinists, he wrote, "have profaned the churches, burned their ornaments and decorations . . . a thing I never heard of having been done in England"—even in England. If Noailles belonged to any party in the conflict just beginning, he was a *politique*; and it was a tribute to the respect which he commanded among the extremists on both sides that he was elected Mayor of Bordeaux in 1561. But the Calvinists were radicals not only in religion but also in political theory, and they were supported by England. It is not strange that the Governor of Bordeaux—Catholic, aristocrat, and royalist as he always was—was accused by his enemies of belonging to the religious reactionaries. Weighed down by ill-health, financial worries, and concern about his country's plight, he breathed his last on March

---

[4] For Renard's later career, see Weiss, I, pp. xxxi *ff*.; "Vunière," *Etude historique*, 101-300; Tridon, "Renard," Part II; Febvre, *Philippe II*, Chaps. VI, XII.

11, 1563. Gilles wrote François the news—"the saddest, most vexing and disagreeable news I could relate: the loss of this great gentleman, our good brother, whom we have a right to call father."[5]

Unlike his brother, François de Noailles was charmed by England. Never had he seen a country "so beautiful and delectable." "To my mind there is nothing more beautiful across the mountains in Italy," he wrote in January 1557, "than in this country." He never lost interest in the scene of his diplomatic *début,* vigorously supporting Anjou's suit for the hand of Elizabeth in 1571, as we have noticed. But his extraordinary talents were required elsewhere and he never crossed the Channel again. While passing through Calais in June 1557 he seized the opportunity to examine the state of the town's defenses, found them inadequate, and wrote a detailed report to Henry II which was confirmed by the investigation of spies. It was apparently on the basis of this report that the King decided, against the advice of his military experts, to attack Calais six months later. In later accounts of the siege it has seldom been noticed that Guise based his attack to the letter on the information supplied by François de Noailles.[6] Space is lacking for even the baldest account of his later career as ambassador to Venice (1557-1561), to Rome (1563), and to Constantinople (1571-1574); as devoted incumbent of what he called "the poorest bishopric in all France"; as opponent of both the League and the Huguenots; and as personal friend of many of the great men and women of his day. Suffice it to say that he became one of the ablest diplomats of his age and that his name still occupies a modest but important niche in literary and ecclesiastical, as well as political history. He lived out his later years in Dax as a sort of elder statesman, the friend of Montaigne and the

[5] Tamizey de Larroque has gathered and printed much of Antoine's later correspondence in his charming little essay, "Antoine de Noailles à Bordeaux" (see Bibliography). The passages quoted are from pp. 481-3 and 527-31.

[6] The evidence is summarized in Vertot, I, 35-7. For the original documents, see Tamizey de Larroque, *Lettres inédites de François de Noailles,* 29; Charrière, *Négociations de la France dans le Levant,* III, 276, note; and Aff. Etr., Corr. pol., Venise, VII, fols. 96-7, 101, 103-6, 111, 117-19, 121-2.

adviser (on occasions) of Henry III, Catherine de' Medici, and Henry of Navarre. He died at Bayonne on September 20, 1585.[7]

If Antoine was born to greatness as head of the family, and if François achieved it by his own talents, Gilles, most modest and unambitious of the three brothers, had greatness thrust upon him. We have seen how unwillingly he entered upon a diplomatic career. Appointments as ambassador to England and Scotland (1559-1561), later to Poland (1573) and Constantinople (1574) came almost as unexpectedly. Elizabeth said of him that she had never known an ambassador "whose conduct was so full of reserve and moderation," and in Poland he achieved the characteristic feat of working with a co-ambassador, Jean de Monluc, without friction or jealousy. In 1585 he succeeded François as Bishop of Dax and spent the remainder of his life in his diocese, where he died about 1597.[8]

As for Mary, her closing days were tragic almost beyond description. After Philip left her for the last time in July 1557 the burden of her failure became well-nigh unbearable. The war was unpopular and the national confidence at low ebb. The fall of Calais in January 1558 was her deathblow, but she tried pathetically to parry it by convincing herself that she was at last to bear the child upon which all her mortal hopes were centered. The people's devotion to her at her accession had changed to hatred, and now the hatred was mingled with contempt; no longer was there any hope of national regeneration or of religious peace so long as the Queen lived. While Mary was dreaming that she saw "many little children like angels play before her, singing pleasant notes, giving her more than earthly comfort,"[9] all eyes, including her husband's, were turning to Hatfield; and when Figueroa arrived in England early in November with secret and urgent instructions from Philip, it was to Elizabeth that he presented them. As the sun rose on

---

[7] François de Noailles deserves, but has not yet found a biographer. Vertot's is still the fullest account of his career (I, 27-78). For additional details, see J.-B. Gabarra, *Un évêque de Dax*, and Tamizey de Larroque, *Lettres inédites*.

[8] Vertot's account of Gilles de Noailles is still unpublished: Bib. Nat., f.f., nouv. acq., No. 9520, pp. 128-52.

[9] Henry Clifford, *Life of Jane Dormer*, 70.

November 17 Mary breathed her last, some twelve hours before Pole too passed away. "That same day at afternoon all the churches in London did ring, and at night [the people] did make bonfires and set tables in the street and did eat and drink and made merry for the new Queen Elizabeth, Queen Mary's sister."[10]

[10] *Machyn Diary*, 178.

APPENDIX I

Noailles's Intercepted Dispatch of January 26, 1554

In his dispatch to Henry II of January 26, 1554, which was intercepted by the English government, Noailles wrote: "J'ay recouvert le double d'une lettre qu'elle [Elizabeth] escripvoit à ladicte royne *que l'ambassadeur de l'empereur a faict traduire* en François, qui est cy enclose." The original dispatch is lost, but this is the reading of the original minute (Aff. Etr., XV, fol. 283), printed accurately by Vertot (III, 44) in spite of Wiesener's conjecture (*Jeunesse d'Elisabeth*, 186, note 1) that Vertot made an error in decipherment. The assertion that Renard was responsible for the translation of Elizabeth's letter which came into Noailles's hands was no slip of the pen. The letter was dictated to a secretary, according to Noailles's usual custom, but several alterations in the ambassador's own hand in other passages of the original minute prove that Noailles corrected the secretary's draft and intended the assertion to stand as quoted above.

When Renard got hold of the original dispatch and began to check Gardiner's decipherment, all that he and his secretary could make of the phrase, "que l'ambassadeur de l'empereur a faict traduire," was "que lres de quel a faict traduyre." Since this made no sense, someone (possibly Renard himself) added a "j" and a "y" on either side of the "a." Thus in the draft decipherment which remained among Renard's papers (Besançon, Bibliothèque Publique, Fonds Granvelle, Vol. 73, fols. 123-4), a copy of which was sent to Charles V, Noailles was made the author of the translation in place of Renard. The decipherment is not in Renard's hand, but the underscoring of Courtenay's name proves that it was his secretary's draft, not Gardiner's. There seems to be no doubt that the original dispatch followed the minute and that the phrase noted was misread by Renard, deliberately or otherwise.

On January 27, however, Noailles wrote Mary of Lorraine, "J'ay recouvert une longue lettre que a escripte Madame Elizabet à ceste royne depuys 8 ou 10 jours, dont je vous envoye le double, *que j'ay faict traduyre* en françoys" (Aff. Etr., X, fol. 169); and on March 17 he wrote Montmorency, "C'estoit ung de mes amys qui me l'avoit donnée [Elizabeth's letter], me disant *qu'elle avoit esté traduite* sur une lettre que Madame Elizabeth avoit escripte à ceste Royne" (Aff. Etr., X, fol. 17). (cf. Gachard and Piot, IV, 374.) In the first passage Noailles may have been referring loosely to the *second* copy or translation which he was sending to the Queen Dowager of Scotland. If Elizabeth's letter was written between January 18 and January 20, as Noailles was informed, there was ample time for the translation to have been made either by Renard or by Noailles's "friend" or by Noailles himself. (cf. the contradictory view of Wiesener, *op. cit.,* 186, note 1.)

There are three possible explanations of the puzzle. (1) The "friend" (one of Elizabeth's servants?) may have led Noailles wrongly to believe that Renard had made the translation, a mistake which Noailles discovered soon afterward. (2) The Queen may have sent Renard a copy of Elizabeth's letter and the "friend" (a French spy in Renard's household?) may have stolen the ambassador's translation of it, a fact which Renard discovered perhaps when he saw Noailles's dispatch and which he attempted to conceal from the Emperor by changing the decipherment as noted above and by simulating surprise at finding the translation in Noailles's packet. (3) Renard may actually have paid the "friend" to give the translation to Noailles in order to cast suspicion upon Elizabeth.

On the whole, I think that the second hypothesis fits the evidence most closely. On January 26 Noailles was sure that Renard had made the translation and said so in a ciphered dispatch which was accompanied (as an added precaution) by a dummy dispatch to be shown to inquisitive officials. It was not important to specify the source of the translation in writing to the Queen Dowager of Scotland next day, hence he spoke of it as his own. Two months later it was dangerous for him to hint to Montmorency that he had spies in the Imperial embassy for fear his letter would be intercepted, so he stated simply that the letter "had been trans-lated" before it reached him. Renard's mistake in decipherment may have been inadvertent rather than deliberate, but he learned through other sources a short while afterward that one of his secretaries was in the French pay (see "French Intrigue at the Court of Queen Mary," *Amer. Hist. Rev.,* XLV (April 1940), 539). Since Renard's negligence seems to account for the known facts, it is unnecessary to presuppose a Machiavellian plot on his part to discredit Elizabeth.

APPENDIX II

Imperial Gifts and Pensions

Five lists of persons receiving gifts or pensions are to be found in Renard's papers:

(1) "A list of names of persons to whom gold chains and gifts have been given," 15 Mar. 1554 (P.R.O., Tyler, 1st half, pp. 245-6).

(2) "A list of persons to whom chains were to be given by Philip" [n.d.] (*ibid.*, 2nd half, pp. 35-6).

(3) "A list of persons to be rewarded" [n.d.] (*ibid.*, p. 36).

(4) "A list of pensions to be distributed" [n.d.] (*ibid.*, p. 36).

(5) A list of pensions actually promised by Renard and communicated to Philip [n.d.] (*ibid.*, 1st half, p. 492; Weiss, IV, 267).

Tyler dates the last four c. July 1554, but internal evidence and careful comparison with the dispatches referred to in Chapter VI, notes 24 and 25, indicate that all four were drawn up by Renard about the end of March 1554, as a result of his consultations with Mary, Paget, and Gardiner. The last, for instance, was undoubtedly drafted about the same time as Renard's letter to Charles V of 3 Apr. 1554 (P.R.O., Tyler, pp. 371-80).

List (1) (gifts of 25 to 200 crowns to each of thirty-eight minor officials, totalling 4,850 crowns) represents the distribution of the 5,000 crowns which Egmont brought with him in March 1554. List (2) (chains worth 100 to 200 crowns apiece to be given to twenty-seven individuals or groups, totalling over 4,700 crowns) represents further small gifts made by Philip after his arrival.

Lists (3), (4), and (5) are concerned chiefly with the pensions to be given to more important persons. (3) may very well be Gardiner's list while (4) is Paget's. Among those included in (3) but omitted from (4) are Cheyne, Thirlby, several judicial officials, and several gentlemen- and ladies-in-waiting; among those included in (4) but omitted from (3) are Clinton, Worcester, Dacre, the Captain of Guines, and the Deputy of Calais. (4) mentions "the Lord Chancellor, to be reserved for some pension or benefice," and "the Lord Paget, to be recompensed as his Majesty knows." (3) is merely a list of twenty-five names and several groups, while (4) specifies the sums (pensions of 600 to 2,000 crowns each, amounting to 23,000 crowns in all) which were to go to each of twenty-three named individuals. If (3) and (4) represent Gardiner's and Paget's lists respectively, then (5) may represent Renard's final list, approved by Mary. Here the names are drawn from both (3) and (4); the total number of persons is reduced to fifteen and they are stated to have been actually promised pensions of 500 to 2,000 crowns, totalling 16,500 crowns in all. Comparison with (2) indicates that many persons suggested for pensions in (3) or (4) eventually received only gifts of chains.

Since there appears to be no final and inclusive list of gifts and pensions actually distributed or promised up to July 1554, it is difficult to estimate the extent of Imperial bribery before the marriage. Allowing for duplications in the existing lists, it seems a safe guess that Renard paid or promised between 30,000 and 35,000 crowns (c. £10,000) before Philip's arrival. After his arrival Spanish money began to flow a great deal more freely. Michiele reported that Philip, his attendants, and the other foreigners who were attracted to England during his stay in the realm spent "upwards of a million in gold" (*Ven. Cal.,* VI, Part II, 1066). The largest item of expenditure was undoubtedly the payment of his own and his followers' expenses, including the salaries of a considerable number of Englishmen (many of them sons of important personages) who were taken into his service (see *Docs. inéds.,* III, 526-7, 529; list of names in P.R.O., Tyler, pp. 495-500, and Gachard and Piot, IV, 442-5). Payment of some of Mary's debts was another large item: 250,000 ducats in the fall of 1554, for example (Muñoz, *Viaje,* 120). Further bribes to English councillors and courtiers constituted a third item, less costly but politically more significant. Noailles heard that Philip gave the English ambassadors who went to meet him in Spain gifts worth

60,000 ducats, and brought 30,000 ducats' worth of chains to be distributed in England (Advis, 1 Aug. 1554, Aff. Etr., IX, fol. 241). In August 1554, Philip distributed pensions amounting to 15,000 crowns or more to members of the Council (Renard to Charles V, 3 Sept. 1554, P.R.O., Tyler, p. 142). The rumor was that the total was actually 30,000 crowns (Muñoz, *op. cit.,* 120); and Renard heard that the King had given something to others not on the list which he sent Charles V (lost), although he did not know "to whom nor how nor why" (Renard to Charles V, 18 Sept. 1554, P.R.O., Tyler, p. 156). In the spring of 1557 Michiele estimated the total annual value of Spanish pensions to Englishmen at almost 54,000 ducats (£28,000) (*Ven. Cal.,* VI, Part II, 1066).

NOTE ON THE SOURCES

I. *French Sources: The Noailles Papers.*

As was the custom in the sixteenth century, the diplomatic papers of Antoine, François, and Gilles de Noailles were considered the property not of their government but of the envoys themselves. Hence these papers eventually found a resting-place in the Château de Noailles in Limousin. The fact that there are very few original letters from François to his brothers—most of them are minutes—and many originals from them to François, suggests that the collection as it exists today was preserved through François's care.

For a century and a half these papers apparently lay undisturbed, then sometime during the last two decades of the seventeenth century, a learned and somewhat erratic antiquary named Antoine Varillas (1624-1696) came across the correspondence of Antoine de Noailles while gathering material on the English Reformation for his most famous work, a "History of Heresy" as it was popularly known.[1] He decided to publish the correspondence and even went to the length of writing a brief monograph on the ambassador's career, based upon a characteristically cavalier examination of the sources.[2] How he obtained access to the Noailles papers and how far his editorial work had progressed by the time of his death, we do not know. Since the subsequent history of the manuscripts which he "discovered" is not at all clear, what follows must be considered merely a tentative sketch of that history based upon study of the only evidence available—that of handwriting and of occasional internal evidence in the manuscripts as they exist today.[3] Space forbids any detailed exposition of this evidence,

---

[1] *Histoire des révolutions arrivées dans l'Europe en matière de religion depuis 1374 jusqu'en 1564* (Paris, 1686-1689). On Varillas, and on the other editors mentioned below, see *Nouvelle biographie générale* (Paris, 1877), and A. Jal, *Dictionnaire critique de biographie et d'histoire* (Paris, 1867).

[2] Bib. Nat., f.f., No. 6948, fols. 241 *ff.* (particularly fols. 241, 246, 257-8). The manuscript is in Varillas's hand with several alterations by Gaignières.

[3] The problem has been to compare six separate hands (Valincour, Valincour's copyist, Gaignières, Vertot, and Vertot's two copyists) in eight manuscript volumes of particular importance: Aff. Etr., corr. pol., Angl., Vols. IX, XII; Aff. Etr., méms. et docs., Angl., Vol. XIV; Bib. Nat., f.f., Nos. 6908, 6948, 20147; Bib. Nat., f.f., nouv. acq., Nos. 328, 9520.

which is excessively complicated and not directly relevant to the present subject; but further research by students of the period may perhaps confirm the conclusions suggested, in substance if not in detail.

Probably it was before Varillas's death in 1696 that two other scholars became interested in the project of editing Antoine de Noailles's correspondence. They were François Roger de Gaignières (1633?-1715) and Jean Baptiste du Trousset de Valincour (1653-1730). Valincour— friend of Bossuet, Racine, and Boileau, member and official historian of the Academy—was the "historian" of the two. He took his share in the task of transcribing hundreds of Noailles's dispatches, but his main interest seems to have been in rewriting Varillas's study of the ambassador's life and career. Four rough drafts of his work have survived, together with the notes (extracts from the sources and from secondary works) which must have served as their basis.[4] Gaignières— collector, antiquarian, and amateur scholar, little known either to his contemporaries or to posterity—was the "editor." He transcribed comparatively few of the documents, but it was he who dated and described the original documents in marginal notes, made corrections in the transcriptions and in Valincour's drafts for an introduction, and indicated whether a document was or was not to be printed by the notations, "imp[rimer]" and "sup[primer]." If one can make a judgment upon the basis of such scanty evidence as is to be found in the manuscripts themselves, it seems clear that Gaignières was the abler scholar of the two.

As the work progressed it grew in scope. Sometime about the turn of the century René Aubert de Vertot (1655-1735), a friend of the Noailles family, was commissioned by the then Duke of Noailles to publish the papers of all three of the latter's famous sixteenth-century forebears, including the numerous embassies of François and Gilles to countries other than England.[5] Whether Valincour and Gaignières were already at work on the documents when Vertot obtained his commission, or whether Vertot obtained their assistance after the Duke had turned the papers over to his care, it is not clear. But one thing is certain: Vertot depended heavily upon the work of the other two in preparing the documents for publication. The evidence indicates that

[4] The most elaborate draft, along with the notes, is in Aff. Etr., méms. et docs., Angl., Vol. XIV. Valincour's copy of Varillas's sketch and various revisions of it are in Bib. Nat., f.f., No. 6948, fols. 270-8, 279-94, 306-13, followed by 297-302. This volume of biographical material on Noailles's life is the chief clue to the problem of editorship.

[5] See Vertot, I, 6; and Nouvelle biographie générale, Vol. XLVI, s.v. Vertot.

he followed Gaignières's judgments as to which documents were worth printing and which were not very closely. He himself recopied practically all the documents which were considered "more important," presumably from copies already made by Valincour and Gaignières, and left the "less important" transcriptions just as they came from the first copyists. Corrections and emendations are to be found in these latter transcriptions, but there are none in those left by Vertot; presumably when Vertot had recopied a first draft of an important letter, he destroyed the earlier copy, since the "less important" transcriptions are the only remaining evidences of Valincour's and Gaignières's work.[6]

Vertot further rewrote Varillas's historical introduction (already revised by Valincour), sometimes borrowing whole paragraphs from the drafts before him. But he changed the proportions frequently, eliminated some of his predecessors' glib historical generalizations, and added considerable detail on François and Gilles de Noailles. On August 10, 1714, he signed the completed introduction, nowhere acknowledging his debt to Varillas, Valincour, or Gaignières.[7]

Vertot's work was not given to the world during his lifetime for reasons which are obscure. After his death in 1735 his manuscripts were sent to the Noailles family and placed with the original documents. Almost thirty years later the major part of his historical introduction, together with all the "more important" documents of Antoine de Noailles's embassy to London (1553-1556), were published by Claude Villaret as *Ambassades de Messieurs de Noailles en Angleterre* (5 vols., Leyden, 1763). Although a few sections of the introduction and a few letters already designated for publication were omitted, the printed work was substantially what Vertot meant it to be, except that *pièces justificatives* from the embassies of François and Gilles de Noailles to London (1556-1561) were not included.[8]

Vertot's *Ambassades,* now a rather rare book, has been used by generations of scholars as a standard source for the history of Mary's

[6] See Table below, p. 349.

[7] Relation des ambassades des Seigneurs de Noailles . . ., Bib. Nat., f.f., nouv. acq., No. 9520.

[8] See Vertot, I, 1-8. About 1888 the Commission des archives diplomatiques decided to publish the correspondence of François and Gilles de Noailles as a sequel to Vertot's book, but the project was apparently abandoned after work on the first volume was far advanced. See Abbé J.-B. Gabarra, *Un évêque de Dax, François de Noailles* (Dax, 1888), 65, note.

reign. As early as three years after its publication, Henri Griffet called attention in a penetrating little essay to the historical inaccuracies and prejudices in Vertot's introductory sketch (Vol. I of the *Ambassades*).[9] But among those who have made use of the book since Griffet's time, there has been little or no recognition of the fact that the documents printed (in Vols. II to V) represented a selection of about two-fifths of the original correspondence of Antoine de Noailles—a selection made by three or four early eighteenth-century savants who were thoroughly imbued with the historical philosophy of the age of the *Roi Soleil,* its fervent patriotism, its hero-worship, and its preference of stylistic elegance to factual accuracy. Careful comparison of the dispatches which Vertot and his collaborators thought "more important" with those which they considered "less important" gives interesting hints about their criteria of selection.

Although Vertot's introduction exhibits some of the worst features of the historiography of his age, many of its most slipshod generalizations can be corrected from the *pièces justificatives* referred to and approved for publication by the author himself. One answer to this seeming anomaly is that Gaignières was primarily responsible for the selection of documents for publication; and Gaignières was apparently more interested in Noailles as a reporter than in Noailles as a diplomatic agent, more concerned about presenting new historical facts than about following the diplomatic process itself. No matter how second-hand or worthless, very few of the ambassador's "advices" or news reports were passed over for publication—and it was fortunate for students of English history that they were not. A dangerous corollary to this principle, however, was that news items which later proved to be false, descriptions of episodes which had no important sequel, and suggestions from the ambassador which were not followed out, all these were thought not worth publishing.[10] This is simply to say that Gaignières was no more interested in propaganda and public opinion,

---

[9] See Henri Griffet, *Nouveaux éclaircissements sur l'histoire de Marie, reine d'Angleterre . . . adressés à M. David Hume* (Amsterdam, 1766), particularly pp. 1-7, 84-93, 99-103, 115, 118, 129. The book is extremely rare, but the British Museum has a copy.

[10] In several cases the editor, probably Gaignières, wrote "fausse-oster" beside some report of Noailles's, for instance several concerning Mary's supposed pregnancy. See Aff. Etr., IX, fols. 445, 461; XVIII, fol. 300. Randall's offer of help to Noailles in 1554 was suppressed, apparently because it had no concrete results. See Aff. Etr., IX, fols. 248, 271, 273.

in diplomatic intrigue and the evolution of foreign policy in general, than most historians of his day.

The editors exposed themselves to a far more serious charge, however. Writing at the behest of the Duke of Noailles, and editing for a public imbued with the glory of France and the divine right of kings, they had motives enough to cover up the dubious and dishonorable in the conduct of Antoine de Noailles and his king. To be sure, they selected for publication enough dispatches to show the attentive reader that the ambassador was deep in the conspiracies of Mary's reign; but they suppressed at least a dozen dispatches of first-rate significance for Noailles's relations with Northumberland, with Wyatt's associates, and with Dudley.[11] Furthermore, they deliberately mutilated a few of the most important dispatches which found their way into print, either by omitting incriminating passages or by altering the phraseology of the original text. It must be emphasized immediately that these spectacular cases of dishonesty are very few, but they are nonetheless important. Not to mention minor cases, three important letters of Noailles were tampered with seriously: (1) his letter to Henry II of July 7, 1554 (a long passage omitted at the close, and several important omissions in the body of the dispatch which are nowhere marked in the printed text); (2) his Instruction to La Marque of January 15, 1554 (several omissions, marked honestly with dots in this case; one phrase—Vertot, III, 23, line 8 from bottom—a deliberate falsification); and (3) his letter to Montmorency of November 26, 1555 (an important omission, marked by dots).[12] I regret that the outbreak of war has made it impossible to obtain final verification of several of these suppressed passages, but I am confident that such verification would not alter any of the general conclusions which I have reached.

In summary, if Vertot's *Ambassades* be judged by the scholarly standards of its own day, it was a fairly honest piece of editing. The

[11] In particular, Aff. Etr., IX, fols. 34, 53, 99, 114, 117, 16, 22, 137, 153, 170, 198, 489, 498. Two of these dispatches (fols. 170, 273) are marked "imp[rimer]" in Gaignières's hand, but the notation has been crossed out and "sup[primer]" substituted. There are other less important cases of the same sort of thing, presumably the result of Vertot's judgment.

[12] Originals: Aff. Etr., XV, fols. 44-5; XV, fol. 267; XVII, fols. 212-14. It should be remarked that the dots which suggest deletions in several other pages of Vertot's *Ambassades* represent merely an unimportant phrase or an undeciphered word in the original.

vast majority of the documents printed were faithfully transcribed; most of the documents necessary for a general understanding of Antoine de Noailles's embassy were published; and most of the letters left unpublished would appear unimportant even to a modern editor. But thanks to the historical tastes and prejudices of Vertot and his collaborators, much material which would be considered significant today was surpressed. Their purpose was to paint the portrait of a man who was at once a pious Catholic, a patriotic Frenchman, and a consummate diplomat; religion, patriotism, and hero-worship were the cornerstones of their work, literary elegance and moral edification its façade. A modern scholar must therefore go back to the original sources, the London correspondence of the three Noailles brothers.

This correspondence remained at the Château de Noailles along with other family papers until the Revolution, when the family archives were confiscated by the government. It is now in the Archives du ministère des affaires étrangères in Paris.[13] Some description of its present state and arrangement is necessary for an understanding of the technical side of the present work.

The collection comprises the diplomatic files of the three Noailles brothers as envoys to the courts of Mary and Elizabeth during the years 1553-1561. The documents—original dispatches from the French court and minutes of the envoys' dispatches—are divided into a "more important" and a "less important" series, just as Vertot left them.[14] With them are the two corresponding series of transcriptions made by Vertot and his collaborators. Although the present numbering of the volumes has no relation to Vertot's, the following table will enable the reader to correlate the references in the text with Vertot's original arrangement.[15]

[13] Correspondance politique, Angleterre, Vols. IX-XX. For the history and present state of the Noailles papers as a whole, particularly the later correspondence of François and Gilles de Noailles, see Léopold Delisle, Inventaire générale et méthodique des manuscrits français de la Bibliothèque Nationale (Paris, 1876), I, p. cxxxii; Louis Paris, Les papiers de Noailles de la Bibliothèque du Louvre (Paris, 1875), I, Preface, and 93-7; and Abbé J.-B. Gabarra, Un évêque de Dax, François de Noailles (Dax, 1888), 4.

[14] The same is true of the documents concerned with the other eight embassies of François and Gilles de Noailles, some of which are in the Archives du ministère des affaires étrangères, some in the Bibliothèque Nationale.

[15] Adapted from Inventaire sommaire des archives du département des affaires étrangères, Correspondance politique (Paris, 1903), I, 161.

1. *"More Important" Series, Originals and Minutes.*

[Vertot, MSS. Volume:]	[Aff. Etr., Volume:]	[Inclusive Dates:]	[No. of Folios:]
I	XV	23 Dec. 1553 to 12 Mar. 1554	346
II	XVI	29 Mar. 1554 to 22 Mar. 1555	397
III	XVII	17 Apr. 1555 to 29 May 1556	340
IV	XIX	9 May 1556 to 7 June 1561	438

2. *"Less Important" Series, Originals and Minutes.*

I	X	16 Mar. 1553 to 12 Apr. 1555	560
II	XI	2 Apr. 1555 to 4 Aug. 1556	384
III	XVIII	15 Dec. 1555 to Nov. 1557	508
IV	XX	24 Mar. 1559 to 20 May 1561	406

3. *"More Important" Series, Transcriptions.*

I, II, III	XII	23 Dec. 1552 to 29 May 1556	510
IV	XIII	9 May 1556 to 7 June 1561	395

4. *"Less Important" Series, Transcriptions.*

I, II	IX	16 Mar. 1553 to 4 Aug. 1556	697
III	[Missing]	[15 Dec. 1555 to Nov. 1557]	......
IV	XIV	24 Mar. 1559 to 20 May 1561	444

Some originals have been lost. A few, still listed in the tables of contents at the head of each volume, have dropped out of their bindings; but copies of most of them survive. Internal evidence indicates that a number of Antoine de Noailles's original minutes for the early months of 1556 are lost, presumably destroyed by the ambassador himself when Dudley's plot was discovered for fear they would prove embarrassing to him if seized by the English government. Over sixty of François de Noailles's more important minutes are missing, but fortunately Vertot's transcriptions of them still exist (Aff. Etr., Vol. XIII). One volume of Vertot's copies has been lost, as is evident from the table. The result is that there are a few undeciphered originals in Aff. Etr., Vol. XVIII, but the cipher can be worked out from Aff. Etr., Vol. XIX. As the table indicates, Vertot's *Ambassades* was published from Aff. Etr., Vol. XII (originals in Aff. Etr., Vols. XV-XVII).

Purely as a matter of convenience, I have followed Wiesener's practice of referring throughout the text to Vertot's transcriptions where they exist, rather than to the originals. In spite of the fact that one volume is missing, the copies are more complete, better arranged, and easier to use for purposes of ready reference; and the corresponding originals can be found in a moment by using either the table above or the detailed tables of contents in the manuscript volumes themselves. In the volumes of originals and copies alike, there are two systems of page-numbering: (1) an earlier notation in longhand, to which the tables of contents correspond; and (2) a recent stamped notation added by the archives. The first system numbers both sides of each folio in the volumes of transcriptions and the recto only of each folio in the volumes of originals; the second system numbers the recto of each folio throughout. Because the second system is more consistent and more carefully applied, I have used it throughout (only the first system was available to Wiesener). References are assumed to be to the recto unless otherwise noted.

The history of the use made by historical scholars of this collection is rather interesting. Froude seems to have known nothing of its existence, but there is some evidence that Lingard did.[16] The first modern historian to use it extensively was Louis Wiesener. In writing his scholarly and delightful study of Elizabeth's youth, he made full use for his purposes of Aff. Etr., IX and XIII. For some reason he never saw the volumes of originals and copies from which Vertot's *Ambassades* was published, and consequently he thought that the originals which formed the basis of Vertot's work were lost.[17] This error was repeated in the *Cambridge Modern History,* II, 803, and found its way into Conyers Read's *Bibliography of British History, Tudor Period* (Oxford, 1933), 53. Wiesener's book is still the ablest study of the diplomatic duel between Noailles and Renard, but it is neither exhaustive nor impartial. Writing in 1878, the author was unable to profit by later publication of Spanish and Imperial material; and in devoting himself mainly to Elizabeth he naturally overlooked a great deal which is of interest to the diplomatic historian. Furthermore, he developed a marked dislike for both Noailles and Elizabeth, and tended at times to exaggerate both the ability and wickedness of the ambassador.

About the time Wiesener's work appeared, Armand Baschet began the task of transcribing the Noailles correspondence for the Public Record Office in London. The work was never completed, but the

---

[16] See Wiesener, 175, note 1; Lingard, *History of England* (ed. 1849), V, 417.
[17] Wiesener, 92, note.

transcription was capably done so far as it went. For the year 1553 the copies are practically complete, but after that they thin out and in April 1554 they stop entirely, except for a few dispatches dealing with Scottish affairs of January-March 1555. Beginning again in June 1556, they include all but about thirty of the "more important" dispatches of Gilles and François de Noailles through June 1557.[18]

So far as I am aware, no English-speaking historian has ever made thorough use of the Noailles papers in Paris, and no French scholar has made such extensive use of them as Wiesener. François Decrue quoted sparingly from them in his *Montmorency* (1885-1889). The casual reader of Abbé G. Constant's article, "Le mariage de Marie Tudor et de Philippe II" (1912), will gather that the author visited both the Archives du ministère des affaires étrangères and the Public Record Office. But Constant quoted only passages from the Noailles papers already quoted by Wiesener and repeated several of the latter's errors; his references to P.R.O., Domestic Papers, were copied (inaccurately) from Pollard.[19] Miss J. M. Stone in her *History of Mary I* (1901) appears to have followed the same practice in borrowing from Wiesener. The relative unfamiliarity of the Noailles papers to students of Mary's reign is largely the result of the fact that a group of eighteenth-century editors published a selection of these papers which was full enough to demonstrate their importance, but not honest enough to reveal the importance of what was left unpublished.

II. *Imperial and Spanish Sources: Renard's Papers.*

Unlike the case of the Noailles papers, two fairly complete files of Renard's correspondence have come down to us: his own and his government's. Again unlike the papers of his rival, all of his correspondence which concerns the present work has been published or (barring the uncertainties of the present situation) will be published ere long.

Shortly before or after his death in 1573, Renard's papers came into the possession of Cardinal Granvelle. About a century later Abbé Jean Baptiste Boisot (1638-1694) bought Granvelle's whole library and

---

[18] P.R.O., Transcripts 3, Bundles 20-3. I am indebted to Professor J. E. Neale of University College for calling my attention to these transcripts. Baschet listed all the Noailles dispatches except for the "less important" documents of 1556-1561 in *39th Report of the Deputy Keeper of the Public Records* (1878), Appendix, 601-18.

[19] See Constant in *Revue d'histoire diplomatique*, XXVI, 60, note 1, and 64, note 6. cf. Pollard, *Pol. Hist.*, 107, note.

undertook the herculean task of sorting, arranging, and deciphering all the manuscripts he found. In 1694 the public library at Besançon which still houses these manuscripts was founded through his generosity.[20] Thanks to neglect before Boisot discovered them, the documents are in a very bad state of repair. Many of Renard's minutes, written in his own rapid and hardly legible hand, are mere fragments; others are torn or stained by dampness. But although nearly everything of interest in the collection has been published, the originals will repay the study of anyone interested in gaining an insight into Renard's character and methods of work.

Charles V's file of correspondence with England during the years 1553-1556 was preserved in Brussels until the Austrian evacuation at the end of the eighteenth century, when it was removed to Vienna along with other hastily-selected documents. It is now in the Haus-, Hof-, und Staatsarchiv in Vienna, and since the manuscripts are in a far better state of preservation than those in Besançon, they often supply the full text of a mutilated document in the Granvelle collection. Since most of the Spanish correspondence in Brussels was removed to Spain during Philip II's reign, some of Renard's letters (mostly originals and copies of dispatches sent to Philip and written in Spanish) are now in the Archives at Simancas. Much of importance for the present subject, however, still remains in the Archives du Royaume de Belgique in Brussels.[21]

These two separate files of Renard's correspondence, now in four different places (Besançon, Vienna, Simancas, and Brussels), became known to scholars only gradually. Boisot published nothing but a brief sketch of Granvelle's career.[22] While Griffet was writing his above-mentioned study of Noailles's career, "someone" brought him a batch of Renard's dispatches from Besançon, which he never returned; he quoted freely from these dispatches and the extracts were used to advantage by Lingard and Froude.[23] Beginning in 1831 the first Record

[20] See the inscription on the bust of Boisot in the reading room. For accounts of Boisot's work, see Weiss, I, pp. xxiv ff.; and Le P. Prosper Lévêque, *Mémoires pour servir à l'histoire du cardinal de Granvelle* (Paris, 1753), I, pp. xvii-xlii.

[21] *Span. Cal.,* X, pp. vii-viii. Napoleon I carried off some of the Spanish correspondence mentioned to Paris, but none of this material concerns Renard's embassy to England (Archives Nationales, Carton K, Nos. 1485-90).

[22] "Projet de la vie du cardinal de Granvelle," in *Continuation des mémoires de littérature et d'histoire* (Paris, Simart, 1727), Vol. IV.

[23] See Griffet, *op. cit.,* p. 48. The implication is that Griffet stole the documents (Tridon, "Renard," 185, note, and 376).

Commission had a set of transcripts made of some of the material in Brussels. These transcripts include dispatches between London and Brussels extending from April 10, 1553, to June 19, 1554; but since they were based upon eighteenth-century copies of originals already removed to Vienna, they are of little value as primary source material.[24] P. F. Tytler published considerable extracts from them in 1839 (dispatches of February 20 to June 19, 1554, only); and both Lingard and Froude made considerable use of them in their chapters on Mary. Bergenroth later transcribed some forty dispatches concerned with Renard's mission to England from the originals in Simancas, but these are of slight value today in view of the progress of publication.[25]

The first publication *in extenso* of certain of Renard's dispatches began in 1843 with the appearance of Volume III of the great *Colección de documentos inéditos para la historia de España*. Some twenty-five dispatches of 1554 were printed, but many of the originals at Simancas were mutilated and the editor's dating of the documents was often faulty.[26] About the same time Charles Weiss published almost all of Renard's papers at Besançon in another great series, the *Collection de documents inédits sur l'histoire de France*; but once again the originals were in bad repair and the dating not always accurate.[27] In 1882 Charles Piot published all the previously unprinted documents which he could find at Brussels bearing upon the Spanish marriage negotiations (July 1553 to December 1554), adding useful analyses of other relevant documents already printed in standard source collections. But he used only the eighteenth-century copies already mentioned, his transcription (or that of the earlier copyist) was careless, and his work as a whole was honeycombed with typographical and editorial errors.[28]

It was not till Royall Tyler undertook to edit the volumes dealing with Edward VI and Mary in the *Calendar of State Papers, Spanish* that anyone made a thorough search for all the relevant Spanish and

[24] P.R.O., Transcripts 8, Vol. 145. See *Span. Cal.*, XI, p. vii; and Wiesener, 90, note.

[25] B.M., Additional MSS. 28597, Nos. 33-63 (fols. 89-213).

[26] *Docs. inéds.*, III, 448-538. These dispatches are all duplicated in originals or minutes at Besançon and Vienna.

[27] *Papiers d'état du cardinal de Granvelle*, 9 vols., Paris, 1841-1852. Vol. IV contains Renard's correspondence of 1552-1556. For a list of all Renard's dispatches at Besançon with those printed by Weiss marked with a "W," see *Catalogue générale des manuscrits des bibliothèques publiques de France, Départements, Besançon* (Vol. XXXIII), A. Castan, ed. (Paris, 1900), II, Part I, 20-5.

[28] *Collection des voyages des souverains des Pays-Bas*, L. P. Gachard and Ch. Piot, eds., (Brussels, 1874-1882), IV, 83-453. See *Span. Cal.*, XI, p. vii.

Imperial material in continental libraries. During the years immediately preceding the first World War he and his wife visited Simancas, Besançon, Vienna, and Brussels, transcribing with a precision unattained by previous scholars everything of interest for the period 1547-1558. The first fruits of their labors were published in Volumes IX to XI of the *Calendar* (covering the years 1547 through 1553), but in 1916 the Public Record Office ran short of funds and the material for 1554-1558 is as yet unpublished, although plans for such publication were under consideration when the present war broke out.

The Tylers' transcripts for the year 1554, all of them translated and ready for publication, were in the Public Record Office when I was permitted to consult them. Those for the years 1555-1558, still untranslated, were at Antigny-le-Château, par Arnay-le-Duc, Côte d'Or, France, in the spring of 1936, when I was permitted to consult them through the courtesy of Mrs. Tyler. The wealth of material for 1554 is in striking contrast to the poverty of the later material—one more eloquent illustration of the decline of English prestige in Spanish eyes after Philip left his bride in the fall of 1554. The transcripts for 1554 are paged in two halves, beginning with January 1 and July 1. Wherever the published version of a document gives a reasonably accurate representation of the original as transcribed by the Tylers, I have given the reference. But reliance has been placed exclusively upon the text of the transcripts, for reasons suggested.

Careful perusal of these two sets of transcripts and conversations with Mrs. Tyler convinced me that she and her husband had exhausted all the material of any importance for a study of Anglo-Imperial and Anglo-Spanish relations during Mary's reign. Considerations of time and money prevented me from visiting Simancas, Vienna, and Brussels during the winter of 1935-1936, although a reading of Renard's day-by-day correspondence in the transcripts suggested that a few dispatches here and there had been lost. But there is every reason to believe that these dispatches will never be recovered, and that nothing of importance in the archives mentioned has escaped the Tylers' notice.

Something of the use made by historians of Renard's papers has already been suggested, and it remains only to notice four special studies of his career. In 1877 a descendant of one of Renard's sons-in-law, an *intendant militaire* named Neuvier who wrote under the pseudonym of Vunière, completed an historical study of the ambassador's life and had a few copies of his manuscript lithographed. Basing himself largely upon Weiss and upon the eighteenth-century transcripts at Brussels, the author produced a fairly good amateur account of his ancestor's career; but his references were careless, his details often inaccurate, and his judgments superficial.[29] Five years later Mathieu Tridon published a more scholarly monograph on Renard, covering both his diplomatic career and his later struggle with Granvelle. Tridon used no sources for the embassy to England which had not been used by Neuvier, Piot's work appearing just too late to be of service; but he made far more critical use of the available source and secondary material than his predecessor, whose book he cited. The chapter on England remained a rather slight sketch, nevertheless.[30] Writing in 1912 upon a broader subject, Lucien Febvre had occasion to investigate certain aspects of Renard's career in the Franche-Comté and Spanish Netherlands, and the result was a disconnected but penetrating account of Renard's character and activities. Febvre was not concerned with the ambassador's diplomacy, but he shed new light on almost every phase of his career at home.[31] By far the ablest and most scholarly account of Renard's activities as ambassador to England is to be found in Tyler's Preface to Volume XI of the *Calendar of State Papers, Spanish,* but it extends only to the end of 1553.

[29] "Vunière," *Etude historique sur Simon Renard, Chevalier et Sire de Barmont* ("autographié," Limoges, 1878). I have used the copy donated by the author to the Bibliothèque Publique of Besançon.

[30] "Simon Renard, ses ambassades, ses négociations, sa lutte avec le cardinal de Granvelle," *Mémoires de la société d'émulation du Doubs,* 5th series, VI (1881), 109-376.

[31] *Philippe II et la Franche-Comté* (Paris, 1913), Chaps. V, VI, and *passim.*

BIBLIOGRAPHY

A. MANUSCRIPTS

[Aff. Etr.] Archives du ministère des affaires étrangères, Paris, France.
Correspondance politique, Angleterre, Vols. IX-XX.
Dispatches of Antoine, François, and Gilles de Noailles, 1553-1561.
Mémoires et documents, Angleterre, Vols. XIV, XV.
Copies of François de Noailles's Journal, extracts from Antoine de Noailles's dispatches, monograph on the latter's career by Valincour, and copies of letters relating to Scottish affairs, 1556-1560.

[Antigny, Tyler] Antigny-le-Château, par Arnay-le-Duc, Côte d'Or, France.
Royall Tyler's transcripts of Imperial and Spanish material relating to English history for the years 1555-1558.

[Besançon] Bibliothèque Publique, Besançon, France.
Fonds Granvelle, Vol. V.
A few letters between Philip and Granvelle, 1555-1557.
Fonds Granvelle, Vols. LXXI-LXXV.
"Lettres et papiers des ambassades de Simon Renard."

[Bib. Nat.] Bibliothèque Nationale, Paris, France.
[f.f.] Fonds français, No. 704.
"Procès verbal de la conférence tenue à Marc," fols. 199-206.
(Transcript by Baschet in P.R.O., Transcripts 3, Bundle 22).
Fonds français, No. 6908.
Personal letters of various members of the Noailles family, 1557-1622.
Fonds français, No. 6948.
"Divers mémoires pris sur les originaux pour la vie d'Antoine de Noailles." Title in Gaignières's hand.
Fonds français, No. 20147.
Journal of François de Noailles, holograph original, fols. 22-25.

Fonds français, No. 20457.
Letters between France and Scotland, 1547-1553, 1555-1556.
Fonds français, No. 32892.
"Généalogie de la maison de Noailles," fols. 56-112.
Fonds français, nouvelles acquisitions, No. 328.
"Recueil de copies de pièces pour servir à l'histoire de la maison de Noailles."
Fonds français, nouv. acq., No. 9520.
Vertot's introduction to the embassies of the Noailles brothers, published with omissions as Vol. I of his *Ambassades*.
Fonds français, nouv. acq., No. 21698.
Letters to the Duke of Guise 1557, including some from Antoine de Noailles.
Collection Dupuy, No. 844.
Several letters concerning Antoine de Noailles.

[B.M.] British Museum, London, England.
Additional Manuscripts, No. 28597.
Transcripts by Bergenroth of a few letters concerning Renard's embassy to England, from Simancas, Spain.

[P.R.O.] Public Record Office, London, England.
State Papers 68, Vols. XI, XII; 69, Vols. I-X.
Correspondence of the English government with its ambassadors and agents abroad, 1553-1557.
State Papers Domestic 11, Vols. I-X.
Especially the documents relating to Wyatt's rebellion and Dudley's plot.
Transcripts 3, Bundles 20-23.
Baschet's transcripts of some of the Noailles correspondence in Aff. Etr., Paris.
Transcripts 8, Vol. 145.
Transcripts of Renard's correspondence from the Archives du Royaume de Belgique, Brussels.
[Tyler] Royall Tyler's transcripts of Imperial and Spanish material relating to English history for the year 1554.

B. Printed Sources

[*A.P.C.*] *Acts of the Privy Council of England,* new series, J. R. Dasent, ed., 32 vols., London, 1890-1907. Vols. IV-VI.

"Baga de Secretis," *4th Report of the Deputy Keeper of the Public Records,* (London, 1843), Appendix II, No. 7.

Calendar of the Patent Rolls preserved in the Public Record Office, Edward VI, and Philip and Mary, London, 1924—.

Calendar of the State Papers relating to Scotland, 9 vols., Edinburgh, 1898 ff. Vol. I.

[Charrière] *Négociations de la France dans le Levant,* Ernest Charrière, ed., 4 vols., Paris, 1848-1860. In *Collection de documents inédits sur l'histoire de France.*

The Chronicle of Queen Jane and of two years of Queen Mary, J. G. Nichols, ed., London, Camden Soc., 1850.

Claretta, Gaudenzio, *Il duca di Savoia Emanuele Filiberto e la corte di Londra negli anni 1554 e 1555,* Pinerolo, 1892. Documents and comment.

[Cobbett] *A Complete Collection of State Trials . . . ,* William Cobbett and T. B. Howell, eds., 21 vols., London, 1809-1814. Vol. I.

Collection of State Papers . . . left by William Cecil, Lord Burghley, Samuel Haynes and Wm. Murdin, eds., 2 vols., London, 1740-1759.

[*Docs. inéds.*] *Colección de documentos inéditos para la historia de España,* 112 vols., Madrid, 1842-1895. Vols. I, III.

[*Dom. Cal.*] *Calendar of State Papers, Domestic, 1547-1590,* 2 vols., London, 1856.

Facsimiles of National Manuscripts from William the Conqueror to Queen Anne, Colonel Sir Henry James, ed., 4 vols., Southampton, 1865. Facsimiles of some of Wotton's dispatches in Vol. III.

[*For. Cal.*] *Calendar of State Papers, Foreign, Edward VI, and Mary,* 2 vols., London, 1861.

Foreign Correspondence with Marie de Lorraine, Queen of Scotland, Marguerite Wood, ed., 2 vols., Scottish Historical Soc., third series, Vols. IV, VII (1923-1925).

Foxe, John, *Acts and Monuments . . .,* George Townsend and S. R. Cattley, eds., 8 vols., London, 1837-1841.

Friedmann, Paul, *Les dépêches de Giovanni Michiel . . . 1554 à 1557,* Venice, 1869. Valuable preface. Dispatches translated in *Ven. Cal.*

[Gachard and Piot] *Collection des voyages des souverains des Pays-Bas,* Louis Prosper Gachard and Charles Piot, eds., 4 vols., Brussels,

1874-1882. Documents on the Spanish marriage negotiations in Vol. IV, Appendix.

Grey Friars of London Chronicle, J. G. Nichols, ed., London, Camden Soc., 1852.

Guaras, Antonio de, *The Accession of Queen Mary,* Richard Garnett, ed., London, 1892.

Journals of the House of Commons, London, 1803 *ff.* Vol. I.

Kennedy, W. P. M., "The Imperial Embassy of 1553-1554 and Wyatt's Rebellion," *English Historical Review,* Vol. XXXVIII (1923), pp. 251-8. Document.

The Letters of Stephen Gardiner, James Arthur Muller, ed., Cambridge (Eng.), 1933.

Lettres et mémoires d'estat [*1537-1559*], G. Ribier, ed., 2 vols., Paris, 1666. Documents concerning French relations with Italy and the Levant.

[Lodge] *Illustrations of British History, Biography, and Manners,* Edmund Lodge, ed., 3 vols., 2nd ed., London, 1838.

The Loseley Manuscripts, A. J. Kempe, ed., London, 1835.

[*Machyn Diary*] *The Diary of Henry Machyn,* J. G. Nichols, ed., London, Camden Soc., 1848.

Mumby, Frank A., *The Girlhood of Queen Elizabeth, a Narrative in Contemporary Letters,* Boston and New York, 1909.

Muñoz, Andres, *Viaje de Felipe II en Inglaterra,* Pascual de Gayangos, ed., Madrid, 1877. *Sociedad de bibliofilos españoles,* No. 15. Includes four letters from a Spaniard who came to England with Philip in 1554, probably Pedro Enriquez.

Nichols, J. G., *Literary Remains of King Edward VI,* 2 vols., Roxburghe Club, 1857.

Nonciatures de France: Nonciatures de Paul IV [*1554-1557*], D. René Ancel, ed., Paris, 1909.

Paris, Louis, *Les papiers de Noailles de la bibliothèque du Louvre,* 2 vols., Paris, 1875. Most of the documents given date from after Antoine de Noailles's death in 1563.

Proctor, John, "The History of Sir Thomas Wyatt's Rebellion" (first printed January 1555), in *An English Garner,* Edward Arber, ed. (London, 1896), Vol. VIII, pp. 37-95.

[Quirini] *Epistolae Reginaldi Poli . . .,* A. M. Quirini, ed., 5 vols., Brescia, 1744-1757.

Relations politiques de la France et de l'Espagne avec l'Ecosse au XVIe siècle, Alexandre Teulet, ed., 2 vols., Paris, 1862.

Relations politiques des Pays-Bas et de l'Angleterre sous le règne de Philippe II, J. M. B. C. Kervyn de Lettenhove, ed., 11 vols., Brussels, 1882-1900. Vol. I.

[*Span. Cal.*] *Calendar of State Papers, Spanish,* 11 vols., London, 1862—. Vols. IX-XI (Royall Tyler, ed.).

Strype, John, *Ecclesiastical Memorials . . .,* 7 vols., London, 1816.

Tudor and Stuart Proclamations, Robert Steele, ed., 2 vols., Oxford, 1910.

[*Ven. Cal.*] *Calendar of State Papers, Venetian,* 9 vols., London, 1864-1898. Vols. V, VI (3 parts).

[*Verney Papers*] *Letters and Papers of the Verney Family,* John Bruce, ed., London, Camden Soc., 1853. Material on Dudley's plot.

Vertot, René Aubert de, *Ambassades de Messieurs de Noailles en Angleterre,* 5 vols., Leyden, 1763. See Note on the Sources.

[*Weiss*] *Papiers d'état du cardinal de Granvelle d'après les manuscrits de la bibliothèque de Besançon,* Charles Weiss, ed., 9 vols., Paris, 1841-1852. In *Collection de documents inédits sur l'histoire de France.* Vols. IV, V.

[*Wriothesley*] *A Chronicle of England . . . by Charles Wriothesley, Windsor Herald* [*1485-1559*], London, Camden Soc., new series, 1875-1877.

C. Secondary Works: Books, Articles, and Bibliographical Aids

Armstrong, Edward, *The Emperor Charles V,* 2 vols., London, 1902.

Baschet, Armand, "List of Dispatches of Ambassadors from France to England, 1509-1714," in *39th Report of the Deputy Keeper of the Public Records* (London, 1878), pp. 601-18. A list of practically all the Noailles dispatches in Aff. Etr., corr. pol., Angl., Vols. IX-XX. Those dispatches actually transcribed by Baschet for the P.R.O. are checked in the copy of the *Report* which is in the Literary Search Room of the P.R.O.

Baschet, Armand, "List of the French ambassadors in England," in *37th Report of the Deputy Keeper of the Public Records* (London, 1876), App. I, pp. 180-94.

Brandi, Karl, *The Emperor Charles V, The Growth and Destiny of a Man and of a World-Empire,* Eng. trans. by C. V. Wedgwood, New York, 1939.

Burgon, John William, *The Life and Times of Sir Thomas Gresham,* 2 vols., London, 1839.

Cambridge Modern History, 12 vols., Cambridge (Eng.), 1903 *ff.* Bibliography (II, 802-5).

Cataloque générale des manuscrits des bibliothèques publiques de France, Départements, Besançon (Vol. XXXIII), Auguste Castan, ed. (Paris, 1900), Vol. II, Part I, pp. 20-5. A listing, not always accurate, of the Granvelle papers at Besançon.

Clifford, Henry, *The Life of Jane Dormer, Duchess of Feria,* J. Stevenson, ed., London, 1887.

Constant, Abbé G., "Le commencement de la restauration catholique en Angleterre par Marie Tudor (1553)," *Revue historique,* Vol. CXII (1913), pp. 1-27.

Constant, Abbé G., "Le mariage de Marie Tudor et de Philippe II," *Revue d'histoire diplomatique,* Vol. XXVI (1912), pp. 23-73, 224-74. Some errors, typographical and otherwise.

Davenport, F. G., "Materials for English Diplomatic History, 1509-1783," *Historical Manuscripts Commission, 18th Report* (1917), pp. 357-402. Description of materials in B.M. and in private collections.

Decrue de Stoutz, Francis, *Anne, Duc de Montmorency, connétable et pair de France,* 2 vols., Paris, 1885-1889.

Dictionary of National Biography, 63 vols., London, 1885-1900.

Dietz, Frederick C., *English Public Finance, 1558-1641,* New York and London, 1932.

Dietz, Frederick C., "Finances of Edward VI and Mary," *Smith College Studies in History,* Vol. III (1917-1918), pp. 61-135.

Duruy, George, *De Pactis Anno 1556 apud Valcellas Indutiis,* Paris, 1883. Doctoral dissertation.

Fage, René, *Les Noailles peints par Oudry,* Brive, 1922.

Febvre, Lucien, *Philippe II et la Franche-Comté,* Paris, 1912.

Forneron, Henri, *Les Ducs de Guise et leur époque,* 2 vols., Paris, 1893.

Forneron, Henri, *Histoire de Philippe II,* 4 vols., Paris, 1881-1882. Not always trustworthy.

Froude, James Anthony, *History of England from the fall of Wolsey to the defeat of the Spanish Armada,* 12 vols., London, 1856-1870.

Gabarra, J.-B. *Un évêque de Dax, François de Noailles,* Dax, 1888. Brief.

Gairdner, James, *Lollardy and the Reformation in England,* 4 vols., London, 1908-1913. Vol. IV.

Garrett, Christina Hallowell, *The Marian Exiles, a Study in the Origins of Elizabethan Puritanism,* Cambridge (Eng.), 1938. "Census of exiles," pp. 61-349; bibliography.

Griffet, Henri, *Nouveaux éclaircissements sur l'histoire de Marie, reine d'Angleterre,* Amsterdam, 1766.

Haile, Martin, *Life of Reginald Pole,* London, 1910.

Harbison, E. H., "French Intrigue at the Court of Queen Mary," *American Historical Review,* Vol. XLV (April 1940), pp. 533-51. Description of Noailles's spies and agents.

Hinds, Allen Banks, *The Making of the England of Elizabeth,* London, 1895.

Hooker, J. [alias J. Vowell], "Life of Sir Peter Carew," in *Calendar of the Carew Manuscripts* (London, 1867), Vol. I, pp. lxvii-cxviii.

Hume, M. A. S., "The Visit of Philip II," *English Historical Review,* Vol. VII (1892), pp. 253-80.

Inventaire sommaire des archives du département des affaires étrangères, Correspondance politique (Paris, 1903), Vol. I, p. 161. Brief description of the Noailles correspondence, 1553-1561.

Knappen, M. M., *Tudor Puritanism, A Chapter in the History of Idealism,* Chicago, 1939.

Lévêque, le P. Prosper, *Mémoires pour servir à l'histoire du cardinal de Granvelle,* 2 vols., Paris, 1753.

Lingard, John, *History of England,* enlarged ed., 10 vols., London, 1849.

Merriman, Roger Bigelow, *The Rise of the Spanish Empire in the Old World and the New,* 4 vols., London and New York, 1918-1934. Bibliography.

Meyer, Arnold Oskar, *Die Englische Diplomatie in Deutschland zur Zeit Eduards VI und Mariens,* Breslau, 1900.

Muller, James Arthur, *Stephen Gardiner and the Tudor Reaction,* London and New York, 1926. Bibliography.

Pacheco y de Leyva, E., "Grave error político de Carlos I haciendo la boda de Felipe II con doña Maria," *Revista de archivos, bibliotecas, y museos,* Vol. XLII (1921), pp. 60-84, 276-92. Documents and comment on Don Luis's suit for Mary's hand.

Paris, Louis, *Les manuscrits de la bibliothèque du Louvre, brûlés dans la nuit du 23 au 24 mai 1871 sous le règne de la Commune,* Paris, 1872.

The Parliamentary History of England, 24 vols., 2nd ed., London, 1761-1763. Commonly called the Old Parliamentary History.

Pastor, Ludwig von, *A History of the Popes from the Close of the Middle Ages,* Eng. trans. by R. F. Kerr, 16 vols., London, 1910—. Section on Mary's reign based upon documents in the Vatican, and upon Constant's "Mariage."

Piot, Charles, "La diplomatie concernant les affaires maritimes des Pays-Bas . . .," *Bulletins de l'académie royale des sciences, des lettres, et des beaux arts de Belgique,* 2nd series, Vol. XL (1875), pp. 817-68.

Pollard, Albert Frederick, *England under Protector Somerset,* London, 1900. Bibliography.

Pollard, Albert Frederick, [*Pol. Hist.*] *The History of England from the Accession of Edward VI to the Death of Elizabeth,* London, 1910. In the *Political History of England* series. Bibliography.

Prescott, H. F. M., *A Spanish Tudor,* New York, 1940. The best recent biography of Queen Mary. (Appeared after completion of present study.)

Read, Conyers, *Bibliography of British History, Tudor Period,* Oxford, 1933.

Romier, Lucien, *Les origines politiques des guerres de religion,* 2 vols., Paris, 1913. Bibliography.

Segre, Arture, and Egidi, Pietro, *Emanuele Filiberto,* 2 vols., Turin, 1928.

Stone, Jean Mary, *The History of Mary I, Queen of England,* London, 1901. Best older biography.

Sturge, Charles, *The Life and Times of John Dudley, Earl of Warwick and Duke of Northumberland,* typewritten doctoral dissertation, University of London, 1927.

Tamizey de Larroque, Philippe, "Antoine de Noailles à Bordeaux," *Actes de l'académie nationale des sciences, belles-lettres, et arts de Bordeaux,* 3rd series (Paris, 1877), pp. 447-535.

Tamizey de Larroque, Philippe, *Lettres inédites de François de Noailles, Evêque de Dax,* Paris, 1865.

Tridon, Mathieu, "Simon Renard, ses ambassades, ses négociations, sa lutte avec le cardinal de Granvelle," *Mémoires de la société d'émulation du Doubs,* 5th series, Vol. VI (1881), pp. 109-375.

Tytler, Patrick Fraser, *England under the reigns of Edward VI and Mary,* 2 vols., London, 1839. Includes extracts from Renard's dispatches of February to June 1554.

"Vunière" (pseudonym for Neuvier), *Etude historique sur Simon Renard, Chevalier et Sieur de Barmont,* lithographed at Limoges, 1878.

White, Beatrice, *Mary Tudor,* London, 1935.

Wiesener, Louis, *La jeunesse d'Elisabeth d'Angleterre,* Paris, 1878. Broader in scope than its biographical title implies.

Zimmermann, Athanasius, *Kardinal Pole, sein Leben, und seine Schriften,* Regensburg, 1893.

Zimmermann, Athanasius, *Maria die Katholische,* Freiburg, 1890.

INDEX

INDEX